MARKETING PAYBACK

rvice

FT Prentice Hall
FINANCIAL TIMES

In an increasingly competitive world, we believe it's quality of thinking that will give you the edge – an idea that opens new doors, a technique that solves a problem, or an insight that simply makes sense of it all. The more you know, the smarter and faster you can go.

That's why we work with the best minds in business and finance to bring cutting-edge thinking and best learning practice to a global market.

Under a range of leading imprints, including *Financial Times Prentice Hall*, we create world-class print publications and electronic products bringing our readers knowledge, skills and understanding, which can be applied whether studying or at work.

To find out more about Pearson Education publications, or tell us about the books you'd like to find, you can visit us at **www.pearsoned.co.uk**

PEARSON
Education

MARKETING PAYBACK

Is your marketing profitable?

Robert Shaw and David Merrick

FT Prentice Hall
FINANCIAL TIMES

An imprint of Pearson Education

Harlow, England • London • New York • Boston • San Francisco • Toronto • Sydney • Singapore • Hong Kong
Tokyo • Seoul • Taipei • New Delhi • Cape Town • Madrid • Mexico City • Amsterdam • Munich • Paris • Milan

PEARSON EDUCATION LIMITED

Edinburgh Gate
Harlow CM20 2JE
Tel: +44 (0)1279 623623
Fax: +44 (0)1279 431059

Website: www.pearsoned.co.uk

First published in Great Britain in 2005

ISBN 0 273 68884 7

British Library Cataloguing in Publication Data
A catalogue record for this book is available from the British Library

Library of Congress Cataloging-in-Publication Data
A catalog record for this book is available from the Library of Congress

10 9 8 7 6 5 4 3 2 1
09 08 07 06 05

Typeset in 10pt Century by 70
Printed and bound in Great Britain by Bell and Bain Ltd, Glasgow

The Publishers' policy is to use paper manufactured from sustainable forests.

CONTENTS

PART I: IS MARKETING PROFITABLE?

PART III: FINANCIAL PLANNING AND CONTROL

PUBLISHER'S ACKNOWLEDGEMENTS

The publishers are grateful to the following for permission to reproduce copyright material:

Figure 3.1 reprinted with the permission of The Free Press, a Division of Simon & Schuster Adult Publishing Group, from COUNTERINTUITIVE MARKETING: Achieve Great Results Using Uncommon Sense by Kevin J. Clancy and Peter C. Krieg. Copyright © 2000 by Kevin J. Clancy. All rights reserved; Table 3.1 from *Marketing and the Bottom Line (1st edition)*, Tim Ambler, © Pearson Education Limited, 2000; Table 3.2 from Rossiter, J.R. and Percy, L., *Advertising Communications and Promotion Management*, McGraw-Hill Education, 1997; Table 5.2 from Lomax, W., Hammond, K., Clemente, M. and East, R., 'New entrants in a mature market: an empirical study of the detergent market', *J. Marketing Management*, 1996; Table 5.3 from Ehrenberg, A.S.C. and Uncles, M.D., 'Dirichlet-type Markets: A Review', South Bank University Business School Working Paper, 1996; Figure 6.1 from *Competitive Strategy*, Warren, K., 2002 © John Wiley and Sons Ltd. Reproduced with permission; Figure 6.6 from Holmes, M. & Cook, L., *Econometrics Explained*, IPA Publications, 2004; Figure 9.2 and Table 9.4 adapted with the permission of The Free Press, a Division of Simon & Schuster Adult Publishing Group, from BUILDING STRONG BRANDS by David A. Aaker. Copyright © 1996 by David A. Aaker. All rights reserved; Figures 9.6–9.8 from Moore, W. L. and Pessemier, E. A., *Product Planning and Management*, McGraw-Hill Education, 1993; Figure 11.2 reproduced with permission of Yahoo! Inc. © 2004 by Yahoo! Inc. YAHOO! and the YAHOO! logo are trademarks of Yahoo! Inc.; Figure 11.3 and Tables 11.1 and 11.2 from Interbrand, *www.interbrand.com*; Table 19.1 adapted with permission from Pearson Education from Richard Stutely, *The Definitive Guide to Managing the Numbers*, FT Prentice Hall, 2003 and the material on the IPA Effectiveness Awards reproduced with the permission of the IPA.

In some instances we have been unable to trace the owners of copyright material, and we would appreciate any information that would enable us to do so.

AUTHORS' ACKNOWLEDGEMENTS

The authors are grateful for the helpful comments and suggestions made by many friends and colleagues. We particularly want to thank Carolyn White for her work on the manuscript, Bryan Finn for contributions throughout the book, and the following people for their support and contributions: Philip Kotler, Malcolm McDonald, Vincent-Wayne Mitchell, Chris Storey, Karl Weaver and Steve Wilson.

1

INTRODUCTION: PAYBACK BEGINS HERE

Is the book for you?

Who should read the book?

Do I need to be Einstein to understand it?

Marketing marketing

The plan of the book

This book is about improving the payback you get from your marketing. Marketing costs lots of money and there are many choices to be made about where marketing budgets can be spent. Good marketing decisions yield substantial profits but bad ones can destroy substantial value. Our aim is to help you make better ones.

Whether you are approaching this challenge from a marketing, finance or general management perspective, it is essential to have a firm grasp of marketing performance and payback. This applies both to marketing people and to agency staff, who should be clear about why they need money and where they should spend it. It applies too to finance people, who need a new perspective to make judgements about marketing's cost-benefits. And of course it applies to general managers and entrepreneurs who need a deep understanding of marketing payback as a key constituent of their strategic thinking.

However, the quest for improved marketing payback goes beyond the routine procedures of marketing and finance. Almost every marketing manager will routinely scrutinize the performance of any agency that they work with, but both parties often find themselves uncomfortable with the process. Budgeting is a time-consuming routine for many marketing and finance people, and the results can seem disappointing for the effort. All too often, reporting seems blind to the important business issues and distracts attention towards inconsequential trivia. Market research manufactures heavy tables of numbers and colourful slide decks, but the number of vital insights they contain are very few. *It's time for a more relevant and dynamic approach to measuring marketing performance.*

If you want to go beyond the flawed control routines and discover effective methods of assessing and improving marketing payback, then you should read this book. It is written for working executives, not for financial experts or statistical specialists. It aims to provide useful tools for everyday management. It covers a wide range of techniques and provides a bridge between the worlds of marketing and finance. It debunks some of the myths about marketing and finance, and spotlights some of the traps set by conventional analyses.

We have highlighted the scope for creativity, obscuration and outright cheating – and show you how to catch and counter this. Throughout the book we discuss current international issues in marketing which are likely to affect you as a manager in the real world. In short, the book gives you the inside track. This will assist you not only in creating your own analyses, but, significantly, in interpreting analyses prepared by others. It will also help you to hold your own when dealing with other departments.

With the fragmentation of channels, expanding product choice and the rising tide of consumer expectations, marketing payback levels are dropping throughout the world. Advertising campaigns only have a positive payback for a minority of cases, and promotions are even more risk-prone. Tomorrow's winners will be those with the courage to change and the discipline to learn new ways of making marketing more accountable.

Is the book for you?

This book is for you if you want a little help with (or a complete guide to) marketing payback. If you are a bit hazy about this subject and you answer yes to any of the following you should definitely read on:

- Pressurized to demonstrate the contribution of marketing?
- Drowning in data yet lacking in deep customer insights?
- Need to predict the performance of brand extensions or range reductions?
- Need to improve the payback from customer acquisition and retention?
- Worried about your advertising's effects?
- Wondering whether your sales promotions are effective?
- Want to value your brands?
- Need an effective marketing plan?
- Want a more reliable sales forecast?
- Have to justify a marketing budget?
- Must respond in a hurry to bad-performance figures?
- Wondering how to allocate the marketing budget?
- Need better historical records of marketing activity and spending?
- Constructing a spreadsheet model?
- Have to make a decision based on the numbers?
- Presenting to your chief financial officer and the Board?
- Want to increase your influence on Board decisions?
- Staking your reputation on a recommendation based on financial analysis?
- Being judged by how you perform against some target or objective?

In fact, the list goes on and on. This book is able to answer so many questions because of the interrelationships between customer insight and financial foresight. You will discover how to unlock these relationships and use them to your advantage.

Who should read the book?

This book is aimed primarily at marketing managers, market researchers, advertising executives, product managers, sales managers and customer service managers. It will help them to discover new and better methods of demonstrating marketing performance and improving marketing effectiveness.

But the book is also highly relevant to accountants, keen to find out how to measure the returns from marketing investments. It will also be invaluable to students of marketing and finance, looking for a real-world assessment of the role of marketing in driving business performance. We might even have some investment analysts turning the pages.

Few managers have any reference point on how to make good marketing decisions, from a financial viewpoint. Although many attend courses on 'Finance for Non-financial Managers', the practical relevance is doubtful. While many go to seminars on branding and customer relationship management (CRM), the economics of these are taken on faith. Most people, in fact, are self-trained in decision analysis and the economics of marketing. This book now provides a reference point.

Do I need to be Einstein to understand it?

There is no need to be ashamed if you are confused and overwhelmed by the deluge of numbers that swamp you or if you find that spreadsheets are overloaded with technical details you'll never use. This book is for you, however, if these problems mean that you are postponing important personal and business decisions because you just don't have the right analysis tools to find the answers.

This book is written for those frustrated and hard-working souls who know they're not dumb, but find that the technical complexities make them feel helpless. We will start from scratch with the basics and try to explain it all as we go along. You can skip over the material that you already know or use it as a refresher for the things you have forgotten.

By the way, we exaggerated a little when we said we would start from scratch. You'll need to be able to start a computer, add and subtract, occasionally multiply and divide, and have a rough idea of what cash is.

Marketing marketing

A big challenge for the marketing community generally is the pessimists and sceptics who challenge that most basic premise of marketing:

A company can take actions that affect its own sales.

Our research shows that, surprisingly, many top executives and Board directors have a fatalistic attitude towards this basic premise. Many believe that sales are beyond everyone's control and they make it difficult for marketing to obtain the budgets and resources that marketing needs. This book will help you answer the fatalists, pessimists and cynics.

Over many years we have come to the view that the best way forward is to demonstrate to the non-marketing community the benefits of marketing in a business, *but in their terms*. This means two things. It means using their language – which is often the language of numbers. And it means accountability, especially financial accountability, for the impacts of marketing expenditure.

We are not alone in this view. Sir Roy Gardner, chief executive of Centrica and non-executive chairman of Manchester United, said in 2004:

> Marketers must be more than functional specialists to win over chief executives. Marketers fail to reach Board level because they are not fluent in the language of finance. Success requires a new set of skills.
>
> I am not saying that customer awareness and brand equity are not important metrics. But as someone who holds the purse strings, I am much more interested in understanding how marketing drives long-term shareholder value. So before I hand someone £10 million to spend on advertising, I want to see a fact-based analysis demonstrating the economic benefits. This is what is required of other parts of the company to justify their investments. And frankly, I see no good reason why marketing should be exempt.

In today's business environment, quantifying the impacts of marketing expenditure in terms that can be endorsed by the non-marketing community is not a passing fad, nor is it an optional extra. Neither is the associated financial accountability. But, as we hope to demonstrate, we do not believe that these are insurmountable hurdles for the marketing community either.

We come to this view from the position of managers, not accountants. We picked up all this numbers and modelling stuff in the early days of our careers as business analysts and modellers in the energy sector – crawling over financials, looking for value and danger signs. Later on we started working with big companies on solving marketing problems using numbers – IBM, Unilever, BP, BT, BA. You come to see and do quite a lot of numbers, and a good chunk of work was budgeting, forecasting, analyzing, interpreting and troubleshooting – and dealing with officials, accountants and Boards in a score of different situations.

Along the way, one of us became a visiting professor at a couple of business schools, and the other headed the training centre for a large corporation. We have personally constructed many complex computer models and developed corporate intranets to communicate numbers and charts to managers in the four corners of the globe. We have also been running a think-tank for five years, the Value Based Marketing Forum, where these issues are debated and analyzed (*www.vbmf.com*).

Our seminars aim to teach excellent decision making, much as athletic coaches teach sports: by explaining the ways in which typical marketing decision makers err. We teach ways to avoid these mistakes and show how people can master the economics of marketing.

We've been able to do this because of path-breaking academic research over the past 20 years by scholars such as Russo and Schoemaker (1989), on how people fall into decision traps, and by Hartley (1995) and Clancy and Shulman (1994) on marketing myths and mistakes. Like good sports coaches, these researchers show that untrained marketing decision makers tend to make a few characteristic errors over and over. We know from our coaching experience and our own research that these discoveries offer enormous value for marketing decision makers. Perhaps the most important lesson of all is that *marketing decision makers have to learn when to distrust their gut instinct and use more formal decision appraisal methods.*

One final thing. We have been observers of the joy of company politics, have seen managers fiddling the numbers and entrepreneurs who pressured others to exaggerate on their behalf. So we think we bring a realistic perspective on today's business environment to the pages of this book.

The plan of the book

You will probably have already skimmed the table of contents and some of the chapters, but we need to explain the logic behind the contents and chapters.

Part I: Is marketing profitable?

In Chapters 2–7 we will help to answer the most basic questions that you will need to master.

- Chapter 2: **Marketing's midlife crisis** helps you assess your own marketing department and how much you are risking from poor marketing evaluation.
- Chapter 3: **Demonstrating success** shows why existing approaches to evaluating marketing success are inadequate and looks at practical ways of demonstrating marketing payback.
- Chapter 4: **The laws of marketing** asks 'Do you believe in marketing laws?'

and shows why it's worth making the effort to read more academic marketing research to find out what the laws are.

- Chapter 5: **Measuring how marketing really works** examines why it's important to understand customer psychology; why the detailed design of market research is something you need to personally decide; and what is the ideal basket of measures for evaluating marketing payback.

- Chapter 6: **Tracking trends and forecasting futures** shows why forecasting is too important to leave to the boffins; how to choose and brief your own modeller; what methods are available to choose from; how to make forecasting bullet-proof.

- Chapter 7: **Avoiding decision traps** shows how to assess your own decision making and avoid repetitive errors and systematic bias.

Part II: Solutions to common problems

With all the foregoing out of the way, you are ready to dig deeper into a range of specific marketing decisions, exploring the methods and techniques available for better decision making.

- Chapter 8: **Expenditure allocation** tells you how to allocate money within your marketing budget to maximize its payback; and how to challenge the common errors that accountants often make.

- Chapter 9: **Brand identity changes** shows how by changing brand identity you can improve business results; and how to decide on the best change to make.

- Chapter 10: **Brand portfolio planning** explains why marketing has a key role in product launch and range consolidation decisions; and how to decide when to expand and when to consolidate your portfolio.

- Chapter 11: **Valuing brands** shows why marketing should be more involved with investor relations; and examines the methods available for putting a financial value on brands.

- Chapter 12: **Integrated marketing communications** shows new and better ways of choosing the best mix of media and creative executions to maximize payback.

- Chapter 13: **How pricing works** explains why marketing should be more involved with pricing; and what are the best ways of setting price to maximize profit.

- Chapter 14: **How promotions work** tells you why marketing should be involved in controlling sales promotion and how to determine the best mix of promotional activities.

- Chapter 15: **Customer equity optimization** shows a new and better way of managing the customer base, by choosing the right number of customers and spending just enough money on customer acquisition, cross-selling and retention.

- Chapter 16: **Getting better value from marketing information** helps you assess the effectiveness of your marketing information management and how to squeeze more value from information.

Part III: Financial planning and control

The final chapters (17–22) review the financial planning and control of the corporation, and the changes needed to optimize marketing payback.

- Chapter 17: **The number wizard's toolbox** investigates the tools you use to hammer the numbers – primarily spreadsheets – and explains how to use them in a disciplined way to construct models.

- Chapter 18: **Marketing planning** describes what marketing plans are and what is an effective planning process.

- Chapter 19: **Better budgeting** covers the budgeting process and the way it needs to be modified to become a useful marketing control tool.

- Chapter 20: **Marketing bookkeeping and accounting** introduces the methods used to keep track of marketing expenditure and activity in a way that can be analyzed meaningfully.

- Chapter 21: **When results go wrong** looks at variance reporting and reviews its limitations and applications for marketing.

- Chapter 22: **Twenty things you'll do differently** now that you've read the book.

part I:

IS MARKETING PROFITABLE?

2

MARKETING'S MIDLIFE CRISIS

This chapter takes a hard look at the way business regards marketing. It describes the roller-coaster of marketing budgets. It looks at the way different functional groups perceive marketing. It discusses the often tenuous links between business results and marketing. And it provides a general warning about spending money on marketing yet ignoring the payback.

As we show through numerous examples, the situation is serious and getting worse. Marketing is too important to be treated as an out-of-control cost item on a profit and loss account, but this is what happens in many firms. The answers lie in a much greater rapprochement between financial and marketing executives, and a clearer understanding of how marketing expenditure drives business results.

Throughout the book we attempt to cut through the jargon surrounding marketing performance, and try to define our terms as accurately as possible. In this chapter the terminology in Box 2.1 is worth noting.

Box 2.1 Marketing performance terminology

Accountability: Form of trustworthiness, the trait of being answerable for one's conduct.

Bias: A partiality that prevents objective consideration of a decision.

Objectivity: The ability to perceive, describe and evaluate things without being influenced by personal prejudices or emotions.

Prejudice: A pre-formed opinion based on insufficient knowledge, irrational feelings or inaccurate stereotypes.

Transparency: The ability to observe things without one's vision being clouded, distorted or obstructed.

Untrustworthy: Behaving in a devious or deceitful way.

Is my marketing department like this?

Only 4% of marketers see marketing as the breeding ground of CEOs. (Shaw and Fisk 2002)

Marketing departments in many companies are suffering a distinct lack of respect and influence. This trend was first highlighted in a *McKinsey Quarterly* article, 'Marketing's Mid-Life Crisis' (Brady and Davis 1993), which quoted one typical CEO as saying: 'Marketing is like a millstone round my neck'. A 1994 survey, from Coopers & Lybrand: *Marketing at the Crossroads*, quoted another executive as saying: 'Marketing is increasingly living a lie in my organization'. Since then, other articles have predicted the death of the brand and the rejection of marketing by Wall Street and the City.

Marketing executives aren't equipping themselves for main Board appointments. Laurie Young, the marketing partner at PricewaterhouseCoopers, says that headhunters find it tricky to fill Board-level marketing vacancies because candidates aren't numerate and lack commercial perspective. Lesley Exley, director of executive search firm Exley Hervey, agrees and comments that marketers don't develop financial acumen early enough in their careers. Consequently marketing is absent from the main Board of the majority of businesses today.

Companies desperately need better marketing leadership. Marketers are allowing their role to be subsumed in other areas or functions (e.g. customer relations by IT and operations, new products by R&D) and marginalized to advertising and packaging design. This shift has been abetted by the tendency of many marketing directors to accede to the prejudices of finance directors and chief executives, instead of taking them on and showing that marketing works. In short, they are wimps.

The work that marketing people do has variously been described as a profession, an art, a science, a sinister instrument of mass persuasion and a ludicrous waste of money. The term 'marketing' is widely used in a pejorative sense in the media, and marketing types are frequently portrayed as false, immoral scoundrels.

Several surveys have provided insight into what this means in practice. For instance, Dr Susan Baker of the Cranfield School of Management used a 'cultural web' framework to show how other departments view marketing (see Figure 2.1). An unflattering caricature of marketing emerged, which unfortunately is widely acknowledged by both marketers and their colleagues in other functions. What is particularly apparent is marketing's perceived lack of accountability, characterized by the words: 'unaccountable, untouchable, expensive and slippery'.

Another survey asked managers to evaluate their marketing colleagues and asked marketing executives to evaluate themselves using the same criteria (see Figure 2.2). The gap between marketing's self-assessment and the perceptions of colleagues must be a cause for concern. If the gaps are real, then fundamental changes to training and career paths are necessary. If they are merely a matter of perception, then it still indicates that there is a significant remedial task to be undertaken, especially in terms of inter-departmental communication.

Figure 2.1
How others perceive marketing

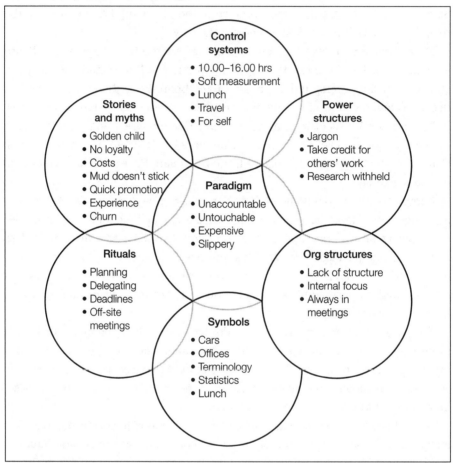

Source: Baker (2000)

Strategic thinking and creative problem solving are where there is the greatest disagreement between the positive marketing self-assessment and the negative colleague assessment. Analysis and measurement is the only area of agreement, with colleagues and marketing self-assessment agreeing – marketing is unaccountable!

Before reading further, ask yourself what the situation is in your company. Here are ten hard questions to ask or be asked about marketing accountability:

1. Have your shareholders been briefed on your marketing performance?

2. Does your finance department understand the contribution of marketing?

3. How much of your market capitalization depends on your marketing?

4. Can your marketing staff be trusted with large sums of company money?

5. Have you eliminated the worse excesses of marketing wastefulness?

6. Do you have specific plans to improve marketing's payback?

7. Is your marketing budget subject to gratuitous cost cutting?

8. Are colleagues critical of marketing's lack of accountability?

9. Do your marketing controls urgently need improvement?

10. What do you need to do to improve?

Figure 2.2
Marketing's capabilities perceived by colleagues and self-assessment

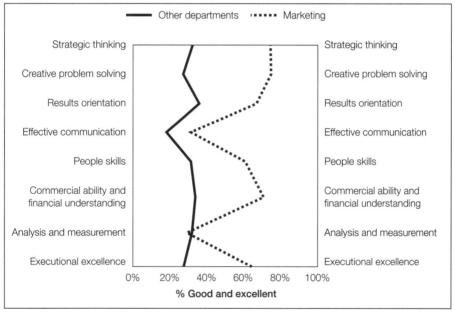

Data from Shaw and Radford (1997)

Can marketing be trusted with money?

The scantiness of marketing clout at Board level isn't because marketing is unimportant – it drives the cash inflow – but because Boards are preoccupied with spending and counting the cash outflow. Management accounts give ten times more information about costs than revenues. While marketing should be equipping the Board with commercial insights into revenue inflows, instead they are preoccupied with surveys of brand awareness and attitudes. Their disinterest in money often leads them to be distrusted with the stuff.

'My colleagues don't trust me' is a complaint we hear all too often from marketing executives. This isn't just an idle moan from tired and emotional executives, it significantly undermines morale and motivation in many organizations. Business cases for marketing spending get blocked by prejudice against marketing, or float past on a wing and a prayer with the blessing of a marketing evangelist.

> A spectre is haunting the marketing world – the spectre of the number crunchers. The pain caused by the decade's bear market has injected a new type of financial rigour into the industry, symbolised by the growing use of complex calculations to measure the impact and value for money of advertising campaigns. (Silverman 2004)

In the UK, the *Financial Times* is reporting an upsurge of activity in accounting for marketing's financial contribution.

Marketing budgets being first for the chop is probably a fact of life. Cuts in other areas involve people and equipment; a marketing budget can be restored next year. So slashing marketing is a knee-jerk reaction for many finance directors (FDs) – see Figure 2.3.

Figure 2.3
Budgets most likely to be cut by finance directors

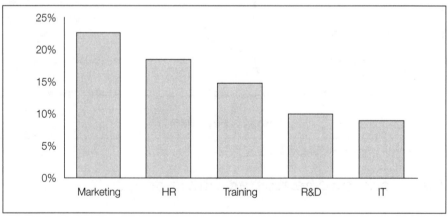

Data from KPMG (1996)

Marketing budgets whiz up and down like a roller-coaster. Whenever the magazine *Marketing* publishes its annual marketing spending survey, this roller-coaster effect is evident from their statistics (see Figure 2.4). Underlying this pattern is an innate distrust of the need for marketing expenditure.

Figure 2.4
The marketing budget roller-coaster

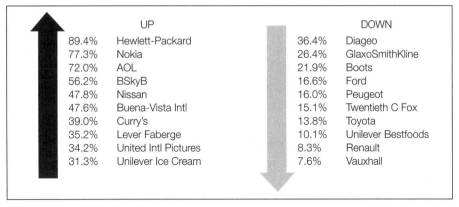

	UP		DOWN
89.4%	Hewlett-Packard	36.4%	Diageo
77.3%	Nokia	26.4%	GlaxoSmithKline
72.0%	AOL	21.9%	Boots
56.2%	BSkyB	16.6%	Ford
47.8%	Nissan	16.0%	Peugeot
47.6%	Buena-Vista Intl	15.1%	Twentieth C Fox
39.0%	Curry's	13.8%	Toyota
35.2%	Lever Faberge	10.1%	Unilever Bestfoods
34.2%	United Intl Pictures	8.3%	Renault
31.3%	Unilever Ice Cream	7.6%	Vauxhall

Data derived from survey in *Marketing* (Feb. 2004)

This raises another question – is anybody controlling things effectively? Another survey attempted to answer this question from the perspective of marketing and finance functions (see Figure 2.5).

Figure 2.5
Effectiveness of controls by function (rated by marketing and finance)

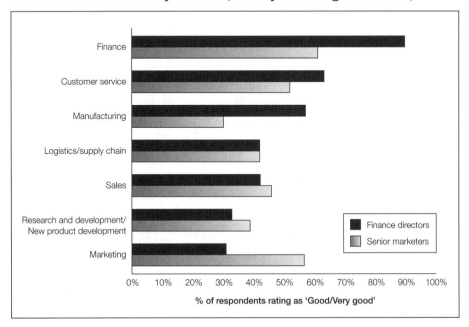

Data from Shaw and Fisk (2002)

The survey results show a significant gap between the functions that finance think are under control, and those that marketing think are under control. There is also an acknowledgement by finance that they have not got a grip on marketing expenditure.

In a recent survey (Shaw and Fisk 2002), 55% of finance directors and 67% of senior marketers agreed that marketing controls were in need of a radical overhaul in the next 18 months.

The need for better marketing controls and accountability is now widely acknowledged, both by marketing and finance. Over the years, this lack of credibility and alignment has meant that marketing metrics, and the marketing executives who propound and defend them, have come to be regarded with less and less respect. The rot set in early in the twentieth century, with Lord Leverhulme's famous remark, 'I know I am wasting half my advertising budget, but the trouble is, I don't know which half.'

However, by the late 1990s, things had got so bad that, in the wake of the various highly critical research studies appearing from consultancies, John Stubbs, CEO of the UK Marketing Council, was forced to admit that, although 'marketing deserves to be valued as the stuff of heroes . . . the beating heart of business', research shows that, 'marketing is isolated, it has too little impact on business effectiveness, it is narrrowly seen as advertising, promotion and bunting, and its professional status is not recognized' (Stubbs 1997).

Healing marketing of its payback myopia

Marketing payback myopia is a common symptom of these structural problems. While most marketers get excited talking about creativity, they get immensely bored when costs and budgets are mentioned; their eyes glaze over and their minds shut down.

This limited attention span is also widely reflected in the treatment of costs and budgets in books on marketing. Examples of the amount of space devoted to the assessment and evaluation of marketing costs and budgets in some leading textbooks is shown in Table 2.1.

Philip Kotler is perhaps unique among marketing experts in recognizing the importance of the issue. Even so, less than 2% of his best-selling book addresses the need. He proposes the idea of a 'marketing controller . . . who is trained in finance and marketing and can perform a sophisticated financial analysis of past and planned marketing expenditures.' Asked why quantitative marketing analysis tools were only to be found in the appendices of his book, he replied: 'Professors were saying to me that this topic was too abstract for a broad course ... but it could be put in an appendix' (quoted in Shaw and Mazur 1997).

Table 2.1

Marketing spending myopia in leading educational texts

Text	Coverage	Percentage of book
Kotler – *Marketing Management*, 7th edn (1991)	Advertising budgets – 1.5 pages R&D budgets – 0.5 pages Total promotional budget – 2 pages Marketing expense to sales analysis – 1 page Financial analysis – 1 page Profitability control – 4 pages Efficiency control – 2 pages Marketing controller – 1 page	1.7%
Aaker – *Managing Brand Equity* (1991)	No mention in the index of budgets, expenditure or marketing spending	0.0%
Day – *Market Driven Strategy* (1990)	No mention in the index of budgets, expenditure or marketing spending	0.0%
McDonald – *Marketing Plans*, 4th edn (1999)	Marketing budget – 1.5 pages	0.3%
Doyle – *Marketing Management and Strategy*, 2nd edn (1998)	Budgeting process – ¼ page Advertising budgets – 3 pages	0.8%
Davidson – *Even More Offensive Marketing* (1997)	How much to spend on communications – 5 pages	0.8%

Aaker is generally acknowledged to be a top expert on brand equity, a concept he developed in the course of several books and many articles. This concept is firmly results focused. The cost of achieving those results, however, is not mentioned.

George Day, who is the father of modern marketing planning, likewise focuses on results and not drivers (i.e. causes behind the results). When he does look at financial topics, he gives a scathing dismissal of value analysis: 'The need for value analysis has been created by the increasingly corrosive influence of traditional capital budgeting methods on long-run competitive performance.'

Doyle, McDonald and Davidson all examine marketing planning at some length. Yet the surprising fact is that none of them devotes any significant attention to the issue of what to spend on marketing, in the short, medium or long term.

How much is at stake?

Lack of control over marketing exposes businesses to massive risk. There are two ways of appreciating the scale of the problem.

First, and obviously, there are the very real, tangible sums of money that are invested in sales and marketing activities of various kinds throughout a business. These investments are emphatically not limited to specific, highly visible items such as advertising budgets, even though those items may indeed be large.

There is IT investment, for example, particularly in customer relationship management (CRM) systems. Worldwide, the value of the CRM sector is estimated to be approaching $1 trillion, according to Oracle CEO Larry Ellison (2004). Unfortunately, there is also a wide consensus amongst analysts that up to 60% of CRM implementations are likely to fail – i.e. not deliver the value that was expected.

Similar black holes of marketing-related expenditure can be identified all over an organization. A survey by consultants Blue Sky, for example, estimated that poor employee retention in call centres was costing employers over £1 billion a year in extra costs. Statistics also show that 80% of new product launches fail every year, according to Professor Michael Baker (1983) – with all the attendant waste of resources that entails.

Another way of looking at the scale of the marketing accountability problem is to look at the value that is placed by investors on intangible marketing-related assets such as R&D, intellectual property (e.g. patents), brands and customer bases. Most companies have little idea how to manage their strategic and operational activities to increase the value of these assets, yet improving performance in this area is vital to maintaining investor confidence.

Although this problem is complicated by the fact that there are, at present, few agreed accounting conventions for valuing or reporting intangibles, nevertheless, stockmarkets are efficient at acquiring relevant information from a variety of sources, drawing their own conclusions and pricing shares accordingly. The law firm Taylor Joynson Garrett has estimated, for example, that 'intangible assets on average account for more than 20% of the market capitalization of UK high technology companies' (Grande 2001). Technology firms' intangible assets are principally related to R&D expertise, and the value of investing in R&D was reinforced by the most recent UK DTI Value Added Scoreboard 2004, which identified a strong positive relationship between increased R&D spending in firms and improvements in their share price performance.

Other examples of companies whose stockmarket valuations bear little relation to the valuation of their fixed assets, but which instead reflect the perceived value of the brands they own, or the quality of their customer base, include Coca-Cola, McDonald's, Manchester United and Microsoft.

Investor confidence is damaged by the poor disclosure of marketing information in Annual Reports and investor briefings. Brand Finance Ltd has surveyed investor demands for marketing disclosure (Haigh 1999), and their figures are reported on the left-hand side of Figure 2.6. Professor Hugh Davidson (1999) has analyzed a sample of annual reports of major organizations, and his findings on the lack of disclosure are shown on the right-hand side of Figure 2.6. There is a worrying gap.

Figure 2.6
Gap between what investors want to know and what Annual Reports tell them

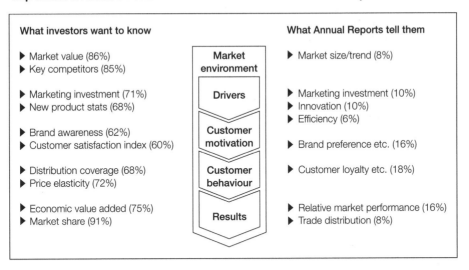

Finally, it is sobering to recall that one of the central reasons for the recent, disastrous worldwide dotcom crash was overvaluation by investors and the markets of essentially *marketing* assets and concepts. Business model after business model in now-bust Internet start-ups has subsequently been shown to be based on poor market research, unsubstantiated connections between customer metrics and results, and overoptimistic forecasts about returns from electronic brands, customer bases and intellectual property.

Even the most conservative estimates suggest that this particular lapse in marketing concentration wiped over $150 billion in value from global stockmarkets during 2000.

Yet, despite the value at risk from poor measurement and control, marketing pays scant attention to them. As Dr David Norton, originator of the Balanced Scorecard, comments (in Shaw and Mazur 1997): 'I find those who have picked up the Balanced Scorecard are strategic planners, finance, quality managers and HR. *My phone doesn't ring much from Marketing.*'

And non-marketing specialists follow customer fads and fashions without the measurement and analysis necessary to make them work effectively. As Professor Malcolm McDonald comments:

> I have worked in 100 plus organizations and I would say in maybe 70% or so you will find they have an inadequate understanding of the customer. At the end of the day, if they don't have a passion for customers they are going to be holding hands and humming when they go over the cliff edge.
>
> All that TQM does is give you a certificate to prove that you can make rubbish perfectly every time (rubbish being goods and services that customers don't buy). And the relationship marketing domain is occupied by happy-clappy, touchy-feely, weepy-creepy, born-again zealots without any underpinning process. Apart from which, 'delighting' or 'exciting' customers is the quickest way to bankruptcy. (McDonald 2000)

The smouldering feud: financial accountability in marketing

The call for financial accountability in marketing has kindled a smouldering feud between marketing believers and the rest of management. Whilst we were writing this book, a worried marketing colleague asked: 'Aren't you playing into the hands of the beancounters writing that book?'

'What exactly is the ROI of marketing?' ask sceptical accountants. The concept of return on investment is a simple one. You look at the results of marketing and compare them with the costs. Yet ROI is an inflammatory subject for marketers.

The passion and sometimes ferocity of the debate about marketing ROI are puzzling and intriguing. Marketing's importance seems straightforward. CEOs routinely say that customers are their top priority, although usually there is a sting in the tail. 'Just show me your numbers,' asks the supportive CEO of his marketing subordinate.

Professor Nigel Piercy is one of the few academics to investigate why there is this difficult relationship. His interviews with marketing managers and directors (Piercy 1992) about budgeting reveal the following emotional issues:

- The **hassle factor** – the sheer difficulty and inordinate amount of time it takes to get resources for marketing, in terms of the papers to be written, committees to be attended and bargaining to be done to get even minor amounts of resource.

- The **conflict over marketing expenditure** with accountants and general management.

- The **lack of control by marketing executives** over resource allocation and actual spending of money.

- The **dead weight of historical views** over how much should be spent on marketing.

- The **imposition of rigid control measures** that link marketing spend to sales, with the interesting effect that when times get hard and we lose sales and market share, we automatically spend less on marketing at precisely that moment when we need to spend more.

The cost of marketing is the crux of the problem, not marketing's effect. Globally we spend $350 billion on advertising (Zenith Optimedia, 2003/4). Add on sales promotion, sponsorship, PR and other costs, and the total bill for marketing is in the region of $1,000 billion.

To financial analysts this amount of expenditure is not an item to be ignored. Despite the distaste that Piercy's marketers feel for the marketing spending debate, it is not going to stop, and marketers must learn how to use the tools needed to evaluate marketing payback.

Why change?

Companies are changing their marketing spending habits. Companies such as Unilever, Kraft and Diageo are declaring war on fuzzy marketing spending decisions:

- because they can;
- because they must.

They *can* change, because new technology and new information sources are available to support marketing decision making. New technologies include automated transaction monitoring, the Internet, new accounting systems and advanced statistical analysis systems. New information sources include scanner data, panel data, customer databases, advertising tracking and promotional tracking. Every consumer has over 50 transactions processed electronically daily (Shaw 1991).

They *must* change because marketing spending is regarded as problematic by many CEOs. Advertising costs are rising steadily and audiences are shrinking and fragmenting. The wisdom of mass advertising is being challenged by alternative targeted media. Direct marketing response rates are gradually falling. Call centres are seen as expensive. Sales forces are becoming ever more costly. Stock-keeping units (SKUs) are proliferating and operational complexity is driving down profits.

Marketing analysis and simulation modelling are methods that equip managers to make better decisions about strategic budget allocation, marketing mix allocation, customer equity, brand support, brand extensions and product development, with several consequential financial benefits:

- *Increasing profitability.* Focused brand investment increases profitability by:
  - Obtaining higher prices, because customers have confidence in the qualities and attributes of brands.
  - Higher volume growth, by selling at an average market price but using the brand's attributes to build higher volume and market share.
  - Reducing waste by increasing the success rates of brand extensions and new product development.
  - Lower costs and better asset utilization, gaining economies of scale from the volume.

- *Increasing brand value over time:*
  - Increasing cash flow through higher profitability, as discussed above.
  - Accelerating the cash flow: focused brand investment can increase shareholder value by generating cash flow sooner than otherwise.
  - Increasing the continuing value of cash flow: brand longevity can generate super profits far beyond the conventional investment horizon. Users of early versions of a product not only buy later versions but also buy new line and brand extensions.

- *Reducing risk:*
  - Strong brands reduce vulnerability to competitive attack.
  - While products are easy to copy, evidence suggests that strong brands are not.

- Brand attributes can provide a significant barrier to entry and so act to reduce the vulnerability of cash flow.

Time and self-discipline are the main costs to marketing managers of this new approach. Realistically, there are development costs too, but these are usually minor compared with the benefits:

■ Initial development costs are incurred once to collect and analyze data and build models. Such projects are undertaken by marketing science departments in organizations like Unilever. Alternatively an outside consultant may be asked to develop and test a model for a fixed fee.

■ Costs of model use are managerial time, the effort to learn the tool and to interact with it.

■ Maintenance consists of refreshing the data and rerunning the analyses, perhaps changing the structure of the model to reflect structural changes in the marketplace.

These costs are a small price to pay for rescuing marketing's reputation. Marketing cannot afford to remain the pariah department, with a reputation for slippery behaviour and unaccountable management.

Key points

■ Unaccountable, untouchable, expensive and slippery are common descriptions of marketing.

■ Marketing faces a crisis of confidence at the top of companies and among investors.

■ Marketing budgets are cut more than any other.

■ Marketing spending is volatile, swinging up and down year-to-year.

■ Marketing controls urgently need an overhaul in most companies.

■ Marketing education needs to address the issue of payback.

■ Marketing people resist the introduction of controls.

■ Marketing information that investors want is not being disclosed.

■ The stakes are high both because of the sums of money spent on sales and marketing and because of the risks to business of not ensuring that this expenditure is effective.

3

DEMONSTRATING SUCCESS

This chapter explains how to demonstrate that marketing expenditure impacts business results. We will look at the various ways of evaluating marketing payback and help you decide which ones work and which don't.

As in other chapters, some terms are used in a specific way, and it is worth noting the definitions in Box 3.1, and referring back to them as you read the chapter.

Box 3.1 Marketing metrics terminology

Demonstrate: Establish the validity of a proposition, by providing evidence, logical arguments or mathematical proofs.

Intuition: The ability to evaluate things without having to apply detailed observation, logic or analysis.

Metric: Numerical summary of observations carried out on a regular basis according to agreed standards of observation and analysis.

Payback: A benefit in exchange for an action or service performed, usually measured in financial terms.

Success: The achievement of the desired aims of a person or an organization.

Waste: A failure to use something wisely, properly, fully or to good effect.

Is there a direct link between marketing and business results?

Marketers insist that there is, and the history of modern marketing is littered with attempts to prove that high scores on metrics such as market share, sales growth, new product launches, brand awareness and customer satisfaction are evidence that they are doing their jobs well and delivering value. In fact, so many sure-fire performance measures have been suggested that Bruce Clark (1999), in a comprehensive review of marketing metrics, comments: 'Figuring out which of many measures are "really important" may drive the conscientious manager to despair.'

Unfortunately, the despair is warranted – using traditional planning and budgeting systems, it is difficult to prove conclusively that any of these measures link marketing activities to business results. For this reason, the various measures proposed by marketing often do not appear credible to finance, nor can they be easily aligned with corporate performance measures. As a result, marketing is often poorly or inappropriately controlled in organizations, frequently with costly consequences – as the late Peter Doyle, former Professor of Marketing and Strategic Management at the University of Warwick Business School, commented:

> The most common criteria for measuring the effectiveness of marketing are increases in sales and market share. Unfortunately, any first year economics student can demonstrate that such growth may as easily decrease, as increase, profits. Sales growth increases profits only if the operating margin on the additional sales covers the higher costs and investment incurred to achieve the growth. Chasing profitless growth has been one of the most common sources of corporate failure. (Doyle 2000)

Given that so much effort has apparently gone into devising measures of marketing performance, what has gone wrong? Thoughtful questioning reveals some deep-seated problems connected to marketing planning and evaluation that companies need to address. For example, ask any executive how they think the system works in their company, and they will most likely voice one of two complaints: the quality of the output and/or the quality of the process.

Underlying this dissatisfaction are several related factors:

- Absence of any apparent benefits from being made accountable;
- Time and resources involved;
- Evident innumeracy of senior managers;
- Reluctance to listen to customers and learn from experience of product failures;
- Cultural disconnect between finance and marketing;
- Short-term financial goals driving decision making;
- Lack of investment in appropriate tools, techniques and systems;
- Fragmented use of available tools.

That there should be these attitudes and problems is not particularly surprising. Historically, little effort has been made to evaluate the full impact of sales and marketing decisions across an organization, and therefore unexpected consequences tend to come as a nasty surprise, and generate an inevitable search for a scapegoat. The impact can range from unforeseen cost and revenue consequences, which 'merely' damage profit forecasts, to quite spectacular disasters which can bring a company to its knees. This lack of foresight happens because sales and marketing are still typically treated as discrete, isolated functional budgets. Their costs can be slashed back or reluctantly accommodated according to the prevailing financial situation, rather than regarded as planned areas of investment, expected to generate future value as part of an integrated strategic initiative.

Second, most sales and marketing personnel, not just senior executives, have frequently been shown to have poor numeracy skills, and often display a lack of interest in understanding or contributing to discussions about corporate financial objectives. The lighthearted comment of the VP of a major credit card company who said (*Marketing Business*, June 1997) 'show me more than two statistics and I'm about as useless as a chocolate fireguard' is by no means an atypical attitude, and epitomizes the very real cultural divide that often exists between sales and marketing staff and the financial decision makers in organizations. Emiko Terazono wrote recently in the *Financial Times* (2004) that 'only 21% of CEOs in the FTSE have worked in marketing' and 'only five FTSE 100 companies have dedicated marketing directors on their boards'.

Third, few organizations have invested enough time and money in appropriate tools, techniques or systems to support marketing decision making adequately. Few executives outside the corporate centre tend to be familiar with routine strategic analysis methods; predictive modelling skills are almost unknown, and few companies have embraced activity-based costing (ABC). All these techniques are almost essential for the accurate evaluation of marketing options and strategies.

As companies face ever-increasing demands to deliver value to investors, it is clear that this lack of accountability and control over marketing cannot be allowed to persist. Marketing's lack of credibility and alignment within the organization undermines the whole company's efficiency and effectiveness. A key objective of successful strategic planning must be the proper allocation of capital and resources in order to balance short-term cash requirements with longer-term growth investment. If marketing is not properly managed as part of this process, it will not only be perceived to be wasteful, it will also be helpless to avoid waste and failure.

Tim Ambler comments:

> Our research showed that most firms do not have a clear picture of their overall marketing performance which may be why they cannot assess it. They prefer to fumble around in the dark. It's easy to see why: fumbling has a lot going for it. More adventure, more creativity, more surprises and more fantasies are all possible. But you may not like what you see when the lights do go on. Clarity of goals and metrics separate the professional from the amateur. Professional marketers quantify results against intentions to keep raising the bar. Professional athletes do the same. (Ambler 2003)

Andrew Ehrenberg agrees:

> What's wrong with marketing is that nearly all of it is rather romantic. Business leaders all talk about growth, but not everybody can grow. Growth is the wrong objective for many. By the self-inflicted goal of 'growth for all', most advertising and also most marketing plans must fail . . . The tendency in consumer research has been to try to explain why consumers behave as they do, without knowing or understanding in any quantitative detail just how they do in fact behave. (Quoted in Shaw and Mazur 1997)

It is worth reviewing how your organization scores on its attitude to marketing accountability. Here are ten hard questions to be answered:

1. How much of your marketing expenditure is wasted?
2. Can you demonstrate that your marketing has positive payback?
3. What exactly is the payoff of your marketing?
4. Do you have too many marketing failures . . . or too few?
5. Does every marketing activity have an expected payoff?
6. How often do you check payback after the event?
7. How transparent is your marketing? Does your agency keep you informed? Do you keep your boss informed of every failure as well as successes?
8. Are your goals realistic? Do you have enough influence on the targets that are set by management?
9. Do short-term results have too much importance?
10. Are you maximizing the right things? Is your goal volume, revenue, growth or profitability?

How should you evaluate your marketing?

There are several approaches to the problem of demonstrating marketing success:

1. The first approach is to tell stories of marketing success and use the evidence to support the general conclusion that 'marketing works'.

2. The second approach is to put a stake in the ground, and track some popular headline measures such as customer satisfaction or brand awareness. Percentage changes in these measures are used as evidence that marketing activities are having a positive (or negative) effect.

3. The final solution is to demonstrate cause-and-effect.

Marketing success: a damn good story

Marketing surrounds itself with damn good stories about its successful track record, and most marketers cling onto them like a life-raft. Coke, IBM and Virgin are icons of marketing success, and their stories are held up again and again to 'prove that marketing works'. The roots of marketing's claims lie deep in a few exemplary brands and associated personal histories – Sergio Zyman, Lou Gerstner and Richard Branson – are star turns in the fabulous marketing story.

To many marketing executives, these stories are useful to silence critics and to intimidate the doubters by blinding them with science. However, cracks are breaking out in the marketing edifice, doubts surfacing about the marketing story, and these flaws are beginning to worry marketers.

Treasure-troves of marketing awards are handed out each year, in ceremonies that attract press and practitioners by the thousand. Success stories sound plausible but they are nearly always conjectural. Where is the proof? Where are the data? Advertising seems self-evident as a driver of success, yet its effect turns out to be very, very hard to catch in the act of changing consumer behaviour, markets being so full of other influences.

Other icons have fallen off their pedestals – British Airways, McDonald's, Xerox – and disintegrated in a miasma of recrimination, intrigue, jealousy, back stabbing and shattered dreams. Marketing stories are losing their power to persuade.

At the core of many of the marketing success stories lie flawed theories, dubious methodologies and wishful thinking. Marketing success is a fraud in the sense that it, marketing, is not demonstrated to be the driver of business success in many cases. There is a real danger of seeing what one believes. Human factors such as ambition, jealousy, rush to publicity, behind-the-scenes manoeuvring – even greed, stress and desperation – are all sanitized out of the reports of marketing's power and its success. Marketers have a lot of credibility invested in particular success stories and want them to prove something.

Marketing success stories are an example of special pleading, a fancy way of equivocating and saying in effect, 'If you look at this, and turn a blind eye to that, then this is a good story for everyone in marketing.' Markets are complex, awash with variables, and analysts must wrestle with levels of complexity only seen elsewhere in fields such as medical research and genetics. We need to dig deeper than the 'damn good stories'.

Case study 3.1

BA – anatomy of a marketing fairy-tale

The British Airways (BA) story has been widely quoted in marketing literature as exemplifying the success of marketing, in fact it has been cited in over 50 textbooks. It is an engaging story about a mammoth struggle for customer rights. Marketing knights Sir Colin Marshall and Lord King are portrayed as fighting with the dark powers of trade unionism to deliver passengers the services they deserve. In a flash of self-congratulation they crowned themselves 'the world's favourite airline'.

BA has also won awards for its advertising. Not only did it invent the 'favourite airline' tag, but its agency M&C Saatchi call it 'the world's favourite advertising'.

Yet hard-nosed economists like Kay (1993) raised doubts a decade ago. He has analyzed success and comments:

> British Airways' competitive strength is largely based on its strategic assets. The most important of these is its dominance of Heathrow Airport, the largest international airport in the world . . . BA advertises heavily. Since its name is already well known and its commitment to its principal markets is not in doubt, the purpose of this advertising, which mostly has little information content, is not apparent . . . BA – whose success was built on cold logic of assets, revenues and efficiencies rather than on anything mystical or intangible – may have fallen victim to its own rhetoric.

A decade after Kay's prophetic words, upstarts such as easyJet and Ryanair have applied their own 'cold logic' and opened a new chapter in asset and efficiency warfare, taking the crown away from the self-congratulatory BA with its expensive marketing.

Even if some success stories are true, we cannot move from the particular to the general to 'prove that marketing works' always. Clancy and Krieg (2000) calculate that, applying the Pareto principle, it is probable that 20% of all marketing spending creates 80% of the value, following the classic performance bell curve (see Figure 3.1).

Figure 3.1
A marketing performance bell curve™

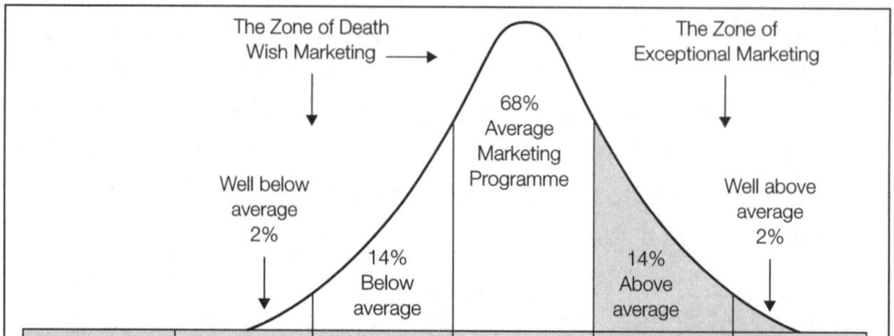

Marketing performance	Embarrassing	Trouble	Disappointing	Pleasing	Amazing
Market share growth	Precipitous decline	Significant decline	Modest decline	Significant increase	Dramatic increase
New product success rate	0%	5%	10%	25%	40%+
Advertising ROI	Negative	0%	1–4%	5–10%	20%
Consumer and trade promotion	Disaster	Very unprofitable	Marginally unprofitable	Profitable	Very profitable
Customer satisfaction	0–59%	60–69%	70–79%	80–89%	90–95%
Customer retention/ loyalty	0–44%	45–59%	60–74%	75–89%	90–94%
Customer acquisitions programmes	Disturbing losses	Significant losses	Marginal losses	Break even	Profitable
Brand equity	Dramatic declines	Significant declines	Modest declines	Stable	Improving

Source: Reprinted with the permission of The Free Press, a division of Simon & Schuster Adult Publishing Group, from COUNTERINTUITIVE MARKETING: Achieve Great Results Using Uncommon Sense by Kevin J. Clancy and Peter C. Krieg. © 2000 by Kevin J. Clancy. All rights reserved.

Clancy and Krieg comment:

The evidence that we have collected over a decade on the performance of marketing programs for consumer and business-to-business products and services incontrovertibly shows that most marketing programs do not provide acceptable return on investment . . . In fact, an astounding 84% of today's marketing programs are unprofitable. . . . Marketing is the engine that drives growth, but the engine is in desperate need of an overhaul. And a major problem we see is *testosterone decision making* – usually male chief marketing officers, advertising directors, and brand managers choosing among alternatives quickly, decisively, and without real information. It's the manly way to screw up. They tell us that their decisions are intuitively appealing. To us this means that it is the same decision everyone else would make. It's the commonsensical thing to do. Yet our research and experience suggest that decisions made on intuition alone rarely lead to successful outcomes. We instead believe that counter-intuitive thinking grounded in rigorous analysis of unimpeachable data is the key to success in marketing.

Marketing's magic numbers

A growing multitude of experts now argue that marketing's success can be assured by gazing at a handful of magic numbers – non-financial numbers such as customer loyalty and brand preference – which are claimed to be inextricably linked to the financial results. The study of a small handful of non-financial numbers is advocated in popular business tracts such as *The Loyalty Effect* (Reichheld 1996), *Brand Valuation* (Haigh 1996) and *Marketing and the Bottom Line* (Ambler 2003).

In these accounts of marketing, just a few numbers are conjured up to provide proof of marketing's success. Ambler has tracked the magic numbers used by marketers over several years. Table 3.1 shows the results of his popularity poll.

Table 3.1
Ambler's marketing metrics popularity poll

Metric	% of firms using measure	% that reach the top board	% giving top rating for marketing performance assessment
Awareness	78.0	28.0	28.0
Market share	78.0	33.5	36.5
Relative price	70.0	34.5	37.5
Number of complaints	69.0	30.0	45.0
Customer satisfaction	68.0	36.0	46.5
Distribution/availability	66.0	11.5	18.0
Total number of customers	65.5	37.4	40.0
Perceived quality/esteem	64.0	32.0	35.5
Loyalty/retention	64.0	50.7	67.0
Relative perceived quality	62.5	52.8	61.6

Source: *Marketing and the Bottom Line (1st edition)*, Tim Ambler, © Pearson Education Limited, 2000.

Ambler notes that many measures such as awareness and distribution are widely used by marketers but not really considered accurate as indicators of performance. He also notes that Boards typically do not receive all the key measures of marketing performance.

The trouble with the 'magic numbers' approach is that inevitably it is quite arbitrary. Macho managers set 'stretch targets' and 'big hairy audacious goals' (BHAG) using these magic numbers as their measures of success. In their planning they claim they will raise awareness from 55% to 57%, their customer satisfaction index from 7.1 to 7.3, and that sales will grow by 2%. Post planning checks are even carried out by a few firms, but what action do they take when the awareness and satisfaction goals fail to materialize?

Many managers use magic numbers to commit acts of intimidation, to support business cases even when they are not in the right. It's easy to forget that magic numbers don't appear out of thin air.

Concerning the measurement of goals, Ambler comments (2003): 'inevitably and quite rightly the goals are bargained'. Concerning the measurement of results, they pop up throughout business without any accompanying account of their origins. But numbers not only come from somewhere, they usually have a substantial history by the time we see them.

Think about the last marketing number you saw before reading this book. Was it the advertising budget? Or the pricing decision for a new product? A brand tracking indicator? Unless it was a telephone number, chances are the last number you saw *measured* something or was the result of a *modelling calculation*. Somebody decides to measure something; that person does so according to certain standards, definitions or specifications, chooses particular units, employs selected measuring techniques and equipment (none of them error free), and then reports them in some format, often after converting it into different units or rescaling it in other ways. When they are modelling, they also make many assumptions, few of which are documented or visible to the casual observer. Or at least, that's the way it goes when things are simple, like when the customer satisfaction report is published.

The story behind a number is often as important and interesting as the number itself. That story is ignored at our peril, because the many steps in creating a number affect what information is captured in that number and how that number is likely to be interpreted and used. So if we really want to understand a number, we must take a hard look at how it was created.

Finance managers know how to dig into numbers. The answers they receive about marketing numbers, or the lack of answers, fuels their scepticism about marketing success. Underlying marketing's magic numbers are layers of unreported facts – facts that could never be reported without legal advice – about U's incompetence, V's burning desire to win a marketing award, W's bonus depending on performance scores, X's dislike of market research, Y's irrational belief in a particular assumption against all evidence, Z's need to please his or her boss.

A multinational in the food business, identity necessarily concealed, witnessed a boardroom struggle between the international marketing Vice President and his opposite number responsible for Europe. The former had research to prove that his new advertising campaign should run. The Europe VP had incontrovertible research to prove it should not. The Group Chief Executive was infuriated that two separate research projects should have been commissioned for the same issue. In fact it was the same single research study. Their two assistants had just picked out the pieces they liked. (Ambler 1996)

There are many things that we can never know about market research and analysis. How much data is presented and how much is suppressed? How did respondents really behave? Can the results be replicated? Researchers are not necessarily frauds, but may just be careless analysts. They go into the field armed with the hypotheses that their all-powerful bosses want to prove.

In the case of marketing, we find analysts and researchers working with marketing managers and agencies, under considerable pressure, to produce the 'right' answers. When Ernest Rutherford discovered the nucleus of the atom, he destroyed 200 years of classical physics. What he found was not supposed to be there, according to the reigning theories of the time, but Rutherford, as director of Cambridge's Cavendish Laboratory, was not beholden to any theorist.

This book aims to persuade you of the need and inevitability of getting behind the stories of marketing's success. It shows you how to get inside the numbers that chart marketing effectiveness. Numbers are not enough; marketing needs diagnostic tools to assess its connection with financial results. Getting inside the numbers will take the reader on a journey into new territory, to areas where only relatively few marketing and finance managers have set foot.

Marketing payback – the final financial frontier

Although the magic numbers approach has the considerable advantages of convenience and internal self-consistency, it has been widely criticized for its lack of alignment with the financial objectives of the business. Representative of these criticisms are the views of Schultz and Walters:

> At the end of the day, top management wants to know what return the organization got back from the resources invested. They want to relate today's spending to today's returns or at least tomorrow's or next week's or the next quarter's. The difficulty is that marketing and brand communication managers are trying to measure communication results based on attitudinal change, not on financial returns to the organization as a result of planned spending. Unfortunately, the two components of attitude and behavior seldom meet in a reliable enough manner with our current measurement systems to provide financial returns.

> We're very good at measuring attitudinal change and we will likely get better in the future. But since the goal of the organization is to be able to relate financial investments to financial returns, our measurement processes do not work very well. And it's unlikely that, without change, they will get much better in the future. So, rather than adjusting, tweaking or restructuring our attitudinal measurements, the time has come to move to behavioural approaches, to measure what the customer or prospect actually does or did in the marketplace based on some sort of transactional (i.e., financial) measure rather than on how they feel or how they felt leading up to that behaviour. (Schultz and Walters 1997)

Behind the facade of the marketing success stories, the awards and the press recognition, the magic numbers and indices, like a monster lurking under a five-year-old's bed, is the bogeyman of finance. To many marketers the call for financial accountability is beyond their reach. However, the demand for financial accountability in marketing is being addressed by a growing number of organizations which reject the purely non-financial measures as inadequate.

The Institute of Practitioners in Advertising (IPA) gives awards each year. Unusually, the criteria for judging are based not on artistic merit, but on profit payback. In briefing entrants for the awards, here is what IPA says (see IPA Awards Guide to Entrants, *www.ipa.co.uk*):

> The IPA Effectiveness Awards reward and showcase the commercial power of marketing communications. They are the only UK awards scheme where entries have to prove that the campaign actually worked in hard business terms.

In their advice to entrants, the IPA offers Top Ten Tips, including:

- Get the client on board
- Show hard evidence that the campaign worked
- Make it a good read

Case study 3.2

IPA judging criteria

Overall, the judges are examining how ideas communicated via one of more channels, have affected a company's commercial performance and how powerfully this has been achieved. The more powerful the idea, the more powerful the effect and thus the greater your chances of doing well.

To help you understand the judging, we have detailed below the criteria on which the judges are asked to examine papers.

- **Clarity of presentation:** How well written, structured, and presented is the case? (NB: one test of award potential is whether the paper would stand up to publication?)

- **Scale of task:** How intrinsically difficult or straightforward is the task that the communication has to solve (e.g. very competitive market or lack of product differentiation) and is the measurement of the communication effect in this market particularly difficult or easy (e.g. type/source of data)?
- **Strength of solution:** To what extent are the strategic solution and subsequent communications idea different and imaginative?
- **Scale of effect:** How great has the effect of the campaign been? How efficient has the campaign been in generating that effect?
- **Explanation and proof of effect:** To what extent does the paper explain and prove how the campaign worked? How well has the case convinced you of the unbreakable logic between the agency's work and the business (or real world) effect?
- **Innovation (measurement):** Has the entry exposed any new ways of presenting data either through its collection, analysis, or use within the argument?
- **Channel exploitation:** Has the effect of the channels of communication used been considered and evaluated? Do we learn about why a particular channel was used?
- **Overall judgement:** How powerful was the idea in delivering a return on investment? What is the overall rating of the paper, taking into account all the above factors?

A presentation entitled 'What Exactly Are You Expected to Prove?', written by Les Binet, Creative Director of DDB Matrix and Convenor of Judges of the 2005 IPA Effectiveness Awards, is included on their website and the rigour of the quantitative assessment is spelled out:

What Exactly Are You Expected to Prove?

Prove that the campaign was effective.
- You must prove, beyond all reasonable doubt, that the campaign was commercially successful.
- It is not enough to show that:
  - Tracking measures improved
  - Consumers' behaviour changed
  - Client objectives were achieved.
- You should also try to show that the campaign paid for itself financially. [Charities etc. excepted.]
- This usually means showing that you generated extra sales.

Prove you generated extra sales.
- It is not enough to measure direct sales:
  - You must prove that those sales wouldn't otherwise have been made by other means.
- It is not sufficient to show that sales increased:
  - You must prove that the campaign was responsible, and not some other factor.

■ It is not necessary to show that sales increased:
  – Sometimes maintaining sales, or slowing a decline, can be a real
    achievement.
■ What you need to show is that total sales were higher than they would
  have otherwise been.

Show that the campaign paid for itself.
■ Having shown that the campaign generated incremental sales, you should
  then show that this increased profits.
■ If possible, look for other contributions to shareholder value, such as
  supporting a premium price or increasing brand value.
■ If your client has a problem with confidentiality, consult the *Guide to
  Entrants*, and/or the IPA.
■ Note: Profit calculations are often flawed, e.g. 'The campaign cost £5m
  and generated £10m of extra sales, so it paid for itself twice over.'

Identify the contribution of each channel.
■ Having shown the total effect of the campaign, you should then
  demonstrate the contributions of the various channels.
■ What roles did the different channels play?
  – Think outside the box: e.g. DM can build awareness as well as generate
    responses.
■ How big was the contribution of each channel?
  – Ideally measure payback from each channel.
  – Difficult to do without econometrics?

Gill Hart, Marketing Director, Europe, Middle East and Africa at the *Financial Times*, comments: 'The awards present the most compelling evidence for clients of ROI and the effectiveness and creative use of media ... in step with FD and CEO thinking and provide thought leadership.'

Ways of improving marketing profitability

There are only three basic ways that marketing decisions can contribute to increasing profits (see Rossiter and Percy 1997):

■ by increasing sales volumes;
■ by increasing price;
■ by reducing unit costs.

Of course, in a recession or in an increasingly competitive market, the objective may be simply to maintain profitability, perhaps by maintaining sales volume, market share or the brand's premium price. However, the overall form of the analysis remains the same.

Note that a key factor in the analysis is that of timescale for delivery of the profit stream. Rossiter and Percy identified three time horizons: 'immediate', 'one year' and 'long run', and proposed the summary of the effectiveness of advertising spend and promotional spend over time given in Table 3.2.

Table 3.2
Summary of effectiveness of marketing expenditure over different time periods

Timescale	Increasing sales volume	Increasing selling price	Lowering cost
Immediate	*Advertising*: use direct response advertising; retail advertising; or classified ads	*Advertising*: justify high introductory price or price increase	*Advertising*: none (immediate cost is increased)
	Promotion: use sales promotions (trade, retail or consumer)	*Promotion*: temporarily discount high introductory price	*Promotion*: none (immediate cost is increased)
One year	*Advertising*: use media advertising	*Advertising*: increase upside price elasticity and decrease downside price elasticity (thereby increasing brand equity)	*Advertising*: partially substitute advertising for sales calls; reduce trade promotion ('pull' strategy)
	Promotion: use trial promotions (for frequent repeat products); achieve decycling; motivate sales force	*Promotion*: 'ratchet' promotions after successful advertising bursts (less price reduction needed)	*Promotion*: increase 'switching costs' and thus lower cost to retain customer
Long run	*Advertising*: defend attained sales rate	*Advertising*: protect brand equity and thus raise average selling price	*Advertising*: lower unit cost via experience curve
	Promotion: none (beyond increasing pool of triers initially)	*Promotion*: offer loyalty promotions (less price reduction needed) and maintain value positioning	*Promotion*: lower unit cost via experience curve

Source: After Rossiter and Percy (1997)

Unfortunately the individual actions outlined in Table 3.2 cannot be used as a simplistic recipe for improving marketing payback. The correct mix of marketing expenditure decisions that is right for a particular company and situation requires some careful calculations in order to achieve the best profit result.

The section that follows provides a more detailed explanation of how to calculate marketing payback in terms that financial executives will understand. All potentially unfamiliar terms and concepts are explained, and if it is new territory for you, making the effort to follow the reasoning will help immeasurably in your next conversation about justifying the marketing budget to colleagues. The terminology and arguments are also core to understanding the content of many of the later chapters in this book.

Why only profit will do

Managers often monitor 'proxy' variables instead of profit, and in this section we consider three of the most pernicious of these:

- volume;
- gross revenue;
- net revenue.

Volume

Tracking sales volumes is a favourite pastime. For example, for the reporting of sales in the drinks industry, the terms litres, hectolitres and barrels are widely used performance measures. Tons or metric tons are widely reported measures in many other sectors.

If you are using volume as your key indicator of performance, variances (usually below target) often cause a response, resulting in sales promotions being applied to increase volumes and balance the budget. Yet widespread research indicates that over 80% of all sales promotions reduce profits rather than increasing them. An obsession with volume can easily take your eye off the profit objective.

Gross revenue

An obsession with gross revenue is also bad. To understand the problem, look at Figure 3.2, which shows a profit–revenue–price curve. Note that this figure assumes that price is kept constant.

Look first at the sales revenue curve. This shows sales revenue increasing in response to marketing expenditure. As more is spent on marketing, however, the incremental benefit to sales revenue reduces. The curve flattens out and begins to approach the maximum uplift for sales revenue achievable by marketing. Now look at the marketing cost line. Because this is a straight line, it will at some point cross the sales revenue curve. At this point, the increased revenue achieved by marketing is exactly cancelled by the cost of the marketing itself.

Figure 3.2

Response curve showing effect of deducting marketing costs from sales revenue

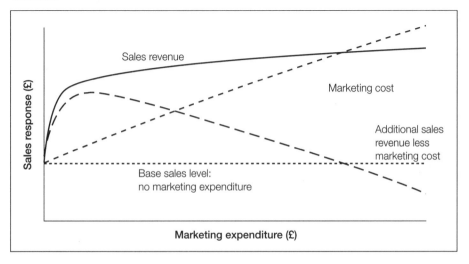

In general, subtracting the marketing cost from the additional sales revenue generated by the marketing gives the effect of the marketing on profitability. This is shown as the third curve in Figure 3.2. Although, as noted above, the additional sales revenues generated by marketing continues to increase with marketing expenditure, when the cost of the marketing is subtracted, the net financial benefit (i.e. the effect on profitability) increases to a maximum and then starts to decrease. At even higher levels of marketing expenditure, the cost of the marketing will exceed the additional revenue generated, and the sales revenue less marketing costs will be lower than with no marketing.

Including the effects of price does not help improve the case for revenue maximization either. As discussed at more length in Chapter 13, the maximum revenue occurs at a lower price than the maximum profit. Cutting price, or increasing promotions, can boost revenues but harm profits. So using revenue as a criterion for evaluating prices and promotions is a bad idea from all viewpoints.

Net revenue

Another performance indicator that is misleading, but quite widely used, is net revenue. This is calculated as:

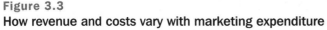

$$\text{Net revenue} = \text{Revenues} - \text{Marketing expenditure}$$

An obsession with net revenue is also bad. This can be seen by looking at what happens when we take into account costs, using the simple fixed cost-variable cost model in Figure 3.3.

Figure 3.3 shows that as marketing expenditure increases, sales volumes will increase and so variable costs will also increase. Consider what happens as we gradually increase marketing expenditure, starting from zero and moving to the right in this figure. Initially net revenue increases and costs also increase. But by the time that we have reached the point of maximum net revenue, by definition net revenues will start to decline and variable costs are continuing to increase. This means that we have already passed the point at which profits are maximized. This leads to the following generalization:

> The marketing spend required to maximize net revenues (i.e. revenues less marketing spend) is always greater than that required to maximize profits.

Figure 3.3
How revenue and costs vary with marketing expenditure

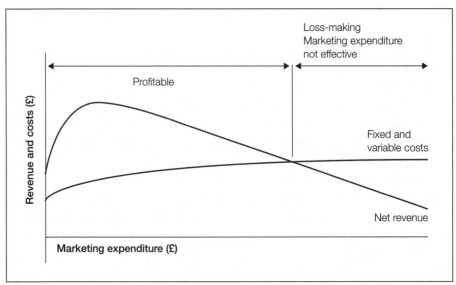

It is hardly surprising, then, that some agencies argue for setting marketing expenditure on the basis of maximizing net revenue.

Using net revenue as a proxy for profit is equivalent to assuming that all costs are fixed costs. This is because, if all costs are fixed, we simply move the net revenue curve vertically downwards in Figure 3.3 by a distance equal to the fixed costs to get to the profit. An assumption that all costs are fixed is seldom a realistic assumption on which to base decisions on the level of marketing expenditure.

What sort of profit is best?

Having shown some of the downsides of using proxies such as volume and revenue as substitutes for measuring marketing payback, unfortunately we have to admit that the use of 'profit' is not as simple as it appears either.

Some of the more sophisticated agencies talk about maximizing profit, but compute profit assuming a fixed profit margin. This, by contrast, is equivalent to assuming that all costs are variable costs and is even more bizarre because it will consistently under-estimate the level of marketing expenditure required for profit maximization!

To appreciate how this happens, consider the comparison discussed in Figure 3.3. Moving from all fixed costs (equivalent to maximizing net revenue) to a mixture of fixed costs and variable costs decreases the level of marketing expenditure that corresponds to profit maximization. If our model of the business is (wrongly) that all costs are variable, then we will conclude that the marketing expenditure required for profit maximization is too low. In effect, we are ignoring the benefit we gain from diluting the fixed costs, by having the higher volumes and revenues that arise from a higher marketing expenditure. There is, then, another general result that we can state:

> The marketing expenditure required to maximize profit assuming a constant profit margin is always less than that required to maximize profit if we take into account both fixed and variable costs.

Overall, there is no short-cut for optimizing marketing expenditure. In order to avoid consistently under-estimating or over-estimating the level of marketing expenditure, it is essential to take into account both the fixed costs and the variable costs of the business. The combined effects of fixed and variable costs are illustrated in Figure 3.4.

Figure 3.4

Response curve showing effects of deducting fixed and variable costs from revenue in addition to marketing costs

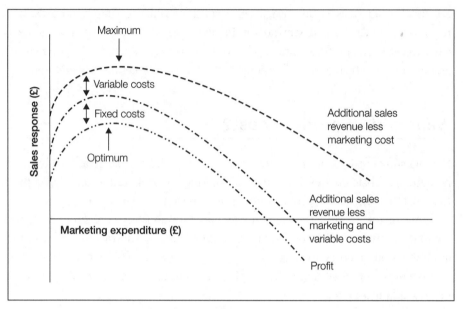

Figures 3.2–3.4 illustrate how a simple response curve can reveal the impact of marketing expenditure. The derivation of response curves usually requires the use of econometric analysis techniques. In practice, response behaviour can be more complex than illustrated in the above example, and we explore below some of the additional factors that may have to be taken into account.

Marketing profit measures compared

Because of the difficulties in defining what is meant by marketing profit in financial terms, a new ratio, Return On Marketing Expenditure (ROME), or as it is often misleadingly called, Return On Marketing Investment (ROMI), has been hailed by some self-proclaimed experts as the new panacea.

Guy Powell in his book *Return on Marketing Investment* (2002) comments, 'ROMI is defined as the revenue (or margin) generated by a marketing program divided by the cost of that program at a given risk level.' Later on in the book he comments, 'For many companies, there is no difference in margin between product lines. In this case the ROMI calculation can be simplified by using revenue only.' Apart from the casual way that he slips interchangeably between revenue and margin, the concept of maximizing ROMI is flawed.

The key feature of ROME is that it is constructed to be analogous to the standard financial ratio Return On Capital Employed (ROCE), used to evaluate the effectiveness of capital expenditure. By putting marketing expenditure on the same basis as capital expenditure and deriving an analogous ratio, the theory is that marketing can adopt a common language with finance that aims to facilitate communications between the two disciplines.

ROME can be defined most easily in terms of the expected effect of a change in marketing expenditure. It is simply the ratio of the change in profitability attributable to the change in marketing expenditure to the change in marketing expenditure itself. This can be expressed as an equation, as follows:

ROME = Change in profitability / Change in marketing expenditure

Or, equivalently,

ROME = (Change in revenue – Change in costs) / Change in marketing expenditure

The advantage of formulating the definition in terms of changes in marketing expenditure and profitability as above is that it gives direct readings on how marketing budgets should be changed in order to maximize profit.

- Applying ROME separately to individual marketing spending line items will establish as priorities for additional expenditure those items that have the highest ROME (or as priorities for spending reductions those items with the lowest ROME).

- In terms of justifying the marketing budget as a whole, all line items with a ROME greater than zero are making a positive contribution to profits and would be retained for profit maximization.

The simplicity of the above definition does not, however, disguise the real difficulties in estimating the change in revenue and costs (and therefore profitability) attributable to the change in marketing expenditure. Amongst the problem areas are the following:

1. Distinguishing the impact of marketing expenditure on demand from that of the other factors affecting demand is not straightforward. For example, the following factors can all have larger impacts than marketing expenditure:
   - price (own price and competitors' prices);
   - seasonality;

- competitor marketing activity;
- economic factors;
- underlying consumer trends.

Identifying the separate impacts of the various components of marketing expenditure is even more difficult than distinguishing the overall effect of marketing expenditure from the other factors listed above.

3. Both direct and indirect effects can occur, for example, sales volume may increase directly as a result of the marketing spend, but also indirectly because distribution increases.

4. Responses to marketing expenditure are not always instantaneous, and can impact over a period of time.

A good solution to some of these problems is to develop a model of market responses that separates out the marketing expenditure impacts from the other factors.

The problem of the timing of the response merits separate discussion. For some types of marketing expenditure, there are clearly long-term effects. Where these are thought to be significant (e.g. product launch advertising, recruitment-oriented short-term promotions, or long-term promotions), the best approach would be to assess the effectiveness of the marketing spend by carrying out a Discounted Cash Flow (DCF) type of analysis on the expenditures and earnings arising from the marketing programme.

What is the best approach to marketing profit?

ROME, ROMI and ROI can all tell you different things about marketing profit. For example, Ambler (2003) comments on the use of return on investment (ROI) as follows: 'When people talk of the ROI from marketing, they usually mean the profit return after deducting the cost of the campaign: it is return minus investment, not return divided by investment . . . The point is that the firm is trying to maximize the net return.'

Graphing the argument, in Figure 3.5, it becomes clear that maximizing ROME will result in lower marketing spend than maximizing profits. As Ambler comments: 'ROI ascribes too much importance to the cost relative to profit.'

We conclude that many organizations are paying too much attention to volumes, revenues, contributions and efficiencies (ROMI, ROME or ROI). The best criterion is to maximize net profit, after deducting the cost of marketing.

Figure 3.5
Profit and return on marketing expenditure

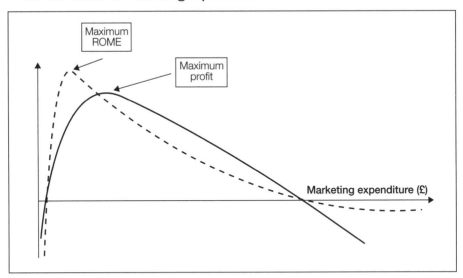

A more precise accounting definition would be EBITDA, or Earnings Before Interest, Tax, Depreciation and Amortization. This may seem to be stating the blindingly obvious, but those familiar with financial ratios will be aware that definitions of profit can get much more complex than this. However, we believe that the arguments in this book are not substantially changed for other ways of calculating profit, such as NOPLAT (Net Operating Profit Less Adjusted Taxes), EP (Economic Profit) or EVA (Economic Value Added).

You should also be aware that there is a growing body of work attempting to understand how improving marketing profits can impact the way markets calculate ratios such as share price (Gregory 1999), shareholder value (Butterfield 2000) and brand value (Perrier 1996; Haigh 1996).

Although this aspect of calculating marketing payback is of academic interest, we have not included a detailed discussion of it here because many managers find it somewhat demotivating.

It is difficult for marketing managers to see how their individual actions count in the overall scheme of world share-price movements and the mysterious workings of investment analysts' minds. Instead, in this book we concentrate on how executives can influence their own company's profits by practical actions and good decisions.

The Diageo way of brand building (DWBB)

Diageo is one of the world's leading premium drinks business with an outstanding collection of beverage alcohol brands across spirits, wine and beer categories. These brands include: Smirnoff, Johnnie Walker, Guinness, Baileys, J&B, Captain Morgan, Cuervo, Tanqueray, and Beaulieu Vineyard and Sterling Vineyards wines. It's global, trading in over 180 markets around the world and listed on both the London Stock Exchange and the New York Stock Exchange.

Accountability and measurement are of paramount importance to marketing, and so too is action. Rob Malcolm, President, Global Marketing Sales and Innovation, has been instrumental in both areas, by spearheading the development of measurement tools and promulgating them throughout the organization.

Measurement tools for marketing

Malcolm (2003) takes up the story:

If we marketers are going to have a seat at the table and have the talent and capacity we need, it can still go pear-shaped if we do not pay attention to government and accountability of what we do.

The good and great sustainable brand-building companies are rigorous in their analysis and in the measurements of the results over time. They improve their track record of delivery by constantly learning, and sharing this learning, embedding this learning in the organization. This rigour takes many forms and needs to be fit for purpose and you are all familiar with many of them; quality business reviews, pre-market testing, concept and advertising research, the right kind of consumer tracking, and some return on investment analysis. Simply stated, we will not earn a seat at the table, nor earn the investment in our brands and the investment in building our functional capability, unless we prove that we deliver a return. It is darn hard, it is time consuming, but the value of strong delivery and the metrics that measures it are inescapable.

If you just think about it in financial terms, if we could improve the efficiency or effectiveness of our marketing spend by just 5% per year, it is a small part of the 50% that we are looking for. The value we can create for the commercial enterprise is tremendous. The supply chain guys in your organizations are killing themselves to find 1% or 2% of cost savings and cover the cost of inflation. They near-constantly radically restructure organizations to get 2% to 3% out of overheads. When you think of the amount of money that is spent in building our brands, the 5% improvement in that efficiency may be the best return your company can get.

Why is it then that so many of us marketers shy away from the cost and efficiency challenge? I have to admit, as a long-term marketer, part of it has not intrinsically been part of our culture. Marketers invent and create stuff and accountants measure it. In my view this is bollocks and is faulty thinking and the sooner we recognize it as such and address it the better. The key thought I would leave you with on metrics and measurement is to make it simple and you will have a chance of getting it done. Make it complex and you won't.

Diageo have invested in a very simple tool for their marketing investments with a bit of rigour behind it (see Figure 3.6). Marketers can understand and buy into it and finance directors love it.

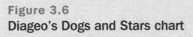

Figure 3.6
Diageo's Dogs and Stars chart

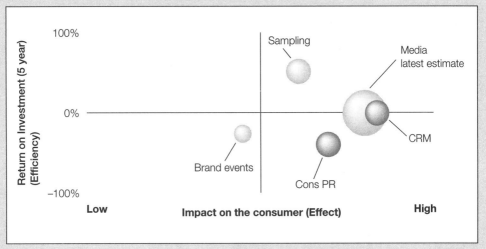

Source: Malcolm (2003)

It's a simple version of the classic Boston matrix, with the return on investment – that is, the sales and earnings divided by the investment – on the vertical axis and the effect on the consumer on the horizontal. Managers plot activities and measure them against those two simple measures, effect on the consumer of the brand building power and the efficiency of the investment. Obviously the stars are those that go in the upper right-hand corner and the dogs are those things that go in the left-hand corner.

Managers then do a very simple exercise. If they have done some great things in the lower right-hand corner that are working with the consumer but are not providing a return, they go to work on how to do them more efficiently. And on the top left-hand side, if they get great return on investment but are not brand building, they look at it and say, 'Why is this not having an effect – a sustainable effect – on the consumer?' They then go to work on that.

Another tracking chart that Rob Malcolm reviews with Diageo's Executive Committee once a quarter is an analysis of the effectiveness of his advertising by brand, by medium and by market for their top eight brands worldwide (see Figure 3.7). When he first shared this chart, he was nervous as it put on the line for all to see one of the most closely guarded marketing secrets – does our advertising really work? Does it really grow the business?

The chart shows advertising that has been running for more than a year and proving itself in business results and equity measures. It also shows advertising that has been running for less than a year but where all the testing and equity measures are positive. It also shows 'We don't know' and 'We have a problem: we know it doesn't work, and we and the agency are working hard to solve it'. The arrows up or down indicate the change from the last quarter. Malcolm reviews this with his Executive Committee every single quarter for all the global brands in every market.

Figure 3.7

How Diageo analyzes advertising effectiveness by brand

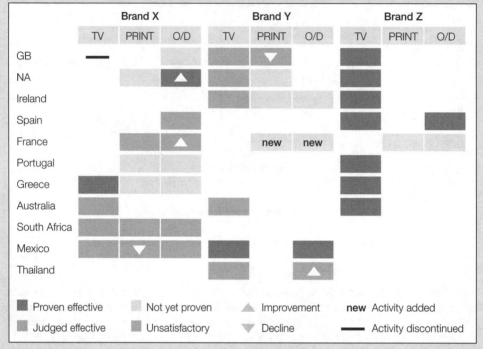

Source: Malcolm (2003)

Malcolm continues:

> I knew we were on our way to building trust by the reaction of the CEO when I first put this chart on the table about eight months ago. Two admittedly imperfect score cards that looked like this and he said, and I quote, 'This is the most honest and transparent presentation I have ever seen for marketing and I really do trust that you are on track to making the progress we need.' That is the start of the journey for the kind of professionalism and trust that we need to build for this function.

Building professionalism and capability

The second challenge addressed by Malcolm is: How do we build marketing professionalism and real functional capability?

This is a long-term commitment, not a quick fix. It requires money, investment, great people, time, tenacity, love, patience and some more tenacity. More than 6,000 people have been trained in five full days' interactive training in the past three years. 100% of all senior management started in the first training programme with the CEO and the Executive Board. 100% of the marketing function, all of the executive teams and all functions in every market, and representatives from global supply and other global functions have been trained. It also includes training our agencies and joint venture partners.

The Diageo way of brand building is not just a programme or this month's seminar. It has become the day job and has permeated the language and approach to the business in every function and at every level of the company.

The corporate commitment in investment terms over the past four years is in the order of £35 million. That includes the cost of the days invested as well as all the programme and training costs. That is a very, very big commitment but one that is felt to have an almost immediate payback. As a percentage of the total investment in marketing, advertising and promotion, that number is actually less than one half of 1% of that asset. If the efficiency or effectiveness of marketing programmes is increased by only 5% a year, the payback is virtually instantaneous.

Rob Malcolm offers the following advice:

■ First enrol top management in the journey. There is no substitute for CEO, Executive Committee and Board ownership and sponsorship. When you have that, you might hear around the organization, 'Hey, these guys are really serious about this stuff.'

■ The second tip is train it yourself internally. Do not delegate this important task to anyone else. Core functional professionalism and capability must be your day job as senior marketing leaders. If you do not live and role-model the values, the tools, the language, the culture and nurture it, you cannot expect anybody else to.

■ Third, make it output and growth-oriented so you can see the results. There is nothing that will embed this more than by people seeing it work and saying, 'Hey, this stuff really does work.'

■ Fourth, make it simple. If it is not simple, it won't happen. It won't stick.

■ Fifth, make it creative and fun. Marketers love to play with fun things and create things. Feed this discipline in a fun, engaging way, so they not only get it but they feel great about it.

These characteristics are the hallmarks of the best sustainable marketing companies and capability programmes. Most are a well-established part of the culture. There is something that every organization can learn from the revolution that is going on at Diageo at the moment.

Key points

■ 'Marketing works' is a blanket claim commonly used to support marketing spending but it lacks credibility.

■ 'Magic metrics' are being used in some organizations to set performance stretch-targets, but the targets are often arbitrary and demoralizing.

■ Diagnosing poor results requires more than a few numbers and there is an urgent need for managers to look more closely at cause-and-effect.

■ Financial payback is the ultimate test of marketing performance.

■ Marketing expenditure contributes to increasing profits by increasing prices and volumes, and reducing operating costs.

- Too many organizations are paying too much attention to sales volumes, revenues, contributions and efficiencies (ROMI, ROME or ROI). Maximizing volume, revenue, contribution or ROME is not the right formula for success.

- The best criterion is to maximize net profit, after deducting the cost of marketing.

4

THE LAWS OF MARKETING

Y ou may be surprised by the suggestion that there are any generally agreed marketing laws, and perhaps cynically assumed that there was only marketing *lore*, a body of half-baked assumptions that could easily be adapted to justify any decision after an event. In fact, there are numerous robust marketing laws that planners ignore at their peril, but they are often not well known, as they tend to be counter-intuitive in nature and often contradict the rules-of-thumb that managers prefer to use every day. For this reason these laws are important, they challenge our complacency, and it is important to study them before reading the more detailed advice given later in this book.

What are empirical generalizations?

Marketing managers often say that experience is the best teacher, and a central theme of this book is that you should learn from past performance to improve future performance – but past performance is not necessarily quite the same thing as past experience.

Most of us learn from personal experience, from colleagues, from competitors and also from teachers. Yet what most of us learn are rules-of-thumb rather than empirical generalizations. To clarify what we mean, some definitions are listed in Box 4.1.

Box 4.1 Marketing laws terminology

Empirical generalization: A pattern of cause-and-effect linking marketing activities to customer responses and payback (e.g. advertising → buying behaviour → payback) that repeats over different circumstances (e.g. product categories, time-periods, geographic areas, etc.) and that can be described simply by mathematical, graphic or symbolic methods. The pattern repeats but need not be universal over all circumstances. It has been established by researching the empirical evidence.

Empirical market response model: A pattern of cause-and-effect based on analysis that applies to a limited set of products, etc. that has been established by analyzing a representative but limited sample of empirical data.

Research: Systematic investigation of an area of knowledge to establish general patterns and rules.

Rule-of-thumb: A way of solving practical marketing problems, regarded as roughly correct but not intended to be scientifically accurate, based on claimed general wisdom from expert experience.

At first sight, rules-of-thumb might seem equivalent to, or at least closely related to, empirical generalizations. They aren't. To understand the rules-of-thumb approach, we suggest you look at Ries and Trout (1993) who claim that: 'After years of working on marketing principles and problems, we have distilled the findings into the basic laws that govern success and failure in the marketplace.'

Ries and Trout's pitch has a strong business appeal:

> Billions of dollars have been wasted on marketing programs that couldn't possibly work, no matter how clever or brilliant. Or how big the budgets . . . So how do you avoid making mistakes in the first place? The easy answer is to make sure your programs are in tune with the laws of marketing.

However, the authors themselves draw attention to the uncertainties surrounding their subject:

> What are these marketing laws? And who brought them down from Mount Sinai on a set of stone tablets? ... There are, after all, many sophisticated marketing practitioners and academics. Why have they missed what we think is so obvious? The answer is simple. As far as we can tell, almost no one is willing to admit that there are any laws of marketing – certainly none that are immutable.

The shortcomings of this rules-of-thumb approach was investigated in depth by Clancy and Shulman (1994). They reviewed a catalogue of 172 'marketing myths' and presented a fierce torrent of counterarguments, suggesting that most of these myths were worth less than the paper they were printed on.

One of the biggest weaknesses of the rules-of-thumb approach is its lack of focus. There is no clear subject matter. The rules encompass sweeping generalizations such as:

- 'Most marketing programs work.'
- 'Faster is better in planning.'
- 'The response of consumers to sales promotions is very unlikely to last long after the promotion ends.'

Their miscellany is a big problem and it becomes very hard for their reliability to be tested or understood without greater focus.

The concept of 'empirical generalizations', as defined above, is much more focused, and the reliability of generalizations can be tested and re-tested in a very systematic way. The focus is on the causal link between marketing activities to customer responses and ultimately payback.

A well-known advocate of the empirical generalization approach is Professor Andrew Ehrenberg. His philosophy is described in his book on *Repeat Buying* (1988), in which he concludes that: 'The fundamental finding in the study of buyer behaviour is that there are simple and highly generalizable patterns. This is by no means an obvious result given the complexities of the buying situation.'

A growing number of other empirical generalizations are being discovered. Analyses of many individual studies are now being compared and contrasted, providing some justification at last for marketing's claim to be a 'science' as well as an art.

All of this work greatly helps in improving marketing payback, because rather than start a market payback study from a null hypothesis, this kind of research enables us to start from a point of real knowledge. This chapter surveys the range of empirical findings and generalizations that have so far been uncovered, and the managerial implications of the work are explained.

Why are empirical generalizations important?

Mainly because they are counter-intuitive. Marketing managers can be terribly complacent, and fail to search out any evidence for their decisions, preferring to sit in their armchairs making intuitive decisions.

Intuitive marketing decisions have a terrible track record, according to Clancy and Krieg (2000):

> Intuitive marketing is our term for the efforts that managers, driven by excess testosterone, unconsciously or unknowingly undertake to kill an otherwise healthy product, service or, occasionally, an entire company. They base their decisions on 'conventional wisdom' and 'common-sense.' Yet conventional wisdom is all too often based on beliefs rooted in marketing myths that permeate business today. Intuitive marketing has led to continued poor performance and brand confusion.

Intuitive marketers are castigated as the "over-and-over-again" managers who feel they don't have time to do it right the first time, but endless time and a company bankroll to do it over and over again.'

Some common symptoms of intuitive marketing cited by Clancy and Krieg include:

- Decisions are based on judgement alone;
- Competitors guide decision making;
- Seeking short-term results;
- Ignoring real customer needs;
- Considering too few alternatives;

- Inability to calculate profitability;
- Ignoring profitability;
- Promoting managers too quickly;
- Flawed research;
- Focus group mania;
- Customer satisfaction study by mail;
- The seven-minute segmentation study;
- Concept testing by telephone;
- Strange, non-representative samples.

Yours will be an unusual organization if you don't recognize some of those symptoms in your own company. It is also worth reflecting on the costly mistakes caused by this kind of decision making. Here are ten hard questions to ask yourself before reading further on how to avoid these mistakes in the future.

1. How confident are we about the rules we apply to evaluating our marketing decisions?
2. Have we fully researched the empirical generalizations about our marketing?
3. Is our marketing based too much on intuition and 'gut feel'?
4. Have we reviewed the marketing journals such as *Marketing Science* and *Journal of Marketing Management*?
5. Do we really understand customer loyalty?
6. Is our understanding of branding set on empirical foundations?
7. Have we taken sufficient account of distribution effects?
8. Do our pricing and promotion decisions take full account of the empirical evidence?
9. Has our advertising agency studied the empirical evidence adequately?
10. Are our new product developments informed by empirical evidence?

Where do empirical generalizations come from?

You probably don't think about empirical generalizations very often, even less study them, so you are probably wondering: Where do I find them? Where have they come from? And should I believe them?

Books on marketing might seem like a good place to look, and yet they aren't. Best-selling texts such as Philip Kotler's *Marketing Management* (1991) make a point of only focusing on management themes. If you want to find any generalizations about how customers respond to marketing activities, you will have to look in the appendices to the book. These are printed on blue paper, to warn the reader 'numbers ahead'. Professor Kotler in discussions with us mentioned that the teaching of quantitative disciplines was unpopular when he first wrote his books, and it got squeezed out of the popular marketing texts.

Books on consumer behaviour are perhaps a better place to look. However, in these books, empirical generalizations tend to be buried in theoretical material. Probably the most accessible book to study is East's (1997) *Consumer Behaviour*.

The best empirical material is to be found in the professional journals, but few executives have the time or patience to study them. Over 100 academic journals are devoted to marketing. Most publish editions four or more times annually, with ten or more articles, and many have been going for 20 years or more. Some are over 50 years old. At a conservative estimate, over 100,000 articles are in print. How can a busy executive find anything that is relevant to the problem at hand? Help is now offered by a few websites.

- The R&D Initiative, producing reusable findings and insight that impact on marketing strategy: *www.marketingoracle.com*
- *Journal of Empirical Generalizations in Marketing Science*: *www.empgens.com*

Many journal publications have much better credentials than practising managers seem to realize. Characteristics to look for are:

- Articles written about a specific cause-and-effect relationship (e.g. advertising → buying behaviour → payback);

- Data collection and analysis to establish the empirical relationship;

- Refereeing of the articles by peer-review prior to publication to ensure they reach adequate standards of rigour;

- Comparison of results with other similar studies;

- Summarization of general relationships that go beyond products, markets and specific situations.

We present some important examples of empirical generalizations in the rest of this chapter culled from this body of research. Many of these are counter-intuitive and fly in the face of conventional wisdom.

Customer satisfaction and loyalty

Customer satisfaction and loyalty is an area where empirical generalizations and popular rules-of-thumb are not always in agreement. The modern doctrines of customer satisfaction and customer loyalty have a bewitching logic. Simply satisfy your customers and they will love you. The more you satisfy them, the more profit they will give you. The more they love you, the better you must treat them. No idea has influenced management more, or for more years, than the concept of 'customers for life'.

Loyal customers cost less to service than disloyal ones, according to Bain consulting guru Fred Reichheld, author of the best-selling book *The Loyalty Effect* (1996):

> Loyalty-based management is a Sunday school teacher's dream come true – an ethical approach to business that pays so well that it puts the unscrupulous approaches to shame . . . we discovered that raising customer retention rates by five percentage points could increase the value of an average customer by 25 to 100%.

And competitors will be kept at bay, according to Harvard Professor Michael Porter (1979), because loyalty 'creates a barrier by forcing market entrants to spend heavily'.

Certainly the influence of these rules-of-thumb can be found in the measurements and targets set by major corporations. A survey we carried out showed that over 60% of all organizations today measure customer satisfaction, making it one of the principal non-financial measures in common use. Yet empirical evidence is sometimes at odds with these doctrines:

> *Loyal customers exist*

Support: People generally buy the same brands again and again. The most prolific research was carried out by Andrew Ehrenberg (1988). Many other studies have established the same pattern.

> *Loyalty is predicted by market share for many consumer products and business consumables*

Support: The percentage of loyal customers for one brand is similar to that of other brands with similar market share in the same market. This generalization is counter-intuitive, and contradicts many of the claims of loyalty gurus (Ehrenberg 1988).

> Monogamous customers exist but they buy less and are less common

Support: There are customers who buy one brand only. However, they tend to have lower consumption levels, and their numbers are not generally high (Ehrenberg, 1988).

> Most buyers are loyal to more than one brand.

Support: This generalization is supported in many sectors where people buy a repertoire of consumer products and services rather than only one. It is also true for many business products and services. Although customers buy several brands, they exclude many too, and are consistent in their loyalty over many purchase cycles (Ehrenberg 1988).

Customer Relationship Management (CRM)

Customer Relationship Management (or CRM) is a fad that has risen and now is on the decline. Its demise is unfortunate, as there are some important generalizations which, had they been heeded, would have put a more successful complexion on CRM.

> Rightsizing the customer base is the best strategy

Support: Many companies think that big is beautiful and try to maximize the size of the customer base. Unfortunately, all customers are not created equal, and as the size of the customer base grows, the incremental value of new customers will fall and eventually become negative. For a review, see Blattberg *et al.* (2001).

> Maximizing retention does not maximize profits

Support: 'Zero customer defections' preach Reichheld and Sasser of Harvard (1990), 'total customer service' sermonize Davidow and Uttal (1989), 'customers-for-life' evangelize Sewell and Brown (1990), 'customer intimacy' declaims Wiersema (1996). Then there's 'customer-centered-growth' (Whitely 1997), 'customer-engineering' (Frigstad 1995), 'customer-inspired-quality' (Shaw 1996), 'customer-one-to-one' (Peppers and Rogers 1996), 'customer-value' (Gale 1994), 'moments of truth' (Carlzon 1989), and many more. Yet the economics of these dogma is poor. Again for review, see Blattberg *et al.* (2001).

Branding

Branding is a topic that can turn a room full of marketers into a herd of experts. Some of the expertise concerns brand loyalty, but as we've already seen, the prevailing wisdom about this must be taken with a pinch of salt.

Emotions, feelings, passions, delight – these are all words that the brand gurus associate with brands. Owning a brand is like having an orgasmatron, that machine in the film *Barbarella* that triggered all her pleasure synapses in chorus. The implication of these romantic ideas is that brand managers see themselves as some kind of latter-day business Casanova. Yet the facts don't really support this fable.

> *People may purchase consistently without any feeling for the brand*

Support: Often a brand is a means to an end but is not valued in its own right. Why should people have strong feelings about brands of bleach or sugar? Their continued purchase is because it is accessible and they know how to obtain it (East 1997).

> *People may like a brand but do not purchase it through lack of need or opportunity*

Support: Many brands are lusted after but not affordable – Porsche or Rolls Royce, for example. People refuse Guinness because they dislike its taste and yet many say they like and admire it (East 1997).

> *Attitudes to a brand may be caused by purchase rather than being the cause of it*

Support: Often the environment shapes behaviour and feelings follow later. Supporters of the local sports team (football, cricket, baseball, etc.) do so because of availability first, and feelings often follow much later. Brands are often bought because of availability first and liking often comes second. See East (1997) and Barwise and Ehrenberg (1985).

> *Awareness of some products may be weak even among consistent buyers*

Support: People's interest and involvement with many products are so low that they cannot recall the brands they use nor even recognize them. Extreme examples would include paper towels (consumer products) and copying paper (business products).

Distribution and availability

Branding and its romantic adherents tend to underplay the importance of distribution and availability. One reason they do so is because the sales force, which they do not generally control, is the dominant force for distribution. Often there is a battle in companies between the importance of selling and marketing.

Yet the evidence is strong that distribution must be rigorously studied in sectors where channels and intermediaries operate. There can be no excuse for downplaying its importance.

> *Increasing distribution increases market share*

Support: This finding has been known for half a century. Distribution can be one of the most potent contributors to sales. Studies include Nutall (1965), Farley and Leavitt (1968), Parsons (1974), Leone and Schultz (1980) and Reibstein and Farris (1995). All these studies found that increasing distribution increases market share.

> *Increasing display has a positive impact on sales*

Support: Availability is only one important distribution effect. Display is also very significant. An early review of 20 publications found strong positive evidence. See Pauli and Hoecker (1952), Muller *et al.* (1953), Cox (1964, 1970), Kotzan and Evanson (1969), Frank and Massey (1970), Kennedy (1970) and Cuhran (1972, 1974a, 1974b). All these studies demonstrated that increasing display space and visibility has a positive impact on sales.

> *Increasing market-share increases distribution*

Support: Channel owners and retailers are influenced by increases in market share to increase availability and display. MacDonald and Lush (1997) have used econometric modelling to show that feedback exists between volume share and front-stock share. The bi-directional sales–distribution relationship creates a momentum for new products which explains their long-term position in the market (Bronnenberg *et al.* 2000).

> High-share brands have more share-points per distributor

Support: The rich get richer is the implication of this finding. Bigger distributors tend to distribute most brands, but as display is more limited for the smaller distributors, they favour the bigger brands. See Nuttall (1965), Farris *et al.* (1989), Borin *et al.* (1991), Verbeke *et al.* (1994) and Mercer (1996).

Sales promotion

Just as distribution is downplayed by branding specialists, so too is sales promotion. Sometimes there is rivalry for funds between sales promotion and advertising. However, in this instance the evidence is not entirely in favour of the sales argument.

> Most sales promotions make losses, even worse than advertising

Support: Sales promotions effects have been extensively studied over the past 50 years. The overwhelming body of evidence is that only a few promotions are profitable in the sense that they cover their costs. See Abraham and Lodish (1990) and Lodish *et al.* (1995).

> Temporary price-promotions have an immediate volume spike

Support: This observation is so commonplace that it hardly needs mentioning, other than the fact that some companies that carry out promotions are seeking a long-term effect and are willing to overlook the absence of short-term effects (a big mistake!). See Ehrenberg *et al.* (1994).

> Sales promotions do not generally have any long-term effect

Support: Many sales promotion agencies can only justify their activities on the basis that their efforts are 'brand building'. Yet the overwhelming evidence is that promotions do not have long-term brand-building effects. See Ehrenberg *et al.* (1994).

> High market-share brands are less deal-elastic

Support: The bigger the brand, the less the effect of promotions. This generalization has been supported by Bolton (1989), Bemmaor and Mouchoux (1991) and Vilcassim and Jain (1991).

> Positive synergy exists between promotions and advertising

Support: When advertising is used to publicize a promotion, the total effect is greater than the sum of the parts. See Walters and Rinne (1986), Gupta (1988), Kumar and Leone (1988) and Walters and MacKenzie (1988).

> The greater the frequency of deals, the lower the deal-spike height

Support: People's desire for bargains is limited and this saturation effect is important. See Raju (1992).

> Crowded categories dilute promotional responses

Support: A study of 108 product categories supports this finding. See Narasimhan *et al.* (1996).

> Trade promotions pass-through is under 100%

Support: Most retailers and channel partners retain some of the promotional money they are given. This has been observed by Chevalier and Curhan (1976), Walters (1989) and Blattberg and Neslin (1990).

Price

Price is what politicians are generally talking about when they refer to 'industrial competitiveness', yet most marketing managers have a half-hearted interest in the subject. Perhaps the reason is because pricing decisions are generally made outside the walls of the marketing department. Even so, price has a vitally important effect on profits, and its effect must be included in any analysis of marketing payback.

> *Cutting prices almost always pushes up sales volumes, but the elasticity varies greatly from case to case*

Support: Numerous studies have been carried out on price elasticity. The general principle is price down → sales up. No general principle exists, however, for the size of the price elasticity (which is the ratio of sales change to price change). Hence, elasticity needs to be measured for each product. See East (1997) for a detailed discussion.

> *Price awareness and knowledge vary greatly from category to category*

Support: Price cannot have an effect on demand if buyers take no notice of it. Price awareness and knowledge should, therefore, be included in any strategic review of a market. Yet in one study it was found that 40% of shoppers did not look at prices (Riley-Smith 1984), while another study found that 82% of housewives could state a price for products that they had bought in the previous week (Gabor and Granger 1961). In the USA it was found that customers knew the price (to within 5%) for only 20% of 60 highly advertised and competitive brands (*Progressive Grocer* 1963).

> *People see prices in terms of acceptable ranges*

Support: Buyers may not know the normal price of a product, but they will have attitudes towards price ranges. When the price is above a certain level, it will be seen as too expensive and poor value; below a certain level, the buyer may suspect the quality to be poor. See East (1997) for fuller discussion.

Advertising effects

Advertising is the beating heart of marketing for many organizations. It is the engine that branding experts fire up whenever they want to shift awareness or attitudes. It consumes vast budgets, exceeded only by sales promotion. Agency staff and client managers measure personal success in terms of their advertising awards. Given its popularity, it would be natural to assume that it is a sure-fire winner.

> *Most advertisements are unprofitable*

Support: In other words, advertising is less than an even money bet. Logically, it should be expected that 50% are worse than average. According to Tim Ambler (1996), the figure is 54%. According to Clancy and Krieg (2000), the success rate is lower. Whatever the precise number, it pays to be cautious about accepting advertising without challenging it.

> *Advertising can drive up distribution*

Support: Distribution is a rather unexciting aspect of the marketing mix and is often downplayed by agencies and client marketing staff. Yet distribution increases are reported in numerous studies of advertising. It is also likely that such effects will be of a longer-term nature than consumer effects. See East (1997) for a summary.

> *Media weight only matters when the creative is effective*

Support: Ineffective creative executions have no significant effect, and so adding media costs to them is fruitless. Conversely, media weight increases do cause sales increases if the creative execution is good. Circumstantial evidence for this is afforded by analyses of several hundred ad tests using IRI's BehaviorScan (Abraham and Lodish 1990).

A criticism of these generalizations is that they fail to take account of the magnitude of the differences – were the creative differences very big, and were the media weights significantly different? Our conclusion is that specific testing is needed to assess your own advertising creative and media weight.

Personal selling

Sales is a stronghold of intuitive decision making and has proved extremely resistant to quantification. Yet for many companies, sales force decisions are at least as important as advertising and promotion.

> *Sales force sizing obeys similar laws to media weight decisions*

Support: Sales force sizing is a fundamental issue and yet many firms continue to employ intuitive methods. There are now several well-tested models available for supporting sales force sizing decisions which have proved very effective, e.g. Lodish *et al.* (1988) and Rangaswamy *et al.* (1990).

Innovation and new products

Another business obsession is the perceived need to innovate. Consumers are deluged with new miracles that they don't want, which don't work, which rapidly pass away – and still the managers yearn for more innovation.

In his 1997 book *The Innovation War*, Christoph-Friedrich von Braun compared business innovation with the arms race, and suggested that R&D was spiralling out of control. He cited the $630 million per day spent on R&D in Germany, Great Britain, France, the USA and Japan. The book has caused a storm of newspaper headlines in Germany and widespread discussion. Charles LaMantia, CEO of innovation consultants Arthur D Little, commented:

> This book is a warning to all those innovation warriors whose business actions are increasingly founded on time-based management. Any escalation spiral that is driven by competitors' actions only is as misguided as was the arms race during the Cold War. (von Braun 1977)

> *Most brand and line extensions fail*

Support: The precise figure varies, depending on which study you use, but 80% failure is about the norm from the studies we have seen. For a survey, see Cooper (1993).

> *Good products fail too*

Support: Well-designed products that have tangible benefits and well-liked features often fail. For examples, see Clancy and Shulman (1994).

> *Early entry advantages*

Support: Numerous studies indicate that there is an advantage to being an early entrant to a new market. For a definitive overview, see Kalyanaram *et al.* (1995).

> *Brand extensions reduce launch costs*

Support: Several studies find that new brands are at a considerable disadvantage compared with existing brands in terms of launch costs. See East (1997).

Key points

- Intuitive marketing is a way of solving practical marketing problems that relies on rules-of-thumb that are regarded as roughly correct but not intended to be scientifically accurate, based on claimed general wisdom from expert experience.

- Intuitive marketing has a terrible track record, but its proponents live in a state of denial of its failures, and pay little regard to empirical generalizations.

- Empirical generalizations are patterns of cause-and-effect linking marketing activities to customer responses and payback, established by rigorous analysis of empirical evidence. The pattern repeats but need not be universal over all circumstances.

- Empirical generalizations are especially important when they are counter-intuitive, and challenge complacent intuitive marketers to ask: Where do they come from? Why should I believe them?

- These laws of marketing, and the supporting empirical studies, provide a body of knowledge with which every trained marketing manager should be familiar. This chapter gathers together a representative sample of these laws, but it does not pretend to be 100% complete and exhaustive in its coverage.

- In any case, empirical generalizations do not tell the entire story. Every market, every product and every marketing activity has distinctive characteristics that need to be measured and analyzed to understand fully how marketing works. We will look at ways of measuring how marketing works in the next chapter.

5

MEASURING HOW MARKETING REALLY WORKS

This chapter explains how marketing really works. We look at the way marketing gets more people to buy more of our product, more often, for more money – the nitty-gritty of consumer psychology, and how it should underpin your marketing planning. We look at how people process marketing stimuli, what they remember and forget, how their attitudes shift, and why this changes their purchasing patterns. We review how the market research industry measures the effects of marketing, and evaluate the strengths and weaknesses of common research methods. Although much of this technical detail is often overlooked by senior executives, or assumed to be the responsibility of junior colleagues, it is essential to understand it in order to make sense of the data you use to make both tactical and strategic decisions.

Why you must measure your customers

Chapter 3 considered both the 'magic metrics' approach and the financial modelling approach, and argued in favour of financial models. However, for the marketing payback analyst, both approaches have practical difficulties to overcome:

- Financial responses to marketing expenditures cannot easily be disentangled from noise created from the other factors that affect demand, particularly when the marketing expenditures are broken down into their component parts.

- Customer awareness, attitudes and other 'magic metrics' can be more readily linked to marketing expenditures, but their link to financial results is less direct.

These practical difficulties can be overcome by combining the insights from both approaches into what is sometimes called a 'triangulation model' (see Figure 5.1). Just as triangulation in surveying enables cartographers to combine observations from several perspectives to get a more accurate measurement, so too can the marketing payback analyst get a better result by combining perspectives.

Triangulation can be considered as a two-stage approach:

1. First, relationships are established between marketing expenditures and customer responses. These relationships are often easier to establish than models of sales volumes because the size of the customer response is greater than the sales effect, and they are less strongly influenced by the economic and competitive environment. For example, awareness and consideration could be modelled in terms of advertising expenditure, promotional activity, PR impacts and sponsorship expenditure.

2. Second, relationships are established between customer responses and sales volumes, but taking into account all of the other drivers of demand (including own price, competitors' prices, seasonality, macroeconomic factors and underlying trends). For example, sales volumes could then be modelled in terms of awareness, consideration, own price, competitors' prices, seasonality, underlying trend, etc.

Figure 5.1
The triangulation process

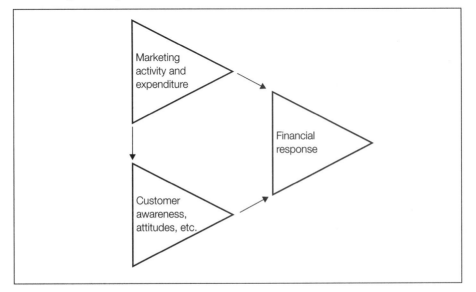

What expert help do you need?

There are many types of experts to choose from (see Box 5.1). Branding experts say it's them. Market researchers say it's them. Consumer psychologists and behaviour researchers say the same. All are correct, but the insights from the three areas must be combined. None of these disciplines offers a complete understanding in its own right.

Distrust is widespread. Branding experts are seen as 'fluffy' and 'abstract'. Market researchers are widely vilified – 'another opinion poll' is a common complaint. Unfortunately, market research is often not well managed, which adds to the complaints. Consumer behaviour researchers are also distrusted – 'ivory tower boffins' is a characteristic epithet. All parties do have their weaknesses, and to get the best from them requires combining the good points from each.

> **Box 5.1** Different types of expert
>
> **Branding experts**: People who work for agencies or consultancies that specialize in branding. Design is the top discipline of these firms, but they also offer a range of associated services. They claim almost mystical insights into the brain, the heart, the mind and the soul of the customer.
>
> **Consumer psychology research**: The academic study of how people buy and consume products and services. It is strongly focused on the mind of the consumer and uses disciplined research methods.
>
> **Consumer behaviour research**: Another name for consumer psychology research.
>
> **Industrial buying behaviour**: The academic study of how industrial purchases occur.
>
> **Market research**: How firms keep in touch with customers and competition. It involves the systematic gathering, recording and analyzing of information about the opinions, attitudes and behaviours of consumers and customers, how they buy, what they buy and what competitors are offering and doing.
>
> **Marketing research**: How firms solve specific marketing problems, by gathering, recording and analyzing information.

Describing and predicting customer responses

It is to consumer behaviour research that we first turn to try and work out a framework that explains the complexity of customer response.

The science of consumer behaviour has developed over the past 50 years alongside the mainstream literature of marketing, but as a parallel and loosely-integrated discipline. The inhabitants of this world have degrees in psychology or sociology, or they are statisticians or economists. For them, researching the problem of consumption takes time and requires real research, cross-checking and literature review. Data are comparatively scarce, and often have to be begged from a friendly client, generally as a favour. As a consequence, many consumer behaviour theorists have developed skills in 'squeezing data' to yield insights.

Insights from work of consumer behaviourists form the basis of the flow chart shown in Figure 5.2. It illustrates how little information we actually take in, and the role that psychological response plays in triggering behavioural response.

We have shown the effect of point-of-sale stimuli (distribution and display) on purchasing as a fluffy cloud on the right-hand side of this diagram. This is because these factors tend to be downplayed in branding and general marketing literature, even though it is clear that brands that are well distributed and displayed have an advantage over those that are poorly distributed and displayed. We shall examine these effects after explaining Figure 5.2 in more detail.

Figure 5.2
Framework for customer response analysis

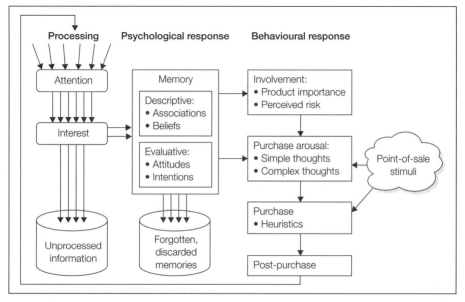

Processing brand exposures

Any analysis of consumer response should begin by asking what factors stimulate people's responses. Factors could include actual experience of the brand itself, plus additional stimuli such as advertising and word-of-mouth. Different people are exposed to different levels of stimuli. Exposure does not guarantee that attention will be paid to the cues or that they will be processed into memory.

You have probably given a great deal of thought to your brand(s). The public at large, unlike you, is not very interested in your or anyone else's brands. The public quickly discovers that what one brand offers today is offered by every brand tomorrow, which means that the rewards resulting from trying to learn which brand is the best are frequently outweighed by the time and effort involved.

Stimuli constantly bombard people's senses and are too numerous to be absorbed in their totality. The two most important stimuli influencing consumer behaviour are marketing stimuli and environmental stimuli. Only a small proportion of stimuli will register in people's minds. This is sometimes called *cut-through* or *stand-out*.

When you try to influence the public, you face an uphill task. Nobody sits in front of their TV set, paper and pen in hand, waiting for a commercial break. People watch or listen to advertising at low levels of attention, and spend little time actively thinking about the information. Instead they store what they see and hear as sensory associations.

Over time, these associations come to define brands in our minds and act to guide intuitive brand choice (see Box 5.2). Thus people buy toilet paper because of a Labrador puppy, insurance because of a red telephone and cigarettes because of cowboys.

Box 5.2 Terms describing processing of stimuli

Attention: The selective process of noticing a stimulus or certain portions of it. People must pay attention to a stimulus when it occurs for it to register in their minds.

Categorization: Tendency of people to place marketing information into logical categories, to process information quickly and efficiently.

Cut-through/stand-out: The ability of some stimuli to register in people's minds.

Generalization: An aspect of categorization with important implications for branding. People have a tendency to generalize from one product to another, and see two products as 'similar'. It allows them to simplify the process of product selection because they do not have to make a separate judgement for each stimulus. The consumer believes that satisfactory past experiences with the brand will be repeated.

Interest: A measure of the level of importance of a stimulus to an individual. People are more likely to process and retain memories of a stimulus that is interesting to them personally.

Recall: A measure of verbal processing, indicating people's ability to remember the names of brands to which they have been exposed in the past.

Recognition: A measure of image processing, indicating people's ability to recognize the identities of brands to which they have been exposed in the past.

Psychological responses

We have said that *brand equity*, in the sense outlined earlier, equates to all the ideas and feelings about a brand, but it is useful to distinguish between different sorts of thoughts and feelings (see Box 5.3). It is useful to make a broad distinction between descriptions (associations and beliefs) and evaluations (attitudes and intentions). For example, beliefs about Kellogg's Corn Flakes range from descriptive (e.g. 'stays crispy in milk') to evaluative (e.g. 'worth paying more for').

Box 5.3 Terms for thoughts and feelings about brands

Associations: Descriptive ideas that people usually associate with the brand.

Attitudes: Evaluative ideas about a brand – positive, negative, favourable or unfavourable. They include feelings about the concept of the brand, and more concrete feelings about buying, owning, using and other actions connected with the brand. Attitudes are sometimes associated with particular beliefs.

Beliefs: Descriptive ideas about the brand that people think are likely to be true.

Purchase intentions: People's beliefs about the likelihood that they will purchase the brand in the future.

Evaluation has been given undue prominence in marketing theories of the buying process, and the importance of descriptive associations is often under-estimated. People buying a product seldom evaluate it as thoroughly as does its supplier. People in the supply company must put aside all their product and organizational knowledge, and put themselves in the shoes of their 'ignorant' consumers and customers.

Descriptions can change people's course of action, despite their more passive nature. Putting a poison label on a bottle, for instance, cannot be described as persuasion but it will almost certainly shape people's actions. Much of branding works in this way, by informing people, rather than persuading them.

Forgetting and the *extinction of memory* are, ironically, more of an obsession with brand managers than are the memories themselves (see Box 5.4).

Box 5.4 Terms used to describe forgetfulness

Extinction: Unlearning of material that has previously been learned (e.g. when McDonald's was criticized, the linkage between McDonald's and 'good for the family' was extinguished). Changing attitudes is an important example of extinction.

Forgetting: The inability to retrieve information from long-term memory.

Inertia: People's resistance to changing beliefs and attitudes.

Interference: Occurs when related information blocks the recall of the relevant information (e.g. competitive advertising often causes consumers to be unable to recall advertising for a related brand).

Retention: The amount of previously learned material that is remembered.

The fastest rate of forgetting occurs soon after the learning has occurred. As the time since the last learning trial increases, forgetting continues but its rate slows down considerably (see Figure 5.3).

Figure 5.3
Forgetting as a function of time

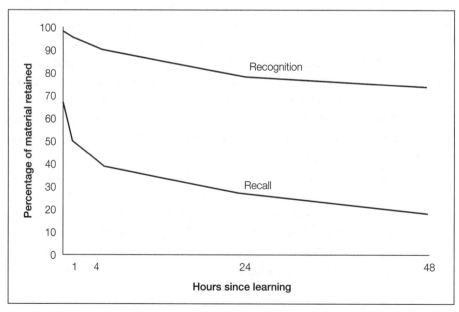

Extinction is a less understood aspect of memory than forgetting. Changing attitudes and beliefs are examples of extinction. Psychological research as well as common experience show that people resist change. Resistance at least partially explains why consumers are slow to change many tastes, shopping patterns and consumption habits. For example, many find it difficult to reduce or eliminate sweets, cigarettes or alcohol. Similarly, others who have developed strong brand loyalties over time resist making changes even if their regular brands are not providing the rewards they once did. This poses a great challenge to brand managers wishing to draw patronage away from the competition.

Inference happens when people develop an *association* between two stimuli. For example, consumers might associate a high price with quality or blue suds in detergent with cleaning power. People have a tendency to fill in the missing elements when a stimulus is incomplete, and in particular they develop their own conclusions from moderately ambiguous information.

Behavioural responses

You have probably heard your advertising or design agency say that branding is terribly important to people when they are in the process of purchasing something. There is a mythology about brand loyalty, suggesting that people love their brands, they virtually worship them, and they cannot bear to be parted from them. The reality is somewhat different.

Nobody pays a great deal of attention to many of the things that they purchase and consume. The great majority of products are of passing interest to most people, most of the time. Observational studies of shoppers indicate that the average buyer takes about ten seconds from first sighting the category-display in the store through to selecting the product. In the great majority of purchases, visual recognition of their 'usual product' or an 'acceptable substitute' is the main process. Furthermore, about 50% of all purchases are impulse choices, where the buyer had not entered the store with the prior intention of buying the product (see Table 5.1).

Purchase stimuli flow in a steady stream into our minds and we actively screen most of them out most of the time. Our buying behaviour is not energized for the main part. *Involvement* seems to be what triggers the purchasing motivation, and in particular directs our thinking in either simple or complex directions.

Table 5.1
Incidence of point-of-purchase brand choices for supermarket products

Type of choice	% incidence
Impulse (neither category nor brand pre-planned)	47%
Brand pre-planned	35%
Category pre-planned, but not brand	15%
Other (e.g. switch of pre-planned brand)	3%
Specific products: point-of-sale choice	
Snack foods	78%
Cosmetics	69%
Soft drinks	67%
Non-prescription drugs and medicines	49%
Cigarettes	33%
Alcoholic beverages	20%
Prescription drugs	0%

Source: POPAI/Du Pont Studies (see Rossiter and Percy 1997)

Some products are intrinsically interesting and occupy our thoughts. Many purchases, however, are boring but the perceived risk of choosing a bad product is slightly disquieting. This disquiet can lead purchasers to pay more attention to their choice than would be the case for other boring products. They are also more likely to be willing to pay a premium price for what is perceived to be a 'good' product. However, the idea that they go through an elaborate evaluation process is generally misleading.

The process of purchasing is something that varies from person to person and from purchase to purchase. Some purchases occur without the guidance of *thoughts* or *feelings*, for example when habitually buying train tickets. Other purchases such as fast food are accompanied by feelings more than thoughts. Some purchases trigger simple thoughts, for example when choosing between a 2-litre bottle or a six pack. Other purchases worry and trouble people for weeks and generate complex thought patterns, for example when buying an automobile or house.

The advertising agency Foote, Cone & Belding developed a grid (Vaughn 1980, 1986; Ratchford 1987) in an attempt to categorize products into high and low involvement types, and also ones where thoughts vs. feelings dominate (see Figure 5.4).

The grid uses an X-axis which divides thinking-centred purchases from feeling-centred ones, and a Y-axis that expresses high and low involvement; the two axes produce four quadrants.

Figure 5.4
The Foote, Cone & Belding grid

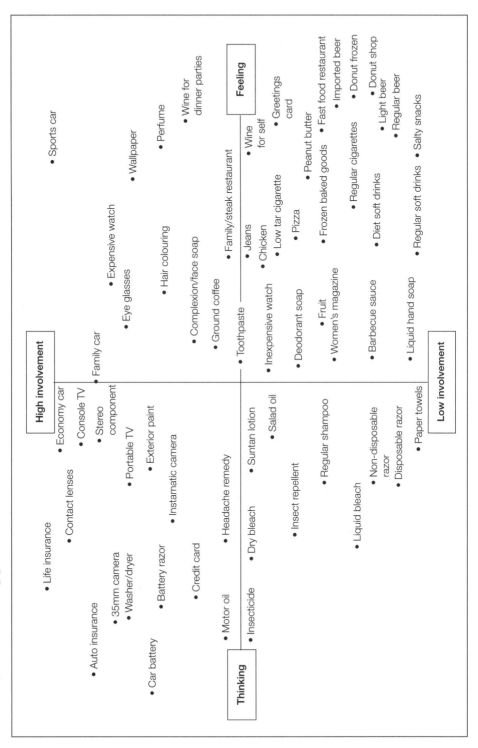

It should be noted that:

- The grid is focused on products, not brands.
- Thought is involved in the definition of both axes.
- Thought and feeling are not necessarily alternatives.

Readers who are responsible for, or associated with, a specific product may find it useful to consider where their product would be positioned on the map.

Purchasing occurs as a result of 'arousal' – something that energizes buying activity. The thoughts that accompany purchase arousal may be complex or simple, but even so, they create an inner state that energizes and directs us.

When people are deciding what to buy, sometimes something relevant about the brand may be remembered. A fleeting interest previously aroused may recur to reinforce the thought that 'perhaps I'll try this today', or 'I'm happy buying what I usually buy'.

People often choose brands because they think they have bought them before, or else they perceive them to be popular. 'My usual please' and 'What's your best-selling brand?' are two common questions asked by buyers of sellers. In these cases, information is sufficient to guide the buying decision, and a more sophisticated statement of benefits is unnecessary.

Complex thought patterns are associated with high-involvement purchases. For example, managers selecting suppliers for a multi-million pound outsourcing contract almost always have complex thought patterns. People seek out information and evaluate options. Evaluative criteria are remembered and organized throughout the process. However, in these cases the complexity of the evaluation may be so great that rules-of-thumb are eventually used to make the selection. Brand popularity or reputation often feature strongly in these complex evaluations when the more rational process fails to resolve the dilemma of choice.

People's final judgements about what brands to select often rely on 'heuristics' or rules-of-thumb which may be used unconsciously in thinking. These range from 'I always buy this brand' (habit) to methods of simplifying complex decisions, such as 'I'm spoilt for choice, so I'll do what I always do and choose the most popular brand'.

Choosing the product that you've bought before, or the first, second or third that you're offered, or simply the market-leading product, can be a sensible way of reducing risk without wasting time. In fact, there is evidence to suggest that this is often how purchasing decisions – even substantial ones such as TVs and motor cars – are made. Box 5.5 describes the terms usually used to categorize behavioural response.

Box 5.5 Terms describing behavioural responses

Market share: The proportion of sales of the brand to total category sales.

Mean population purchase rate: The number of purchase occasions in the period made by an average member of the population.

Penetration: The proportion of all category buyers in a population who buy the brand at least once in a period.

Purchase frequency: The average number of purchases made by those who purchase at least once in a period.

Repeat purchase %: The percentage of buyers last period who also buy this period.

Share of category requirements: The proportion of category sales accounted for by a particular brand among those who purchased it. The denominator excludes category volume taken by those who did not purchase the brand, and it is therefore higher than market share.

Trial purchase %: The percentage of the population who have not previously bought the brand (say within the last two years) but who buy it this period.

Professor Andrew Ehrenberg has been looking at behavioural data since the 1950s. At first, facts and figures were extremely scarce and hard to assemble, so Ehrenberg's findings were not readily confirmed by other researchers. During the last five or so years much more evidence has started to emerge in Britain, Germany, France, the United States and Japan, as computer data on customer purchasing behaviour have become much more widely available. Evidence of loyalty has been studied in over 50 product categories as diverse as biscuits, beer, cars, cosmetics, cleaning materials, OTC medicines and pharmaceutical prescriptions, supermarkets and TV programmes.

Four questions about loyalty, as raised by Scriven and Ehrenberg (1994), are answered by the behavioural studies:

- Is there such a thing as loyalty?
- Is loyalty predictable?
- Does the degree of brand loyalty differ much among brands?
- Are highly loyal buyers worth having?

First, loyal behaviour does exist. People tend to buy the same brands again and again, but their loyalty is polygamous; that is, they habitually buy a repertoire of several brands, one of which is dominant.

Second, different possible measures of loyalty tend to correlate with each other: Table 5.2 shows this pattern in the powdered detergent market. Loyalty measures such as quarterly repeat purchase, first-brand loyalty, share of category requirements all correlate. The pattern of variation in loyalty is predictable from market share alone. The bigger the brand, the more loyal the customers.

Table 5.2
Loyalty measures and market share in UK detergents

Brand	Loyalty measures			Market share
	Share of category requirements	Quarterly repeat purchase	First brand loyalty by brand	
Persil	47%	75%	78%	30%
Ariel	35%	66%	75%	18%
Bold	32%	64%	72%	13%
Daz	26%	57%	68%	10%
Surf	26%	56%	58%	10%
Average	33%	64%	70%	16%

Source: Lomax et al. (1996)

Third, loyalty depends on market share, but differs little between brands with similar market share. This rather contradicts the wisdom of the gurus. For example, according to Rapp and Collins (1987), 'no matter how small or how large your business is, a key to making it work is "customer development" . . . customers are identified, located, persuaded, motivated, converted and cultivated in a way that maximizes sales and profits.' And Bain's Reichheld (1996) proclaims: 'Revenue and market share grow as the best customers are swept into the company's business, building repeat sales and . . . customer spending tends to accelerate over time.' Yet the evidence from categories as diverse as cars and cosmetics paints a rather different picture.

Differences in purchase frequency are small between brands. This can be seen in the analysis of US instant coffee purchases in Table 5.3. Even 100% brand-loyal customers differ little in purchase frequency. No brands enjoy abnormally high purchase rates, whether in coffee, cars or cosmetics.

Fourth, brand-loyal customers are few in number, and they do not buy much compared with the average buyer. They are not heavy buyers of the brand, and are light buyers of the category. For example, only 15% of Nescafé customers are 100% loyal. They buy coffee 4.3 times per year, as compared with the average coffee buyer who buys 9 times per year (across a portfolio of brands). There are more loyal customers for large brands than small ones.

So, this would be a typical pattern of brand loyalty. About 20% of people who bought Maxwell House in a year are 100% loyal (i.e. bought Maxwell House exclusively). Loyal customers bought a little more than the average brand customer, 4.2 Maxwell House purchases per year versus 3.6. Loyal buyers are also lighter coffee buyers than average – 4.2 coffee purchases versus 9 coffee purchases per year.

Table 5.3

Purchase frequency and brand loyalty in the US instant coffee market

Buyers of	Purchase frequency (annual)			Number of 100% loyal buyers	Market share of brand
	Of any coffee	Of brand	Of 100% loyal buyers		
Maxwell House	9	3.6	4.2	20%	19%
Sanka	9	3.3	3.2	20%	15%
Tasters Choice	9	2.8	4.2	24%	14%
High Point	8	2.6	1.8	18%	13%
Folgers	9	2.7	3.3	13%	11%
Nescafé	11	2.9	4.3	15%	8%
Brim	9	2.0	2.4	17%	4%
Maxim	11	2.6	3.9	11%	3%
Average	**9**	**2.8**	**3.4**	**15%**	**11%**

Source: Ehrenberg and Uncles (1996)

Average buyers of Maxwell House made 9 purchases of any instant coffee in the year, but bought Maxwell House only 3.6 times (a share of category requirements of 40%). Which other brands Maxwell House buyers also bought is in line with these other brands' market shares and market penetrations, and is not partitioned or segmented. In other words, Maxwell House is not particularly like or unlike any other coffee, it's just bigger.

Branding and the supply chain

Channels and trade customers are neglected in most brand-tracking studies. This is probably a reflection of the rivalry between sales and marketing in most firms –

sales representatives and managers claim most of the credit for sales volumes, and put their success down to their relationships with trade customers. Marketing people generally take a contrary position and claim that it is their brilliant brand advertising that sustains sales volumes. Whatever the cause, the trade customer perspective is generally kept in the dark by brand-tracking research studies. The consumer is king in the competitive drama as written by the brand manager, and the trade customer is a minor player, which is a gross distortion of reality.

The analysis of several leading grocery brands in Figure 5.5 shows clearly that trade customers treat them like royalty, giving far more shelf display and charging a price premium. These factors are bound to influence consumers and they deserve tracking.

Figure 5.5
Relative price and share of shelf space for leading brands and followers

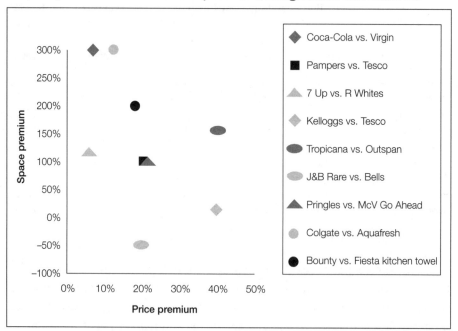

How well does branding theory measure up?

Badly, in our experience. You have probably listened to branding experts holding forth on the psychology and sociology and semiotics of brands, and the language you have heard almost certainly contained many fancy words and phrases. These theorists claim be able to unlock the inner secrets of how brands create value.

Brand equity is the key to much current thinking and it's the starting point of our terminological journey. Here are some commentaries and definitions:

> In the 1980s the hard-nosed businesspeople began to notice that brands appeared to be changing hands for huge sums of money . . . Suddenly the brand stopped being an obscure metaphysical concept of dubious relevance. It was something that was worth money. The shift of perception was reflected in the way that the traditional term *brand image* (with its suggestion of ghostly illusion) was increasingly displaced by its solid financial equivalent, *brand equity*. (Feldwick 1999)

> The continuity of brand loyalty and brand evaluation provides some guarantee of continuing profit, and this has led us to treat brands as an asset that should be conserved and exploited by the holding company. (East 1997)

> Brand equity is a set of associations and behaviours on the part of the brand's customers, channel members and parent corporation that permits the brand to earn greater volume or greater margins than it would without the brand name and that gives a strong, sustainable and differential advantage. (Srivastava and Shocker 1991)

> The reservoir of results gained by good marketing but not yet delivered to the profit and loss account. Awareness, attitudes, associations, memories and habits, which cause people to choose/recommend the brand more often, and in larger quantities and/or at higher prices than would otherwise be the case. Also trade availability and brand information stored in IT systems. (Ambler 2003)

The trouble with all these definitions is their imprecision in specifying what 'results' or 'things' in people's heads are relevant or irrelevant, and what should be measured. People carry round many things in their heads, and most are irrelevant to branding.

Branding theory can also be criticized for lacking an underlying rationale linking its ideas together. The many different approaches that have been published can, for the most part, be described as using one or a combination of the types of measures listed in Box 5.6.

What emerges is not so much a theory of how brands influence people but, instead, a ragbag of poorly defined, overlapping and inconsistent ideas, paying little or no regard to the consumer behaviour theory upon which the branding authorities often claim their subject is founded.

David Aaker's is perhaps the best-known theory and is by far the most sophisticated. In his earlier work, for example his 1991 book *Managing Brand Equity*, he describes brand equity as having five components:

- brand loyalty;
- brand awareness;
- perceived quality ;

- brand associations;

- other proprietary assets.

Aaker's 1991 framework is useful and pragmatic, but mixes apples and oranges in a way that is not entirely satisfactory. It includes twofold measures of memory (recall/recognition); descriptive ideas (Low and Lamb 2000); specific evaluative ideas (quality) and specific behaviour (loyalty), and omits numerous others. Most incongruous of all is 'other proprietary assets' which isn't a measure of what is in people's heads.

Aaker's 1996 book *Building Strong Brands* sets the agenda for the more sophisticated analyses of brand equity. He lists ten categories of brand equity measures and in his Figure 10–7 he lists over 40 subsidiary measures, about which he comments:

> Clearly tapping the Brand Equity Ten can require dozens of measures (see Figure 10–7) . . . When tracking effort is needed within a brand context, the set of 10 measures summarised in Figure 10–7 will provide a good point of departure. However, the measurement should be adapted to include brand specific information. . . . There will usually be a trade-off between completeness and cost. A 40 or 50 item inventory may provide useful diagnostics. Even a few judiciously chosen questions, however, can provide helpful indicators of a brand's health.

A problem with most of the existing branding theories is that they make a poor job of explaining how many of the main instruments of marketing – advertising, promotions, direct marketing, sales forces and product development – fit into their frameworks

Advertisements generally feature brand names and marks, but they are often not prominent. Many advertisements aim to launch new products, and many others describe features and benefits that are specific to particular products. While the effect of the advertising may be reflected in sales increases for these products, the effect of the brand image within the advertisement is more questionable.

Sales promotion barely refers to brands at all, and branding enthusiasts often comment that sales promotion damages the brand image, yet promotion commands far more budget today than does advertising. Dramatic sales spikes result from promotional activity, something that apparently is divorced from branding.

Direct marketing is growing faster than advertising, and yet it is widely regarded as a medium that does not grow brand image. Responses to direct marketing are readily measured and campaigns are often profitable, despite being divorced from branding.

Sales forces, too, can be highly sceptical of the importance of branding, and consider product price and quality to be marketing priorities, along with their own personal expertise at closing sales and managing customer relationships. Product managers also point out the importance of innovation and technical differentiation. Many products available today are genuinely different, and despite the claims about ease of 'replication' of products, in reality consumers can choose between a wide array of truly different products. Once again the question arises: If products are really different, why do we need brands?

Box 5.6 Common branding measures

Brand associations: Components of brand image, usually assessed by qualitative research techniques, e.g. free association.

Brand awareness: The ability of a person to remember a particular brand either spontaneously (recall) or prompted (recognition).

Brand equity: A highly ambiguous term, covering whatever ideas and feelings people carry around in their heads about the brand. David Aaker restricts it to cover loyalty, awareness, perceived quality, other associations and other brand assets.

Brand essence: The smallest compression (six words or less) of what is special about the brand. Derived from 'interrogate the brand until it confesses its essence'.

Brand experience: The ideas and feelings that people associate with the brand as a result of use of or contact with the brand. In practice difficult to separate from general brand equity.

Brand identity: The descriptive ideas that brand owners wish people would associate with the brand.

Brand image: The descriptive ideas that people actually associate with the brand. See also *brand associations*.

Brand loyalty: An ambiguous term: (1) a measure of how much people buy one brand rather than another in the category; (2) a measure of the degree to which people have positive attitudes to one brand rather than another; (3) a measure of people's brand allegiance.

Brand perceived quality: A measure of how positively people perceive the quality of products that bear the brand.

> **Brand personality**: The fundamental characteristics of the brand, a shorthand that people use to categorize the brand. Brands are often anthropomorphized in this way. See also *brand soul*.

Brand preferences: An ambiguous term: (1) a measure of how many people buy one brand rather than another in the category; (2) a measure of how many people have positive attitudes to one brand rather than another.

Brand soul: An extreme view of brand personality, where it is claimed that 'consumers treat brands just like people, and people have souls'.

Brand strength: An extremely ambiguous term. Among its many meanings: (1) a measure of people's positive attitudes towards a brand; (2) a measure of a brand's large relative size; (3) a measure of a brand's long-term sustained profitability.

Brand value: The financial expression of brand equity.

Brand values: The positive feelings that the brand generates in people's minds.

Branding: Strategy to differentiate products and companies and to build economic value for both the consumer and the brand owner.

Other brand assets: Patents, trade marks, channel relationships, etc.

How good is your market research?

> All is not well in the land of market research, although many of its inhabitants are prospering and industry turnover increased. (Davidson 1997)

Market research today is a large industrial concern. Its day-to-day interests are managing its 'interviewing factories' and its data collection and tabulation plants. Tens of thousands of interviews are conducted daily, and for a market research manager, the sheer difficulty of the process is a major distraction. The vast bulk of the data is daunting, and research managers heave a sigh of relief when the data tables come off the printer.

Here are ten hard questions to ask about your market research:

1. Do you have an ideal basket of measures?
2. Are you drowning in detailed market research data?
3. Is your research agenda balanced and unbiased?

4. Does your market research provide insights for innovation and improvement?

5. Are you spending your market research budget wisely?

6. Do your researchers apply the latest methods?

7. Are you squeezing the maximum insights from the raw data?

8. Does your market research improve the accuracy of your forecasting?

9. Have you customized your research to fit the distinctive features of your brands?

10. Are market research reports as important as financial reports?

As a consequence of the lack of conviction about market research within client companies, interpretation and diagnosis of the market research data are of secondary importance to many research firms. Standardized surveys that will be bought by multiple clients are what's attractive to many of the larger research firms. The mass production ethos of the research world does not easily accommodate the unique selling points of a particular brand.

A useful distinction has been made in the past between *market research* and *marketing research*, the key point of which was that the term 'research' is inappropriate for describing the data gathering and tracking activities that make up a lot of the industry's output, which is more akin to journalism and news gathering than military intelligence or laboratory research.

> A new piece of consumer research should be an exciting voyage of discovery, opening up new perspectives for innovation and improvement. Marketers should anticipate the outcome with the same excitement as the result of a major sporting event . . . Too often, though, research pursues a disappointing journey through old and familiar scenery, creating no excitement, charting no new frontiers. (Davidson 1997).

Hugh Davidson's point is well made, for most market research serves no more useful purpose than the morning newspaper, merely a comforting illusion of being in touch with the world.

Expectations about customer response measurement are generally formed on-the-job. To most marketing managers, and their in-house market researchers, the drab mass-produced product of the market research 'factories' represents the standard. Few have raised their expectations and enquired into the world that is alluded to by the phrase 'marketing research'.

Numerous market research firms now offer their clients the opportunity to buy brand and advertising tracking studies that survey consumer perceptions of brands on a regular periodic basis (usually quarterly, monthly or weekly) – see Table 5.4.

Table 5.4

Factors and questions typically used in brand tracking surveys

Factor	Question
Brand associations and beliefs	Series of questions concerning brand associations and beliefs
Brand attitudes	Series of questions about people's attitudes to the brand
Brand recall	What brands of beer can you think of?
Brand recognition	Which of these brands of beer have you heard of?
Category use	Which of these alcoholic drinks do you drink nowadays?
Future purchase intent	How likely are you to buy brand X in the next three months?
Past purchases	Have you ever tried any of these brands?
Recent purchases	Which of these brands have you bought recently?

The data are typically collected by questionnaire surveys of independent samples because it would be inappropriate to ask the same people about their awareness of a brand on a regular basis. The sample must be gathered to include a specified proportion of all key segments, including users and non-users.

Many brands in each market are often surveyed. For example, the first such studies in the UK were carried out by Millward Brown for Cadbury in 1977 (and subsequently continued for 15 years). Cadbury had many brands in the same market and needed to compare them with each other and their competitors. Usually only one or two firms carry out surveys of a given market.

Since the work of Lavidge and Steiner (1961) and Colley (1961), one of the most widely used models of marketing impacts has been the linear progression of the customer through a series of psychological stages known as a 'purchase funnel'. This funnel can take many forms, some examples being illustrated in Table 5.5.

We have examined many such surveys over the past 15 years, and one of the limitations we have found with 'off-the-shelf' surveys is that they can be highly generic and overlook the nuances of brand associations and beliefs that are specific to individual brands. However, adding brand-specific questions can raise the survey costs to levels that are not generally acceptable to clients.

Brand managers also need to be cautious about interpreting the survey results, especially in view of empirical studies of survey validity. Barnard *et al.*

(1986) found that only half the people who credited a brand with a particular attribute on one occasion did so on a second occasion. There is a high random element to people's descriptions and evaluations of brands. Their research is based on fast-moving consumer goods (FMCGs).

Table 5.5
Alternative definitions of purchase funnel stages

Step	Schultz and Walters (1997)	Fill (1999)		Rossiter and Percy (1997)	
		High involvement	Low involvement	Advertising	Promotions
1	Media advertising	Awareness	Awareness	Exposure	Exposure
2	Attitudes/ awareness	Extensive information search	Short internal information search	Processing	Processing
3	Knowledge	Attitude/ intention	Trial/ experimentation	Communication effects and brand position	Communication effects and brand position
4	Preference	Trial/ experimentation	Attitude/future intentions	Need arousal	Usage
5	Conviction	Long-run behaviour	Long-run behaviour	Information search and evaluation	
6	Purchase behaviour			Purchase	
7				Usage	

People are much more likely to have positive attitudes towards a brand if they have previously bought it. Most of the fluctuations in attitudes can be explained by people's prior purchasing behaviour (Barnard 1987). Immediately after buying, people's attitudes tend to be positive, but over time this reverts to the random pattern (Sandell 1981). Again, most of these empirical generalizations tend to apply to frequently purchased goods.

Beyond FMCG there is evidence that positive attitudes precede purchase and therefore are potentially predictors of purchase (Pickering 1984; Eagly and Chaiken 1993; Korgaonkar *et al.* 1985).

Our general advice is to dig deeper than the summary tabulations. Small changes in survey-sample composition can cause larger changes in average index numbers, and this noise can be eliminated only by using more rigorous statistical analysis on the original source data.

Statistical analysis of the data can also help establish connections between cause-and-effect in the framework shown earlier in Figure 5.2. In particular, links between the brand identity cues and exposures on the one hand and the purchasing process on the other require analysis of data that goes beyond the limits of most brand tracking studies.

An ideal basket of measures

So, what is the ideal basket of measures? Our recommendation for a comprehensive set of measures for a consumer products company would cover the factors in Table 5.6. The important point is that these data should be brought together into a single database so that it can be analyzed and used for modelling.

Table 5.6
Basket of measures for a consumer products company

Factor to be measured	Relevant research
Macroeconomic factors	Government and industry statistics
Stimulus exposure – media weight (inc. competitor)	Media audits and research
Stimulus exposure – message/treatment (inc. competitor)	Campaign tracking
Stimulus exposure – field sales activity	CRM system call reports
Stimulus exposure – retail price (inc. competitor)	Retail audit/consumer audit
Stimulus exposure – sales promotion (inc. competitor)	Retail audit/consumer audit
Stimulus exposure – distribution/display (inc. competitor)	Retail audit/consumer audit
Processing and psychology (see below for detail)	Brand and ad tracking
Consumer buying behaviour	Consumer panel data/EPOS/ loyalty card
Total market retail sales (inc. competitor)	Retail audit/consumer audit
Trade sales	Ex-factory sales
Profit	Company finance calculation

This basket of data is needed in order to create an audit trail leading from marketing expenditure to customer responses and ultimately to sales and profits. Many companies have this data, but few make the effort to assemble the audit trail in a structured way that is suitable for analysis (see Figure 5.6). As a consequence, the potential insights from a structured analysis of the audit trail are lost.

Figure 5.6

An audit trail from marketing expenditure to sales and profits

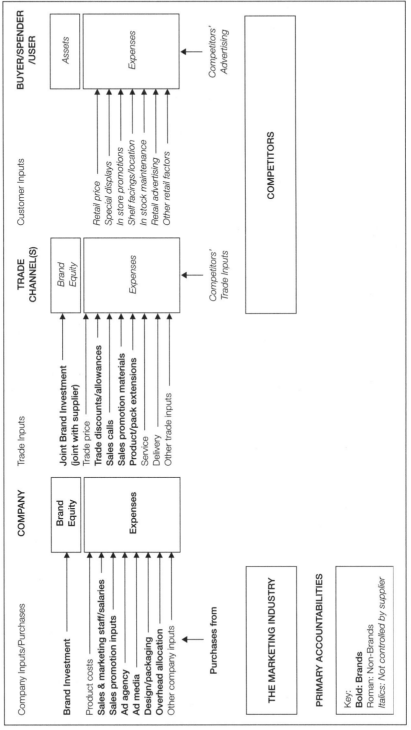

Data from Shaw and Mazur (1997)

There is not one standard basket of measures that fits all industries. Contrast Table 5.6 with the basket of measures needed for a credit card company, in Table 5.7.

Table 5.7
Basket of measures for a credit card company

Factor to be measured	Relevant research
Macroeconomic factors	Government and industry statistics
Stimulus exposure – ATL media weight	Media audits and research
Stimulus exposure – ATL message/treatment	Media audits and research
Stimulus exposure – direct marketing campaign	List statistics/database extract profile
Stimulus exposure – direct marketing treatment	Campaign tracking
Stimulus exposure – direct marketing offer	Campaign tracking
Acquisition success	Response rates, sources and offer when acquired
Processing and psychology (see below for detail)	Brand and ad tracking
Customer segment statistics	Customer database analysis
Product holding statistics	Customer database analysis
Balance interest payments	Customer database analysis
Non-interest charges	Customer database analysis
Add-on sales	Customer database analysis
Card transactions and merchant fees	Customer database analysis
Defaults	Customer database analysis
Dormants and lost customers	Customer database analysis
Profit	Company finance calculation

The aim of collecting this basket of data is not just to create a snapshot at one point in time, but to create a dynamic picture of developments over time. Figure 5.7 illustrates this concept.

So far we have not looked in any detail at the customer response data. Our experience of the market research industry is that it does, at best, a barely adequate job in this area. This is the final area that we shall examine in this chapter.

Three main methods are available:

1. **Panel method:** To diagnose the causality through every step in time, the theoretically preferable method is to interview the *same* people over time. Unfortunately this can prove expensive. Also there is a practical difficulty, as respondents are sensitized over time and interviewing bias is likely be a problem.

Figure 5.7

Recording the dynamic picture developing over time

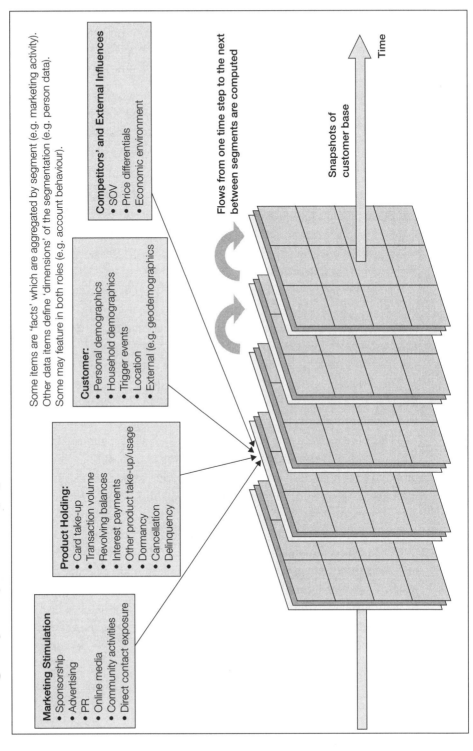

2. **Wave method**: Typically used before, during and after a campaign. Separate samples of respondents are interviewed each time. Survey waves are typically at three- or six-month intervals. We cannot causally track the same person over time and instead must make inferences.

3. **Continuous method**: Small samples of respondents are interviewed on a regular basis, say daily or weekly, for example 50 interviews weekly. To smooth out noise from the small sample size, market research firms often plot moving averages, something they call 'rolling the data', for example a four-week roll of 200 respondents.

An issue with survey methods concerns the use of telephone and web surveys. Strictly speaking, face-to-face interviews are needed because the interviewers have to show brands and ads to respondents to measure processing and recognition. However, in the USA and Australia, telephone interviews are a much lower-cost alternative, but a much less reliable source.

The scope and order of measures are vitally important. An idealized sequence is shown in Table 5.8. We have used as an example a brand of synthetic motor lubricant, which is a category of high-specification engine oil that reduces wear and prolongs engine life. One of the challenges for the marketer, especially in a category such as this, is that knowledge of the category itself may be poor.

The reason for being cautious about the sequence of questions is to eliminate as far as possible 'order bias', which is caused when earlier questions give hints to respondents about the expected answers to later questions.

The challenge with this ideal survey is practical. The survey is inevitably long, if all these questions are included. This gives rise to high costs, which may be prohibitively high for some market research departments. It also adds to interview fatigue, and can result in poor response rates or incomplete answers. So the market research manager and their agency must, understandably, select carefully from the idealized set and choose what is affordable and practical.

Our final recommendation to users of these surveys is that they should obtain original source data from survey questionnaires, as we have found that the insights from analyzing individual response data goes far beyond the limited insights available from tabulated and moving-average data. A cause-and-effect analysis is, strictly speaking, only possible with panel data. However, strong inferences and insights are yielded by analyzing single respondent data for continuous tracking.

Table 5.8
Ideal sequence of interview questions

Factor	Example of survey question
Category need: Respondent's acceptance that the category is relevant and necessary to them	Do you intend to buy a synthetic motor lubricant next time you buy engine oil for your automobile?
Category advertising cut-through: Respondent's ability to recall an ad for that category	What ads have you seen recently for synthetic engine oils?
Category prompted brand awareness: Respondent's ability to recall a brand for the named category. Known as 'unaided'	What brands of synthetic engine oil first come to mind?
Brand recognition: Respondent's ability to recognize a number of brands	Which of these brands have you seen before?
Brand prompted advertisement recall: Respondent's ability to recall an advertisement for a given brand	What advertisements have you seen recently for Castrol Syntec?
Action (reported purchase): Respondent's recall of recently purchased brands in the category	Which brand of synthetic lubricant have you bought recently?
Brand purchase intention: Respondent's opinion of the likelihood of purchasing the brand in future	If you were going to buy a synthetic lubricant for your automobile, how likely would you be to buy Castrol Syntec?
Brand attitude: Respondent's assessment of their loyalty to the brand	Overall, how would you rank Castrol Syntec for use in your automobile – the single best, one of several you'd consider, or you'd refuse to buy it?
Brand benefit beliefs: Respondent's beliefs about product benefits	How does Castrol Syntec rate on protection against engine wear, high-price, etc?
Brand purchase inhibitor beliefs: Respondent's beliefs that might inhibit purchasing	How likely do you think it is that once you have used synthetic motor oil in your car, you cannot switch back to conventional motor oil?
Advertisement recognition: Respondent's ability to recognize an advertisement	Have you seen this commercial on TV before?
Profile variables: Demographic information about the respondent	What is your age, gender, etc.?

Uncovering the true value of market research at BT

It's rare for market research to discover completely new consumer behaviours, but that is precisely what happened at BT, one of the world's leading telephone companies.

It happened at a time when stringent regulatory pressures on price – requiring a basket of call charges to be reduced by retail price index minus 7.5% – were driving revenues down. In response, the telecoms services provider looked to encourage adoption of products likely to stimulate calls, such as second phone lines and answerphones, used R&D to create new services which would stimulate calling, such as Call Return 1471, and applied advertising to call stimulation.

The breakthrough came when BT's researchers discovered that negative attitudes towards calling friends were suppressing latent demand (see Figure 5.8). Central to this was research that showed major differences between men and women's use of the phone. While women tend to use the phone to chat as an end in itself, men view the phone as a means to an end for delivering functional messages.

One consequence of this difference in view is that in a large proportion of households, men act as 'gatekeepers' of the telephone. Cost is generally used to justify this control.

Figure 5.8
Social pressure of men on female partners suppresses latent demand

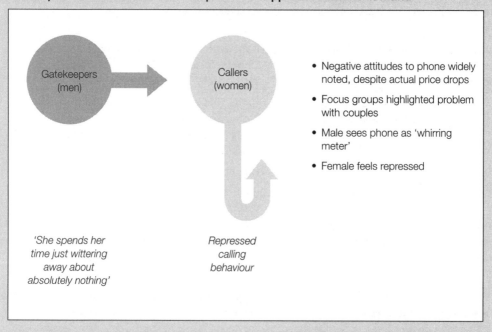

BT identified two major opportunities for its new advertising campaign. The first was to promote the value of 'female' phone calls, especially among men. This would legitimize women's behaviour and free-up their usage of the phone by softening attitudes among gatekeepers, while also encouraging men to change their own calling behaviour.

The second target was to reduce price perceptions. Despite the steady reduction in cost of calls, perceptions that BT's charges were high had risen. Research revealed that this was a result of rises in the average quarterly bill – which had increased by 71% between 1986 and 1994 – rather than knowledge of actual call charges. Line rental costs had risen faster than inflation, while call volumes were growing. Competitors' emphasis on price was also fuelling the impression that BT was expensive. Typically, costs were over-estimated by 400%.

A new advertising campaign, combining TV commercials starring Bob Hoskins, press advertising and price-led poster ads, was launched in May 1994. A £44 million budget was invested through to June 1995. Proving the effectiveness of the 'It's Good to Talk' campaign was complicated, because of the range of other factors in the market. These include growing penetration of other services, competitor activity and the growth of telephone-based services.

BT's research is much more sophisticated than many similar studies. In particular it has good descriptive data as well as evaluative. During the campaign period, recall stood at very high levels, occupying the number one slot in *Marketing* magazine's Adwatch survey for a record 22 out of 30 weeks. There were also substantial rises in agreement with important attitudinal statements. In the early stages of the campaign, 16% of consumers agreed that 'advertising reminded me to call someone and I rang them' – this rose to 31% by the end of the campaign. While 12% agreed that 'I have spent longer on some calls as a result of seeing the advertising' in the initial stages, 19% agreed at the end. The biggest shift in agreement was among women aged 35-plus, whose calling behaviour had been suppressed by male gatekeepers beforehand.

Shifts in opinions towards the phone were also created. While 44% agreed 'it's fun to pass time chatting on the phone' before the campaign, 54% agreed afterwards. Among men over 35, there was a 24% increase in agreement with this statement, compared to 14% for men overall and 10% for women. In the same period, women felt less guilty about chatting on the phone (down to 44% from 48%). There was also a steep fall in perceptions that BT's call charges are too high.

In addition to the consumer attitude data, an econometric study was undertaken to calculate the financial payback. Because of the complex range of charging bands offered by BT, it was necessary to build eight different models for the econometric analysis. These showed the impact on both calls-per-line and call duration for four key charge bands: local calls at standard rate; local calls at cheap rate; national calls at standard rate; and national calls at cheap rate.

These were applied to all campaigns over nine years. Perceived price of calls and general consumer expenditure were included in the models. The advertising variable allowed for the delayed impact of advertising. The regression analysis estimates were then validated against known data and were shown to have a good fit.

As a further way of proving that the econometric model was a reflection of reality, a control area was set up in which no ITV airtime was bought for the first three months of the campaign. By comparing national increases in calls per line with the Central TV region, it could be seen that local calls rose by 1.34% in areas exposed to the campaign compared to the area which was not. Likewise, national calls rose 1.72% and international calls 1.48%.

The sales uplift from the campaign was calculated to have provided incremental revenue of £33,000 per TVR. When multiplied by the total number of TVRs bought in the campaign (10,566 in all), less the cost of airtime and production, it was shown that the campaign yielded incremental revenues of £297 million – a return on investment of nearly 6:1. This excludes any impact on international calls or business lines.

Key points

- People are bombarded with information about products and brands all the time, and take very little notice of most of it.

- It is all too easy to focus on tracking 'stuff' in people's heads and ignore the bigger picture of the mechanisms by which branding influences buying behaviour.

- *'Cut-through'* (or the related measure, *'stand-out'*) is important for brands to register in people's minds, and it depends on (a) *attention* being gained (b) *interest* being elicited.

- Brand-*recognition* and brand-*recall* are widely available in brand tracking research, but better measures are needed to help diagnose the reasons behind trends in brand stand-out.

- People's minds hold two types of information about brands – *descriptive* (associations and beliefs) and *evaluative* (attitudes and intentions). Most brand-tracking research is inadequate in its tracking of descriptive measures, and pays too much attention to hierarchical evaluative scales that provide only limited diagnostic insights.

- Trade customers' thoughts and feelings are rarely captured in brand-tracking studies, and this is an area that urgently needs attention.

- The contribution of market research can benefit significantly from: better briefing to ensure that all of the relevant diagnostic measures are captured; better analysis, especially combining data from different research sources including marketing inputs (e.g. media tracking), consumer awareness and attitudes (e.g. opinion surveys) and consumer behaviour (e.g. panel research).

- There are significant advantages in obtaining individual respondent data where available as these provide much deeper insights than aggregate and moving-average data.

- Market research departments need to do a better job in unlocking value from brand-tracking research, by demanding more insights from their market research firms and by subjecting the data to rigorous statistical and econometric analysis.

- Market research firms tend to design brand-tracking studies on a basis that can be sold to the maximum number of client firms, with the consequence that the data are biased towards generic questions and lack questions that are specific to characteristics of individual brands.
- Marketing research as a 'tool for analyzing marketing decisions' should displace market research as a 'news and current affairs service'.

6

TRACKING TRENDS AND FORECASTING FUTURES

This chapter focuses on analyzing market trends and using the insights gained to forecast sales. This is perhaps the core of the book with regard to understanding the numbers. With the advent of spreadsheets, this type of analysis is remarkably easy to do and very instructive. It gives you a good feel for what is happening with your business. It also helps you find relationships between sales and other variables. Understanding the relationships between your numbers will help you make better use of forecasting models and other associated decision support tools.

Can you really make accurate sales forecasts?

While most business people recognize the need for effective forecasts, there is a tendency to take extreme views about forecasting:

- Fatalists take the view that forecasts are always wrong.

- Then there are the ostriches, who bury their heads in the sand, see all forecasts as a 'black art' and refuse to look at the explanations.

- Instinctive forecasters, on the other hand, claim that calculations and formulae are not needed, and instead rely on a mix of intuition and rules-of-thumb to predict outcomes.

- Finally, there are the statisticians and economists who use complicated formulae and baffle their colleagues with jargon.

We believe a rigorous approach is essential, but there is no need to bury the techniques and concepts in impenetrable jargon. Essentially, forecasting and predictive modelling set out to answer three key questions, which can be stated quite simply, as follows (see Figure 6.1):

- Why are we where we are today? What has caused us to follow the path we have undertaken to arrive here?

- Where are we going if we carry on along the same path, bearing in mind the competitive environment?

- How should we get from our current performance to a better level of performance? What changes do we want to make?

You may not be an expert statistician or econometrician, but don't be intimidated. You are an expert in your own field. Forecasts and models require teamwork between you (the 'client') and the technician.

It's important that you understand what the technician is doing, which is why you must read this chapter. Admit that you don't understand how all the mathematical technicalities work, but don't let that put you off, because a good technician will explain what they are doing and why.

Think of the technician as a detective, not an accountant. Give them a decent brief, spend time with them, involve them in the decisions you are making, encourage them, provide them with what they need, give them a realistic timetable.

Figure 6.1
Three key questions answered by forecasting and modelling

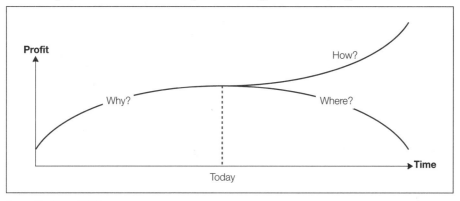

Source: After Warren (2002)

Get your brain going by reading the empirical generalizations (see Chapter 4). Discuss the mechanisms that may be at work (see Chapter 5) and canvass points of view among your colleagues. Think about the evidence. Ask yourself what you can and cannot establish with the data you've already got. Think laterally about where you might find additional evidence.

Check that your brief is good. Does it specify what effect you are predicting – sales, image or both? Does it specify all the likely causes of the effect – advertising, price, promotion, distribution or competition? Have all the key decision makers been involved in reviewing and agreeing the brief – the finance director, the CEO? Do they believe in the methods you are using?

Talk often with the technician, don't just leave them to get on with the analysis. Fill them in on the decision that you're using their analysis to support. They will probably discover things that may help you with other decisions. And they'll probably want to discuss what they are finding as it emerges and before the study is officially complete.

Cutting through the jargon

To understand what constitutes a good forecasting and predictive model, we first need to clarify the basic concepts and terminology used in the forecasting and modelling world (see Box 6.1).

All disciplines have their jargon, and that of statisticians and econometricians can be more impenetrable than most. It was Disraeli who first coined the phrase 'Lies, damned lies and statistics', and the passage of time has done little to improve the reputation of statisticians and forecasters. Precision in terms of language will help penetrate some of the mist of uncertainty surrounding the forecasting and modelling process.

Box 6.1 Terminology used in modelling and forecasting

Aims, goals, objectives and targets: The opinion of an individual or organization that business performance will reach a particular level at a stated future time. Achievement of a target is usually contingent on the individual or organization making changes in activities or resources that will cause the performance to change.

Best-case/worst-case: An opinion about the likelihood of good and bad future performance.

Cause-and-effect: Distinction between events, where the occurrence of one (the cause) is supposed to bring about or produce an occurrence of the other (the effect).

Confidence: An opinion about the likelihood of a forecast being correct.

Correlation: The degree to which two variables change together. The occurrence of correlations does not necessarily imply causation.

Econometrics: The application of psychological, sociological and economic explanations to understanding business financial and economic performance.

Explanation: An intelligible account of why something happens. The scientific explanation of an event has the form of an argument whose conclusion is the event to be explained and whose premises includes both causes and assumptions.

Forecast: A statement about probable future performance.

Forecasting model: A simulation of business performance (e.g. profits) and its causes (e.g. advertising) used to make predictions about future performance, assuming specific patterns of future causes.

Hockey-stick: A forecast where past trends show declining performance, but future performance is predicted to improve. An extreme form of best-case.

Pattern: A regular or repetitive form in data (e.g. advertising) that may be useful as a guide for making another pattern, such as a pattern of sales over time. The occurrence of patterns does not necessarily imply causation.

Simulation: The technique of imitating the real world with a computer program, which is suitably analogous in terms of representing cause-and-effect.

Trend: A general tendency of data to move in a particular direction. The occurrence of trends does not necessarily imply causation.

At the outset, it is especially important to understand the difference between a forecast and a predictive model:

- **A forecast** is usually defined as an estimate of an actual value in a future time period. 'Where are we heading in the future under current policies?' is the key question. It normally refers to a time series, which is a collection of values observed sequentially through time. The term 'forecast' is widely used to imply extrapolation of past time series into the future, without reference to underlying driving forces causing the patterns.

- **A predictive model** usually refers to a representation of the future based on an attempt to identify and quantify the fundamental driving forces causing the patterns in the data (for example predicting how promotions drive sales). 'Why has contribution followed the time path that it has?' is one key question, along with 'How can we alter that for the better?'

Patterns in data

Primary schoolchildren are taught from an early age to recognize patterns. It is one of our most fundamental mental skills, and it is not terribly difficult. Time patterns such as daily routines, weekly patterns and the seasons are familiar to all of us, and we know how to project them into the future.

The starting point for analyzing a pattern is to collect historical figures over time. You will have seen in the previous chapter what that involves. Sales are the most fundamental data that need to be analyzed in this way. You can either choose sales volume (i.e. quantity) or sales value. If you have data available on price and volume, we'd generally recommend that you analyze sales volumes, as the analysis is usually more straightforward.

Obviously the longer the run of the historical data available, the deeper the insights it reveals. Ten years is the length of time many investment analysts study. Three to five years is common in marketing plans. Twelve months is the norm in budgeting. Our advice is to get as long a run as possible.

Having collected the data, you should plot a graph. Spreadsheets are the tool of choice for this, and most novices can plot graphs. Even with limited data, there are some patterns that you may notice:

- **Trend** which rises (or falls) steadily over the time period you are examining;
- **Seasonal pattern** which repeats, more or less the same, every 12 months;
- **Short-term peaks** that are the effects of events such as price-promotions or important sporting fixtures.

These features are illustrated in Figure 6.2.

Figure 6.2
Patterns in time-series data

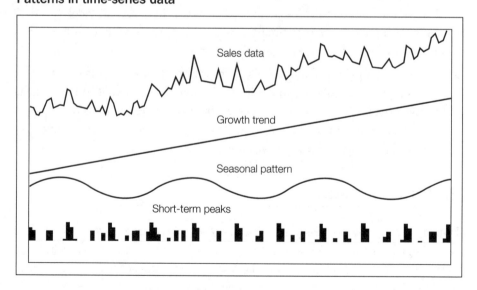

Forecasting methodology decision tree

Choosing the appropriate method or technique is a key element in the forecasting process. There are a number of key criteria that should be considered in choosing which method or methods to use. These include:

■ Availability of data;

■ Quality of data;

■ Availability of resources;

■ Access to experts;

■ Time horizon for forecasting purposes.

Forecasting practitioners often use a decision tree diagram as shown in Figure 6.3 to help them select the best forecasting technique for a particular situation.

Figure 6.3
The forecasting methodology decision tree

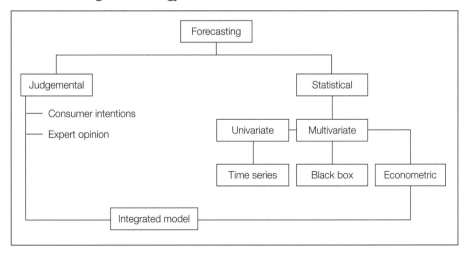

The decision tree nature of the diagram is somewhat misleading in that it implies that it is an 'either/or' decision when choosing a forecasting technique. In fact, there is often much merit in employing more than one forecasting technique, and there is plenty of evidence to suggest that combining the results of different forecasting procedures can increase the accuracy of the forecast. Similarly, it is important to recognize that it is possible to mix and match forecasting techniques.

The forecasting options available depend critically on the pool of knowledge known as the fact base (Shaw 2003). Here lie the data, the sources of information and the collective knowledge of the organization. The first decision to make is whether to choose a technique that relies primarily on judgement or on a statistical analysis of the data (or both). If there are little or no data available, then the judgement route is the only one available. If the data are available, then statistical modelling is feasible, and can either be the sole basis of the forecast, or can be complemented by a judgemental technique.

Judgemental modelling

Let us follow the judgemental route for a moment. There are two types of judgemental forecasts: those that rely on experts and those that seek to canvass the views of the consumer. Surveying the intentions of potential consumers is an obvious and often powerful technique that is especially useful in predicting the demand for a new product or service. Conjoint (or trade-off) analysis seeks to explain these intentions by reference to various aspects of the product or service (price, level of service, design, etc.) and can provide insights into the causality of consumer behaviour that can be built into the forecasting process.

The main judgemental forecasting approach is to have a single expert, or group of experts, who are familiar with the situation and produce a forecast based on their own judgement. It is the most widely used forecasting method in marketing and is especially popular in markets where new technology is changing the landscape radically. In these circumstances the past will not necessarily be a reliable guide to the future (invalidating a statistical approach), and the consumer may not be able to make an informed judgement on choices that rely on features that are too novel to appreciate (negating a survey of intentions).

In many instances the judgement of the expert, or panel of experts, is used directly and explicitly in the forecast. But a number of studies have shown that expert opinion is subject to bias and hence can be a most unreliable method, according to extensive research on judgemental forecasting (Russo and Schoemaker 1989; Wright and Goodwin 1998).

Studies of sales revenue forecasting (e.g. Fildes and Hastings 1994) highlight many problems with frequently used judgemental approaches:

- Innumeracy among those responsible for forecasting;
- No training, or minimal training;

- Poor data quality and quantity to inform forecasters;
- No use of computers in many cases;
- No monitoring for accuracy because of poor record keeping;
- Not treated as a specialized professional function;
- Infrequent, minor duty of those making the forecasts;
- Not line management duty, often lower-level peripheral staff.

More sophisticated methods, such as Delphi techniques, where a panel of experts is fed the results of previous rounds of forecasts and then asked to re-forecast in the light of this information, can improve forecasting accuracy significantly.

Similarly, techniques such as judgemental bootstrapping, which uses successive rounds of the experts' opinions together with their assumptions to formulate a model, can also lead to improved forecasts. This technique was first used in the early 1900s to improve crop forecasting but is currently an under-utilized technique in modern business forecasting. Box 6.2 shows a simple exercise to illustrate how judgemental forecasts work.

Box 6.2 The marketing evaluator

Basic financial structure

For your selected brand or business, write down an approximate breakdown of total revenue into profit, marketing spend, variable costs and fixed costs in the table below. These can be in actual currency values or as percentages.

Profit	Marketing spend	Variable costs	Fixed costs	Total revenue

Market response factors

Then, for each blank cell in the table below, write in the approximate percentage changes in sales volumes that you would expect to result from the changes in price and marketing spend.

Marketing spend	Price		
	Down 10%	Unchanged	Up 10%
Up 25%			
Unchanged		+0%	
Down 25%			

For example:

Marketing spend	Price		
	Down 10%	Unchanged	Up 10%
Up 25%	18%	+5%	–%10%
Unchanged	+15%	+0%	–20%
Down 25%	+6%	–10%	–29%

Response curve

Spreadsheet programs can then be used to interpolate the response curve at other values than those estimated. Then the profit curve can be plotted. An example is given in Figure 6.4.

Figure 6.4
Contour chart mapping profit responses to cost and price changes

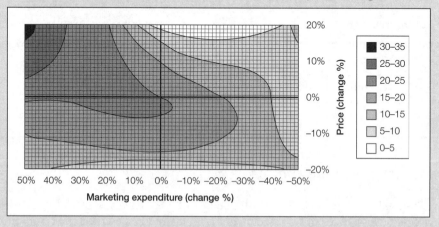

This contour chart of profits illustrates how profits will change with marketing or advertising expenditure and price changes. What is perhaps surprising is that the contours do not follow a simple pattern, but map out complex landscapes. Starting at the current position (i.e. 0% change in marketing expenditure and price), the path to maximum profitability involves first reducing price (by heading south) to get onto the profit ridge. As the marketing expenditure increases, profitability increases as we move up the ridge in a west-north-westerly direction. This means that we can begin to increase price. In the example shown, the optimum strategy for a 20% increase in marketing expenditure is to return to the original price. Beyond this, further increases in marketing expenditure will support a premium price.

Statistical modelling

Statistical analysts are faced with a choice of *univariate* or *multivariate* techniques.

Univariate means that only prior values of the single variable to be forecast are used in the model. Thus, in our sales forecasting example, only past sales of the product determine future sales, whereas in a multivariate technique we would also consider price, advertising, competitor activity and all the other factors outlined in this chapter. This approach is also described as time series analysis.

Multivariate techniques are potentially more powerful than univariate ones, in that they make use of all the information available about the product or market to be forecast.

There are circumstances, however, when univariate methods are the most appropriate, especially for short-term forecasts. In the short term, it may be appropriate to assume the economic, technological and competitive environment will not change, and that the company itself will continue to behave as it has in the recent past. In this case, a univariate technique will deliver a valid forecast. Univariate techniques, which include moving averages, exponential smoothing and curve fitting, are relatively simple to use and easy to understand. They can fairly easily be carried out in standard spreadsheet packages.

Econometric modelling

The application of the best available statistical methods to obtain explanations in economic and social psychology models is a science known as *econometrics*.

Specifically, in marketing, econometrics has come to mean a body of statistical theory that has developed alongside consumer theory, which aims to explain patterns of consumer and trade purchasing. Econometric techniques force analysts to formulate hypotheses about the relationships between business results and marketing drivers, and test them against theory and data.

Four skills need to be combined to be effective at econometrics, which explains why it takes many years to become proficient at it:

- **Consumer behaviour theory:** Models are formulated according to hypotheses that make sense in terms of consumer behaviour theory (the term is rather misleading, as industrial buying is also included in the theory). Much of the learning in this field arises from pragmatic analyses of actual consumer situations, but there is also a body of customer psychology theory that borrows from the field of social psychology (see Chapter 5).

- **Mathematical statistics:** As discussed in the previous section, this describes a set of mathematical techniques that are able to give rigorous guidance on how one variable is affected by others.

- **Data:** Numerous problems need to be resolved to obtain effective data, and these practical issues are not prominently addressed in consumer behaviour theory. Market research theory provides answers to many of these issues.

- **Business results:** Financial analysis needs to be understood and incorporated into the modelling process.

Econometric modelling is therefore a powerful technique that allows the analyst, in theory at least, to incorporate assumptions about all the key drivers of a market or a company's sales into the forecasting process. It has the advantage therefore of relating directly to the planning processes in an organization, where decisions about product, price, advertising, promotions and distribution can be replicated within the model.

The limitations of econometric modelling as a forecasting tool are that it is a data-intensive process, and that it requires accurate forecasts of each of the assumptions to produce an accurate forecast of the variable of interest.

Case study 6.1

Analytics at Kraft

Kraft is the largest branded food and beverage company in North America and second largest in the world. Core categories include snacks, beverages, cheese, grocery and convenience meals.

Like several of its peers, Kraft uses analytic modelling to inform many key decisions. A key problem they solved was resource misallocation: brands driving over 80% of corporate growth were receiving only 20% of marketing resources.

Tom Lloyd, Group Market Analytics Manager, comments: 'This is not merely an exercise in justifying expenditure, it is a vital element in staying ahead in the competitive game.'

Analytic models are used to determine responses to every element of the marketing mix: price, advertising, consumer promotion, trade promotion, distribution, new products. Regular pricing has declined in recent years as a major driver, as the retail trade becomes more powerful in determining the price to the consumer. Advertising is ever important, but its effectiveness is constantly being challenged. Consumer promotions are a very expensive way of getting incremental volume. Trade promotions are also a costly source of incremental volume. New products are costly to develop, with a high failure rate.

In North America, the company has developed cross-portfolio allocation models to improve the effectiveness of spending. The model includes:

- advertising;
- trade merchandising;
- consumer promotions;
- events and outdoor;
- consumer attitudes and beliefs;
- retail sales.

ROI by market and mix-element is calculated by the model to show the return on all expenditure.

Objectives are set by a Business Team Planning Group, with representation from:

- Finance;
- Advertising;
- Media Planning;
- Consumer Promotions;
- National Sales;
- Logistics/Manufacturing;
- Market Research.

Kraft uses modelling as an integral part of its marketing planning process. Unlike many companies whose marketing plans have little connection with financial goals, Kraft's is fully aligned financially. The scale and impact of analytics are shown in Table 6.1.

Table 6.1
Integrating modelling with market planning at Kraft

Business area	Frequency	Types of decisions
Regular pricing	Twice a year	EDLP vs. Hi–Lo strategies
Media plans	Annual	Optimum flighting – burst vs. continuous Effective frequency – coverage vs. OTS Allocation by media channel
Consumer promotions	3–4 per year	Cost per adopter Effectiveness of promotions
Trade promotions	Annual Quarterly Weekly	Annual activity plans Business reviews Selecting activity to plug gaps
NPD	2–3 times per year	Opportunity assessment

Key: EDLP = Every Day Low Pricing; OTS = Opportunities To See; NPD = New Product Development

Tom Lloyd has the following advice to offer about working with econometric modellers:

- Start with the problem, not the tool.
- Don't get sidetracked by 'black box' debates.
- Choose a modeller you trust and want to work with.
- Use models to get insights, not merely to prove a point.
- Don't be phased by clever people; if it doesn't look right, then say so.

The process of econometric modelling

> Any astronomer can predict just where every star will be at half past eleven tonight. He can make no such prediction about his daughter. (Adams 2001)

There are six steps to good econometric modelling, and they are described in Figure 6.5.

A key point to the process depicted in Figure 6.5 is that it is a *learning* process. Knowledge gained in the information-gathering stage may result in a rethink in the formulation of the objectives of the project altogether. An evaluation of the model may lead to the selection of a different technique to be used in the modelling process. Using the model in one forecasting round may influence the whole process in the next round of forecasting.

Figure 6.5
Steps in the forecasting and predictive modelling process

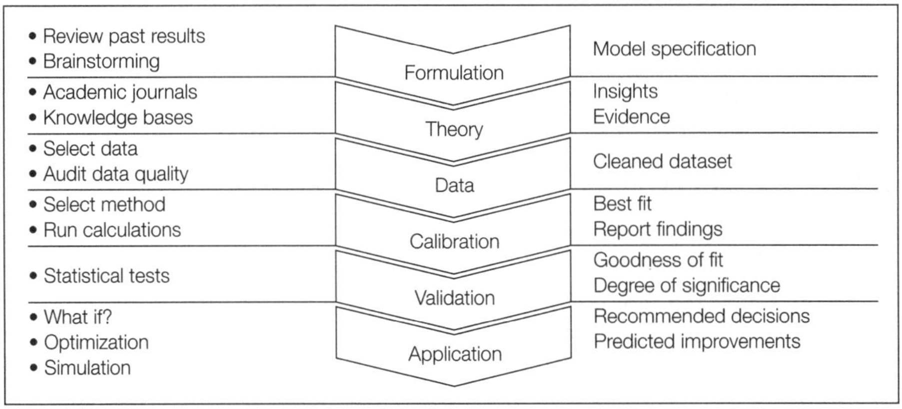

• Review past results • Brainstorming	Formulation	Model specification
• Academic journals • Knowledge bases	Theory	Insights Evidence
• Select data • Audit data quality	Data	Cleaned dataset
• Select method • Run calculations	Calibration	Best fit Report findings
• Statistical tests	Validation	Goodness of fit Degree of significance
• What if? • Optimization • Simulation	Application	Recommended decisions Predicted improvements

Formulation

Always formulate the model clearly at the outset. A written brief should be agreed with the sponsors of the modelling process, as this makes them articulate their requirements as clearly as possible, in terms of:

■ Business objectives of model (e.g. marketing mix allocation);

■ Hypotheses being tested (e.g. brand ads drive premium prices);

■ Parameters being estimated (e.g. price elasticity, ad elasticity);

■ Information sources (existing data, list of sources);

■ Information sources (new, e.g. survey);

■ Data quantity and quality requirements;

■ Controls and benchmarks to be established;

■ Expected use of results (budgeting process in four months' time);

■ Decision criteria (e.g. shareholder value improvement);

■ Approach to modelling (e.g. not black box);

■ Deliverables (e.g. report and simulator).

Brainstorming and reviewing past performance can help specify the business objectives of the model.

Hypotheses that must be tested should be clearly articulated at the outset, since this will impact the design of the methods used.

Scope and parameters need to be specified in terms of:

- Products/markets to include:
  - countries;
  - regions;
  - total market;
  - company sales;
- Exact specification of variable(s) to be forecast:
  - volume, value;
  - sales, profits, stocks;
- Time horizon and frequency:
  - 1 year, 3 year, 5 year;
  - annual, quarterly, monthly;
- Uses of the model:
  - budgeting;
  - scenario planning;
  - marketing evaluation.

As part of this process, it is often useful to set out clearly what decisions might be affected by the outcome of the modelling process. This will help determine at what level of detail the outputs of the model need to be reported. Similarly, it focuses attention on the key information to be collected, and adds a degree of precision to the data-gathering process.

Theory

At this stage, it is often useful to conduct some brainstorming sessions, engage in some mapping exercises that will tease out some of the key drivers of the process, and identify some of the causal relationships and feedback loops that underlie senior management's perceptions of the market dynamics in which they operate.

Each key decision maker will have a 'mental model' of his business, and getting them to map how the market works for them will help to build a shared understanding of the problem or identify where a consensus needs to be forged.

Drawing a causal loop model can be helpful. Progress from a simple input–output diagram to more complex diagrams. 'Triangulation' involves linking three (or more) variables together, including intermediary variables. Eventually a fully integrated model is produced.

A literature review can help put these mental models and market maps into context by providing examples of mappings, quantifications and outcomes from other markets and organizations.

The output of this process should be (a) insights into likely relationships and null-relationships, and (b) evidence of these effects found in other research studies.

Data collection

Collecting, collating, analyzing, reconciling and understanding the data is probably the most important step in any forecasting or modelling project. This subject is dealt with in more detail in Shaw (2003).

It is worth reiterating here, though, the importance of understanding the provenance of the data. Statisticians refer to a concept known as the 'data generation process' which describes accurately the idea that all data are manufactured, and knowledge of the manufacturing process is vital if we are to understand the 'product'.

For example, a series may be labelled 'sales of chocolate in the UK in millions of grams per year', but you should consider the following:

- Is it a complete sum of sales from all outlets and from all suppliers?
- Is it a sample survey of a panel of consumers?
- Is the survey once a year or continuous?
- Was the sample random?
- How big was the sample?
- Has the sample been weighted to reflect the composition of the total population?

Calibration

At its most basic, an econometric model is just an equation (or a set of equations). The equation predicts a value (the *dependent variable*) that we are interested in, such as sales volume, sales revenue, awareness, etc. from a set of other values (the *independent variables*), such as price, advertising, disposable income, etc. The weights given to the independent variables in the equation are called the *coefficients*.

The model is usually constructed, and the values of the coefficients obtained, using a computer. Software for econometric modelling is widely available today for no more than a few hundred pounds. Spreadsheets such as Microsoft Excel have statistical tools available and these can be useful for many forecasting needs.

Statistical packages for more complex econometric analyses are also available. The two leading general statistical packages are SAS and SPSS. More specialist econometric packages include EViews, RATS and Microfit. Although software vendors claim that they have de-skilled the job of econometrics, we strongly advise against taking these claims seriously and do not advise non-statisticians to venture into this minefield alone.

Examples of econometric models are given in the excellent paper by Holmes and Cook (2004). They quote the following example of the type of equation that could be obtained by econometric analysis:

$$
\begin{aligned}
\text{Sales} = \\
+0.2 \times \text{Temperature} \\
+0.8 \times \text{Distribution} \\
-0.5 \times \text{Price} \\
+0.1 \times \text{Advertising}
\end{aligned}
$$

The minus sign in front of the coefficient of price ensures that the sales predicted by the equation fall when price increases, and vice versa.

Holmes and Cook illustrate how the above model can show the separate effects of the dependent variables in Figure 6.6.

The chart shows the clear effects of a seasonal pattern that corresponds to temperature variation, an upward sales trend that corresponds to an increase in distribution, and a step change in sales when the relative price falls. The effects of advertising are less apparent.

Validation

The next step is to carry out a thorough evaluation of the model. This involves analyzing both the inputs to the model and the outputs from the model (see Figure 6.7).

If it is a statistical model, we can look at how closely the model predictions follow what actually happened over a period of history. This measure is known as the R squared (R^2), and measures the explanatory power of a model. An R^2 of 0 means the model explains nothing of history.

Figure 6.6
Econometric analysis illustration

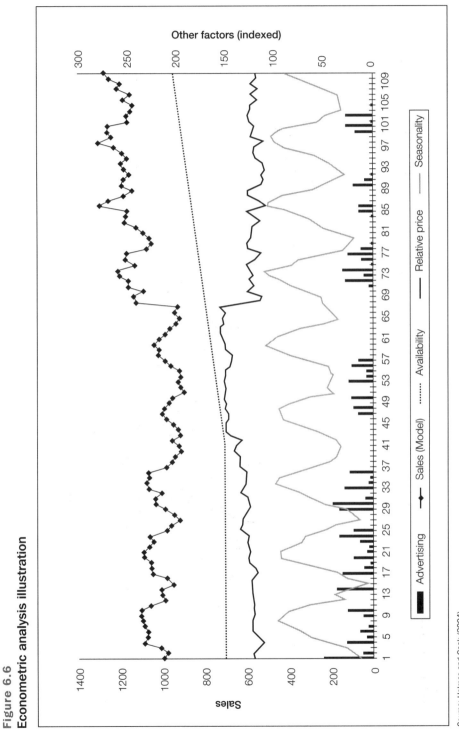

Source: Holmes and Cook (2004)

Figure 6.7
Validation illustration

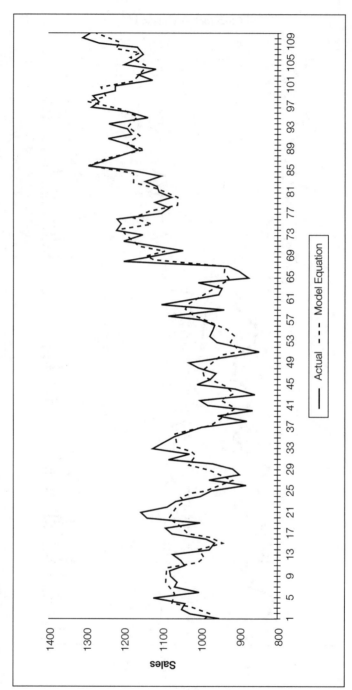

An R^2 of 1 means that the model is perfect and explains all the variation in history. In practice, a wide variation in R^2 is experienced in modelling different markets. If the series is fairly stable, then an R^2 of 0.9 or more (i.e. 90% of the variation in history is explained by the model) is common. If the series is erratic, then an R^2 of 0.5 (i.e. 50% of the variation in history is explained by the model) would be acceptable.

The R^2 is a useful overall descriptive measure of a model, but it is better to test it in action by getting the model to predict what would have happened in an 'out of sample' period.

For example, let us assume we have sales data monthly for the years 1997–2002. We would then build the model using only data for 1997–2001, saving the final year for testing the model. We then get the model to predict what happened in 2002, and look and see how close the prediction was to reality. We can calculate the Absolute Percentage Error (APE) by subtracting the prediction from the actual, to get the forecasting error, and, ignoring whether the result is positive or negative, expressing the result as a percentage of the actual:

$$\text{Error} = (\text{Actual} - \text{Prediction})$$
$$\text{APE} = \text{Absolute (error)/Actual}$$

The R^2 and APE are measures describing the output of a model. We can also test how good the inputs to a model are by their degree of significance. The T-statistic tests whether an estimate of a variable is in fact reliable, or whether it could in fact plausibly be zero, and therefore insignificant. If the T-statistic is greater than 1.95 then we can be 95% confident that the variable is significant, and therefore should be included in the model.

Application

The final step in the process is to use the model for its intended purpose: to make predictions about the future based on a defined set of assumptions. It is often convenient to build a spreadsheet version of the model that contains the key inputs to the model, the key relationships in the model in the form of a set of equations, and the relevant outcomes in the form of predictions of the key variables to be forecast.

The use of macros, hot buttons, and charts and tables can transform the spreadsheet model into a highly interactive forecasting modelling instrument, which can be used as a sophisticated scenario planning tool. This can also be developed into an optimization model that will calculate the optimum level of, for example, expenditure on advertising under different circumstances, and allow the user to seek the level of advertising expenditure needed to achieve a certain level of sales.

Integrated forecasting and predictive modelling in action

> If you bet on a horse, that's gambling. If you bet you can make three spades, that's entertainment. If you bet cotton will go up three points, that's business. See the difference? (Sherrod 2003)

The holy grail of forecasting is an *integrated* forecasting system which combines both judgemental and statistical forecasting techniques. This requires an evaluation of all of the forecasting techniques for each of the forecasting situations. Surprisingly, there is little evidence that organizations employ formal evaluation procedures on a systematic basis, although the principles for conducting such a review are fairly intuitive and easy to implement. Of course in practice, organizations often combine formal statistical techniques and then informally adjust them using judgement, but this procedure is by definition not documented and hence loses much of its validity:

Here are ten hard questions to ask or be asked about the way you conduct forecasting in your organization:

1. What controllable factors (e.g. marketing expenditure, pricing) drive the patterns in our sales data?
2. What are the most important influences outside our control (e.g. competitor activity) that drive the trends?
3. How much confidence do we have in our best-fit formula?
4. Do we understand where the data have come from? Are we clear on the data definitions?
5. Is the correlation a genuine cause-and-effect relationship or a complete coincidence?
6. Do we understand the relationships in our econometric model? Do they accord with common sense?
7. By how much can we realistically change the controllable factors in a week, month, quarter, year?
8. What is the baseline forecast?

9. What is the maximum improvement we can make to profits in a quarter, year, three years?

10. Have we learned from previous forecasting errors?

Much attention has been devoted over the years to forecasting how sales of new products may perform over the whole of the product life cycle. Forecasting the success of a new launch is particularly difficult in that there are no historical data to work with. Intentions surveys and conjoint analyses are techniques that have had much success in providing forecasts of new products and services. Similarly, expert opinion is also used successfully for new products and services, especially in the field of new technology.

Once the product or service has passed the launch phase, then in many markets sales undergo a period of rapid growth, followed by a slowdown and eventually saturation. This S-curve shape of the product life cycle is a common assumption in marketing, and this type of curve can be built into the modelling process.

To calculate the optimum expenditure allocation, sophisticated marketing managers estimate the sales response functions and then find the level of expenditure that maximizes payback (see Box 6.3 for some additional terminology definitions).

Box 6.3 Sales response definitions

Optimization: Fine-tuning of several continuous factors under a manager's control in order maximize (or minimize) a dependent variable. For example, fine-tuning of advertising and sales promotion expenditure to maximize net profits.

Constrained optimization: Optimization when there are limitations placed on some of the variables. For example, when the total marketing budget is fixed; this also corresponds with an allocation decision.

Sales response function: A mathematical formula that connects the likely sales volume during a specified time period and the different possible levels of a marketing mix element.

Response curve shapes

In an ideal world, sales of a brand would increase in proportion to the marketing spend on the brand. Provided that our starting point is profitable, we could then spend more and more on marketing, driving up sales and profitability until we became immensely rich and opted to retire to our yacht in the Caribbean.

Unfortunately, the overwhelming view of the literature on marketing expenditure is that life is not like that. Instead, the responsiveness of brand sales to brand marketing expenditure decreases the more we spend. This gives rise to the so-called 'saturation' curve illustrated in Figure 6.8 (from Batra *et al.* 1996).

Figure 6.8
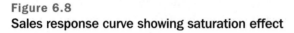
Sales response curve showing saturation effect

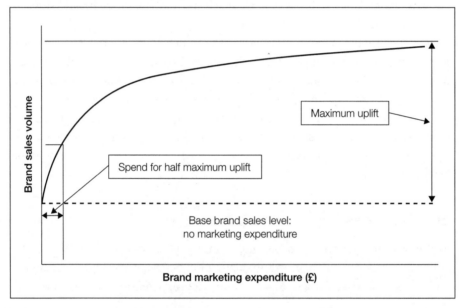

As shown in Figure 6.8, the response of brand sales volume to brand marketing expenditure can be characterized by two parameters:

- The maximum increase in brand sales volume that can be achieved if 'money is no object' for marketing expenditure (clearly, a highly theoretical concept!)
- The marketing expenditure required to achieve half of the maximum increase in brand sales volume.

Sometimes, more complex response behaviours are described in the literature, the most common of which is the S-curve (see Figure 6.9). The idea of the S-curve is to capture the effect of there being a threshold to marketing expenditure. As noted above (and, for example, described by East 1997: 280–3), this reflects the idea that marketing expenditures are ineffective below a certain level.

A further optional refinement is that, at high marketing expenditures, consumer 'wear-out' begins to occur, and the consumer response to the brand begins to fall. This feature is illustrated by the broken line in Figure 6.9. Although they describe effects that are widely believed to apply, S-curves are technically difficult to handle, and most analysis and optimization is carried out using the simpler saturation curve described earlier. We shall not depart from this convention.

Figure 6.9
Sales response curve showing wear-out

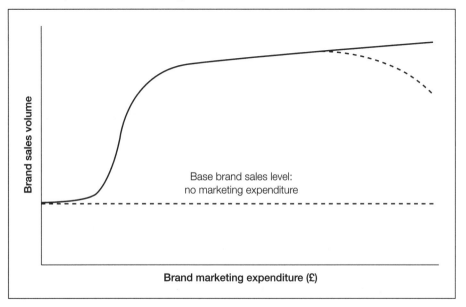

A further simplification is also widely adopted. The response curves are almost always defined in terms of the brand sales volume response, assuming that prices remain constant. In practice, of course, the purpose of the marketing expenditure may be to support a premium price for the brand at the same level of sales as much as to increase sales volume.

For example, the illustrative plot in Figure 6.10 shows the relative price against share of market. The power brands all enjoy a premium price position as well as high shares. By comparison, the follower brands have low share and price. Also there is a group of Every Day Low Priced (EDLP) brands that have high share but low price.

Figure 6.10
Relative price and share of market

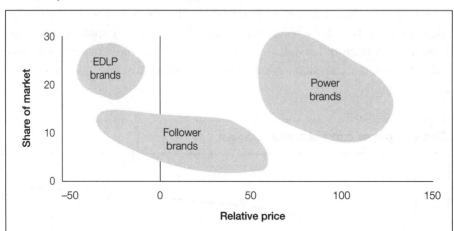

In this book, we shall conform to the convention of optimizing marketing spend assuming no change in prices, but note that this approach can be extended to an overall optimization of price and marketing spend if required.

Forecasts of profits

The sales forecast can be translated into a revenue forecast by making assumptions about the price of the product or service. Adding a cost element to the process will therefore generate a forecast or prediction of profit. This is becoming increasingly common as both the marketing team and the finance team want to know the financial implications of marketing and other actions. Many organizations will already have quite sophisticated financial models that can be adapted, simplified or bolted on to the forecasting model. The key requirement for the cost model is to make a distinction between fixed costs and variable costs. Fixed costs do not vary with sales whereas variable costs do.

Judgemental methods are usually the most appropriate technique for forecasting costs. Expert opinion in finance and marketing is invaluable in predicting future costs. If major changes in costs are expected, then outside expert opinion could be sought. In some markets, particularly those where regulation is important, econometric techniques have been used successfully in forecasting longer-term trends in costs.

It will be clear from all these examples that there are many useful applications of forecasting and modelling techniques in marketing. Whilst some of the processes will require the support of expert technicians, it is essential that business executives in both marketing and finance take charge of such initiatives, both in terms of design and common-sense evaluation of the final results. Many aspects of the process can be carried out using functions supplied on any standard spreadsheet program, and it is worth the extra effort involved in learning how to use these features.

Key points

- Every organization needs forecasts and targets.
- Forecasts are statements about probable future performance.
- Targets are management judgements that business performance will reach a given level at a future time as a consequence of specific decisions and actions.
- Patterns in data can easily be analyzed using spreadsheet technology.
- Forecasting accuracy can be improved by using judgemental methods and statistical ones.
- Econometric modelling incorporates explanations from economics and social psychology into the statistical analysis.
- Forecasting should be carried out in a systematic and disciplined way, but it is rarely done like this.

7

AVOIDING DECISION TRAPS

This chapter discusses the mistakes that decision makers make over and over again, but should be able to avoid. It starts by looking at the habitual ways in which decision makers spend their time, and argues that better management of decision making can improve success rates. It then examines the traps into which we fall, and shows how to avoid them. It finishes by listing the seven habits of highly effective decision makers. Some of the rules have been introduced in earlier chapters – after all, common sense should know no boundaries. Here, the same kind of thinking is applied to the political subtext of decision making, to help you make the right decisions, even under difficult circumstances.

Decision making in the real world

When we look at how decision makers and analysts really behave, the pressures they work under, and the errors they make, there are some striking insights. Academics who study this 'behavioural decision theory' have published numerous articles and made their insights available to other scholars, but until now this important work has not been made readily accessible to the general reader.

We know from our experience that decision analysts are mostly middle-ranking managers, often in staff roles, providing advice and support to line management and decision makers. As such they are under intense pressure from interested parties to make 'politically correct' recommendations.

You will recognize these pressures:

- *'Only tell me the good news'*: some managers make it clear to analysts that they do not wish to receive negative news.

- *'You don't have enough experience'*: senior decision makers often make it clear to the analysts that their rank is subordinate.

- *'We shoot messengers'*: in many companies there is a culture of punishing the bringer of bad tidings.

Objectivity is particularly questionable when advertising agencies, media shops or promotional agencies are told: 'Do an assessment of your own performance and let us know the results.' We have personally examined dozens of flawed analyses, where the findings did not seem to us to be supported by the available evidence. Common errors include:

- Omission of negative findings;
- Suppression of problem data;
- Selective reporting of results.

Errors like these are avoidable; we call them decision traps. Most decision makers commit the same kinds of errors. So whatever kind of decision you have to make, you can probably use the insights a small group of researchers have developed to prevent those mistakes. As in every other chapter of this book, before you start, check you are familiar with the terminology we are using (see Box 7.1).

Box 7.1 The terminology of decision making

Decision: A choice between two or more alternatives resulting in the selection of the one that is judged to be the best.

Decision analyst: Person who provides analyses of the alternatives, to support the decision maker in choosing the best one.

Decision trap: Widespread methodological errors that people frequently commit when making decisions.

Decision maker: Whoever makes such a choice.

Model: A representation of the most important elements of a perceived real-world situation.

Auditing and improving your decision analysis

'Ad hoc' is a good description of real-world decision analysis. And the bigger the decision, the more ad hoc it tends to become. Really big decisions, such as mergers and acquisitions (M&A), new products and new brands, are often terribly ad hoc and as a consequence the failure rate is high. If you look back over the past year or two at the big decisions you have made, I'm sure you'll agree.

Ten hard questions to ask about your company's decision making:

1. What marketing decisions have you regretted the most?
2. What were the circumstances?
3. What lessons did you learn from the experience?
4. What types of decisions are you especially bad at making? How can you improve your judgement?
5. Which of your decisions carry the highest risks? Which have the highest potential for regrets? What mitigating actions do you take?

6. Have you ever lied with statistics? Have you ever been caught out? What were the circumstances?

7. Do you always interrogate the figures to establish their validity?

8. How can you squeeze more insights from your marketing information?

9. Do you sometimes discover mistakes in your analyses? What are your most persistent analysis problems?

10. Are you good with numbers? How can you improve?

A decision audit can help you identify the areas that have insufficient time and talent allocated to them, and those that absorb more time and talent than is totally justified. This is not something you need do often. But once a year it is a useful discipline to audit your decision making and identify key improvements.

The various types of decision a manager has to make include routine, recurrent major decisions, step-change decisions and emergency decisions. Different approaches to choosing the best alternative should be selected to fit the circumstances (see Table 7.1). Not all decisions merit detailed analysis, but many decisions which receive quick and dirty analysis should be treated with more respect.

Some decisions are easy to make, and we tend to make these fast. Others are difficult and those are the ones we put off for as long as possible, or until there is no decision to be made because someone has taken it out of our hands. Just because the decision is easy does not mean it is the right one.

Marketing managers often use rules-of-thumb for decisions. For example, if a competitor launches a promotional campaign, the brand manager will have a strong instinct to react by spending promotional budget to restore competitive parity. We tend to follow the same path for many of these decisions, and yet we should ask ourselves, have we defined the decision correctly?

It's easy to get an easy decision wrong

Your research agency tells you the advertising tracking research shows the campaign is wearing out. Easy – pick up the phone and give the advertising agency a roasting. Actually, this was a brilliant opportunity to rethink whether or not you need that campaign to that audience.

Table 7.1

Auditing and categorization of decisions

Type of decision	Examples	Methods of analysis
Routine decisions: Many decisions are routine: the same circumstances recur	• Responding to competition • Responding to advice from sales managers, finance, product developers, etc.	• When they arise, you apply a rule-of-thumb
Recurrent major decisions: A number of major decisions recur on a periodic basis. They are major because they involve the commitment of funds and budgets for 12 months or more into the future. They involve fine-tuning and allocation of resources. Often they are irreversible once made	• Financial planning • Allocation of budgets across brands and products • Allocation of budgets across marketing mix	• Construct a model • Analyze historical data • Seek agency advice • Hire consultants
Major step-change decisions: Some decisions do not recur. They are major because they involve a major commitment of funds. They tend to be either/or decisions	• New brand launch • Brand extension • Product launch • Creative change	• Construct a model • Analyze historical data • Seek agency advice • Hire consultants • Pre-testing
Emergency decisions: Some situations are, however, without precedent – you make the decision on the spot as events unfold. This is emergency decision making and can take up most of a manager's time	• Re-forecasting • Disaster recovery	• Construct a model • Tracking and feedback

Don't be satisfied with just a list of decisions; categorize and group them and ask yourself the following questions:

- **Avoidable failures**: Did we fail more than we should have in some areas?
- **Data quality problems**: Were the problems related to poor data?
- **Data gaps**: Were the problems related to gaps in the data?
- **Analysis errors**: Were the analysis methods weak?
- **Bias**: Did we allow too much bias to creep into particular decision areas?
- **Rules-of-thumb**: Are we worried that our rules aren't working properly?
- **Reinventing the wheel**: Could we have grouped our analyses better, by pooling resources and sharing methods?
- **Talent**: Did we put the right people on the right decisions?

Allocating analysis time and resources better

The widely respected business guru Chris Argyris points out that even the most intelligent individuals can become ineffective decision makers (Argyris 1998). Why? Because we are so busy working that we fail to learn to improve our decision making. We get sucked into patterns of behaviour that have produced success for us in the past, not realizing that they may not be appropriate for us in the fast-approaching future. What's worse, we spend too much time on the wrong things.

I have seen salesmen agonizing over many weeks to decide which car to choose, collecting automobile magazines, soliciting the views of colleagues and friends, even asking customers. The same people spend the best part of 60 seconds updating the monthly sales forecast, manipulating orders promised by customers but not received, and creating a document that has almost no value in predicting the future and may have catastrophic effects on operations and inventory.

An important question to ask yourself is: 'What time and resources am I putting into my key decisions?' We ask managers to do this at the end of our seminars. Then we ask them how they want to divide their time in the future, and how, being realistic, they expect to. This gives a basic indication of how each individual wants to change the decision process. Table 7.2 shows some typical time allocations for the managers we talked to.

Table 7.2
Time allocated to key stages in decision making

Key decision stages	Actual time allocation	Intended time allocation
1. Specifying the decision	5%	15%
2. Gathering intelligence	65%	35%
3. Squeezing out insights	15%	20%
4. Evaluating options	10%	15%
5. Monitoring and learning	5%	15%
	100%	**100%**

We would like to invite you to consider the same questions. Ask yourself what barriers hinder proper allocation of time and how can they be removed? Start by evaluating your use of time against the decision stages in the table. For example, do you spend too much time collecting data? Most marketers are drowning in data, yet frustrated by the lack of insights. Do you squeeze out the insights from the data you already possess? Most marketers groan audibly at the thud of their monthly data 'fix' arriving. People usually react to such data overload in one of two ways:

- Many senior marketers shut down the flow of information because it's overwhelming. People with this reaction are afflicted by too little information. They rely on old knowledge and rules-of-thumb, and make bad decisions because they close off the flow.

- Some marketers become data junkies. They keep scanning the numbers and never shut off the flow of raw data. Their hope is that something new will emerge to help them solve the problem at hand. They may even purchase 'data mining' software to help them sift the grains of data. They get paralysed by too much information and rarely squeeze useful insights out of the data mountain.

Numbers don't speak for themselves; you have to interrogate them to yield insights.

Do you spend enough time evaluating options? Many marketing decisions conform to the TINA (There Is No Alternative) school of thinking. Often so much time is consumed gathering intelligence that none remains for fine-tuning, even though decisions are often improved by examining the alternatives and fine-tuning.

Overcoming the hurdles

Why are some decisions so difficult? There are several reasons why we put off making decisions, and several steps we could take to remedy this. The five stages listed in Table 7.2 provide the backbone of good decision making. Unlike the parts of a golf swing, or other physical effort, the decision steps need not be rigidly sequential. Indeed, insights discovered at the information squeezing stage should sometimes inspire you to go back and re-specify. Also, complex problems such as the relaunch of a brand may demand a series of smaller decisions, each of which will involve several specifications, several intelligence gathering efforts and so forth.

1. Specifying

As in the advertising example described earlier, we are not sure what we are trying to achieve. Specifying means defining what must be decided, and determining, in a preliminary way, what are the options and the criteria that would cause you to prefer one option over another. Good decision makers think about the viewpoint from which they and others will look at the issue and decide which aspects they consider important and which they do not.

2. Gathering intelligence

You do not have all the information you really need to make the right choice. (Nor, like waiting for the trains to run on time, will you ever have the perfect set of data to work with.) Gathering intelligence involves both seeking the knowable facts and the reasonable estimates of 'unknowables' that you will need to make the right decision. Good decision makers manage intelligence gathering with deliberate effort to avoid such failings as overconfidence in what they currently believe and the tendency to seek evidence that confirms their biases.

3. Squeezing out insights

You are drowning in data and suffering analysis paralysis. Squeezing out insights means analyzing the fact base to discover patterns that will impact your decision. Most people are bad at squeezing the last drops of insight out of existing data. Good decision makers use tools and tricks to sift and tease out insights from intransigent data, working among mountains of data without falling under an avalanche.

4. Evaluating options

Most people have particular trouble with assessing the financial implications of a decision. Sound specification, good intelligence and clear insights don't guarantee a wise decision. People cannot make sound decisions using seat-of-pants judgement alone, even with excellent data in front of them. A systematic approach to evaluating the options forces you to examine many angles and often leads to better decisions than would weeks of unorganized worrying. Is it possible to make a realistic estimate of the financial value of each marketing strategy? Experienced people would say 'yes' to this, but acknowledge that it's a trick issue and that you might need to use certain tools and devices to evaluate options.

5. Monitoring and learning

Few decisions get re-visited after the event. Most of us decide, declare victory and move on to the next decision. Everyone needs a system of learning from past decisions. This usually means keeping track of what you expected would happen, systematically guarding against self-serving explanations, then making sure you review the lessons your feedback has provided the next time a similar decision comes along.

At a minimum, marketing directors should sit down for a few hours twice a year with their associates to look back. Have they been collecting the right data to keep track of the lessons of experience? Are there empirical generalizations from the past to illuminate the future? What have they learned in the past six months? How should it change their future work?

Becoming a better judge

The nature of judgemental forecasting makes it particularly prone to certain types of error. The empirical evidence (e.g. Arkes 2001) suggests that overconfidence is endemic in many forecasting situations that include judgement. Makridakis and Gaba (1998) list 12 types of judgemental bias, and, most helpfully, ways of avoiding their negative impact (see Table 7.3).

Table 7.3
List of judgemental biases

Type of bias	Description of bias	Ways of avoiding or reducing the negative impact of bias
Inconsistency	• Inability to apply the same decision criteria in similar situations	• Formalize decision-making process • Create decision-making rules
Conservatism	• Failure to change opinion in light of new information	• Monitor changes and build procedures to address them
Recency	• Most recent events cause earlier events to be downgraded or ignored	• Realize that cycles exist • Consider the fundamental factors affecting each event
Availability	• Reliance on easily recalled events, excluding other pertinent information	• Present compete information, pointing out all sides of situation being considered
Anchoring	• Predictions unduly weighted by initial information	• Start with objective information • Discuss types of changes • When changes are proposed, ask for reasons
Illusory correlations	• Mistaken belief that patterns are evident/ two variables are related	• Verify statistical significance of patterns • Model relationships in terms of change
Selective perception	• People influenced by their own circumstances	• Ask people with varied backgrounds to suggest solutions independently
Regression effects	• Apparent trends might be spurious, i.e. due to random variations	• Look at a range of scenarios • Make contingency plans or have 'fall-back' positions • Take a longer-term view
Attribution of success and failure	• Success is attributed to one's skill and failure to bad luck or another's error. This inhibits learning as it omits recognition of one's mistakes	• Do not punish mistakes; encourage people to accept them and make them public so others may learn to avoid similar pitfalls

Table 7.3
(continued)

Type of bias	Description of bias	Ways of avoiding or reducing the negative impact of bias
Optimism, wishful thinking	• People's preferences for future outcomes affect their forecasts	• Have the forecasts made by a disinterested third party • Have more than one person independently make forecasts
Searching for supportive evidence	• People search for and remember information in accord with their beliefs and opinions	• Collect disconfirming evidence • Have someone play devil's advocate
Underestimating uncertainty	• Excessive optimism, illusory correlation and need to reduce anxiety lead to under-estimating future uncertainty	• Estimate uncertainty objectively • Consider many possible future events by asking different people to come up with unpredictable situations/events

Becoming a better statistician

Statistical modelling itself is also subject to a range of decision traps. We list below some of the main problem areas.

Omitted variable(s)

If a factor that should be in the model is omitted, the effect will be to introduce bias into the model. The importance of the factors that are in the model will be distorted as they will try to compensate for the effect of the omitted variable(s), giving misleading results. Although there are a variety of statistical tests that can detect such bias, the common-sense approach of asking the question 'Shouldn't this factor be included?' is the most powerful analytical tool available.

Spurious correlation

Just because it appears that there is a statistical relationship does not mean that there is a causal link. Again, common sense should be applied and the question asked 'Should this factor really be included?'

Outliers

Outliers are points that do not agree well with a statistical relationship. There is always a temptation to disregard them, and a statistical relationship can always be made to look better by so doing. However, it is often worth taking the time to investigate the reasons why a point does not fit well before adopting the extreme step of excluding it. The reason may, of course, be that it is a data error. If so, then you need to ask: Is it a one-off error, or does it affect other data as well? But equally, the outlier may also be real, and represent a factor that we have not taken into account in the model – all the more reason for understanding it and taking it into account.

Correlated variables

If two of the explanatory variables that we think should be important always change together, then statistically we will not be able to establish a relationship containing both of them. Consider, for example, the problem of trying to predict sales volumes for a brand from television and press advertising activity. If television and press advertising always occur at the same time and in the same proportion, we will not be able to identify their separate effects in a statistical model. The most that we may appear to find is that, for example, television is significant but that press is not. But this is misleading because, in such a model, television will be representing both its own impact and that of press.

Model accuracy

Clearly the extent to which the model fits the historic data is an important consideration. This is often measured by the R-squared or the Rbar-squared, which are numbers calculated using standard formulae as a test of model accuracy. But, beyond the overall fit of the model, we will also wish to know that all of the variables used in the model are significant – indeed, in some cases, the significance of the individual variables will be as interesting as the overall model itself.

Statistical validity

The methods used in econometrics are valid only if certain conditions hold. For example, there should be no trend or pattern in the errors of the model – they should appear completely random. It is always good practice to look at the errors (often called 'residuals' by statisticians) to see if any patterns are apparent to the eye. Another condition is that the coefficients of the explanatory variables should be stable over time. If these conditions are not met, then the model cannot be considered statistically valid.

Seven habits of highly effective quantitative thinkers

Our goal in this book is to introduce you to the quantitative concepts, skills and habits you need for successful marketing spending evaluation. To some of you this sounds easy; to others it sounds dreadful.

If this sounds like remedial maths, we've got good news. It turns out that formal maths is not the best way to teach quantitative reasoning, and superior decision analysis is not restricted to those who aced at high school or university maths.

But if maths isn't the key to good quantitative decision evaluation, what in the world is inside this book? Here is a sneak preview. What distinguishes good quantitative decision analysts is not their skill with pure mathematics, but rather their approach to quantitative reasoning. Effective quantitative thinkers possess certain attitudes, skills and habits that they bring to bear whenever they need to make decisions based on numbers. Thanks to Steven Covey's best-selling book, *The Seven Habits of Highly Effective People* (1990) and its offshoots, seven has become the canonical number for lists of good habits.

Habit 1: Only trust numbers

Accepting numbers as evidence is more difficult than it sounds. We tend to trust what we experience, and seeing a number on a piece of paper is not much of an experience. Numbers after all are just symbolic representations of quantities that themselves are more abstract than real.

Do you really understand what it means when your service has a customer satisfaction index of 5.1, other than higher is better? But if you want to be a good quantitative thinker, you must learn to make decisions on the basis of numerical information, even when that information conflicts with your instincts and perceptions.

How? Try to raise your level of trust in careful quantitative analysis, and reduce your confidence in hunches, rules-of-thumb and casual observation. Sublimate your impulse to leap to conclusions, transforming it into an urge to seek hard data. Don't accept verbal strategies, such as 'invest heavily' or 'invest selectively'. In short, only trust numbers.

Habit 2: Never trust numbers

Before we try to reconcile this next, apparently inconsistent piece of advice, first we will explain why numbers are not worthy of your trust. It's because numbers can be wrong, are frequently misleading, and all too often have an agenda.

People lie and cheat. Some quantitative deceit is obvious, as when the agency submits expenses for a lunch that got cancelled. Other deceit is harder to spot, as when the researcher submits interviews that never occurred, or gaps in respondent answers are completed by the researcher.

Numbers are also wrong for innocent reasons. People are slow to update databases. People misremember figures, and punch the wrong keys. Scanners and electronic processors develop faults. Computer models have bugs.

Habit 3: Ask 'Who says so?'

We should be careful in assessing the validity of a measure on the basis of the presumed credibility of its source. Marketing expert Drayton Bird recently recounted how McKinsey & Co. had asked him for a forecast of something (Bird 1998):

> Flattered I wrote a thoughtful document for them, which we discussed in their grand New York offices. They didn't go so far as to pay me, but I thought I might use the story – 'Guess who the consultants consult when they want to know about marketing?'

So, even when a reputable name like McKinsey is cited, make sure that the authority stands behind the information, not merely somewhere alongside it.

'The computer says so' is one of the most worrying answers. Putting it on a computer is one of the commonest tricks to avoid investigation or detection of poor data. If your best measures come from some faceless electronic brain, it may pay you to have a computer expert check out its electronic sanity.

Habit 4: Ask 'How does he know?'

Experts often purport to use scientific measurements. But a truly scientific one is based on equations derived from proved laws of nature that specify how a phenomenon at point A now will move to point B in the future. Among the things that affect business there are only a few events that can be predicted using scientific forecasts.

Rather than relying on science, most managers look for past trends or statistical correlations which they use to extend into the future, and predict cause-and-effect. For example, the Profit Impact of Market Strategy (PIMS) database contains the largest collection of business performance data that has ever been assembled (Buzzell and Gale 1987). Statistical analysis of PIMS has been widely used to identify factors that correlate with good or bad performance.

Although trends and correlations are to be taken seriously, we should be careful to consider that correlations often do not amount to cause-and-effect, and trends will some day cease. For example PIMS analysis in the 1980s showed correlation between market share and performance. However, it is dangerous to confuse manifestations of good performance with the causes. Firms with competitive advantages are likely to have both high market share and high profitability, but it does not follow that a firm without a competitive advantage will increase its profitability by increasing its market share. The PIMS analysts pointed this out, using the analogy of height and weight, pointing out that height and weight are closely correlated but you will not grow taller by eating more. This cautious advice, however, never stood in the way of many ambitious top executives, eager to justify their corporate acquisition sprees by citing PIMS as evidence.

Habit 5: Ask 'What's the track record?'

Perhaps foremost in establishing the credibility of measures is their track record. But track records are not easy to judge, especially when your factor is one of many that are changing, all of which may be important. Watch out for evidence of bias, such as a biased sample, one that has been selected improperly or has selected itself. Most textbooks cite only success stories to prove their theories. Failures are usually more common, and may be more important, but are rarely studied.

Testing is a common technique among marketers. New products, advertisements and promotions are frequently and routinely tested. Yet few companies maintain proper records of past successes and failures. Since marketing managers typically change jobs every eighteen months to two years, the organization has no means of learning from past failures. We have long advocated that organizations keep long-term records of past failures and successes (see Shaw and Stone 1990), but have rarely found this in practice.

Habit 6: Ask 'Does it make sense?'

This will often cut a result down to size when the whole rigmarole is based on an unproved assumption. Many statements that are made on the subject of customers are blindly accepted by management, yet may seem absurd to the casual observer.

'The well-served customer is an appreciating asset. Every small act on her or his behalf ups the odds for repeat business, add-on business, and priceless word-of-mouth referral' wrote Tom Peters (1987). Another guru, Fred Reichheld, wrote (1996): 'We discovered some years ago that raising customer retention rates by five percentage points could increase the value of an average customer by 25 to 100%.' 'So why isn't every company doing that?' asks the casual observer, applying common sense.

Habit 7: Build models

Superior quantitative thinkers are habitual model builders, constantly creating numerical models that simulate the real-world situations they are trying to understand.

Especially in marketing, the elements of the real world are complex. Models are intended to capture the most important elements of this complexity. Managers get a better understanding by focusing only on the most crucial elements. We can represent the real world not only by choosing the most important elements, but also through the form in which the elements are connected.

Computer models usually provide more reliable answers than mental models and mental arithmetic. This is even the case when the parameters in the model are based on management judgement. This sounds magical, but it works because of one simple idea. When a person makes a prediction or quantitative judgement, you get wisdom mixed in with random noise. Intuitive judgements suffer from serious random inconsistencies due to fatigue, boredom and all the factors that make us human.

The ideal decision process would eliminate the random noise but retain the real insights that underlie the prediction. This is precisely what modelling does. It eliminates the noise and retains the core wisdom of the human expert. Moreover it produces a standard procedure for judgement. And dozens of studies show that this odd system does produce excellent judgements.

This chapter concludes the first part of the book. The seven chapters in this section have mapped out the main principles of our recommended approach to improving marketing payback. In the next part we examine all these techniques and concepts in more detail, and apply them to many familiar marketing activities and situations.

Key points

- Auditing decisions periodically and learning from them is an important discipline.
- Time is the decision maker's biggest enemy – manage it effectively.
- Biases and prejudices can be forestalled if you are watchful.
- People who lie with statistics can be caught out.
- Data can be systematically interrogated to yield insights.
- Persistent analysis problems can be remedied.
- You can be trained to improve your judgement if you are self-aware and honest.
- Mitigating action can be taken against most risks.
- Quantitative thinkers can cultivate their good habits.

part II:

SOLUTIONS TO COMMON PROBLEMS

8

EXPENDITURE ALLOCATION

This chapter looks at the critical practical decisions that need to be taken on how much marketing expenditure to allocate, and on what. We review common practices in expenditure allocation, and we set out some guiding principles that can help obtain maximum payback from expenditure decisions, including specific techniques that are available for rightsizing expenditure allocation in order to maximize payback.

The principles of expenditure allocation

In order to ensure that the allocation process fully supports the governing objective, maximizing payback, we have found that these five principles of resource allocation work well at all companies.

1. Rightsizing expenditure allocation;

2. No expenditure rationing;

3. Waste elimination;

4. Funding projects not people;

5. Consolidating and fragmenting.

The question most managers constantly ask is about balancing budgets: 'How much expenditure should we add to sales promotion and how much should we take away from advertising?' The question we think they should be asking is: 'What is the right amount of expenditure to have on advertising and what is the right amount on sales promotion to maximize payback?' This second does not refer to how much was previously spent on this or that – it refers to the future. It refers to rightsizing the budgets.

Rightsizing involves asking important questions that seldom get raised. Am I over-sized with too many customers or too much market share? Am I over-advertised with too much exposure in all the media? Am I over-distributed in every grubby outlet? Am I over-mailing my customers? Am I over-promoted with too many price cuts or promotional gifts? Am I over-selling with too many representatives covering every location? Am I over-priced?

It is surprising how many companies operate as though marketing expenditure must be rationed. The general practices we observe seem to be based on the belief that money is a scarce resource, the proper uses of which are only understood by a few wise men and women, all of whom work in the finance department. We argue that the opposite is true – money is plentiful but expensive in the sense that there must be payback for all money used. This principle is absolutely essential to an understanding of marketing payback.

Waste is constantly arising, due to the inflexibility of our budgeting processes. Parts of the business that previously were profitable become loss-making, and yet we are slow to adjust to these changes. Consequently we continue pouring money into chronically unprofitable areas of the business. Marketing needs to wake up to this problem, and liberate expenditure from products and services that no longer justify the outlay.

The other source of funding is essentially external. The capital markets stand ready to fund growth-projects via new debt or equity fusions. If management stands by the business cases for new products, brand extensions and line extensions, then it should be prepared to give them adequate funding in totality, including their marketing.

Yet the reality is the common practice of raiding the brand maintenance budget to pay for product launches. (Brand maintenance is the advertising and promotion that is necessary just to keep the brand at its current sales level.) This is illustrated in Figure 8.1, where the overall marketing budget is 'balanced' at a fixed level. Whenever there is a burst of launch activity, the cost of marketing for the launch is taken out of an overall marketing budget 'pot'.

Figure 8.1
Raiding the brand maintenance budget to pay for product launches

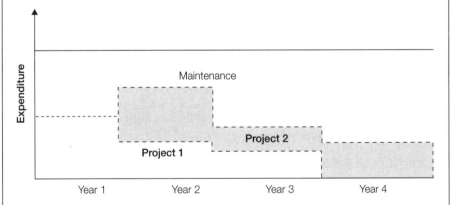

Yet the principle of rightsizing says that either the maintenance budget is right or it is wrong. If it is right, then the maintenance budget should not be 'raided' to pay for a launch. Also, if the launch is the right decision, then the launch activity should be funded as a project and the cost of marketing for the launch should be included in the business case for the project. This approach is illustrated in Figure 8.2.

Figure 8.2
Expenditure levels when projects are funded

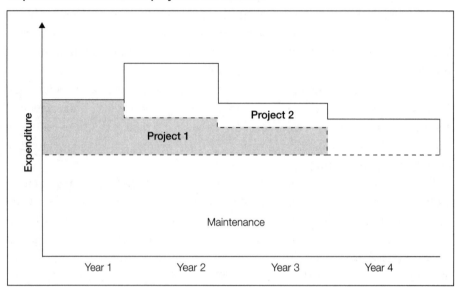

The final allocation principle that marketing needs to decide is whether the budget should be split into many small tactical activities, or consolidated into a few large strategic ones (see Figure 8.3). Yet most managers seem to decide this by default, responding to the approaches of more junior managers, each of whom wants their 'own' budget. Fragmentation of spending can end up frittering away millions on minor tactical activities, none of which accomplishes much, but which gives the individual managers a sense of 'having my own budget'.

Before continuing, it is worth asking ten hard questions about how budget allocation is managed in your company:

1. Do you exercise the power of the purse?
2. Do you understand the five principles of expenditure allocation?
3. Is finance committed to the principle of 'rightsizing' the marketing budget?
4. Are you actively eliminating marketing waste?
5. Is your growth budget managed separately from brand maintenance?
6. Is your budget fragmented across too many small projects?
7. Are you using models to optimize expenditure allocation?

Figure 8.3
Deciding how much to fragment the total budget

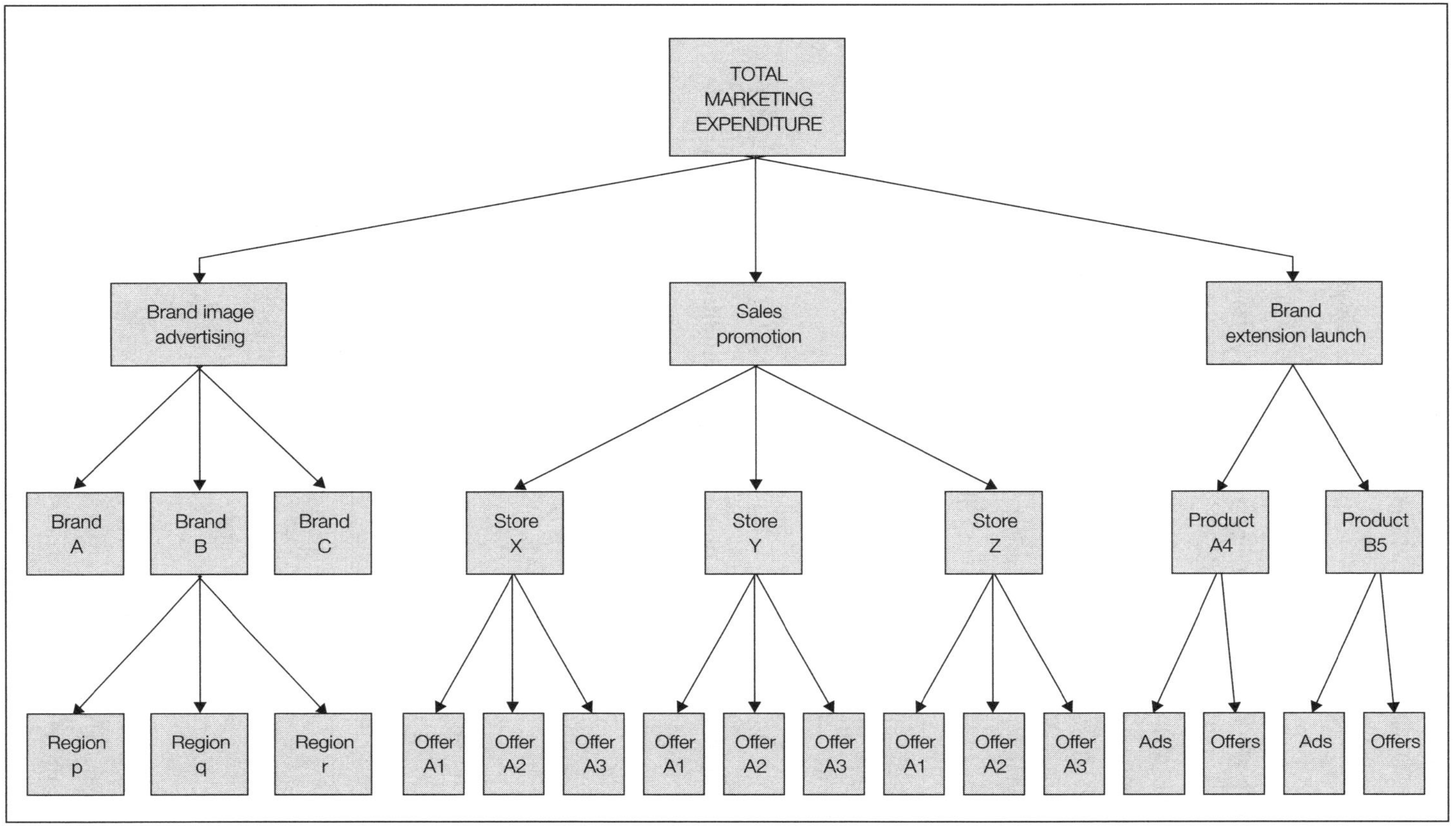

8. Do you build judgemental models?

9. Have you used econometrics?

10. Have you identified the optimum allocation?

What exactly do we mean by 'allocation'?

The term 'allocation' itself can be confusing, because to cost accountants its meaning is different from its meaning to marketing managers. Before examining the types of decisions, this terminological point requires clarification.

Allocation of expenditure is a planning decision, aiming to maximize the payback from the marketing budget. In assessing the best decision, the manager has to consider cause-and-effect, and to weigh up many alternative expenditure allocations, and then choose the allocation that is predicted will yield the most payback. This is illustrated schematically in Figure 8.4. For each market and brand, a sliding scale of expenditure levels is possible, on advertising, sales promotion, etc.

Figure 8.4
Schematic illustration of marketing expenditure allocation

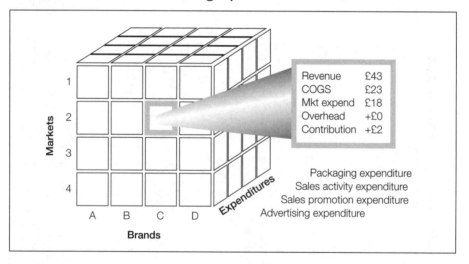

Contrast this with the cost accountant's common usage of the term – distributing overhead costs among business units on a 'fair' basis. This is not a planning decision, in the sense that it does not direct or guide business activities. Rather, it is a methodological decision about the humdrum details of the business unit profitability calculation. This is a different sense of allocation, and it is essential that you make it clear to your colleagues in finance what you are talking about.

Determining the right quantity of marketing budget to allocate to particular brands, products, channels, media and sales territories lies at the core of marketing budgeting.

By the 'right' quantity, we mean the budget expenditure levels, and associated activity plans that will maximize the payback – no more and no less (see Box 8.1 for terminology). How much money should be spent on brand A versus brand B? Sales promotion versus advertising? Television versus press?

In our view, the proper exercise of the power of the purse, by which we mean the power to fund or not fund marketing activities, is so critical that it should never be delegated. It is the marketing director's primary responsibility to ensure that all the company's marketing expenditure is put to the best possible use. The responsibility is difficult or impossible to fulfil if the expenditure decisions, or the process for making those decisions, are determined by other executives.

Box 8.1 Expenditure terminology

Allocation (finance and cost accounting): A methodological decision about the distribution of overhead costs between the various departments of a business, taken when defining the profit function.

Allocation (marketing mix): A planning decision to systematically distribute the limited marketing budget over markets, brands and types of expenditure.

Business unit allocation: Distribution of expenditure across business units; heads of each business unit can then decide how to allocate expenditures.

Corporate marketing budget: A total figure is set for the marketing budget, and the head of marketing decides how to allocate it.

Functional allocation: Distribution of expenditure across functions, such as sales (selling), advertising, direct marketing, etc. Heads of functions can then decide how to allocate expenditure more finely.

Marketing budget: The total amount of money earmarked in the budget for marketing expenditures.

Marketing mix: The mixture of marketing activities and expenditures – traditionally the 'four Ps' of product, price, promotion and place (distribution).

> **Strategic brand/marketing allocation:** A total figure is set for each brand/market, and then brand/market directors decide how to allocate it.
>
> **Tactical marketing-mix allocation:** Each brand/market manager decides what is the most appropriate expenditure allocation across advertising, promotion, etc.

Before looking in detail at the principles of marketing budget allocation, it is worth distinguishing between two interrelated aspects of decisions on the marketing budget:

1. The decision on the overall marketing budget;

2. The allocation of that budget among markets, brands and expenditures.

In our experience, only a minority of marketing directors take the lead in overall budget decisions. The total marketing budget is often decided outside the marketing department, by a budget committee consisting of the Board and its financial advisors. Although the marketing director will put a budget recommendation to this committee, his influence is diluted by the other interests represented. Other factors such as cash flow, investor sentiment and changes in the economic or market environment are more likely to influence the Board's decision on the overall level of marketing spend. However, this is not an argument for failing to undertake marketing budget optimization calculations. If the results are compelling enough, even the most short-sighted Board must take them into account, or they are failing in their duty to shareholders to maximize return on investments.

It is equally true that only a minority of senior marketing managers actually make decisions about allocating the available marketing budget. All too often, these decisions are made elsewhere in the organization, typically by finance or business unit managers (Shaw and Fisk 2002). Why should this be so? Allocation appears complicated, due to the cumbersome spreadsheets that have to be manipulated. Often marketing directors and their staff are not spreadsheet literate. Sometimes they appear to be relieved that they are able to sidestep responsibility for these allocation decisions, and readily accept the rather arbitrary budgeting and allocation done on their behalf by budget managers, spreadsheet technicians and marketing agencies. This is an all too common dereliction of duty.

Yet spreadsheets are an extremely effective tool for dealing with allocation calculations, and we strongly advocate their use in making allocation decisions. Later in this chapter we shall look at some effective approaches to marketing budget allocation that require at most a simple spreadsheet for implementation.

Traditional 'top-down' approaches

Decision processes

The expenditure allocation process at many companies can defy description. When we try to figure out how allocation decisions are made at companies we work with, it is not uncommon to find that no executive, including the CEO, is able to describe to his or her satisfaction the set of principles or processes that the company actually uses (as opposed to what it says it uses) to determine how much money to allocate where.

As with many business management decisions, a first look at the processes at work in marketing budget allocation decisions tends to categorize them into 'top-down' or 'bottom-up' approaches. Top-down approaches tend to be popular, especially when linked with a budget-setting mechanism that bases this year's budget on what was budgeted (or spent) last year, with minor 'fine-tuning' adjustments.

In part, this is because allocation can be an emotive issue. People often see the size of their budget as a measure of their importance. For this reason, allocation is often not done in the manner of the logical calculation that we present in this chapter.

Strategic allocation across brands and markets is more often a matter of tradition rather than logic. How much to spend on Dove versus Sunsilk? How much to spend on Europe versus North America? Only 20% of senior marketers in a recent survey (Shaw and Fisk 2002) considered themselves good at evaluating and reallocating resources effectively.

Business unit allocation

Most firms today have predominantly business unit allocation procedures, similar to those shown in Figure 8.5. Each business unit head has an overall expenditure budget, covering all operating expenses.

Marketing is often low down in the priority for business unit heads. Furthermore, if a brand is shared across business units, then each unit will be asked to make a contribution to the brand budget, as an allocation out of their business unit marketing expenses. In effect the expenditure 'trickles down' from top to bottom, and the brand gets what's left over at the end of this process. The volatility of brand budgets in many organizations is a direct consequence of this trickle-down model.

Figure 8.5
Business unit 'trickle-down' model

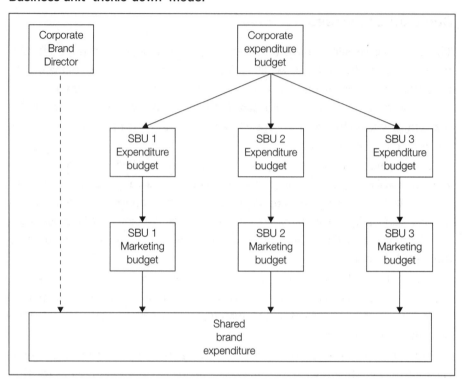

Functional unit allocation

Functional allocation of individual brand's marketing mix elements is also subject to pressures and biases from agencies who are trying to sell things to the marketing department and from sales managers who have sales bonuses at stake. How much to spend on advertising versus sales promotion? How much to spend on consumer promotion versus trade promotion? Figure 8.6 illustrates this functional allocation approach.

The functional allocation method has similar elements of arbitrariness to the business unit method. It produces particular problems in fixing brand budgets, since they are controlled by multiple departments.

Worse still, the expenditure objectives are likely to be inconsistent. Sales departments often target their performance on volume or revenue. When volumes are low, they are likely to push for increased sales promotion expenditures. Marketing is often pressurized to concede advertising cuts to pay for the increased sales promotion. This approach is sometimes called 'raiding' the brand budget.

Figure 8.6
Functional expenditure allocation

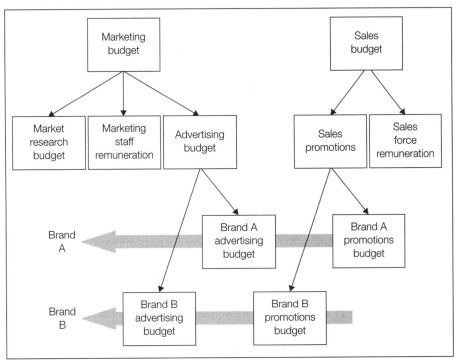

The 'above-the-line' and 'below-the-line' expenditure split

One of the most hotly debated aspects of expenditure allocation concerns the split of money between above-the-line expenditure (mainly on 'brand advertising') and below-the-line (usually sales promotion and direct marketing). And it's unlikely that most financial managers, or sales managers for that matter, will have the knowledge or techniques to assess the above-the-line brand budgets effectively.

Brands need money to sustain them and, what's more, the money needed goes beyond what's required just for selling products. Although many brands, such as Coca-Cola, Microsoft and Disney, have brand names and marks that were created decades ago, the brand authorities tell us that money must keep on being poured into something called 'branding' to feed people's minds and keep the 'brand equity' in good shape.

'In essence, selling seeks an immediate order for the product: it aims to increase the revenue line of the profit and loss account right away,' comments Ambler (2003). The immediacy of the results of selling contrast strongly with the time delay associated with branding. 'Brand equity is what the brand has earned but has not yet paid out in profits,' Ambler remarked in an earlier publication (1996).

Yet separating brand-building expenditure and selling expenditure is not as easy as it first appears. Some activities such as direct marketing and sales promotions are mainly aimed at selling things, and are not considered to be brand building. Conversely, some communications are distinctly brand building and are not obviously selling something. Some products have an extra something added to them to support the brand image. Service has also become an area where extra expenditure can help improve brand image.

Yet most activities, even those that sell things, do positively influence brand image and equity. The reason for this is that brand attitudes are positive among brand owners and users, compared to non-owners and non-users, hence anything that increases numbers of owners and users will inevitably raise brand equity.

Our conclusion is that there is a spectrum of brand building forces from strong to weak. Therefore it would be a mistake to pre-judge what activities are brand building or not. The only way to establish the strength of brand-building effects is to carry out research.

Expenditure strategy research

Strategy research is concerned with long-term shifts in expenditure and associated shifts in consumption and sales.

The starting point should be to audit the brand's history, together with comparative data on the market and competing brands. Annual data are gathered covering at least five years, preferably ten. Where the brand covers several segments (e.g. premium and everyday prices) the data should be split to reflect this (see Table 8.1).

Table 8.1

Data to be included in a brand history review

Brand	Competitive	Market/segment
Total A&P spend	Competitor A&P spend	Total market A&P spend
Promotion/total A&P	Relative promotion index	Promotion index trend
Total media spend	Share of voice	Media price index (CPM index)
Brand loyal ad exposure	Comp. exposure to brand loyal	Market ad exposure levels
% of volume on promotion	Competitor volume on promotion	Market promotional index
Volume by price	Volume share of market	Market volume
Price (point of sale)	Relative POS price	Price POS index
POS/trade price ratio	Relative trade price	POS/trade price ratio
Cost of goods	Relative cost of goods	Market cost of goods
Profit as % of revenue	Relative profit	Market profitability
Awareness	Relative awareness	Involvement in category
Trial purchase rate	Switching in/out rate	Market churn rate
Repeat purchase rate	Relative loyalty	Purchase cycle rate
Average purchase quantity	Relative purchase quantity	Market average purchase quantity
Product launches, formulation changes, new packaging	New entrants, exits, substitutes	Weather conditions, economic indicators and trends

Key: A&P = Advertising & Promotion; POS = Point-Of-Sale

Trade distribution data are also important to include (see Table 8.2).

Table 8.2

Trade distribution data for a brand history review

Brand	Competitive	Market/segment
Availability	Relative availability	Market availability trends
Features and displays	Relative features and displays	Trends in features and displays
Visibility	Relative visibility	Trends in visibility

Without actually modelling the data, you will see averages, trends and correlations. These will help you understand the dynamics of the market and the part played by advertising and promotion. This review may help you to estimate the effects of different marketing budgets.

Starting from the brand: 'bottom-up' approaches

Two bottom-up brand-based analysis methods often yield useful insights:

- Share of revenue analyses;
- Share of voice analyses.

The 'share of revenue' approach

With this approach, marketing expenditure is set as a percentage of revenue. There are some powerful advantages to this approach:

- It is simple.
- It is easily understood.
- If revenue increases, then marketing expenditure increases, giving a double whammy to the feel-good factor in marketing department (note, however, that the converse is also true).

Perhaps not surprisingly, therefore, Batra *et al.* (1996) report that over 70% of companies use the percentage of sales revenue as their preferred criterion for setting advertising budgets.

The main weakness of this approach is that it lacks sensitivity to what is happening to the brand or the external environment. An extreme example is new product launches or product repositioning. In one example of a strategy for a new brand launch, the advertising expenditure in the first year was twice the gross profit, falling to 50% of gross profit in the second year and 30% of gross profit in the third and succeeding years!

Brand histories over five or ten years should be plotted as a time series. Examination of these series often reveals important trends.

Figure 8.7 shows the combined share growth of the six leading brands in a market. The trend analysis shows that in this situation, the 'power brands' have come to dominate the lesser brands. Yet further examination of these brands shows that they spent less proportionately on marketing than did the smaller brands (this point is also made in the discussion of Figure 8.8). This trend analysis provides further insights into the relationship between marketing expenditure allocation and brand size and growth.

Figure 8.7
Growth of the most powerful brands in a market (illustrative)

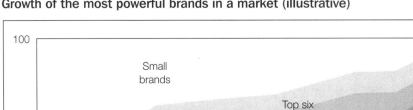

The 'share of voice' approach

This approach tries to overcome the inability of the 'share of revenue' approach to take into account competitor activity by targeting spend on the brand as a proportion of total marketing expenditure in the sector (i.e. the share of voice). If your competitors are shouting loudly, the argument goes, then you also have to shout loudly to make yourself heard. Of course, the question that this begs is whether you can afford to shout quite as loudly as your competitors or, indeed, whether you need to shout even more loudly still to achieve your objectives for the brand!

Hence a popular simplification – to benchmark 'share of voice' by the market share of the brand. The argument is that the higher the market share, the larger the audience you have to address, and the more you have to spend on marketing to maintain your position.

Well, up to a point. There are two main problems:

- The first is that the above analysis applies only in a steady state. A recent market entrant with a small market share may well decide to 'punch above its weight' in terms of marketing expenditure in order to build the brand and gain market share; conversely, the major market players may feel that their brand is sufficiently robust for them to spend proportionately less than their market share and still maintain their position.

■ The second is thresholds; there is a widespread belief that, below a certain level of media activity, you might as well not bother – either because you will not get the reinforcement necessary for the message to stick, or because you will be drowned out by the other players.

These factors were taken into account by Broadbent (1989), who proposed the relationship between market share and share of voice illustrated in Figure 8.8. The figure captures the effect that brands that occupy a larger market share tend to support their position with a larger share of voice, although not proportionately so. For example, a brand with a 5% share of market typically has a share of voice minus share of market of 4%, and therefore a share of voice of 9%. Similarly, a brand with a 20% share of market typically has a 20% share of voice, and a brand with a 30% share of market typically has a 24% share of voice.

Figure 8.8
Relationship between share of voice and market share

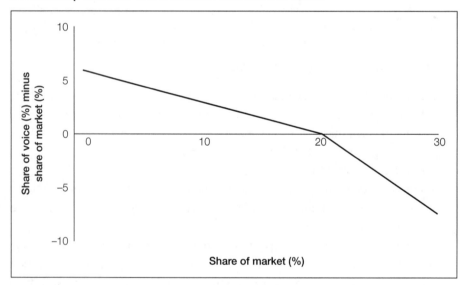

Plotting individual brand data on this type of chart enables groupings and correlations to be identified. For example, in Figure 8.9 the large brands (with high share of market) have a share of voice that is less than share of market by anything from 2% to 8%. The smaller brands have a relatively much higher share of voice, because of the media dilution effect mentioned earlier. The highest share of voice of all is for the launches; the cost of these would be prohibitively high were it not for the anticipated growth and profit in future years. Finally there are a few brands that invest relatively little in advertising, and it is likely that much of this will be sub-threshold and therefore wasted.

Figure 8.9
Scatter plot of share of voice and market share

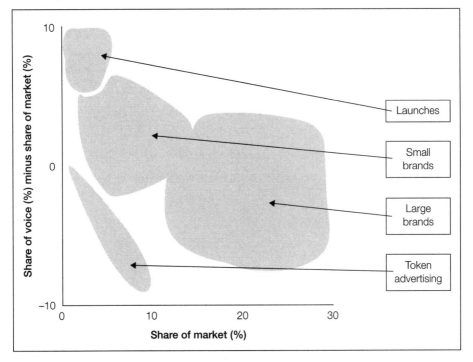

A general disadvantage of all the approaches outlined above is that they provide no quantitative calculation of the relationship between marketing expenditure and payback. Just because we have always spent 10% of revenue on marketing is not necessarily a good reason for continuing to do so. Equally, just because our major competitors are spending a certain amount on their brands, it does not necessarily mean that they have optimized their return either! We shall now therefore consider brand marketing approaches that are based on the rate of return.

Techniques for optimizing expenditure allocation

The word 'optimization' implies maximizing or minimizing something. The main techniques used to do this are:

- Trial and error with a real system;
- Simulation;
- Mathematical programming techniques.

Trial and error

The simplest approach is trial and error, where marketing managers try to learn from experimentation on a real system. They change one factor and observe what happens. For example, they may wish to experiment with different weights of advertising or with different service factors. Trial and error approaches are widely used in marketing, but there are a number of problems with them:

- There may be too many alternatives to explore.
- The cost of making errors, which is intrinsic to this approach, may be high.
- The time taken to do the experiment in the real world may be too long to make such an experiment practical.
- Trialling can alert competitors to new strategies.

Simulation

Because of the problems intrinsic to the trial and error approach, the second alternative, a mathematical approach to optimization, may be preferable. The mathematical approach to optimization modelling tends to break down into two main areas of activity: defining the function which is to be optimized (which is then expressed as some form of mathematical calculation), and identifying the optimum value once you know the main variables.

In attempting to solve optimization and prioritization problems, computer models of varying degrees of complexity are generally used for the following reasons:

- **Time compression**: Models enable the compression of time; years of operations can be simulated in minutes or seconds of computer time.
- **Ease of manipulation**: Changing the decision variables or the environment is much easier in a model than manipulating the real system. Experimentation does not interfere with actual activities.
- **Cost**: Modelling is much cheaper than the cost of experimentation conducted on a real system.

- **Risk reduction**: Mistakes made during the trial and error period of modelling do not have the impact they would in reality, and by modelling, managers can more safely estimate the risks resulting from specific actions.

- **Data analysis capacity**: Models enable the analysis of large, sometimes enormous, numbers of possible solutions. This is helpful when dealing with marketing problems, as managers often have a large number of alternatives from which to choose.

- **Learning reinforcement**: Models reinforce learning and training.

Given a computer model, you can change the values of the key input variables to find out what happens, and to try to work towards an optimum. This is also known as 'what-if' analysis.

The problem with 'what-if' analysis, however, is that it gives no guarantee at all that the selected option is actually the best possible. Moreover, as models get more and more complex, the weakness of this approach in determining the optimum becomes more pronounced.

Mathematical programming

The third approach, usually described as mathematical programming or simply optimization, is a more sophisticated approach to the problem. Essentially, computers use a variety of mathematical techniques to search efficiently for an optimum solution to complex problems.

Optimizing the right variable

In the context of optimizing brand marketing expenditure, a key question is 'What are we optimizing?' An initial response to this question is sometimes 'sales volume'. On closer examination, however, this is seldom a sensible approach. Unless the 'wear-out' effect discussed earlier is visible, you can always obtain a small increase in sales volume by spending more on marketing. What is in doubt, of course, is whether this additional expenditure is cost-effective.

A similar objection also arises to the concept of optimizing sales revenue – sales revenue can always be increased by spending more on marketing. But again, the question is – at what cost?

A better approach is to focus on net revenue – that is, sales revenue less marketing costs. The use of net revenue as the criterion for optimization allows for a real trade-off between expenditure and revenue and therefore a true optimization. This is because net revenue does not continue to increase as marketing spend increases. At some point the additional marketing spend becomes ineffective and the net revenue starts to decline.

A commonly-used variant of optimizing on net revenue is to assume a constant profit margin on sales revenue, and to optimize on operating profit net of marketing expenditure (for convenience, we shall refer to this as net operating profit). This is a seductive option because it gives the impression that profitability is being optimized.

Both of the two previous options (optimizing net revenue or net operating profit under the assumption that the profit margin on sales revenue is constant) by implication assume that the fixed costs of the business are zero. In view of the popularity of this assumption, it is perhaps ironic that this will always result in a lower 'optimal' marketing spend than if the true (i.e. non-zero) fixed costs had been taken into account.

> Ignoring fixed costs when estimating the level of marketing expenditure for maximum profitability will always lead to the level of marketing expenditure being under-estimated.

A rigorous mathematical proof of this is beyond the scope of this book. However, the logic of the proposition can be appreciated by considering that ignoring fixed costs ignores the beneficial effect of scale in diluting the fixed costs. A higher marketing expenditure brings greater volumes, a greater dilution of the fixed costs and improved overall profitability.

As a result, our preferred approach for optimization (and the only one that we will discuss here) is to focus on the profit contribution of the brand, taking into account both variable and fixed costs. This gives a meaningful optimization, avoids the bias introduced by assuming a constant profit margin on sales volume, and aligns well with the concept of return on marketing expenditure (ROME).

Optimizing expenditure for a single brand

The simplest case is where we want to optimize the marketing expenditure for a single brand. Given that we are optimizing profit contribution, we need to know how to relate sales volume to profit. Our preferred approach is to adopt a simple 'fixed cost/variable cost' model. In other words, the non-marketing costs for the brand (say, down to the level of EBITDA [Earnings Before Interest, Taxes, Depreciation and Amortization]) are divided into:

- Fixed costs that do not vary with sales volume;
- Variable costs that are directly proportional to sales volume.

There are many ways of specifying this model, but one of the simplest is in terms of the 'gross margin' (i.e. the profit contribution expressed as a fraction of revenue) and the proportion of costs that are fixed costs. If these two parameters are known, together with the two parameters that describe the response curve (discussed earlier), then the calculation of how the profit contribution varies with marketing spend is fairly straightforward (see Box 8.2). A typical result is shown in Figure 8.10.

Figure 8.10
Profit response curve for one brand

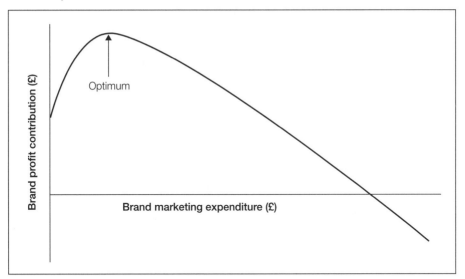

What the curve shows is that initially, as marketing expenditure increases, the brand profit contribution increases until the optimum is reached. After this point, the effect of additional marketing expenditure may well be to continue to increase the sales volume, but these increases are no longer cost-effective. The increased revenue does not match the additional variable costs plus the additional marketing costs. The brand profit contribution then begins to decline, and will make the brand less profitable than it would have been without marketing expenditure and, eventually, will make it unprofitable.

Box 8.2 Four key parameters

The curve shown in Figure 8.10 can be derived from just four parameters:

- Brand response curve parameters:

  - The maximum increase in brand sales volume that can be obtained from marketing expenditure;

  - The marketing spend required to achieve half of the maximum increase in brand sales volume.

- Brand financial parameters:

  - Gross margin;

  - Proportion of costs that are fixed.

The four parameters above are also all that is needed to calculate the optimum marketing spend for a brand. Consider, for example, the following case:

- The maximum increase in sales volume is 50%.

- The marketing spend required to achieve half this increase is 10% of revenue.

- The gross margin is 60%.

- Fixed costs are 30% of total costs.

The optimum marketing spend for the brand works out at 7.2% of sales revenue.

Sometimes there is no optimum spend for a brand. Instead the chart above heads south from the start, indicating that no level of marketing expenditure will ever give a positive return. An example of this behaviour is the following set of parameters:

- The maximum increase in sales volume is 50%.

- The marketing spend required to achieve half this increase is 30% of revenue.

- The gross margin is 30%.

- Fixed costs are 30% of total costs.

The optimal mix changes as expenditure changes, as shown in Figure 8.11.

Figure 8.11
Changes in the optimum marketing mix as expenditure changes

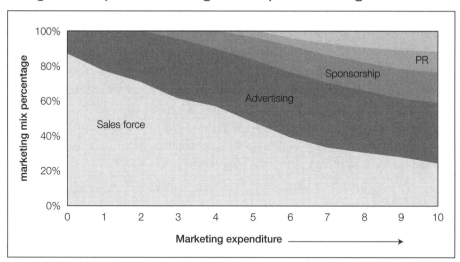

A small number of mix elements dominate when expenditure is low. Initially the mix is dominated by sales force expenditure and, as the expenditure grows, advertising becomes the next important mix element. Then as expenditure grows, and the incremental effects of sales and advertising fade, so sponsorship and PR enter the mix. The mix becomes richer as expenditure is increased.

Optimizing expenditure for a portfolio

What if you do not just have one brand, but a portfolio of brands? Given the response curves and the financial parameters for each brand, we could, of course, apply the approach described above to each brand. We could add up the optimum spends and derive an optimum spend for the brand portfolio as a whole.

However, we seldom encounter the utopian situation where marketing funds are unlimited. In the real world we are more often constrained by budgets. As a result, a more common question for a portfolio of brands is not what is the overall optimum spend, but what is the optimum allocation of the (fixed) marketing budget across the brands?

The good news is that this question can also be answered by an extension of the approach for a single brand. As might be expected, it requires estimates to be available of the four parameters listed above for each brand. The mathematical analysis is complex, but conceptually the process is fairly straightforward.

Figure 8.12 shows that a small number of brands and countries dominate the expenditure when the budget is limited, because these few brands offer the best return in terms of profitability. As more is spent on these brands, the returns fall as we move up the saturation curve. There comes a point where the return for the initial brands can be matched by a small spend on the next best brand. As the budget increases, however, expenditure on the initial batch of brands and countries approaches saturation and it becomes optimal to diversify the expenditure across more brands and countries.

Figure 8.12
Changes in the optimum brand/market allocation as expenditure changes

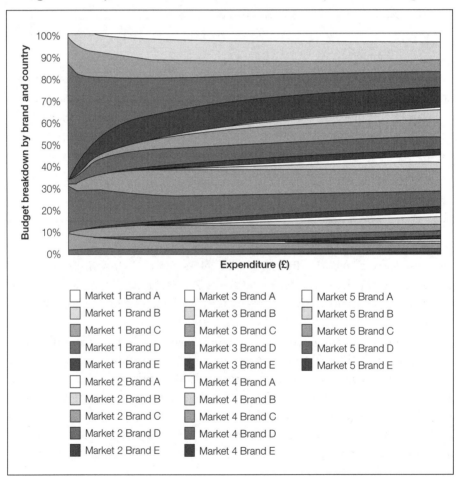

Another difference between a single brand and a portfolio is the possibility of 'halo effects' in which marketing expenditure on one brand has a positive effect on other brands. Clearly this complicates the mathematics behind the analysis, but the same basic approach can still be used effectively.

The same analysis applies to a mixture of several brands in several geographic regions. An example of the results that can be obtained from a brand portfolio expenditure analysis is given in Figure 8.13 (Merrick and Weaver 2001).

Figure 8.13

Profit from best allocation of marketing expenditure, at various levels of total spend

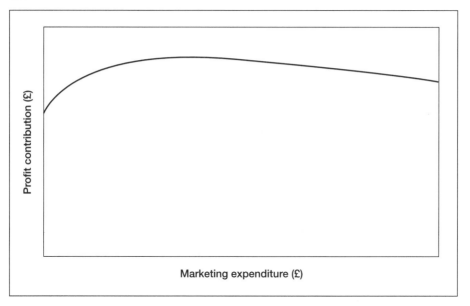

This shows how profit contribution varies with advertising spend for Ford's portfolio of major brands across the major markets in Europe. It is interesting to note that the curve is not symmetrical, but is steeper to the left of the optimum than to the right. A budget that is much lower than the optimum will therefore have a more damaging impact on the profit contribution than a budget that is higher than the optimum by the same margin. This conclusion arises from the specific characteristics of the brands in Ford's portfolio; the shape of the curve may be quite different for other brand portfolios.

This graph needs thoughtful consideration. Although at first sight it seems to imply that, within a certain range, the level of marketing expenditure is unimportant, there is a complication that must not be overlooked. The curve is actually a 'best allocation curve'. In other words, the allocation of the spend changes as we move along the x-axis (i.e. increase advertising expenditure) as indicated in Figure 8.14.

Figure 8.14
Best and worst allocations of marketing expenditure

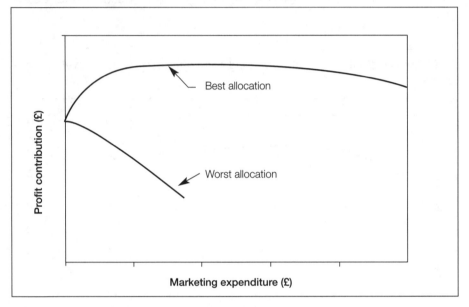

The worst allocation of marketing expenditure would yield declining profits from the outset, because the margin uplift was less than the marketing expenditure. So, far from concluding that payback is not sensitive to marketing expenditure levels, we conclude that it is vitally important that every 'cell' in the model receives the optimal allocation of marketing expenses.

The important lesson to take away is that the local allocation problem is of paramount importance. Getting peak payback from local expenditures will ensure peak global payback.

Local managers only need to estimate the four key parameters for this optimization to be assessed: peak volume increase, expenditure increase to gain half the peak, gross margin and fixed costs. As long as local analysts do their homework and pinpoint the local payback peaks, the Board will have all the data necessary to solve the marketing mix optimization problem.

Case study 8.1

Samsung's optimal marketing revolution

Firms selling many products in many regions face the complex issue of how to allocate marketing resources. Identifying the best solution is only half the battle, for there is also the problem of shifting the budgets around between the budget holders. Samsung overcame these challenges by using hard data, not intuition, to allocate its marketing dollars.

Management launched an intensive 18-month project to gather varied and detailed data on more than 400 possible product-category and country combinations. They did not simply impose a 'robot reallocation', instead they sought the marketers' seasoned judgement, which informed some important adjustments, and they re-examined performance expectations, roles and incentives so that a lack of resources would not unfairly limit anyone's personal success in the organization.

The project started when Eric Kim joined the company in 1999. He faced the challenge of turning the biggest electronics firm that consumers had never heard about into a global brand that would rival Sony. The firm had been the behind-the-scenes supplier of electronic goods to powerful branded multinationals and it needed to become a household name. He was given just five years to succeed.

The good news was that Kim was given $1 billion in marketing budget. The bad news was that this would evaporate into thin air if misallocated. Kim's team would have to reap maximum returns on every dollar spent. On a global scale that's an extraordinary challenge. Selling 14 product categories in 200 countries, there were 476 product-category combinations to evaluate.

Creating the fact base

At the outset, Kim's team faced the challenge of creating a fact base. Although relevant information resided in each country in several departments and office locations, pulling it together into a consistent fact base presented a Herculean task. It would be necessary to collate population levels, GDP per capita, growth forecasts, and product information such as penetration rates, market share and profitability, media costs and competitor dynamics.

The 14 category managers each had their own facts bases, but they were generally not consistent, nor entirely complete. With little or no standardization of data, Samsung couldn't make the comparisons needed to allocate budgets.

The solution was to build a marketing fact-base repository, called M-Net, where every country would store the following data:

- Overall population and population of target buyers;
- Per capita spending on product categories;
- Category penetration rates;
- Overall growth of categories;
- Share of each of the company's brands;

➤
■ Media costs;

■ Previous marketing expenditures;

■ Category profitability;

■ Competitor metrics.

Benchmark data were collected so that Samsung could compare itself with competitors. Expert judgement was used – from brand managers, category managers, etc. – to augment and expand the hard data.

Gathering the fact base was only the starting point, however. Insights still had to be squeezed out of the data. Given the scale of the database, this was another challenge. Clearly the analysis and synthesis of these ideas was beyond the computational powers of a human brain, and so the next step was to build analysis and simulation models into M-Net.

Computer optimized marketing

The analysis and simulation models allowed Samsung's managers to experiment with alternative budget allocation levels and to forecast their effect on business results. By performing numerous 'what-if' analyses, better budget allocations were discovered and misallocations pinpointed.

Three key learnings emerged from these analyses:

1. overinvestment in two regions;

2. underinvestment in two regions;

3. overinvestment in three product categories.

North America and Russia had received 45% of the budget, yet the models indicated that they only merited 35%. Europe and China had only received 31% but the model showed they merited 42%. And over half was going to mobile phones, vacuum cleaners and air-conditioners, and the model suggested that a 22% reallocation would produce better results.

Misallocation was revealed in a very significant way. Over $150 million needed to be reallocated to places with greater profit potential. Kim commented (Corstjens and Merrihue 2003): 'There was no way we could continue without a methodical approach to ensuring that marketing investments were targeted at the highest return opportunities.'

Winning management support

The final challenge that Kim overcame was winning management support. Executive pay and compensation had tended to reward large-sized or fast-growing business units. Budgets were seen as a sign of success; so reallocating budgets could hurt local managers, in the head, the heart and the purse.

Local managers cared little about the global organization, especially when their evaluation was focused locally. The rewards system encouraged managers to grow their own businesses without regard to others.

This phase of change relied less on computers and more on leadership and communication skills. M-Net had a vital role to play, for it allowed local managers to compare themselves with other managers, in different countries and different product categories. Televisions in Brazil were comparable with DVD players in France.

Workshops and meetings were held to discuss the insights and changes needed. In total there were 121 such sessions to test and hone the findings of the modelling. Once the findings were validated and changes identified, it was time to re-set allocations in the field.

Kim decided to embark on a global roadshow to assure people that a reduction in budget was not a vote of no-confidence, no matter how clear the modelling behind it: 'In a project such as this, there is no substitute for effective communication when it comes to implementing change.'

The roadshow was instrumental in implementing the allocation changes smoothly. Local managers appreciated upper management's openness and willingness to take the time to meet and explain the changes, as well as the opportunity to meet and ask questions. They liked the personal touch much more than the 'robot reallocation'.

Annual sales rose 25% between 2001 and 2002, from $27.7 billion to $34.7 billion. Net income also increased from $2.5 billion to $5.9 billion between 2001 and 2002. Samsung believes that this growth is sustainable and is committed to embedding the optimal marketing approach into its management processes.

Key points

- Allocation of the marketing mix is a planning decision aimed at maximizing payback from the marketing budget. Misunderstandings between finance and marketing need to be avoided by making clear the sense in which mix allocation is being performed.

- The twin practices of allocation by business unit and allocation by function are likely to result in decisions that do not maximize marketing payback and which institutionalize marketing waste.

- Five principles should be applied to allocation: rightsizing, no rationing, waste elimination, funding projects not people, and consolidation vs. fragmentation.

- Marketing mix allocation involves making numerous detailed quantitative assessments of how much marketing money to spend and where to spend it.

- Marketing directors should exercise the power of the purse (i.e. to evaluate which areas to fund), and they should not delegate these important decisions to finance staff, spreadsheet technicians and outside agencies.

- Expenditure strategy research is important to gain insights into the general patterns of brand expenditure and payback; however, it does not provide exact numbers for calculating optimal allocation.

- Sales response models are the basis of rigorous mix allocation; they are needed for every brand-market combination.

- Strategic and tactical allocation problems can be solved using judgemental models that need only four key parameters to be estimated by local marketing managers.

- Econometric modelling provides a more rigorous alternative to judgemental models, as long as sufficiently detailed sales volume and mix history are archived for analysis.

9

BRAND IDENTITY CHANGES

This chapter discusses brand identity and the decisions associated with changing identity and image. It starts by looking at the practical situations when brand identity decisions are required. There follows a discussion on the main brand identity frameworks that have been developed and how they can be applied. The focus then shifts to examine how strategic research can help establish a stronger brand identity. Finally we review how changes in brand identity should be tested and tracked.

The approach taken in the chapter deliberately challenges a number of pre-conceptions about brands and questions the truth of some widely cited examples of brand-building success.

Branding basics

You may have been at the receiving end of the verbal excesses of branding enthusiasts and authorities, and perhaps you have ended up bemused and confused. We certainly have been. Yet your puzzlement is a natural reaction to a subject that is still in transition from alchemy to science.

Brands and branding are among the most fashionable areas of marketing today. Authorities on branding make extravagant claims about the untold wealth that their alchemic skills can release. In particular, they lay claim to the mineral rights of the consumer's brain.

Unfortunately these alchemists have cloaked their subject in some of the most obscure terminology found anywhere in management today (see Box 9.1). Worse still, in the rush to impress friends and colleagues with their knowledge and wisdom, the same terms are used in ambiguous ways, definitions are rarely written down, and inconsistencies are brushed aside with creative postmodernist disdain.

Box 9.1 Branding jargon

Brand equity	Brand stretching
Brand essence	Brand valuation
Brand identity	Brand warriors
Brand image	Cannibal brands
Brand personality	Power brands
Brand positioning	Super brands
Brand soul	Tomorrow's brands
Brand strength	Umbrella brands
	Yesterday's brands

However tedious it may seem to gifted, creative people, standards and definitions are imperative in this subject if it is to be analyzed rigorously. So, as you progress through this chapter, you will find sections set aside for language and definitions. We'll begin with some of the easier terms – see Box 9.2.

Box 9.2 Branding terminology

Brand: Name, term, sign, design or symbol, or a combination of these, intended to identify the goods or services of one seller or group of sellers and to differentiate them from competitors.

Brand mark: That part of a brand that can be recognized visually but is not utterable, such as a symbol, design or distinctive colouring or lettering.

Brand name: That part of a brand that can be vocalized.

Product: Anything that can be offered to a market for attention, acquisition, use or consumption that might satisfy a want or need.

Product line: Group of products that are closely related because they perform a similar function, are sold to the same customer groups, are marketed through the same channels or make up a particular price range.

Product mix: Set of all product lines and items that a particular seller offers for sale to buyers (also known as range or assortment).

Trade mark: Brand or part of a brand that is given legal protection.

On the face of it, then, a brand is rather a mundane thing, and for many people the fuss that's made over brands and branding can seem excessive and exaggerated. After all, it's just a name, term, sign, design or symbol.

Substantial amounts of money are paid from time to time for the redesign of brand marks, such as those created recently for Abbey or BP. Refurbishing a business with these brand marks is expensive too. Brand names also get changed, such as when the UK Post Office (briefly) became Consignia. Yet the sums paid to design agencies and branding consultancies are relatively small when compared to other marketing costs. At the same time, the impact of other marketing expenditure, such as sales promotion or direct marketing, is more self-evident.

What is brand identity?

You probably don't take brand identity decisions often, but when you do they will have momentous impact on your marketing, your customers and your shareholders. For this reason, the majority of the content of most books and papers on brands and branding seems to be devoted to this topic. It's about the questions: 'What is my brand? Who am I? What do I symbolize? With what is my brand associated? What makes my brand identity strong?' These concerns seem to obsess marketing managers.

The marvellous thing about these questions is how inconclusive they are to answer. Unlike the question 'What's the payback from my advertising?', identity decisions seem to rely a great deal on gut instinct and emotions. Perhaps this observation goes some way towards explaining why brand identity has taken over from advertising as a creative marketing preoccupation. Brand identity is the perfect playing field on which people with artistic temperaments can kick around their creative ideas without questions being asked or criticisms getting voiced.

Cases of strong brand identity are widely heralded by the branding authorities – Coca-Cola, Microsoft, IBM, Nokia, Disney, McDonald's and Virgin are regularly cited. Yet the more you dig into the subject, and the more you compare business performance with claims about brand strength, the more difficult it becomes to accept the glib explanations about strong brands. Yet despite your reservations about the mechanisms underlying brand identity, its importance must not be completely denied.

Yardley had many characteristics of a strong brand – its name, its heritage, its loyal customers. Founded in London in 1770 by William Yardley as a lavender business, the brand identity is quintessentially English, conservative and old-fashioned. Unfortunately, shortly after SmithKline Beecham had paid £110 million to own Yardley in 1990, it discovered that most of Yardley's loyal customers were reaching old age and they no longer bought perfume. By 1997 the situation had got so serious that SmithKline decided to give Yardley an identity makeover, using advertising that featured supermodel Linda Evangelista in chains and shackles. But the makeover failed to win back its old customers or gain any new ones and so in 1998 the company went into receivership. Although bought by Wella, and subsequently targeted by P&G, the jury is still out as to whether the Yardley brand has any value remaining.

A disproportionate amount of management time and effort is devoted to worrying about brand identity, given the infrequent nature of brand identity decisions. Most companies leave their identity well alone for many years, sometimes many decades. Yet brand identity is fascinating because the risks and consequences of bad or ineffective brand identity are so large. Nonetheless, the prominence identity receives is out of all proportion to the frequency with which identity decisions about it are made. Other decisions, concerning brand portfolio planning and expenditure allocation, are often neglected and deserve greater prominence and attention.

Ten hard questions to ask about the way you manage your brand identity:

1. Can your colleagues in finance understand what you say about branding?
2. Is there adequate legal protection of your brand identity?
3. Does your risk management team assess the risks associated with the brand?
4. Have you been tracking the changes in your brand image over the long term?
5. Do you have an effective framework for managing your brand identity?
6. Is there a clear direction in which you plan to shift your brand image?
7. Have you used research to determine your current positioning?
8. Do you use perceptual mapping to define your brand positioning changes?
9. Are you satisfied with the progress you have made in repositioning your brand(s)?
10. Do all elements of the marketing mix support your brand positioning?

Diagnosing your brand identity problems

Six situations have a bearing on brand identity, listed in order of frequency:

- Launch;
- Physical identity changes – name, trade mark or other distinctive feature;
- Disaster recovery – environmental, health, scandal, etc.;
- Major communications changes – core ideas, strap lines and slogans;
- Ingredient changes – product formulation or service quality;
- Price repositioning.

In each of these situations except new launches, brand identity decision-making processes are generally triggered by two things:

- **Sales problems:** Disappointing results often trigger diagnostic analysis.
- **Brand image problems:** Tracking studies may reveal a declining image.

Once the problems are recognized, then a number of tools and techniques can be used to resolve the issues. These approaches may be formalized, but often are not. Typically they are applied in this order:

- **Diagnosis**: Root-cause analysis pinpoints the real source of the problem.
- **Options**: Several potential solutions are proposed.
- **Pre-testing**: Solutions are tested in simulated market conditions.
- **Forecasting**: Sales and profit improvement are forecast for each option.
- **Decision**: Agreement is reached as to the best solution.

Table 9.1 shows the typical triggers and relevant solutions to the six major situations which have a bearing on brand identity, together with some notable examples of what we consider to be successes and failures.

Table 9.1
Recognizing and solving brand identity problems

Brand situation	Diagnosis and analysis	Success	Not a success
Launch	Growth forecasts Gut instinct Pre-testing	Amazon, Egg, PC World, Pret A Manger, Red Bull	Ford Edsel, Virgin Cola, Radion, Planet Hollywood
Physical identity changes	Sales problems Brand tracking indicators Pre-testing	Accenture	Consignia
Disaster recovery	Press comment Sales problems Brand tracking indicators	Tylenol	Barclaycard, Ratners
Major communications changes	Brand tracking indicators Advertising tracking Pre-testing	IBM Global Services	British Airways, Yardley
Ingredient changes	Quality/value tracking Pre-testing	Castrol, Virgin One, Barclays OpenPlan, Sainsbury Local	New Coke, Kodak, Polaroid, Levi's
Price repositioning	Price/value tracking Pre-testing	Budweiser, BT	British Airways

The six brand identity situations are now discussed in some detail in the following sections.

Launches

These decisions are rare, and they are usually taken on the basis of growth forecasts. Forecasting inaccuracies can have disastrous financial consequences. As we have noted in a white paper on forecasting (Shaw and Finn 2003), forecasting inaccuracies can be significantly reduced by following a series of procedures. Unfortunately this advice is not observed by many companies.

The Ford Edsel is a widely cited example of a launch failure that offers many lessons (Haig 2003). Pre-testing showed numerous problems – unattractive appearance, high price, silly name, fictitious customer needs – but management chose to ignore the early warning signs and ploughed hundreds of millions into a misconceived brand.

Amazon, Egg, PC World, Pret A Manger and Red Bull are examples of relatively recent brand launches that have attracted more positive comments, and appear to be successful. With hindsight, the reasons for success can generally be explained. What we don't know for certain is how much formal analysis preceded their success, and how often it was only gut instinct that guided their development.

Physical identity changes

These decisions are less rare, and most brands have a physical identity makeover every few years. This usually involves hiring a specialist consultancy or agency that will recommend a name change, or redesign the logo or trade mark.

Accenture, Monday and Consignia are recent examples of name changes. Sometimes physical identity is changed for legal reasons, as in Accenture's case. More often the reason for change is sales or brand image problems, as in the case of Monday, the short-lived renaming of PricewaterhouseCoopers' consultancy arm.

The UK Post Office had become a conglomerate of businesses, including logistics, call centres and postal services. 'We were researching hard into what this organization was facing,' commented Keith Wells, a brand consultant, to BBC Online, 'what we needed was something that could pull all the bits together.' They followed the fashion of creating a mysterious name (Amazon, Google and Yahoo! are recent examples). Quite what research they undertook is unclear, but the public reaction after the change in January 2002 was universally hostile. By May 2002 management did a U-turn and the Consignia name was dropped.

Disaster recovery

This is another problem that is particularly prevalent for corporate brands, but can also trouble product brands. Major firms today often take insurance cover against 'brand risk' and also put aside resources for disaster recovery.

Arthur Andersen, Enron, Exxon, Pan Am, Perrier, Ratner and Tylenol are commonly cited examples of brands that faced disaster recovery situations, with varying degrees of success. It would be a mistake to bracket them all as branding problems, as in the case of Arthur Andersen and Enron, the disasters were far more pervasive than brand identity.

Press hostility is the early warning of impending problems, followed in short order by falls in brand tracking indices and sales. Analysis is rarely formalized, and decisions are often based on judgement and lessons from history. Tylenol successfully recovered from malicious cyanide poisoning by recalling the product and maintaining active press contacts until the culprit was caught.

Major communications changes

These happen much more often, but are less visible to the outside world. Reasons for communications changes are:

- **Disappearing customers:** Yardley faced this problem as its older, more conservative customers dwindled in numbers.
- **Image wear-out:** Attention and interest in a brand can decline over time and the brand can then be perceived as boring. Smirnoff is a brand that revives its image every few years to ensure attention and interest.
- **Gap between image and desired identity:** IBM had to give its image a major makeover to become a credible player in the lucrative services market.
- **Low perceived value:** British Airways has suffered when low-price airlines such as easyJet and Ryanair challenged its value. BA's attempts to communicate the non-financial benefits of flying with them have so far met with only limited success.

Ingredient changes

These happen frequently, and reflect themselves in perceived quality and value for the customers. Rejuvenating the product formulation and revitalizing tired service standards are common approaches, both at brand and product level.

Castrol has successfully exploited its R&D programme by reminding the public through its advertising and communications that the lubricant products are constantly changing and at the cutting edge. Although lubricants are intrinsically dull, boring products to most people, Castrol's ability to inject some excitement into a dull item has helped it to maintain premium pricing and a high market share over decades.

New Coke is a classic example of a disastrous ingredient change. Blind tasting tests of Coke versus Pepsi have always favoured Pepsi, and for a period in the 1980s Pepsi began to gain share. Coke's management became obsessed with the taste issue and reformulated the taste of Coke. They carried out extensive pre-testing, but only focused on taste. Signs that the public did not want the original Coke to be scrapped were ignored, and they went ahead. The outcry against the decision was huge, and even President Ronald Reagan joined in. Within a couple of months the decision was reversed.

Service is another ingredient that can have an important impact. Recent new product launches, such as Virgin One, Barclays OpenPlan and Sainsbury Local have all been successful and their success provides a 'halo' effect for the parent brand.

Price repositioning

This is a related brand decision, also reflecting itself in perceived value. These issues can be addressed in two ways: by changing actual price-positioning (relative to competition) or by communicating differently.

Every financial service organization today faces a constant battle with these issues. Relative price is a key factor in the minds of many customers, who see some brands as expensive, or good value for money, or worth paying more for, etc.

In 2003, despite being the boss of the country's biggest credit card, Barclaycard, with nine million customers, Matthew Barrett told the UK House of Commons Treasury Committee that credit cards were too expensive as a means for him to borrow money and that he had advised his four children not to use them for this purpose as well. This story stayed in the news for weeks and has since become part of public folklore.

British Telecom faced a related issue when customers' perceptions of the price of telephone calls did not line up with actual prices. Without actually changing prices, BT ran a successful advertising campaign, called 'It's Good To Talk'. It was described by the press as 'social engineering', such was its impact on customers' price perceptions.

Describing and measuring your brand identity changes

Making sense of these changes requires learning a language about brand identity, both tangible and intangible.

Tangible factors in brand identity

Building a brand identity is costly and at times it can seem ephemeral. Yet there are tangible aspects of branding and these can be protected in law, although there is no cohesive body of law that protects the overall concept of a brand (see Box 9.3).

Box 9.3 Legal ways of protecting brands

Copyright: Rights that protect a brand from being copied that are created without registration. For example, labels and graphic surface patterns on products are protected by copyright (e.g. Burberry, Yves St Laurent).

Distinctiveness: The degree to which confusion between one brand and another may be avoided.

Look-alike: One brand which may be confused with another due to similarities in name, symbols, logotypes and visual presentations.

Patent: System of registering an inventive idea that protects it from being copied.

Passing off: Using a name, mark or symbol that looks like or may be confused with another one, which is not protected by trade mark registration. In some countries, for example in England under common law, there is some legal protection, depending on the degree of confusion (e.g. United Biscuits vs. Asda in the case of Penguin and Puffin biscuits).

Registered design right: System of registering a design to protect it from being copied.

Trade mark: A badge of origin which identifies a product as having come from a particular source, which is registered under law. Trade marks do not travel between countries without registration.

The brand owner must rely on a contrived mixture of copyright, design right, registered design right, trade marks, common law rights (passing off) and trading standards legislation for protection. A brand can incorporate several common elements, which include:

- names;
- symbols;
- logotypes;
- trade dress and packaging;
- strap lines.

Each attracts a different form of legal protection. These forms of protection must be combined together in order to evaluate the level of legal protection that a brand attracts as a whole. Within each of these components there are numerous subcategories which must be considered individually, for example:

- colour;
- sound;
- shape and decoration;
- product design;
- trade secrets;
- inventions.

Intangible factors in brand identity

Less tangible aspects of a brand's identity are more important to its success than the tangible factors, even though protecting the brand in law is important to sustaining its long-term success. Here is how David Aaker (1996), one of the world's top brand authorities, defines some of the main intangible factors:

- **Brand identity:** A unique set of brand associations that the brand strategist aspires to create or maintain. These associations represent what the brand stands for and imply a promise to customers from the organization.
- **Brand image:** How customers and others perceive the brand.
- **Value proposition:** A statement of the functional, emotional and self-expressive benefits delivered by the brand, which provides value to the customer.

You should note that the 'brand identity', as defined by David Aaker, corresponds to the descriptive ideas (associations and beliefs) discussed in the previous chapter, and his 'value proposition' corresponds to the evaluative ideas (attitudes). One of the major challenges of branding is to define a brand identity (Chevalier and Curhan 1976) that creates strong positive attitudes (evaluative).

The importance given to identity and perceptions often surprises engineers and financial managers, especially given the substantial costs associated with brand. As an example that illustrates why they are important, we examine the often quoted example of the blind tasting of Coke and Pepsi.

This example shows clearly that consumers are willing to ignore their sensory experiences when choosing a brand, a finding that runs counter to the expectations of engineers and financial managers, who often believe that people choose products based on tangible experiences.

Colas are nothing more or less than fizzy brown liquids that people choose to drink as an alternative to water. Unimportant compared with many things in life, such as sport, politics or religion, colas represent a low-involvement purchase. We would go further and say that colas are 'dull and boring', although their manufacturers would perhaps disagree with us.

What is at first sight remarkable is that Coca-Cola is bought more often than Pepsi throughout most of the world, despite the product being dull and boring. But that's the point. Choosing something that's intrinsically dull and boring is difficult, especially when the products are similar.

Why not choose water? In some situations, water would be the drink of choice. But in many situations, water is just too dull and boring, and so people choose something that is less dull and boring. People actually react against the boring-ness of the liquid and 'not boring' seems to factor in their choice.

Figure 9.1
Cola selection in blind and named situations

	Blind	Named
Prefer Pepsi	51%	23%
Prefer Coke	44%	65%
Equal	5%	12%

Consider now how people reacted when offered a choice of two colas, which were not labelled (Figure 9.1). When the only brand-identity clue was taste, more people chose Pepsi than Coca-Cola. When the name of the brand was shown, more people chose Coca-Cola than Pepsi.

We overrule our senses when selecting a brand, as this example clearly illustrates. Although people's sensory experiences of a product can have some effect on their brand choice, other factors can often dominate the brand selection decision, much to the surprise of the engineers and financial managers who create and evaluate the products.

Aaker (1996) has closely studied numerous different brands in many markets and has catalogued the recurrent brand image associations he found. His excellent book *Building Strong Brands* is an essential guide for anyone wishing to develop a knowledge of brand associations. Figure 9.2 illustrates Aaker's catalogue of associations; the terms used in the diagram are explained in Box 9.4.

Figure 9.2
Brand identity and value system

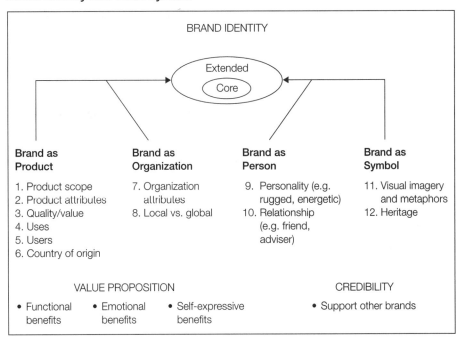

Box 9.4 Definitions of terms used in Figure 9.2

Brand as organization: Associations connected with the organization to which the brand belongs (e.g. Marks & Spencer returns policy).

Brand as person: Associations with a type of person, which symbolizes the brand (e.g. Kwik Fit – fast, helpful, professional).

Brand as product: Associations connected with the products within the brand (e.g. HP printers).

Brand as symbol: Associations with specific symbolic images (usually tangible, such as the Nike swoosh) or heritage (e.g. Wedgewood).

Core brand: The central timeless essence of the brand.

Credibility: The brand promise is supported by other attributes such as trustworthiness.

Emotional benefits: Positive feelings that the brand evokes (e.g. Häagen-Dazs is seductive, sensuous and stylish).

Functional benefits: Benefits of the way the brand functions (e.g. Volvo is a safe, durable car).

Heritage: The brand has a long history, rich in symbolic significance.

Imagery: Specific images that are coupled strongly with the brand.

Metaphors: One concept that stands for another (e.g. the Energiser bunny for long battery life).

Self-expressive benefits: Benefits associated with self-expression and self-image – public – aspirational (e.g. Tango was relaunched as in-your-face rebelliousness).

Value proposition: The evaluative associations of the brand.

Differentiation or salience?

Brand strategists have long claimed that differentiation is important. Yet there is a rising tide of opinion that challenges this rule-of-thumb. One of the most eloquent critics is Andrew Ehrenberg, and his arguments warrant our attention (Ehrenberg *et al.* 1997).

> Competitive brands seldom differ from each other in a big way, since any innovation with selling power is usually copied. Nor does the brands' advertising usually give them very different images or values, despite what tends to be said about brand differentiation. Nevertheless, brands differ greatly in their market shares. This is explained by the very different numbers of people to whom each brand is 'salient' (e.g. in their consideration set). Such salience is in practice reinforced and/or nudged by advertising which in effect merely says in impactful ways 'I'm a good example of the product' or 'here I am.'

Salience is a rather neutral term, meaning the extent to which the brand 'sticks out from the crowd' and is on the agenda of potential customers. A salient brand does not have to be 'valued' much more than rival brands or encourage feelings of warmth or affinity (i.e. be a brand 'for people like me'). It merely has to be noticed.

The differentiation or salience debate is strongly emotive. There is also a strong element of vested interests, because agencies base their appeal to clients on their ability to differentiate the client's brand from its competitors. However, putting aside these vested interests, the salience argument deserves our attention.

Researching your brand identity strategy

Strategy research is concerned with long-term shifts in consumption and competition – over many years – and is used as a basis for major branding decisions. This analysis is not commonplace, but it is imperative for the following decisions:

- Launches;
- Physical identity changes – name, trademark or other distinctive features;
- Major communications changes – core ideas, strap lines and slogans.

Strategy research essentially consists of three types of analyses: marketing audit, qualitative research and quantitative research.

Marketing audits

Marketing audits look at long-term trends – 10 to 20 years – in all factors that do, or could, affect our profits, sales and market share, and the impact of brand image and identity (Table 9.2). The long-term perspective is what makes them unusual.

Table 9.2

What to look for in a marketing audit

What to look for	Example
Market size trends	Alcoholic drinks – shift from growing to mature market
Relative price increases	Beer – becomes 50% more expensive than other alcohol
Disappearing market segments	Yardley – traditional grannies are disappearing
Declining segment share	British Airways – loss of economy customers
Declining consumption rates	Guinness – declining consumption of strong-tasting beer
Recognition declining	Ovaltine – fewer and fewer people recognize it
Recall declining	Kodak – digital brands are rising to top-of-mind
Attitudes hardening	McDonald's – attitudes towards diet and health
Purchase intentions declining	Guinness – people like the image not the product
Competition rising	Barclaycard – entry of MBNA, Capital One, etc.
Acquisition opportunities	Sainsbury Local – buying up the corner shops

Market size and revenue trends are important, especially viewed over long periods, where product life-cycle trends may be apparent. Spending patterns provide useful clues about how people are prepared to allocate their disposable income (see Figure 9.3).

Relative price is an important driver, and it should be analyzed for long-term trends. For example, in the UK the price of beer has increased by 50% in real terms compared with other types of alcoholic drink, a factor that explains some of the significant decline in beer's share of the alcoholic drinks market (see Figure 9.4).

For existing brands (i.e. excluding new product launches), we can assemble market and revenue share data for our brand and competing brands and assess the trends. Our brand may be losing share, in which case the aim of the audit is to diagnose why.

Segment data should also be assembled wherever possible. Our brand may be losing share predominantly in certain key segments, and this bias may be important when diagnosing the problems. For example, Yardley suffered in the early 1990s when 'traditional grannies' modernized their attitudes and behaviour. British Airways' losses of share began in its economy class, before spreading more widely.

Figure 9.3
Trends in alcohol spend in the UK – shift from growth to maturity

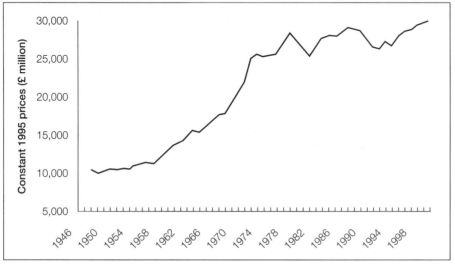

Figure 9.4
Relative real price trends for competing alcoholic drink categories in the UK (including taxation)

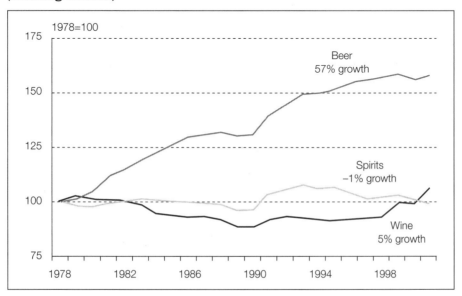

Consumption rate statistics also provide evidence, especially viewed over ten years. In Britain, beer drinkers have been shifting away from strong-tasting darker beers, and towards milder flavoured lagers. Guinness responded to this trend by introducing Guinness Extra Cold, because low temperatures chill-out our taste buds.

Recognition statistics are readily available and should be examined for long-term trends. Ovaltine's customers fell asleep during the 1990s and by 2002 the factory was closed and the brand put up for sale. The trouble is that few people today even recognize a brand that was once to be found in every household. Without brand recognition, it is hard to see why anyone would wish to buy the brand.

Recall statistics are also revealing. Kodak's recall figures tell us how few people can remember the brand when asked 'What makers of photographic products can you recall?' They have been declining for several years, since the digital camera manufacturers Canon, Fuji and Sony became top-of-mind.

Attitude statistics are also revealing, not only for the brand but also the category. For example, McDonald's has taken heed of consumer attitudes to diet and healthy eating, and has recently announced changes in product size and ingredients in response to consumer attitudes towards healthy eating.

Purchase intentions can reveal gaps between attitudes and behaviour. For example, Guinness track the numbers of people who refuse the product, buy occasionally, buy often, and always choose Guinness. They find that although many people have positive attitudes to Guinness, and think it's cool, many of them would refuse the product itself.

Competitive entry and intensity also should be tracked. Barclaycard and other UK credit cards have been strongly impacted by MBNA and Capital One entering the UK market and changing people's expectations about credit cards.

Finally, some brand decisions are opportunistic, for example Sainsbury Local. The opportunity to enter the corner-shop market has existed for decades!

Qualitative strategic research

Qualitative research consists of 'groups' and 'depths' – focus groups and depth interviews – to develop an understanding about brand associations, beliefs, attitudes and evaluative ideas (see Table 9.3). One of the major strengths of qualitative research is its ability to uncover factors that have gone unmeasured in tracking research.

Table 9.3
What to look for in qualitative research

What to look for	Example
Key associations	Banks – associated with big profits and poor value
Growing expectations	MBNA – easy for people to switch card provider
Shifting customer values	easyJet – in-flight extras not essential
Changing interests and pastimes	Alcopops – the rise of clubbing
Disposable income changes	Pret-A-Manger – the rise of the affluent office worker
Confusion choosing between product features	Renault Megane – the importance of self-image
Changing beliefs about brands	Virgin One – the decline of trust in banking heritage
Shifting attitudes	easyJet – the affordable long weekend break
Growing competitive intensity	Barclaycard – the fragmentation of the card market
Acquisition opportunities	Sainsbury Local – buying up the corner shops

Qualitative strategy research provides data rich in ideas, hypotheses, insights, explanations and connections. It answers questions of how, what, why, when, where but not 'how many'. For this reason it is often used as a preliminary to larger-scale quantitative research.

The choice of format – group or depth – is important. So too is the technique of eliciting answers. The main techniques are: association; completion; transformation; construction.

Association techniques include word associations ('What do you associate with the word . . . ?') and collage building (from a wide variety of materials cut from magazines). For example, banks have been found to be associated with words like: greedy, untrustworthy, bad service, annoying call centres, closing branches, etc.

Completion procedures include sentence completion, story completion or bubble cartoons (fill in the bubble). For example, 'When I change current account provider, I expect the bank to . . . '

Transformation procedures involve inviting respondents to imagine transforming brands into people (e.g. 'If this brand came to life as a person, what would he be like?'). For example, Accenture was transformed into 'The A Team' and the 'Green Berets' in some groups we have run.

Construction procedures ask respondents to construct a role (e.g. acting out the buying of a round of drinks) or to construct an obituary for a brand, saying what it would be remembered for and so on (e.g. in the obituary for Microsoft, what would it be remembered for?).

Interpreting responses to these procedures clearly requires skill, insight and imagination. The main steps are: transcription, mechanical analysis and interpretive analysis. Most tape recordings are transcribed in text first. Mechanical analysis classifies what they said to bring together similar comments. Several passes are often needed as the classification emerges. Interpretive analysis attempts to work out the meaning of what has been said.

Language used by customers should be noted carefully. Often brand owners do not communicate with their customers using appropriate language.

IBM commissioned one of the authors in 1996 to survey the global services market. Customers were asked to describe in their own words the services that they bought. Over 4,000 purchase instances were described, the language was catalogued and listed, and the terms were then compared with the language that IBM had been using (see Figure 9.5). When IBM realized how inappropriate was the language it used to talk to customers, it decided to overhaul its entire communications strategy.

Figure 9.5
Language differences between customers and suppliers at IBM

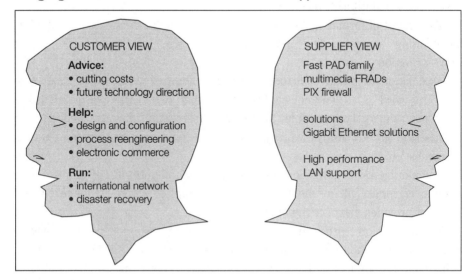

Quantitative strategic research

Quantitative strategic research involves asking a sample of respondents a series of predetermined questions and analyzing the answers. This research attempts to address questions such as:

■ Does your brand have a better image in terms of product quality?

■ Is a competitor's product perceived to be better in terms of value for money?

This information can help in determining how to position your product, and to understand the underlying reasons if you are losing market share.

Perceptual mapping is a powerful technique for displaying the relationships between a set of brands and a set of attributes. The attributes can be:

■ Image characteristics, such as 'prestigious' or 'basic';

■ Perceptions of different target groups;

■ Overall similarities with other brands.

The technique has been used for about 30 years. Its popularity stems from its ability to communicate in a visually compulsive way the complexity of a marketplace with a large number of brands and attributes.

Perceptual mapping originates from the observation that people seem to use a few core attributes when they think about a product class, even though they may be aware of hundreds of specific attributes. The objective of perceptual mapping is to identify the relevant dimensions and to locate the positions of existing and potential new brands on these dimensions.

We commonly want to reduce the large number of potential attributes to a manageable number of principal factors. The analysis should suggest answers to the following four questions:

■ How many different principal factors are needed to explain the pattern of relationships?

■ How should the principal factors be named and what is their significance?

■ How do the detailed attributes map onto the principal factors?

■ How do brands map onto the principal factors?

Moore and Pessemier (1993) provide the example in Figure 9.6 of a perceptual mapping of the beer market. This combines quality attributes such as 'heavy' and 'pale colour' with the perceived preferences of various groups of consumers. The analysis uses two principal factors: a 'budget–premium' dimension on the horizontal axis and a 'light–heavy' dimension on the vertical axis.

The usefulness of the technique is enhanced when the attribute plot shown above is overlaid with the competing brands, as in Figure 9.7.

Figure 9.6
Perceptual mapping of the beer market – attributes

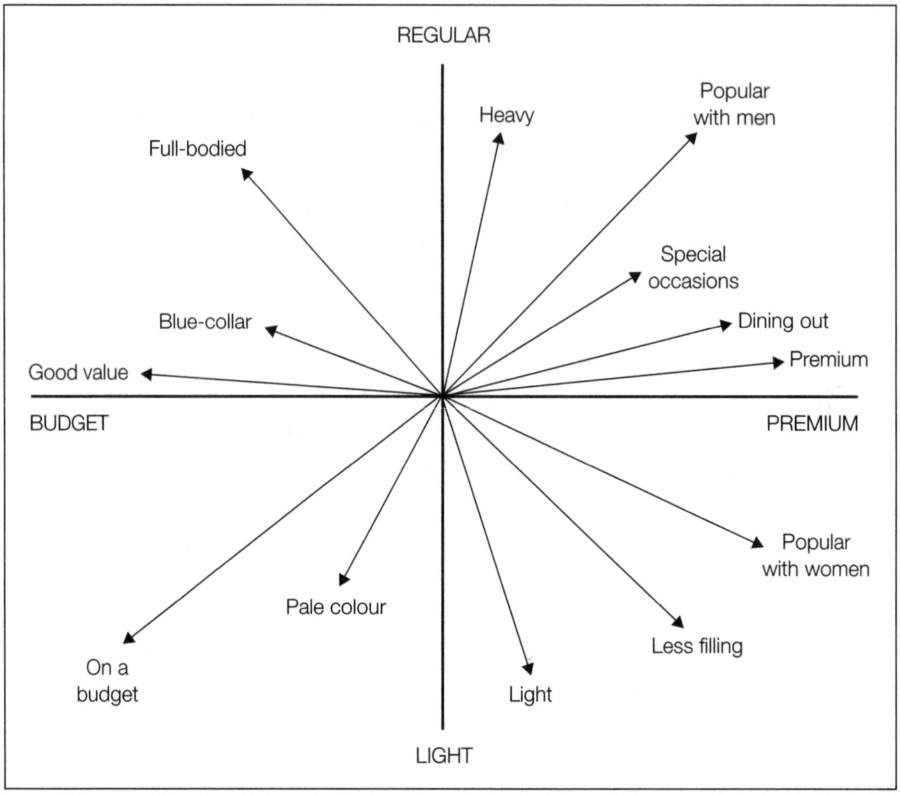

Source: Reprinted with permission from *Product Planning and Management*, Moore and Pessemier, McGraw-Hill, 1993

In order to read perceptual maps, and particularly to understand the relationship between brands and attributes, look at the perpendicular distance between a brand and the attribute line. For example, Miller Lite is 'less filling' and Coors is associated closely with 'dining out'. Also, Budweiser is 'popular with men' and Coors Light is 'popular with women'. Note that, because the attribute lines for men and women are almost perpendicular to each other, the popularity of a beer with men indicates nothing about its popularity with women.

Finally, we can plot the brands without the attribute, as shown in Figure 9.8. This sort of chart is also called a *similarity mapping*.

We can use this form of perceptual map to look for clusters of brands. Such clusters can help to identify subcategories of beers that may differ from the usual segmentations of the marketplace.

For example, Becks and Heineken are clearly positioned closely together. By contrast, Old Milwaukee Light is not near any other brand and therefore has little direct competition. This may indicate the opportunity for a new beer to compete with Old Milwaukee Light in the 'pale colour' and 'on a budget' segment.

Figure 9.7
Perceptual mapping of the beer market – attributes and brands

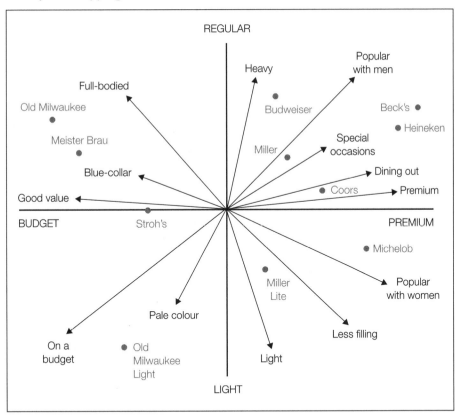

Source: Reprinted with permission from *Product Planning and Management*, Moore and Pessemier, McGraw-Hill, 1993

Figure 9.8
Perceptual mapping of the beer market – brands

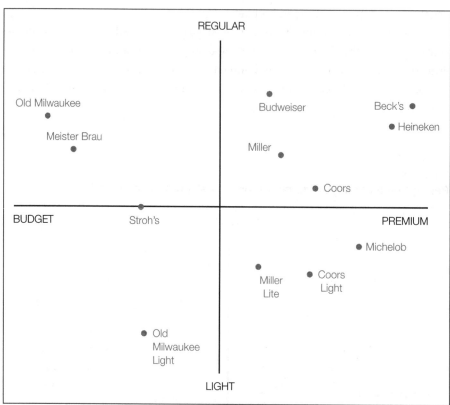

Source: Reprinted with permission from *Product Planning and Management*, Moore and Pessemier, McGraw-Hill, 1993

Testing your brand identity decisions

Brand identity testing is concerned with providing assurance to the creative team that the new brand identity will work, or not. It is also called pre-testing. Testing is carried out in connection with the following decisions:

- Launch testing;
- Physical identity testing – names, trade marks, logos;
- Major communications testing – core ideas, strap lines and slogans;
- Product testing – new formulations;
- Service testing – new service elements;
- Price testing – repositioning.

There are three stages that brand identity changes pass through, and at each stage, a variety of techniques are available. First, *concept development tests* help select ideas. Second, *rough testing* is conducted with rough executions to decide which is worth finishing. Third, *finished testing* is used to screen the final creative executions before they go live.

Concepts are tested using individual depth interviews amongst the target audience group to obtain a private opinion or rating of each idea presented. The skill of the researchers is of paramount importance in ensuring that all eventualities are investigated and that comments are effectively interpreted.

New Coke's disastrous launch in 1985 provides important lessons about the management of concept testing. About 200,000 consumers were contacted in the test programme. While interviews showed a willingness to try a new Coke, other tests disclosed the opposite. In particular, respondents were unaware that the traditional product was going to be withdrawn.

Rough testing involves mocking up the final product. Simulating market conditions as much as possible is important. Making rough models of one aspect of the new brand can be misleading.

New Coke was rough tested on the basis of taste. But out of 200,000 tests only 30,000 tasted the new formulation, the rest tasted other experimental formulations. These tests were generally positive. However, they ignored the intangible aspects of the brand and its heritage in particular.

The symbolic value of Coke was the sleeper. Probably this should have been foreseen, and been tested as part of the test design. The 100-year-old formula and American heritage were being interfered with! Even worse, the tradition was being abandoned. Strong feelings about this traditional heritage were ignored, to management's cost.

Finished testing involves exposing a research sample to the finished product before it is launched. The same techniques as for rough testing are used, but using a finished execution not a rough.

Following testing, the researchers assess the test scores and decide which creative executions of the brand identity to accept, which to reject, and where changes should be made.

Tracking your brand identity

The final stage of brand identity evaluation is tracking. *Brand identity compliance* is the first stage of tracking. This entails checking all creative executions to ensure that the brand identity guidelines are being followed. To facilitate compliance checking, *brand standards manuals* are developed by many organizations. These provide a detailed specification about how the brand identity is to be implemented in advertising, packaging, direct mail, etc.

IBM carried out a review of its brand identity executions in 1995. It discovered several hundred local interpretations of the brand identity, all of which were in manifest violation of the branding guidelines. Lou Gerstner ordered a major programme of change as a consequence of this finding.

Structure and *activity tracking* will be covered later in the book, and we do not deal with them here.

The main purpose of *brand image tracking* is to ensure that the identity, as planned by the marketing department and its agency, is creating the expected image in the minds of the target audience(s) (see Table 9.4). Brand identity is aspirational, reflecting perceptions that the company wants to have associated with its brand.

Table 9.4

Tracking actual brand image and comparing it with plan

Dimension	Brand identity (Goal)	Brand image (Current reality)
Product	Premium Beer	Premium Beer
User	Young (in spirit or body)	Middle-aged
Personality	Fun, humorous	Fun, humorous
Functional benefit	Superior flavour	Superior flavour
Emotional benefit	Social group acceptance	(none)

Source: Adapted with permission of The Free Press, a Division of Simon & Schuster Adult Publishing Group, from BUILDING STRONG BRANDS by David A. Aaker. Copyright © 1996 by David A. Aaker. All rights reserved.

In this example, tracking reveals that the brand image needs attention in the areas of perceived user (middle-aged) and social group acceptance. This may be achieved by softening the middle-aged imagery and reinforcing the fun, humorous personality.

Throughout this chapter we have suggested a rather more rigorous approach to brand identity planning than is usually advocated by brand gurus and media agencies. Executives adopting this style of thinking may well be labelled boring and unimaginative by colleagues who are more interested in the emotive side of the subject, but they should have the courage of their convictions. More money is wasted on high-profile brand adventures than in almost any other area of marketing spend.

Key points

- Major decisions on brand identity are made infrequently, either in connection with a major disaster (e.g. environmental, health, scandal), or because of declining performance that is attributed to 'wear-out' of the brand's strength.

- Risks associated with brand identity decisions are high, and many high-profile failures are widely known (e.g. New Coke, Consignia, Yardley).

- Legal protection for tangible brand identity is important and large teams of lawyers are employed by many successful brands (e.g. Disney, Coca-Cola, McDonald's).

- Intangible factors in brand identity are commercially more important than tangible factors, although harder to protect in law.

- Strategic research tools are available to support brand identity changes. Most marketing departments lack the in-house skills to carry out these analyses, and generally consultancies are employed. Marketing departments need to develop a deeper understanding of these techniques and how they work, to ensure that the consultants' work is properly supervised and evaluated.

- Rigorous concept testing should be carried out prior to any major brand identity investment. Marketing departments need to ensure they have the necessary technical knowledge internally before embarking on risky brand identity testing.

- Brand identity tracking surveys enable marketing departments to follow up the effects of brand decisions and, in particular, to assess whether the identity as planned is reflected in the perceptions of customers or potential customers. They tend to reveal relevant information only if managers personally dig deep into the survey data and subject it to detailed analysis to squeeze out significant insights.

10

BRAND PORTFOLIO PLANNING

The previous chapter provided an overview of brand identity planning. This chapter looks at brand portfolio planning – decisions relating to stretching, extending, compressing and rationalizing brands. Brand portfolio planning is one of the main drivers of marketing payback. We look at how to describe and measure the shape of the brand portfolio, its depth, breadth and length. We show how to analyze portfolio decisions, and how to test and track them.

Throughout this chapter, we have illustrated key points by reference to specific examples. However, as we note in the section on international decisions, only seven of the top 100 FMCG brands are global in the sense that they are represented in the USA, Europe and Japan. We realize that readers may not always recognize the brands used in the examples, but the key points are common across the world.

Stretching your brand portfolio

You may resist the idea of pulling your carefully created brands out of shape, but, in truth, your company probably stretches, extends and distorts your brands every few months, or even weeks, by adding new products or even new brands. Sometimes they compress and rationalize them. Generally these moves are intended to grow sales volumes and revenues, or to cut excess costs, but it is important to realize that all of them result in portfolio choices.

Continuously reviewing, developing and changing brands is an important activity because it can grow profits. Stretching brand structure, extending it, segmenting it – these are the reasons why spending serious sums of money on branding is so important. A brand that stays in its original box is unlikely to generate super-profits, but one that jumps out of its box can create significant new value. The structure of a brand needs to be distorted, stretched and pulled. Doing this effectively requires lots of thinking and deciding. Where can a brand be stretched to? How many product variants are needed? What gaps in the market should be covered? When will stretching fail? When will it succeed? How successful will it be?

Only a minority of marketing managers take the lead in assessing these portfolio choices. Often the decisions are taken at Board level or by departments such as strategic planning (to exploit M&A opportunities), R&D (to exploit technological advances), operational managers (to make better use of capacity) and even sales managers (to offer products that match the competition) – see Shaw and Fisk (2002).

The financial incentives to add new products, packs and variants are considerable, especially just after a brand has been acquired. When, for instance, Cavenham Foods bought Bovril in the 1960s, Chicken Bovril appeared soon after. Part of the financial attraction is the economies of scale, when costs associated with the new product or variety can be shared and spread across the portfolio.

Risks, unfortunately, are high too and the failure rate of these decisions is about 80%. A primary reason for this high failure rate is that branding questions are seldom effectively analyzed, with technical, operational and financial analyses tending to dominate the decision making.

Case study 10.1

Bic – a brand extension too far?

Bic has fallen under the spell of brand stretching gurus a few times. The Bic name is French, but misplaced emphasis on French heritage and shelf placement led to a dreadful brand extension mistake – Bic perfume. It did not work because associations with cheap and disposable pens, lighters and razors were a handicap in the perfume category. It destroyed shareholder value, although the damage was limited by swiftly withdrawing it.

Bic didn't stop there. Bic underwear was a line of disposable pantyhose it tried to sell and failed. Management argued that the disposability and the Bic brand were synonymous. Consumers were unable to see the links between Bic's other products and pantyhose, because of course there is no link.

Usually structural decisions, such as the Bic ones above, are made elsewhere than the marketing department. Although marketing people may be consulted, their opinions are often not given the weight they deserve. The fact that about 80% of product launches fail is testimony to the problem.

Given the importance of structural decisions in driving brand value, it would be reasonable to expect that branding books and literature would cover this topic well. Yet the branding literature has little to say on the subject, other than stressing its importance. Instead, the strategic planning literature, and particularly portfolio theory, is a better guide to structural issues. Before reviewing that advice, it is worth putting the theory in context by asking ten hard questions about your own brand portfolio planning approach:

1. Do you plan your portfolio in a systematic way?

2. Is your brand portfolio in a healthy shape? Or is it too long or too short? Is it too deep or broad? Or too short, shallow or narrow?

3. Can you relate your financial performance to the shape of your portfolio?

4. Have range-filling, stretching and extension had the profitable results that you expected?

5. How many of your products are really new, and how many are merely technical upgrades of existing ones?

6. Do you copy competitors' new products too much, too reactively? Do you analyze the financial consequences of copying what your competitors do?

7. Are you doing enough to cut back the bad performers in your brand/product portfolio?

8. Do you know how much cannibalization has eaten into your results?

9. Are you using testing effectively to screen portfolio decisions?

10. Is there a tracking programme to learn from past portfolio decisions?

Portfolio language and terminology

You or your firm will periodically need to make product and brand portfolio decisions and answer a number of associated branding questions, some of which are summarized in Table 10.1. This two-by-three matrix has product decisions along one axis and brand decisions along the other.

Product decisions fall into three main groups: totally new categories of product; extending the product beyond its current range; or adding new variants within the existing range. Brand decisions entail a choice between launching a new brand or using an existing one.

Table 10.1
Types of product branding decisions

	New category	Extended range	Current range
New brand	Brand Proliferation Diversification (e.g. the AA; One.Tel)	Brand Proliferation Category Filling – Positioning (e.g. First Direct)	(e.g. Utterly Butterly)
Current brand	Brand Extension	◄——— Line Extensions ———► Brand Stretching (e.g. Ariel Liquid)	Brand Gap Filling (e.g. new pack sizes)

Understanding the terminology of these decisions, and the rationale behind them, is a useful starting point in any analysis (see Boxes 10.1 and 10.2). There are two main perspectives: product and brand.

Product terminology

The *product mix* is the set of all product items that you offer. Product mix can be quantified in terms of *breadth, depth, length* and *consistency*. For example, in Table 10.2, Dairy Crest has a breadth of three product categories. The depth of the product mix is the total number of brands in its mix – 13 (excluding own-label and unbranded). The resulting average depth per category is 4.33.

Table 10.2
Dairy Crest product mix dimensions – breadth and depth

←	Breadth	→
Spreads	**Cheeses**	**Liquid products**
Country Life	Cathedral City	Frijj
Clover	Davidstow	
Willow	Wilson's	
Utterly Butterly	Wexford	
St Ivel Gold	*specialty blue cheeses*	
Vitalite		
Golden Churn		
Special Soft		

(Depth axis runs down the left side)

Data from Dairy Crest Website, 2004

The *length* of product mix refers to how many SKUs there are for each brand/product-line. *Consistency* of product mix refers to how closely related the products are in terms of end-use, production, distribution, etc.

> **Box 10.1** Product terminology
>
> **Category:** A manageable group of products that consumers perceive to be interrelated and/or substitutable in meeting needs satisfied by the category. Taking the consumer perspective tends to introduce alternatives and ambiguity. For example, Muller Vitality Probiotic can be categorized as yoghurt, a drink or a health food.
>
> **Item or SKU (stock-keeping unit):** A distinct purchasable item that is distinguishable by attributes such as size, shape, colour, flavour, price or promotion. Each item has a unique design and may carry bar codes to

➤ distinguish it from other items. For example: Utterly Butterly 500g; Ford Mondeo ST220; HSBC Bank Gold Credit Card.

Need family: The core need that underlies the product family. Alternative categorizations are possible and should be considered. For example, travel (e.g. walking), transport (e.g. buses and rail), owning a means of transport (cars and bicycles).

Product family: A grouping of product items that can satisfy a core need with more or less effectiveness. For example, grocery products and banking services are product families.

Product line: A subgrouping of the product family, of products that function in a similar manner. For example, spreads (butter and margarine) and credit cards. This approach to products tends to focus on tangible features and functions.

Styles: A subgrouping of items that is not registered in the product codes. Particularly important for mass-customized products such as automobiles. There may be many style features, for example within the Ford Mondeo ST220: body style (4-door saloons, 5-door hatchback and estate cars), engine size, colour, trim, optional extras (e.g. sunroof).

Brand terminology

Brand proliferation helps large firms dominate their product categories and enter new ones. It can occur in two ways:

1. **Within existing categories**: First Direct, for example, extended the range of Midland Bank (later to become HSBC) into telephone banking. Dairy Crest's acquisition of the St Ivel Spreads range, including Utterly Butterly, enabled it to cover a larger proportion of the spreads market.

2. **Diversifying into a new product category**: For example, when Centrica, a UK gas company, acquired the AA, a roadside rescue business, it was acquiring both a new brand and a new category of business. It also launched One.Tel, a telephone business under a different and new brand, and a credit card, Goldfish. The AA business has subsequently been sold. In general, there are relatively few successful examples of diversification.

Brand extensions concern the breadth decision. It gives an existing brand name to a product in a new category. This is a risky strategy and many of the failures such as the Bic perfume mistake mentioned above, and others such as Coors Spring Water, Cosmopolitan Yoghurt, Frito Lay Lemonade, Harley-Davidson Perfume, Heinz Cleaning Vinegar and Ponds Toothpaste are brand extension failures.

Line extension means lengthening the product mix by adding new items. Companies wanting high market share tend to carry longer lines. A company can extend its line in two ways (see Figure 10.1):

- *Stretching* occurs when the length of the product line goes beyond its current range (for example, when Ariel stretched from powdered detergent to liquid and to tablets).

- *Filling* occurs when items are added within the existing range (e.g. new pack sizes).

Figure 10.1
Branded product families

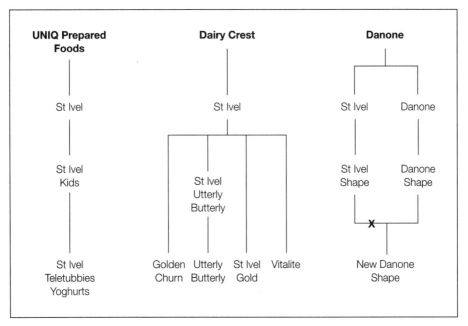

Box 10.2 Brand terminology

Branded product family: such as St Ivel, where there are common themes linking the products (see Figure 10.1). St Ivel sub-brands include: St Ivel Kids (flavoured yoghurt drinks), Utterly Butterly, Golden Churn, St Ivel Gold and Vitalite (spreads) and Shape (yoghurt in pots). The St Ivel sub-brands in spreads were sold to Dairy Crest in 2002 and Danone acquired Shape in 2002. Danone decide to drop the St Ivel brand connection with Shape, and it was rebranded as Danone Shape.

Companion products or range products: A grouping of product items that are perceived by consumers as having some similarities. For example, banking services (Abbey, HSBC – current account, credit card, savings, mortgages, loans, home insurance, motor insurance, life insurance), automobile services (the AA – roadside rescue, motor insurance).

Corporate brands: The company name and logo, for example Dairy Crest, Danone and Uniq.

Individual branded products: such as Cornetto or Magnum ice cream, where flavour variants are allowed, or Utterly Butterly buttermilk-based spread, where pack size variants occur.

Product line brands: such as fabric detergents Bold, Daz, Ecover, Fairy, Persil, where liquid, powder and tablet forms are available as well as different pack sizes and biological/non-biological and colour varieties.

Range brand: such as British Gas, which offers a group of companion products connected to the theme of 'the house': gas, electricity, home phone and mobile, broadband Internet, maintenance and breakdown care, home appliances, central heating systems, loans, fires and fireplaces, home security, home improvement, home insurance.

Analyzing the effects of your portfolio decisions

We commented earlier that brand portfolio decisions are often taken without adequate analysis. This is because the decision maker needs to learn how to do several different kinds of analysis, depending on the nature of the decision. Only a few managers learn the necessary skills. These key decision analyses are:

- Financial cost-efficiency;

- Brand proliferation and consumer 'mindspace' segmentation;

- Brand consolidation;

- Brand extension;

- Trade 'shelf space' segmentation;

- International decisions.

Financial cost-efficiency

'Big brands provide economies of scale' is an argument that financial managers are likely to raise in connection with brand extensions and line extensions. Note that these cost-efficiency arguments do not apply in the case of brand proliferation strategies.

Economies of scale have been observed for at least one hundred years and assumptions about scale economies clearly should be built into any models. The three dominant effects are:

- The dilution of fixed costs and overheads;

- Achieving high capacity utilization;

- Advertising efficiency effects.

Capacity utilization is widely understood in the case of capital equipment capacity. Advertising capacity utilization is a less well known but equally important effect. There is often a threshold below which advertising is no longer useful. For advertising to support brands, the larger the brand, the more efficient the advertising payback is likely to be.

The alternative approach – brand proliferation and extensions – can enliven a business's annual report, but the action seldom lives up to the talk. For example, a statement in an annual report that '25% of our sales volume this year has come from new products developed in the past five years' may disguise a breakdown of 'new' product innovation that looks like Figure 10.2.

New brands and products, line extensions and even product improvements are often confused by companies wishing to appear radically innovative. The reality is that real growth in GDP is only a few per cent per annum in most western economies, and corporate growth is seldom much higher. The conjuring trick for those wanting to appear radically innovative is to hide the withdrawal of old products (15% of volume in this example) and cannibalization of old volume by line extensions, flanker brands and new brand names (7% in this example). The key to correct definition of innovation is consumer perception, rather than degree of technical change.

Figure 10.2
Illustrative analysis of true effects of portfolio decisions

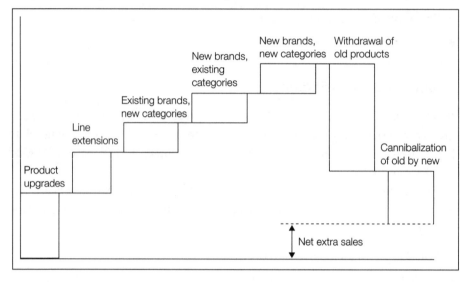

Brand proliferation and consumer 'mindspace' segmentation

Segmentation of consumer mindspace is often held up as an important guiding principle behind brand proliferation as well as extensions. Over a long term, brands will build up a web of associations, images, evaluations and buying habits, which is sometimes called 'mindspace' or brand equity. This takes a long time to build, and it is a competitive asset in the sense that more mindspace for you means less mindspace for competitors.

For example, Nestlé holds over half of the UK's £500 million instant coffee market by having proliferated a portfolio of product brands that cover all the main segments (Table 10.3).

A segmentation scheme divides the buyers in the market into groups with common needs – both rational and emotional needs. Brand management is sometimes defined as finding appealing and legally acceptable ways to discriminate between customers with different needs.

Brand proliferation and line extensions have one major drawback, however, and that is *cannibalization*. This term refers to the internal competition between own-brands and line extensions within a category – new brands 'eating' old ones. Adding new brands and lines to the same category inevitably takes away sales from existing brands and lines – some of which are your own. The economics of proliferation and extension are therefore critically dependent on the size of this cannibalization effect.

Table 10.3
Nestlé brands in the UK coffee market

Consumer segments	Brands
Low price, old-fashioned, spray-dried powder	Fine Blend
Mainstream, spray-dried granules	Nescafé
Decaffeinated, mainstream, spray-dried granules	Nescafé Decaffeinated
Premium freeze-dried	Gold Blend
	Blend 37
Decaffeinated, premium freeze-dried	Gold Blend Decaffeinated
	Blend 37 Decaffeinated
Super premium freeze-dried arabica	Alta Rica
	Cap Colombie
Decaffeinated, super premium freeze-dried arabica	Alta Rica Decaffeinated
	Cap Colombie Decaffeinated

Case study 10.2

Segmentation of detergents market

Liquid detergents provide a revealing example of evidence of consumer behaviour towards innovation. These liquid detergents were developed by scientists as an alternative to the traditional powdered ones, such as Persil and Surf (from Unilever) and Ariel, Bold, Fairy and Daz (from Procter & Gamble). Technically, the new products were revolutionary, with seven years' of R&D to develop a fatty acid with water-softening capabilities equivalent to a phosphate, and new 'builders' to prevent redisposition of dirt in the wash. But the key question is: How did consumers perceive the innovation?

First to market was Unilever, and it faced the question of differentiation: Given the technically different basis of liquid detergents, how different would consumers perceive it to be? Tom Peters, Gary Hamel and Michael Porter all seem to favour differentiation: it avoids consumer confusion and cannibalization, according to them. They also favour being visionary and first to market. So Unilever was first to market, and with a radically different identity.

The new Unilever brand was named Wisk. Its growth from launch in the final quarter of 1985 was slower than is typical for line extensions, but after a year it had achieved a share of 10% (for line extensions it often takes only three to six months to reach peak share). Growth was achieved by stealing share from existing products, including Persil and Surf. It cannibalized 4% from Persil's 33% share, but also stole share from Ariel (3% from 19% share), and all brands lost share to the new entrant in direct proportion to their size before the launch. At first this seemed to vindicate the decision to differentiate under a new identity.

Procter & Gamble responded in the first quarter of 1987, but quite differently from Unilever. The differentiation was minimized in this case and the product was launched as Ariel Liquid, a line extension. Within one quarter Ariel Liquid climbed to share levels that it took Wisk a year to achieve. And contrary to the theories of the consultant gurus, Ariel Liquid did not cannibalize the parent brand more than other brands. It cannibalized 2% from Ariel Powder's 16% share, but also stole 5% from Persil and 2% from Wisk. Again the losses in share were in direct proportion to brand sizes before the launch.

Unilever responded to the success of Ariel Liquid rather belatedly in the third quarter of 1988, by which time the share of Persil had deteriorated from 33% (just prior to the launch of Wisk) to 24%. It launched Persil Liquid. By mid 1989, Persil Liquid had 6% share and Persil Powder 23%, Wisk had decayed to 5%, and Ariel Liquid and Powder had 9% and 11% respectively. The more strongly differentiated product, Wisk, ended up in the weakest position.

This case suggests that strong differentiation can be less effective than hiding behind an existing identity, even when the new product is technically quite different, contrasting with the widespread view that stronger concepts favour a new brand name and strong differentiation. It is particularly valuable to note the differing fortunes of Wisk and Persil Liquid in the UK, since they are actually the same product.

The key determinant is whether consumers see the differentiation. Despite all the technical innovation, most consumers saw the liquid as an example of the detergent category, not as a new category, and there were no barriers to consumers switching from powder to liquid or back again. The key to success was for a large enough number of consumers to see the liquid detergent as relevant to them as a detergent.

This is not an isolated case. Hundreds of studies suggest that radical innovations are only occasionally adopted by creatures of habit, even when the innovations have real benefits. Internal problems, such as lack of organizational commitment, can exacerbate the market issues. But the real challenge is to get the 'ugly duckling' out into the waters, see whether real customers will part with real money, and have the measurement systems needed to monitor results early, and evaluate fast whether you have a winner or loser.

Brand consolidation

Brand extension, stretching and consolidation are three associated strategies that have come to challenge the conventional wisdom of proliferation as a strategy. The main thrust of the argument is that 'big brands have a disproportionate share of consumers' mindspace'.

Companies such as Procter & Gamble, Colgate-Palmolive and Unilever have shown that consolidating overlapping brands can cut costs, increase market share and boost shareholder value. As long as a brand 'fits' the needs of consumers, then there is no compelling reason to go to the added expense of proliferation.

Successful consolidation might take two brands, each possessing 10% share and turn them into a brand with 22% share (because the marketing expenditure is more focused, effectively doubling the level of brand support, and the positioning of the two brands A and B does not overlap significantly) as illustrated in Table 10.4. The cost of goods is reduced because of greater buying power, and duplicated overheads are stripped out. Profits more than double.

Table 10.4
Realizing value through brand consolidation

| | Initial P&L | | New P&L |
	Brand A	Brand B	New Brand
Market share %	10	10	22
Cost of goods sold % revenue	60	60	55
Gross margin %	40	40	45
Advertising and promotion % revenue	25	25	25
Overheads % revenue	10	10	7
Profit (EBITDA) % revenue	5	5	13

Brand extension and leveraging

Extension and leveraging means using the initial brand to move into other opportunities. Ivory soap, for example, has used its base – soap bars – to move into liquid hand soaps, body washes, dishwashing liquids and washing powders. These use the brand's core characteristics as a basis for extension.

Virgin, by contrast, appears to have leveraged its brand in quite unrelated ways into airlines, financial services and cola drinks. The unifying factor that connects these ventures is that of fun, value and rebellion.

McKinsey & Co. has published a study of leveraging the Ralph Lauren brand (Court *et al.* 1999). Consumers were asked how receptive they were to extending the brand: would it be appropriate for this brand to offer a product or service in a particular area; and would respondents expect the brand to perform better, the same or worse than currently available brands?

Consumers believed that within the men's clothing market it would be appropriate for Ralph Lauren to increase its presence in accessories (78%), casual clothing (73%) and business clothing (71%). But they thought leverage would be less appropriate in the women's clothing sector and still less in children's clothing, travel and linens.

The study shows that taking home furnishings as an example, although 60% thought the Ralph Lauren brand to be appropriate in this sector, only 22% thought it would compete effectively against existing home furnishing brands.

Within its category, 39% of respondents thought that it would compete effectively in accessories. As it moved away from its core area, the analysis showed that competitiveness fell rapidly outside the core category.

Two dimensions that can help in these kinds of assessment are 'roles' and 'umbrellaness' (Corstjens and Corstjens 1995), as illustrated in Figure 10.3.

Figure 10.3
Branding solutions for retail brands

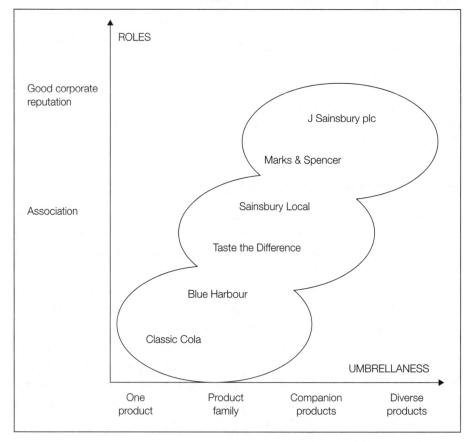

For example, Sainsbury plc and Marks & Spencer are umbrella brands, covering diverse products. To consumers they offer a badge of quality, associated with a good corporate reputation. Sainsbury Local is a convenience store format, with less variety than the full store. Corporate advertising and PR are now widely used and have an umbrella effect that stretches across all products sold in stores.

Taste the Difference is a product branding used by Sainsbury that denotes higher-quality ingredients for a wide range of Sainsbury's own foods. It is occasionally featured in advertising and PR. It is a smaller umbrella than the corporate brand which represents a set of diverse products, grouped around the high-quality theme. Be Good to Yourself is another similar grouping from Sainsbury.

Blue Harbour is a range of men's casual clothing created by Marks & Spencer for sale in its own stores. It responds to the growing recognition that the older St Michael brand is no longer 'cool' and some consumers are embarrassed to wear clothing bearing the Marks & Spencer label. It covers a specific type of men's apparel. A hypothetical stretching decision for the company might be whether it can stretch to women's casual wear.

Finally, Classic Cola is a cola brand created by Sainsbury for use in its own stores; at time of launch it was so successful that Coca-Cola threatened legal action. The potential for stretching is limited. It is easily identifiable on the shelf by its distinctive packaging.

Trade 'shelf-space' segmentation

Segmentation of channel space, also called 'shelf space', is another key factor to be analyzed in assessing brand structure. In many channels, such as financial service intermediaries, channel space is a scarce resource, but does not consist of physical shelving; however, we will use 'shelf space' as a convenient shorthand.

Physical shelf space

In physical channels, shelf space has many important aspects:

- Eye-level displays, hand level, foot level;
- Number of facings;
- Depth of inventory;
- Position compared to traffic flow;
- Special displays;
- Features;
- Special labelling.

Manufacturers develop their brand and product portfolios to maximize the potential of their shelf-space allocation. *Category management* concerns the shelf-space decision. It is, ideally, the organization of brand identities and images within a category to maximize the shelf space for the category, together with the selection of product items within each brand. For example, in the spreads category, Dairy Crest has Country Life, Clover, Willow, Utterly Butterly, St Ivel Gold, Vitalite, Golden Churn and Special Soft. Dairy Crest category managers face important structural issues about the number and position of their brands and the product variants for which channels will provide shelf space.

Sophisticated category managers deploy brands to block competitors and stop them gaining strength. For example, Smirnoff's owner in the 1970s, IDV, faced a threat from Vladivar vodka from Warrington, Cheshire. 'IDV introduced Popov to match the Vladivar positioning and thereby reduce its differentiation. The price was the same, regionalization was also in the north-west and the most crackpot PR agency was hired to out-zany Vladivar' (Ambler 1996).

Channel owners employ research firms, such as ACNielsen, to analyze consumers' categorization of shelf space, and these analyses are being used to an increasing degree to determine shelf-space decisions.

Psychological shelf space

Where shelf space is not physical, as in PC components sales, automobile servicing, financial services and pharmaceutical sales, there are psychological aspects of how a product is presented to the end consumer. Depending on the regulatory situation, these may include:

- Share of display space (e.g. Dell web pages; bank branch display space);
- Recommended brand (e.g. auto servicing choice of lubricant);
- Sales script priority (e.g. pharmaceutical selling).

International decisions

Global markets and international brands have been an important issue from the time Ted Levitt published 'The Globalisation of Markets' in 1983. His argument was that people around the world were more alike than different. The world was becoming a global village. Marketers would make more money by concentrating on the similarities and forgetting the differences.

Multinational brands offer the same branded products in multiple countries around the world. For example, Dove soap is sold in 80 countries globally. Although these are widely cited in textbooks, they are comparatively rare as success stories (see Figure 10.4).

Figure 10.4

Extent of overlap of the top 100 FMCG brands in Europe, USA and Japan

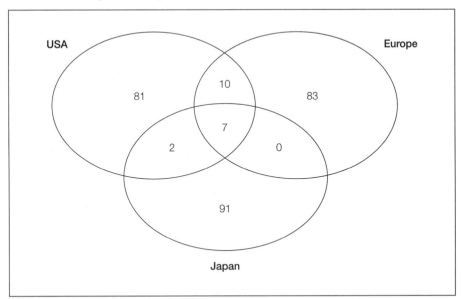

In the triple overlap are Coca-Cola, McDonald's, Kleenex, Nestlé, Sony, Panasonic and KFC. The two common to the USA and Japan but not Europe are Lipton tea and Band Aid. Even true Euro brands are rare – few major brands are major in more than three European countries.

Brand portfolio decisions are risky and pitfalls abound. You must therefore evaluate them carefully through strategy research, testing, and tracking.

Researching your brand portfolio strategy

Strategy research is concerned with long-term shifts in consumption, channels of distribution and competition. In particular, strategy studies provide a framework for evaluating the potential rewards and risks of structural decisions.

Empirical generalizations

Studies of past launch decisions have sought to determine whether any discernible patterns exist. Failure levels reported seem to vary considerably (Table 10.5).

Table 10.5
Assessments of portfolio decision failure rates

High-risk assessments	Low-risk assessments
US Dept of Commerce: over 90% failure	The Conference Board: 20–40% failed
Angelus: over 80% failure	Booz Allen Hamilton: 30–40% failed
Dodd: over 80% failure	UK Govt: 40% failed
Rosen: over 80% failure	Helene Curtis: 43% failed

Data from Crawford (1977)

Booz Allen and Hamilton (1982) were among the first to explain these large differences and provide a framework for assessing new markets and products. They surveyed 700 companies and found that some types of new product were much less risky than others. They identified six categories of new products, in terms of their newness to the marketplace and to the company, in order of increasing risk:

- Cost reductions (11% of new products);

- Repositionings (7%), e.g. Nescafé Beverage Sachets (for office dispensers); Hewlett-Packard Laserjet 5L (for home users);

- Revisions to existing products (26%), e.g. New Persil, Hewlett-Packard Laserjet 6P (replacing the 5P);

- Additions to existing product lines (26%), e.g. Chum Turkey, Hewlett-Packard Laserjet Remote Control;

- New product lines (20%), e.g. Mars Ice Cream, Hewlett-Packard Support Pack;

- New to the world products (10%) e.g. Quorm, the Network Computer.

ACNielsen has developed a tool called BASES which accumulates data on product tests and launches since 1977. It has data on 43,000 tests and 10,000 launches in 60 countries (see Figure 10.5).

Brand/category audits

Marketing audits look at long-term trends in the structure of the categories in which you currently participate. Where brand extensions and diversification are being considered, they must also include potential categories.

When carrying out a structural audit, focusing on three key competitors is a useful discipline. Selecting the appropriate basis for comparison is important.

You should take on the market leaders, provided you are strong enough. Structure is related to strength, and vice versa. Unless you are strong enough to take on the brand leaders, it is better to find a niche to build on the brand's strength, rather than attacking competition on every front.

Where you are present in several product categories, then you will need to undertake an analysis for each of your categories. In situations where a large number of categories is involved, it is sensible to restrict the audit to between seven and ten categories which are most important to you strategically (see Table 10.6).

Figure 10.5
Coverage of BASES data analysis

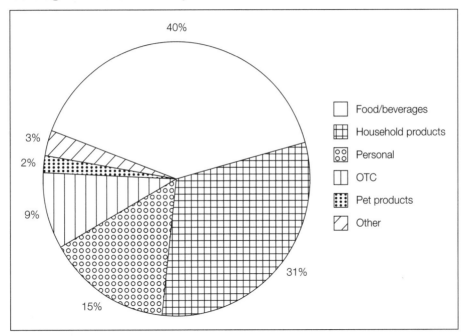

Channel/distribution audits

Many markets depend on distribution channels and intermediaries to sell the product or service to customers. Auditing and mapping the distribution channels that link end consumers to the category of product they buy is another important analysis. Usually it is necessary to audit the top five trade customers or, when the channel is fragmented, the top five trade segments (see Table 10.7).

Table 10.6
What to look for in brand/category audits

What to look for	Example
Category depth – number of your brands in each category	Scottish Courage had over 100 ale brands in the beer category
Category tail – number of your brands that individually has under 1% share of category	Scottish Courage also had over 100 ale brands with under 1% share of beer volume
Brand mix – breadth	All Scottish Courage brands were product brands. None spanned ale and lager
Product line length	Kronenbourg in the UK had fewer lines than its nearest competitor, Stella Artois
Consolidation of the market	Six UK beer brands have doubled their share over the past decade
Premium segmentation	Premium lagers in large bottles have emerged as a distinct segment, mainly for on-trade sales, e.g. Asahi, Cobra, Hoegaarden – typically priced at £3.00 to £4.50/litre
Low-price segmentation	Skol and Tennents lager typically priced at £1.20/litre (cheaper than alcohol-free brands)
Niche brand emergence and growth	Hoegaarden in specialist continental lagers
Category diversity growth – number of lines that are routinely available as mainstream products	Beers show less diversity than other categories, except in the minor niche ales and lagers. e.g. Shampoos and conditioners for normal, dry, greasy, fine, volumizing, curls, frizz, smoothing, dandruff, natural, protecting, revitalizing, hydrating, greasy roots/dry ends, etc.
Pack size diversity growth	Stella Artois in 4x440ml cans; 12x440ml cans; 24x440ml cans; 4x568ml cans; 10x25cl bottles; 20x25cl bottles; 6x330cl bottles; 24x330cl bottles; 66cl bottle; 1 litre bottle; 5 litre barrel
Downward line stretching	Carlsberg Special Brew in multipack cans (£2.64/litre at Tesco on 8 March 2004). Still not stretched to the low-price level of £1.20/litre
Upward line stretching	Carlsberg Special Brew has extended into the premium large bottle segment (£4.62 per litre at Tesco on 8 March 2004)
Share of category – for each segment, variety, style, etc.	Higher or lower than average shares should be reviewed to assess whether they are explained by structural issues (e.g. gaps in the range)

**Table 10.6
(continued)**

What to look for	Example
Own profitability figures	These help us decide whether the trade-off between volume and profit is worthwhile
Competitive intelligence on profitability	Where available, these help us decide whether the trade-off between volume and profit is worthwhile

**Table 10.7
What to look for in channel/distribution audits**

What to look for	Example
What changes have occurred in the number of outlets and the structure of them?	Consolidation of channels, with smaller, low-volume outlets closing
What changes have occurred in the ownership of the channels and what has been the effect on suppliers?	Active buying and selling of large blocks of on-trade channel capacity to 'chains'. Sophistication of channel management has greatly increased. Many more on-trade chains exist than in food retail sector
How much channel penetration do we have? What is the significance of that?	Budweiser has 80% distribution in the on-trade, whereas Stella Artois has only 40% distribution, even though Stella has the highest market share. Therefore Bud sells less per outlet
Is our penetration deeper in some types of outlet than others?	Stella Artois tends to have better distribution in the high-volume outlets, and is not well represented in the sticky-carpet, low-volume end of the market
How much display space is given to each brand? Is its prominence in proportion to its market share?	Guinness gained extra space at the bar by introducing Guinness Extra Cold, requiring a separate font and display
Do specialist channels exist that tend to carry a different range of brands?	Hoegaarden beer is sold predominantly in up-market bars
Growth and decline of specialist channels	Up-market bars have gone through cycles of growth and decline during the past 50 years
Share of added-value: have suppliers or channel owners gained more from profit growth during the decade?	On-trade has gained all of the profit growth over the past 10 years and brewers have not grown their profits significantly in real terms. Most of the growth has come from price rises to consumers

Channel qualitative research

Qualitative channel research consists of depth interviews to develop an understanding of the way trade customers decide on the range of brands and product lines to stock and display. An audit guide is shown in Table 10.8.

Figure 10.6
Brand and channel profitability curves

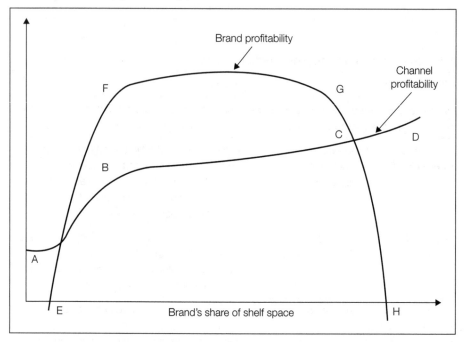

Figure 10.6 illustrates how profitability of the brand and the channel change as the brand gains share of shelf space. The channel is generally less profitable (in percentage margin terms) than the brand. However, at low shelf space (A) the retailer can extract sufficient 'listing allowances' that it has positive profitability, even though the brand is making a loss for its suppliers (E).

As the shelf space is increased, so the product sales grow, and profits rise for the brand owner and the channel. At point (B) the profit growth gradient for the channel flattens, as it does for the brand (F). Between points (B) and (C) for the brand owner and (F) and (G) for the channel, they negotiate prices. Eventually, a point (C) will be reached where the channel is unwilling to give the brand any further exclusivity, unless it is paid an extra allowance. If shelf space increases above this point, the brand owner's profits would decrease sharply, whereas the retailer continues to increase its profits, up to the point (D).

Table 10.8
What to look for in channel qualitative research

What to look for	Example
What factors do trade customers use to categorize brands?	Factors that are commonly important are: volume traffic (e.g. top 6 beers); profitability (e.g. Hoegaarden); essential brands (e.g. Guinness); variety-seeker brands (e.g. minor specialty ales)
What criteria are used to decide which brands, product lines and SKUs to select?	Category management is an important discipline in retailing and channel management. It is important to gain an understanding of how it operates
Why do channels distribute some brands and items more than others?	Turnover and profit are common reasons. Stella Artois gains a large share of supermarket beer display because of the strength of the brand. Displays change rapidly as deals change
Does my brand portfolio have enough clout with the channel to gain serious attention?	Minor beer brewers have steadily been squeezed out of the distribution chain. However, some specialty brands (e.g. Hoegaarden) are given prominent display
What is the role of corporate reputation in relationships with trade customers?	Top suppliers may gain an exclusive relationship as 'category captain', advising the trade on the category

Consumer qualitative research

Qualitative consumer research consists of focus groups and depth interviews to develop an understanding of the role of all the brands, product types, packs and varieties in consumers' lives. It can also involve observational studies of consumers choosing the products; Table 10.9 provides an audit guide.

Consumer quantitative research

Quantitative strategic research involves asking a sample of respondents a series of predetermined questions about the brand portfolio and product mix. Perceptual and preference mapping are the two main results of these studies.

A brand leader in the frozen foods market carried out a perceptual mapping study of the mid-week mealtime selection (see Figure 10.7).

Each product was rated for different factors, such as natural, satisfying the appetite, etc. and a perceptual map was plotted. Most frozen fish proved positive on the natural scale, but was poorly rated on satisfying appetite. The exception was fish and chips – presumably due to the presence of chips. At the time, this combination was not offered, and as a result of identifying the gap, a product was launched.

Table 10.9
What to look for in consumer qualitative research

What to look for	Example
How aware are consumers of the choice of brands and product lines available in the category?	Awareness will vary considerably, with some consumers only aware of a small range of brands and product lines, others with wide knowledge
Are consumers segmented in their approach to the range of brands?	Variety seekers are an important group in some markets, and understanding what drives them can help assess the product mix. For example, repertoire drinking is normal in beer, and understanding the nature of people's repertoire is important
Who buys the product, as opposed to who consumes it?	On-trade buying of beer happens in rounds, and this separates buying and consumption. Status can be an important factor in selection of drinks in a public arena
How much pre-planning of purchasing occurs and how much is impulse buying?	Beer is often an impulse purchase in the off-trade. Choosing a bar is often an impulse decision, although most drinkers have a repertoire of bars
How willing are consumers to accept an alternative to their favourite brand?	Some brands (e.g. Guinness) have such a loyal following that their consumers will switch to another outlet if it is not offered
Are some items habitual impulse purchases?	Some consumers will habitually buy certain items if on promotion (e.g. beer bargains)
What are people's attitudes to various pack sizes and other product variants?	Premium packaged lagers became 'cool' some years ago, and consumers were willing to pay almost double the price of draught lager

Figure 10.7
Perceptual map of fish-based foods

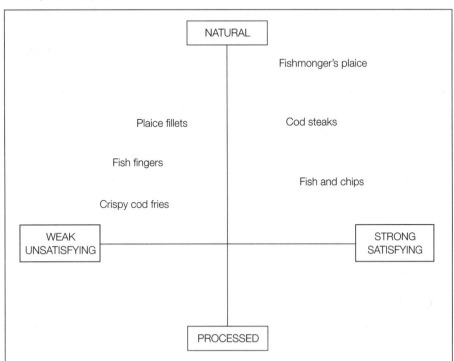

Summarizing the strategic research

Data overload is one of the consequences of strategic research and it can be challenging to pull insights out of the data. Several summary chart formats should be considered to summarize the data.

The first of these is shown in Figure 10.8. This new matrix provides a map of the markets in which you participate, or plan to participate, in terms of how fragmented they are and how easy/difficult they are to enter:

■ In the top-right quadrant are consolidated markets with high entry barriers. Entry through organic growth may not be an option, and acquisition may be the best strategy (this is how IBM grew its share of the global services market).

■ In the bottom-right quadrant, where entry barriers are lower and participants are consolidated, the best strategy may be to launch new products. Kettle

Crisps adopted this strategy, taking on the giant snack manufacturers, in what had previously been a highly consolidated market.

■ In the top-left quadrant, where the entry barriers are high but the market is fragmented, the best strategy may be to acquire and consolidate under a strong brand. This is how SAP and Siebel have grown, moving the ERP and CRM markets from fragmented to consolidated.

■ In the bottom-left quadrant, there is a low barrier to entry and the market is fragmented. To survive you have to be cost-competitive, otherwise it may be best to exit this quadrant.

Figure 10.8
Matrix summary of strategic research – market assessment

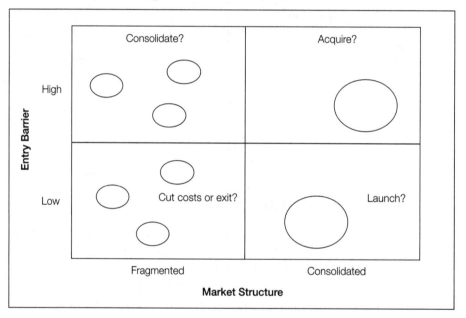

Figure 10.9 is another summary chart that is useful for communicating the risks of brand development projects. The risks increase as one moves from the bottom left to the top right of the chart. Bubbles represent the estimated profits of the projects. The chart shows that there are some high-reward, low-risk projects in gap-filling. By contrast, there are brand extension projects that also have high projected profits, but the risks attached to them are greater since they involve moving into riskier markets that are also new to the company. Table 10.10 gives an example of the underlying analysis.

Figure 10.9
Risk–reward chart for brand development projects

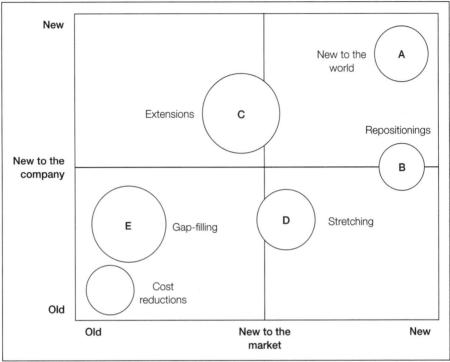

Table 10.10
New market portfolio assessment

	A Totally new brand	B Totally new reposition	C Extensions	D Stretching	E Gap-fill
Market size (next year)	–	–	Medium	Small	Medium
Market size (3 years)	Large	Medium	Large	Medium	Large
ROS (mean scenario)	20%	10%	11%	12%	15%
ROI (mean scenario)	50%	25%	28%	30%	35%
Chance of success	40%	90%	50%	90%	70%
Likely timescale	4 years	1 year	1 year	3 months	6 months
Initial investment	High	Medium	Medium	Low	Low
Cannibalization	None	None	Medium	High	Low

Testing your brand portfolio decisions

Structural decisions are risky, and it is therefore important to test them as much as is practically possible before making any significant financial commitments. The objectives and methods of testing depend on the type of decision.

Testing requires market investigation, but it also needs financial and operational analysis. For a more comprehensive treatment of the subject, you should consult Cooper (1993). Some of Cooper's objectives of testing are outlined in Table 10.11.

Table 10.11
Testing objectives for brand extensions

Structural decision	Market test objectives	Financial/operational test objectives
Product upgrades – revised specification	• Will consumers buy it more than the old specification? • Will trade customers support it? • Can the sales force sell it as effectively?	• Will new formulation increase or decrease profits? • What will it cost to launch? • Can our supply chain deliver it as effectively as the old product?
Elimination, consolidation and withdrawal of features	• Will the withdrawal of a feature or the elimination of products be resented by consumers? How will they respond? • Will the trade respond negatively to a withdrawal? • How will the sales force handle customer protests?	• What effect on profits will the withdrawal have? • Will overheads really be reduced by the withdrawal? • Will the supply chain benefits be realized?
Brand range gap-filling	• Will the new product cannibalize the existing one? • Will trade customers list the extra items, and what will they expect in return? • Will the sales force make the effort needed to sell the extra items?	• What is the trade-off of more revenue vs. higher costs for extra products? • Are there marketing costs associated with the launch of the extra items? • Can our supply chain deliver the extra SKUs effectively?

Table 10.11
(continued)

Structural decision	Market test objectives	Financial/operational test objectives
Brand stretching and extension	• Is our brand appropriate outside its usual range? • How competitive is our brand outside its usual range? • Will trade customers list the extra items, and what will they expect in return? • Can the sales force be stretched beyond their usual competency?	• What is the trade-off of more revenue vs. higher costs for extra products? • Are there marketing costs associated with the launch of the extra items? • Can our supply chain deliver the extra SKUs effectively?
Brand proliferation – existing categories	• How much will additional brands cannibalize our existing brands? • Will trade customers list the extra brands, and what will they expect in return? • Will the sales force have time to sell the additional brands?	• What is the trade-off of more revenue vs. higher costs for new brands? • Are there marketing costs associated with the launch of the new brands? • Can our supply chain deliver the extra SKUs effectively?
Brand proliferation – diversification	• Why do we need new brands? • How much better will new brands perform than extending existing brands? • How long will it take to grow the new brands to an effective size?	• What is the trade-off of more revenue vs. higher costs for new brands? • Are there marketing costs associated with the launch of the new brands? • Do we have the core competencies in these new categories?

Market research is needed to answer the market test questions. It is difficult to assess accurately people's likely responses. What they may, in good faith, tell an interviewer during a market research survey will be different from what they actually do in a buying situation. Test marketing has to be skilfully designed and performed for its conclusions to provide reliable guidance to decision makers.

Test marketing is now widely accepted by leading consumer product manufacturers as standard practice. There is obviously a need to reduce the substantial risks inherent in marketing new products and brands, and this can be done by some form of test marketing. A sequential approach should be followed:

1. **Define the objectives**: As with other management problems, the principal step is to get the objectives right. Reviewing Table 10.11 shows some possible objectives.

2. **Set the criteria for success**: Again, modern management demands that a yardstick for success should be defined *beforehand*.

3. **Integrate tests with operational marketing**: It is vital to ensure that the test fits in sufficiently with existing marketing activity. A detailed plan of test mechanics should be drawn up early in the process.

4. **Establish controls**: Two aspects of control are important. First, the time period must be split in three: before, during, after. Data must be collected before the test, after it, as well as during the test. Second, the market must be split into cells: some where the test is carried out, others where there is no test.

5. **Select representative areas**: The test must reflect, in miniature, the total market. A common flaw of test marketing is choosing unrepresentative test areas.

6. **Decide number of test markets**: Where there are several variables being compared, at least two cells must be tested for each alternative.

7. **Establish duration of tests**: The length of time allowed for tests depends on the buying frequency of the product. Seasonality also needs to be taken into account.

8. **Interpret the results**: The interpretation of the results is often not self-evident. In particular, they will need to be turned into a forecast.

Selecting the precise method to use requires experience. Some techniques, such as simulated test marketing, seem to be good at weeding out failures, but not as good at predicting the upside potential. The test could be undertaken via any of the following methods:

- In-home or at work by personal call by an interviewer;
- Sent by post, with a postal questionnaire;
- Sent by post, with a telephone follow-up;
- Sent by fax;
- Sent by fax with a telephone follow-up;
- Sent by email, with a web-based questionnaire;
- Sent by post, with an email follow-up;
- In a hall test, van test or test centre.

The concept test could either be *monadic* (one product) or *paired comparisons* (several alternative product options), *ranking* of options, *trade-off* (conjoint analysis), and *comparison with existing products*.

The design of questions also demands care and skill. Typically questions will cover the following aspects:

- Understanding the product idea;
- Perception of its attributes;
- Its believability (especially of the branding);
- Its perceived advantages and disadvantages;
- Its rating on specific product attributes;
- When and how it might be used;
- How often;
- What products it might replace;
- The sort of people it might appeal to.

Test marketing is a versatile tool of brand management. By using it intelligently, a wide range of information may be gathered. Like all research techniques, it does not guarantee success, but in skilled hands it can reduce failure risks considerably, while at the same time providing reliable forecasts of successes.

How DirecTV predicted market size for satellite TV

In 1992, when satellite TV was still in its infancy, DirecTV developed a forecast for the market potential. Here's how they did it . . .

1. Test research study (phone–mail–phone) to determine consumer purchase intentions. Panel was initially qualified by phone; then mailed a brochure with features and price points; then called again to determine purchase intention.

2. Adjusted the reported purchase intentions based upon years of research in correlating intentions to actual behaviour in both durable and non-durable goods categories (Figure 10.10).

Figure 10.10
Cumulative research into consumer durables

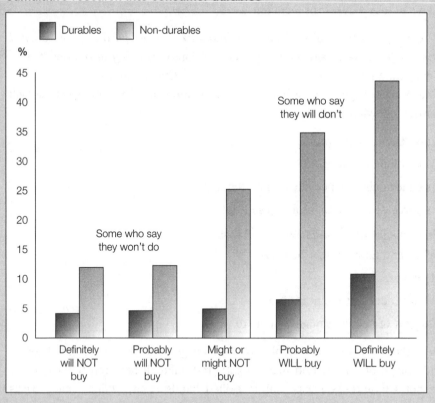

3. Used the adjusted intentions data to forecast the potential size of the market over time, making assumptions about the availability (65% US household coverage area) and affordability (price point) of the service.

4. Reviewed multiple 'benchmark' products/service diffusion curves to determine which were most likely to have had adoption patterns similar to what satellite TV might expect. Ultimately selected cable TV as the benchmark and used the innovation and imitation scores from cable TV penetration to build the satellite TV forecast.

The result was a forecast which closely (and conservatively) predicted market penetration for the next 8 years (see Figure 10.11).

Figure 10.11
Market penetration forecast for satellite TV

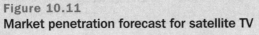
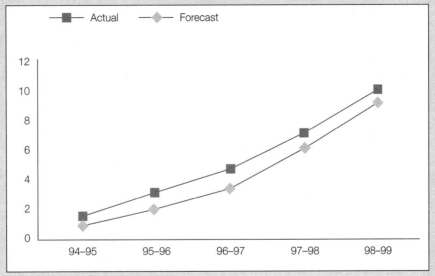

Tracking your brand portfolio

The final stage of evaluation is tracking. The purpose is to assess the accuracy of forecasts of brand structure changes. For the example in Figure 10.12, tracking reveals that product upgrades and line extensions have exceeded forecast. All other decisions are worse than forecast. In particular, extending existing brands into new categories has performed especially badly. The net result of the changes is to perform worse than forecast.

Figure 10.12
Tracking variances between actual performance and forecast

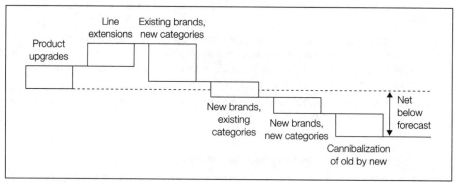

You will want to diagnose why some initiatives underperformed, and for that you will need some more detailed diagnostic tracking. A good approach for each test marketing study is to establish a tracking study that checks the validity of the test marketing results. An illustration is given in Table 10.12.

Table 10.12
Types of diagnostic tracking studies

Factor tested	Forecast	Actual
Understanding the product idea	65%	52%
Perception of its key attributes	32%	22%
Its believability (especially of the branding)	25%	12%
Its perceived advantages and disadvantages	20%	8%
Likeability rating on specific product attributes	15%	5%

For this particular example, the tracking research indicates that there are problems with the perception of the key product attributes – people simply 'don't get it'. Nor do they believe it and like it as much as the test marketing had suggested. A likely explanation of these scores is that the communications campaign has not explained the product effectively to its target audience.

Tracking structural changes is important, not only to make decisions about recent initiatives, but also to learn to make better ones in the future. It is important that the tracking is designed with the specific brand strategy in mind. All too often, off-the-shelf brand tracking does not offer good diagnostic insights.

Key points

- Brand portfolio decisions generally are taken outside of marketing – by Boards, finance, strategic planners, R&D, operations and even sales – with consequently poor success rates.

- Product mix can be measured in terms of length (number of items or SKUs), breadth (range of product categories), depth (number of brands in each category) and consistency (how closely related products are).

- The financial impact of portfolio decisions is often diluted by product withdrawals and cannibalization.

- Brand proliferation growth strategies need to be balanced against the cost-inefficiencies of servicing many small brands.

- Brand consolidation can improve cost-efficiency, but the withdrawal of the eliminated brands must be managed carefully to avoid loss of sales volume.

- Brand extension, stretching and gap filling can improve both cost-efficiency and sales volume, but the appropriateness and competitiveness of the extensions must be analyzed before taking action.

- Strategic research should be carried out periodically to assess the health of the brand portfolio and product mix, and it is important to take a long-term perspective.

- Testing should be carried out before adding or subtracting from the brand portfolio. Often testing is poorly designed, and so it is important to ensure that the testing methods used are effective.

- Tracking of structural changes to the brand portfolio needs to be designed so that it provides early warnings of potential problems.

11

VALUING BRANDS

The context for brand valuation

Corporate reputation

Company valuations

Brand valuations

Importance of brands as value drivers

How are brands valued?

Is brand valuation useful to you?

Key points

This chapter looks at brand valuations. We begin by discussing their significance in the context of company accounts and valuations and corporate reputation, and then consider how brand valuations are carried out in practice. We include some sample calculations based on different methodologies and highlight the key assumptions that have to be made in these calculations. The chapter ends with a brief discussion of the alternatives to brand valuation and a means of brand health monitoring, budget setting and brand development.

Although few companies use brand valuation techniques as a routine management tool, nevertheless, understanding how the calculations are done is helpful in understanding more about how the stockmarkets and investment analysts view your business. Many of the interim calculations, prior to valuation, are identical to those discussed in other chapters of this book, for example for forecasting marketing costs and revenues.

The context for brand valuation

One of the frustrating things about the topic of marketing value, to many managers, is just how difficult some of the ideas are to pin down (Box 11.1).

Box 11.1 Terminology used in the financial evaluation of marketing

Customer value: The perceived worth of something to a customer, expressed as a set of evaluative statements. Not necessarily connected or correlated with economic value, despite what the pundits say.

Economic value: The monetary worth of an entity, established by a valuation method.

Market capitalization: The overall value assigned to a company by a stockmarket (equal to the share price multiplied by the number of shares).

Net present value: A single value that represents the profit stream (or other financial flow), summarized using a method such as Discounted Cash Flow (DCF).

Profit: Revenues minus costs measured over a specified period. There are several accounting definitions of profit, probably the most useful for general marketing use being EBITDA or Earnings Before Interest, Tax, Depreciation and Amortization.

Profit maximization: Making brand management decisions in order to maximize profit over a specified period.

Profit stream: A series of profits over a period of time. Investment analysts often look at profit streams over three, five, ten years or more.

Share price: The price at which company shares are traded on a stockmarket.

Valuation: A method of estimating the monetary worth of an entity. Its main applications concern how companies and shares are valued.

Valuation method: The rules and calculations used in the valuation process. Different methods are available, so it is important when reviewing something's value to know the method used.

Value based marketing: A disciplined process of evaluating marketing decisions, based on robust financial valuation principles and market response analysis. The result: optimal marketing decisions, strategy and implementation.

It may seem paradoxical to many marketing people that most finance people spend little or none of their careers thinking about economic value. On the other hand, economic value is something that investment analysts, concerned with trading shares, think about a good deal. Understanding this conceptual gap is a good starting point.

Corporate reputation

The concept of assigning a value to a brand is closely associated with whether the valuations assigned by the market to companies depend in part on the good or poor corporate reputation of the company. The main determinants of company valuations will naturally be the current and expected future financial performance. But are the perceived strengths in areas such as marketing skill, financial management and the ability to recruit and retain staff also a factor, over and above their direct effect on the financials? A detailed statistical analysis reported by Finn (2004) shows that corporate reputation is a statistically significant explanatory factor in both market capitalization and credit risk ratings.

A full discussion of corporate reputation is beyond the scope of this book. However, as brand valuation and corporate reputation are clearly related (especially when the 'brand' is synonymous with the company), it is relevant to note the following important differences:

- Unlike brands, quoted companies have freely available market values and credit risk rating scores every day.

- Working at the company level avoids the approximations involved in trying to dissect a company's accounts to attribute costs and revenues across a portfolio of brands.

The assessment of the impact of corporate reputation on the market value of a company is therefore a more rigorous and statistically robust process than brand valuations although, of course, it does not provide information on the individual brands in a multi-brand company.

Before reading further on the various different methods of brand valuation, it is worth asking ten hard questions about how your company values its brands:

1. Do we know the value of our brands?

2. What methodologies can we use/have we used to assess these values?

3. Why do we/don't we show brand valuations as part of our intangible assets on the balance sheet?

4. What assumptions do we make when disaggregating the company accounts to estimate the financial performance of our brands?

5. What assumptions do we make about brand performance in the long term (beyond five years)?

6. How much of the value of our brands depends on their long-term performance (beyond five years)?

7. What discount rate or earnings multiple do we/would we use for brand valuation calculations?

8. On what is this based?

9. Do our brand valuations carry different messages from our market research metrics?

10. How do we score in terms of corporate reputation?

Company valuations

Company valuations are readily available on a day-by-day or even minute-by-minute basis for quoted companies, i.e. companies whose shares are traded on a stockmarket. However, valuation calculations are required for businesses in a number of situations, including the sale or acquisition of:

- Some or all of the shares of an unquoted company;
- Part of a company (even if the company is quoted);
- A quoted company where the buyer believes that the market valuation of the company does not reflect the company's true potential.

Valuation of companies has become highly refined over the decades. The classic text is *Valuation* by McKinsey (Copeland *et al.* 2000).

The analyses behind company valuations involve examining the financial history over many years and assessing the credibility and risks associated with financial forecasts (which may have been prepared either by company management or by consultants) – see Figure 11.1. This assessment is then used to estimate the net present value of future distributable profits. The methods and conventions used have been improved over time in light of actual experience, but these details need not concern us here.

Figure 11.1
Illustration of the factors used in valuation calculations

The practical implications of valuation calculations can be understood by looking briefly at The Walt Disney Corporation and its share price, illustrated in Figure 11.2. Although Disney is a brand, its presence in this conglomerate is diffused. The value of The Walt Disney Corporation is clearly not just 'the brand'.

Investment analysts rely upon published annual reports on the Disney business, plus interim statements and future projections. These generally aggregate the results of numerous subsidiary businesses. For the analysts, the aggregate figures must be disaggregated for them to assess the future potential, since each component business has different growth rates and profit performance.

The Disney brand operates in several different product categories – filmed entertainment, consumer products, theme parks, property, broadcasting and live entertainment. Business performance goes up and down as a result of the changing fortunes of the sectors in which Disney operates, as well as due to the 'brand performance'. For example, weather conditions have a significant effect on the performance of the theme park sector.

Figure 11.2

Historical development of the Walt Disney Corporation and its share price

Period	Consumer products	Filmed entertainment	Live entertainment	Broadcasting	Theme parks	Vacations, resorts and property
1920s	Animation; character licensing	Animated feature films				
1930s						
1940s	Music publishing	Live action films				
1950s	Book publishing	Television shows			Disneyland	
1960s						
1970s	Disney stores	Touchstone			Walt Disney World; EPCOT	Hotel property and resort development
1980s	Direct mail; Hollywood records; Hyperion books;	Home videos; Hollywood pictures		Disney channel; KCAL-TV;	Tokyo Disneyland; Disney/MGM Studios; EuroDisney;	Disney Institute vacations
1990s	Software development; ESPN stores	Miramax	Hockey; live theatre; baseball	ABC TV network;	Animal Kingdom	Planned communities; cruise liners

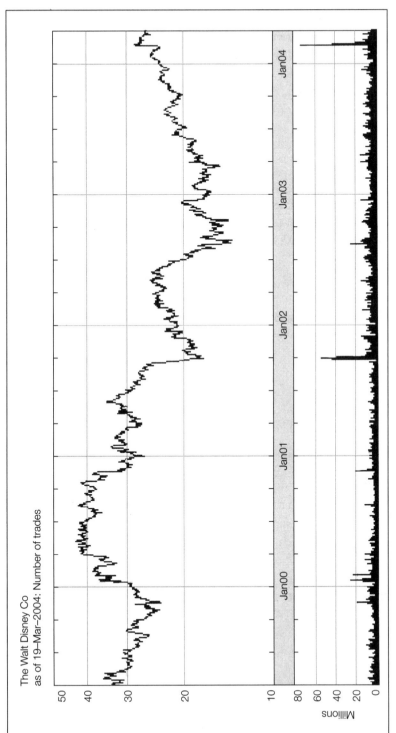

The Walt Disney Co
as of 19–Mar–2004: Number of trades

Valuing the Disney brand is therefore a matter of analyzing and valuing the individual portfolio elements, and then aggregating up to a total value figure. As a consequence, the rises and falls in Disney's value are not driven by a simple set of macroeconomic variables, but its value is driven by a complex portfolio of microeconomic factors. Although it is tempting to paint a simple picture of any brand, it would be misleading to do so, as this Disney example illustrates.

Brand valuations

Brand valuation was introduced in the 1980s, initially as a response to the vulnerability of sound but financially sleepy businesses to the attentions of acquisitive conglomerates. What would otherwise appear to be a lacklustre balance sheet could be improved significantly by making explicit recognition of the values of the brands owned by the company as intangible assets.

Valuing brands necessitates the disaggregation of the company into its component brands, and the application of valuation methods to each component brand. Brand valuation was controversial when it was introduced and remains so today.

Its advocates argue that it is perfectly natural to recognize the financial value of a company's brands on the balance sheet, given that these are durable assets that deliver real financial benefits to the business in terms of a higher price or market share than would otherwise be the case. Its critics, in equal measure, maintain that, whatever the theory, brand valuations are arbitrary, subjective and opaque, and consequently of limited use.

The final difficulty for brand valuation is that brands are sold infrequently. Businesses or business units are sold regularly, so company valuation theory can be tested against many cases. Brand valuation theory has been subjected to much less rigorous testing because there are relatively few test cases.

Importance of brands as value drivers

Before looking in detail at brand valuation, it is worth defining the minimum requirements for a 'brand' to be worthy of consideration for a brand valuation analysis (Haigh 1996). The following criteria need to be satisfied:

- The brand must be clearly identifiable.
- The title to the brand must be unambiguous.

Figure 11.3
Financial performance of branded companies

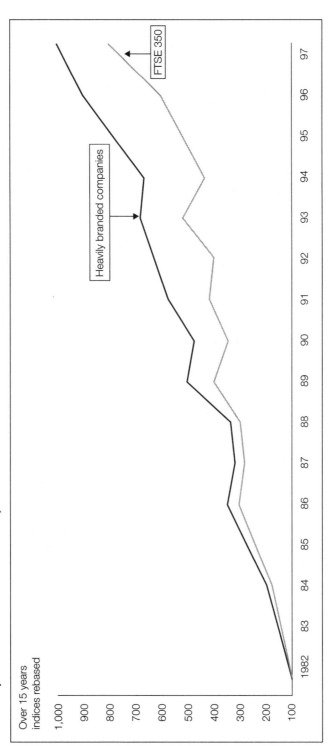

Over 15 years
indices rebased

FTSE 350

Heavily branded companies

Source: Interbrand/Citibank

- The brand must be capable of being sold separately from the business (otherwise the brand valuation becomes identical to the valuation of the business).

- There must be a premium value over the equivalent commodity product.

If these criteria are met, there seems little doubt that such brands will have a value. For example, Figure 11.3, taken from some research by Interbrand and Citibank, shows how the stockmarket performance for heavily branded companies compares with the FTSE 350 index over a 15-year period.

Although Figure 11.3 provides powerful evidence that heavily branded companies have outperformed the market, the key question is: can we attach a robust financial value to a brand?

Table 11.1 shows how *BusinessWeek* values the world's strongest brands, again using an analysis from the brand consultancy Interbrand.

Table 11.1
Interbrand/BusinessWeek's 2004 best global brands

2004 rank	2004 brand value $ million	Brand	2003 rank	2003 brand value $ million	Percentage change
1	67,394	Coca-Cola	1	70,453	−4%
2	61,372	Microsoft	2	65,174	−6%
3	53,791	IBM	3	51,767	4%
4	44,111	GE	4	42,340	4%
5	33,499	Intel	5	31,112	8%
6	27,113	Disney	7	28,036	−3%
7	25,001	McDonald's	8	24,699	1%
8	24,041	Nokia	6	29,440	−18%
9	22,673	Toyota	11	20,784	9%
10	22,128	Marlboro	9	22,183	0%
11	21,331	Mercedes	10	21,371	0%
12	20,978	Hewlett-Packard	12	19,860	6%
13	19,971	Citibank	13	18,571	8%
14	17,683	American Express	15	16,833	5%
15	16,723	Gillette	16	15,978	5%
16	15,948	Cisco	17	15,789	1%
17	15,886	BMW	19	15,106	5%
18	14,874	Honda	18	15,625	−5%
19	14,475	Ford	14	17,066	−15%
20	12,759	Sony	20	13,153	−3%

Source: *Interbrand/BusinessWeek*, 2 August 2004

Table 11.2 is another estimate of the importance of branding published by Interbrand for various markets.

Table 11.2
Relative importance of brands and other assets (%)

Market	Brand	Other intangibles	Tangibles	Total
Luxury goods	70	5	25	100
Food and drink	55	5	40	100
Financial services	30	50	20	100
Automotive	30	20	50	100
Information technology	20	50	30	100
Retail	15	15	70	100
Pharmaceuticals	10	50	40	100
Industrials	5	25	70	100
Utilities	0	30	70	100

Source: Interbrand, *www.interbrand.com*

The message of these figures is certainly not being ignored by finance directors. Figure 11.4 encapsulates where they saw the main sources of company value in a survey undertaken in 2001.

Figure 11.4
Finance directors' views on sources of market capitalization

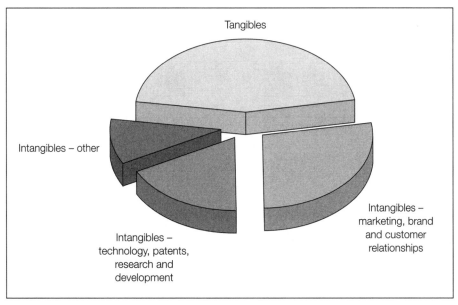

Data from Shaw and Fisk (2002)

But how do these enormous valuation figures translate into day-to-day branding expenditure decisions? The fact that other companies have high valuations for their brands does not necessarily mean that your branding expenditure will generate a lot of money for your company.

Part of the problem is that many brands operate in a diverse set of markets, and it is important to differentiate between those markets where branding is important and those where it is less important. Figure 11.5 illustrates the situation for a large bank.

An organization chart provides a useful way of illustrating the relative importance of branding in different parts of the organization. Thus for consumer banking, there is greater importance to be effectively branded, but even within the consumer division, different areas are affected differently by branding.

Figure 11.5
Importance of branding as indicated by shading intensity

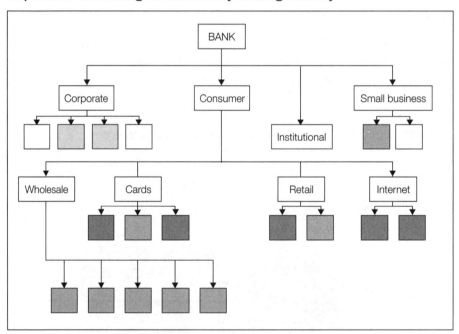

You may find it useful to develop a similar chart for your own organization. This is best done by getting several colleagues to make an assessment of the relative importance of branding. Then pool the results, checking for areas of agreement and areas of disagreement. Where there are differences of opinion, discuss them to understand the reasons behind the differences.

How are brands valued?

The major brand valuation technique in use today was pioneered by Interbrand, who have developed and refined the 'economic use' method of brand valuation. We will look at this in detail later but we first consider some of the other approaches that have been put forward over the years, together with their advantages and disadvantages (see Dresdner Kleinwort Benson & Interbrand 1997 for a fuller discussion).

Historical cost

This approach values the brand as the sum of the costs incurred in bringing the brand to its current state.

The main disadvantages are:

- The historical costs of creating a brand appear to bear little relation to the current value of the brand, based on the other approaches to brand valuation (and are often considerably lower).

- In practice, it is difficult to identify the costs involved in creating a brand and, in particular, to separate out that part of marketing expenditure responsible for brand building.

Replacement cost

This approach values the brand at the cost of creating a new but similar brand.

The main disadvantage is:

- The difficulty in estimating how much it would cost to create a new equivalent brand now. It would be a questionable assumption to base the estimate on the cost of creating the original brand as the existence of the original brand will often have changed the marketplace. However, even if this assumption were to be justifiable, then the approach suffers from the same disadvantages as the historical cost approach.

Market value

The market value of the brand is what it might be sold for in the open market, assuming a willing buyer and willing seller.

The main disadvantages are:

- There is scant information available about sales of brands.
- Even where such information is available, it is difficult to extrapolate from one brand to another.

Premium price

This approach values the brand in terms of the premium price that it commands over an unbranded or generic equivalent. A premium price can be used to calculate the additional profits earned by the brand (after allowing for any additional production or marketing costs), and these can be used in a Net Present Value (NPV) calculation to arrive at the value to the business now of the profit stream attributable to the premium price.

The main disadvantages are:

- It is not always easy to find an equivalent unbranded or generic product.
- The effect of the brand is not always or entirely reflected in a premium price. It may also be reflected in sales volumes or, equivalently, market share. Indeed, the profit-maximizing optimum for a brand will normally be to use the brand strength to gain some combination of a premium price and market share.

Royalty relief

The royalty relief approach values a brand at the NPV of the royalty payments that the business would have to pay to license the brand if it did not own the brand. In other words, the brand is valued as the amount by which ownership of the brand 'relieves' the company from the need to pay licence fees or royalties.

Where royalty data are readily available, this approach is workable. However, royalty data are generally applicable only to specific sectors and markets, and are not easily extrapolated beyond these boundaries.

Economic use method

This method of assessing brand value attempts to calculate the value of the brand to its owner in terms of the NPV of the profit stream attributable to the brand.

This is the approach of choice for brand valuation companies such as Interbrand and Brand Finance, and will be described in more detail below.

The 'economic use' method of brand valuation has been implemented in a number of ways and various proprietary techniques have been developed to estimate some of the key factors. Here we present a simplified form of the approach, broadly following the methodology of Brand Finance, as described in the excellent review by David Haigh (1996).

All 'economic use' methods start with an analysis of the profitability of the brand to the business. It should be emphasized that all of the analysis that follows is based on separating the finances of the brand of interest from other brands that may be owned by the company, and also from any unbranded products that may be produced in parallel by the company.

The economic use/historical earnings approach

The simplest 'economic use' method is the 'historical earnings' approach, the main steps of which are set out below:

- Starting with the revenue attributable to the brand, multiply by the profit margin for the brand to get the operating profit for the brand (or, equivalently, deduct from the revenue the operating costs associated with the brand).

- Estimate the capital employed by the brand, including both fixed assets and working capital. Multiply this by an appropriate capital charge to obtain the charge for capital employed by the brand.

- Subtract the charge for capital employed by the brand from the operating profit for the brand to get the earnings after capital charge.

- Not all of these earnings are attributable to the strength of the brand itself – there could well be some earnings after capital charge even if the brand were weak. Therefore multiply the earnings after capital charge by the proportion of the earnings that are attributable to the strength of the brand to obtain the brand earnings.

- Multiply the brand earnings by the tax rate to get the tax payable on the brand earnings. Then subtract the tax payable from the brand earnings to get the brand earnings after tax.

- Finally, multiply the brand earnings after tax by a factor ("the multiple") to obtain the brand valuation.

This calculation method is illustrated in Table 11.3.

Table 11.3
Calculating economic use/historical earnings

Step	Item	Calculation	Year 0
1	Revenue attributable to the brand	A	140.0
2	Gross profit margin of the brand	B	30%
3	**Operating profit for the brand**	C = A * B	42.0
4	Capital employed by the brand	D	220.0
5	Charge rate for capital	E	10%
6	Charge for capital	F = D * E	22.0
7	**Earnings after capital charge**	G = C − F	20.0
8	Proportion of earnings attributable to the brand	H	50%
9	**Brand earnings**	J = G * H	10.0
10	Tax rate	K	30%
11	Tax payable on brand earnings	L = J * K	3.0
12	**Brand earnings after tax**	M = J − L	7.0
13	Multiple	N	10.0
14	**Brand value**	P = M * N	70.0

Apart from the technical difficulties associated with disentangling from the other aspects of the business the revenues, profit margin (or operating costs), fixed assets and working capital associated with the brand, there are three factors in the table that have a critical impact on the brand valuation:

- The charge rate for capital;
- The proportion of earnings attributable to the brand;
- The multiple of brand earnings after tax used to obtain the brand value.

Although most companies will have a fairly narrow range of expectations for the charge rate for capital, the proportion of earnings attributable to the brand and the multiple used to obtain the brand valuation are, at the very least, much more difficult to estimate.

The economic use/future earnings approach

In theory, the multiple used in the 'historical earnings' approach should reflect both the growth prospects for the brand and the uncertainty attached to future earnings from the brand. Although the calculation method could be improved by calculating a weighted average of earnings over recent years, the preferred and most widely used approach for brand valuation is to estimate the brand value as the NPV of the future brand earnings after tax.

For this method of brand valuation, the procedure is as follows:

- Calculate the brand earnings after tax as per steps 1 to 12 in the table above, but do this not only for the current year (Year 0), but also for the next 5 years.

- Discount the brand earnings after tax for Years 0 to 5 back to the current year.

- Estimate the 'terminal value' of the brand (representing the NPV of after-tax brand earnings from Year 6 through to infinity). This is usually calculated by assuming no further growth beyond Year 5.

- Estimate the brand value as the discounted brand earnings after tax for Years 0 to 5 plus the terminal value.

This method of calculation is illustrated in Table 11.4.

Table 11.4
Calculating economic use/future earnings

Item	Year 0	Year 1	Year 2	Year 3	Year 4	Year 5
Revenue attributable to the brand	140.0	147.0	154.4	162.1	170.2	178.7
Revenue growth		5%	5%	5%	5%	5%
Gross profit margin of the brand	30%	30%	30%	30%	30%	30%
Operating profit for the brand	**42.0**	**44.1**	**46.3**	**48.6**	**51.1**	**53.6**
Capital employed by the brand	220.0	230.0	240.0	250.0	260.0	270.0
Charge rate for capital	10%	10%	10%	10%	10%	10%
Charge for capital	22.0	23.0	24.0	25.0	26.0	27.0
Earnings after capital charge	**20.0**	**21.1**	**22.3**	**23.6**	**25.1**	**26.6**
Proportion of earnings attributable to the brand	50%	50%	50%	50%	50%	50%
Brand earnings	**10.0**	**10.6**	**11.2**	**11.8**	**12.5**	**13.3**
Tax rate	30%	30%	30%	30%	30%	30%
Tax payable on brand earnings	3.0	3.2	3.3	3.5	3.8	4.0
Brand earnings after tax	**7.0**	**7.4**	**7.8**	**8.3**	**8.8**	**9.3**
Discount rate	15%	15%	15%	15%	15%	15%
Discount factor	1.00	1.15	1.32	1.52	1.75	2.01
Discounted cash flow	**7.0**	**6.4**	**5.9**	**5.4**	**5.0**	**4.6**
Value to Year 5	34.4					
Terminal value	30.9					
Brand value	**65.3**					

This approach has two important advantages in that it provides:

- A more rigorous methodology for taking into account the future growth of the brand, and;

■ A mechanism for taking into account the effect of brand strength on the level of risk associated with future earnings.

However, the advantages of this approach come at a cost:

■ It requires that a forecasting model for the brand be developed. The forecasting model has to include estimates for the next 5 years of revenues, margins (or costs) and total capital employed attributable to the brand.

■ It introduces another key factor that has to be estimated, namely the discount rate to be used in the NPV calculation.

■ It introduces a further arbitrary factor in the choice of a 5-year period for the forecasting model.

■ It frequently exhibits the behaviour (exemplified in the table) that the terminal value is of comparable importance to the NPV of the brand earnings after tax for the initial period of 5 years, emphasizing the importance of the assumptions made for the period more than 5 years into the future.

The general principle behind 'future earnings' systems of brand valuation is that strong brands benefit not only from a favourable combination of a premium price and a high market share, but are also more resilient in adverse market or economic conditions. This means that they have a lower risk profile and therefore that a lower discount rate should be used in calculating the present value of future earnings.

Both Interbrand and Brand Finance have developed proprietary methodologies based on ranking and rating systems to assess brand strength and to map this parameter onto the discount rate to be used in the NPV calculation.

Alternatively, a widely adopted approach is to start with the Weighted Average Cost of Capital (WACC) for the company, and to adjust this value upwards or downwards for each brand in the company's portfolio based on the relative position of the brands as measured by consumer perception metrics.

Comparison with the 'royalty relief' approach

Finally, for comparison, we carry out a brand valuation using the 'royalty relief' method of calculation referred to earlier. The calculation is illustrated in Table 11.5.

Table 11.5
Calculating 'royalty relief'

Item	Year 0	Year 1	Year 2	Year 3	Year 4	Year 5
Revenue attributable to the brand	140.0	147.0	154.4	162.1	170.2	178.7
Revenue growth		5%	5%	5%	5%	5%
Royalty rate	5%	5%	5%	5%	5%	5%
Royalty income	**7.0**	**7.4**	**7.7**	**8.1**	**8.5**	**8.9**
Tax rate	30%	30%	30%	30%	30%	30%
Tax payable on royalty income	2.1	2.2	2.3	2.4	2.6	2.7
Royalty income after tax	**4.9**	**5.1**	**5.4**	**5.7**	**6.0**	**6.3**
Discount rate	15%	15%	15%	15%	15%	15%
Discount factor	1.00	1.15	1.32	1.52	1.75	2.01
Discounted cash flow	**4.9**	**4.5**	**4.1**	**3.7**	**3.4**	**3.1**
Value to Year 5	23.7					
Terminal value	20.7					
Brand value	**44.4**					

In addition to an estimate of the royalty rate that would apply for the sector and market, key features of this approach are as follows:

■ It requires forecasts of future revenues (but not of operating costs or capital employed).

■ It requires a discount rate.

■ The terminal value can be of a comparable magnitude to the NPV of the royalty payments for the first 5 years, implying that the assumptions for the period beyond 5 years also have an important effect on the estimated valuation.

Is brand valuation useful to you?

The principal advantage of brand valuation is that it reduces the complexity of assessing the worth and attributes of a brand to a single financial number. Difficult and imprecise though this process is, in some situations it is essential. For example, in mergers and acquisitions or legal and tax cases, this is exactly what is required.

What is more debatable is whether brand valuation is a useful tool as a means of brand health monitoring and as a way of informing decisions on budget setting and brand development processes. Although it can be used in this role, the balance of opinion currently seems to weigh significantly in favour of more direct and transparent measures for these purposes, based mainly on two approaches:

- Forecasting models of brand revenues, costs and profitability – but without the additional calculations and assumptions necessary to extend the forecasts to produce a brand valuation.

- Metrics derived from market research on customer opinions and attitudes towards the brand.

Key points

- There needs to be cooperation between marketing and finance to solve the problems of calculating financial results from branding expenditure.

- Brand valuation as a topic is an offshoot of company valuations, and has evolved in order to explain the sometimes large discrepancies between a company's market valuation and the value of its tangible assets.

- There is no doubt that the value of intangible assets, which include brands, now has a significant impact on the value of most major traded shares.

- To carry out credible brand valuations, certain criteria need to be met – for example, it must be possible for a brand to be sold, as an entity, separately from its parent company.

- There are numerous different methods of calculating brand value, all of which have various advantages and disadvantages. None is entirely satisfactory as a method of guiding day-to-day brand expenditure decisions.

- An approach based on statistical forecasting methods and market research is preferred as the best route for managers attempting to understand the impact of brand expenditure on future sales and profitability.

12

INTEGRATED MARKETING COMMUNICATIONS

This chapter looks at the various types of marketing communication, and traces the development of a marketing communications campaign through the setting of objectives and tasks, the choice of creative executions, the key issues in media planning and the tracking of the effects of the campaign. The chapter closes with a discussion of how the responses obtained from tracking can be used to improve and optimize future similar campaigns.

Information about marcoms planning is fragmented across many sources. This chapter pulls together best practice advice into one integrated framework, orientated around maximizing marketing payback.

Objective and task frameworks

Setting objectives and tasks for marketing communications is generally acknowledged to be the best way of bringing financial discipline into marketing communications, an area which is usually badly in need of discipline of all kinds. Before going further, ask yourself ten hard questions about how marketing communications is run in your company:

1. Can your communications executions be clearly grouped according to their objective and tasks?

2. Do you maintain a historical archive of past creative executions, including associated media details?

3. Can you tell which executions work and which don't?

4. Do you use pre-testing effectively?

5. Is your media planning scientific?

6. Are you using Payment By Results (PBR)?

7. Do you track communications effectively?

8. Can you diagnose the causes of communications problems?

9. Are you using communications modelling effectively?

10. Have you identified the half of your advertising spending that is wasted?

It is worth starting by looking at the framework for analyzing different types of marketing communication shown in Table 12.1.

Table 12.1 provides the communications planner with a checklist for organizing their activities. This 'objective and tasks' framework should be used to describe the unifying characteristics of the creative executions within a campaign. Table

12.2 shows an example of its application. The first step is for the communications planner to decide the primary objective of the campaign. In order that the campaign is measurable, it is important that it has one primary objective.

Table 12.1
Communications responses and stimuli framework

Behavioural response (objective)	Psychological response (tasks)	Communications stimuli
• Convert non-users to users	• Category need reminder	• Hard sell
• Attract new users	• Category need sell	(e.g. buy now)
• Increase repeat-purchase	• Brand recognition	• Soft sell
frequency	• Brand recall	(e.g. brand image)
• Increase amount bought	• Brand attitude – create	• Factual
• Increase consumption rate	• Brand attitude – improve	• Informational
• Increase usage of product	• Brand attitude – maintain	• Rational/logical
• Maintain repeat purchases	• Brand attitude – change	• Emotional
• Maintain usage of product		• Offers
• Accelerate next purchase		• Demonstration
• Decrease defection		• Problem solution
• Persuade consumers to		• Product features
choose lower-cost		• Lowest prices
interactions with supplier		• Greatest value
• Better product distribution		• Product popularity
• Improve product display		• Status
		• Entertainment

Table 12.2
Objectives and tasks for recruiting new cardholders

Behavioural response (objective)	Psychological response (tasks)	Communications stimuli
Convert non-users to users	Category need sell (problem avoidance)	Hard sell (e.g. buy now)
		Demonstration
	Brand recognition	Problem solution
	Brand attitude – create (high involvement, problem avoidance)	Product popularity
		Status
		Entertainment

Table 12.1 column one (behavioural response) provides a checklist of possible objectives. It is good practice to define the campaign objective in terms of the behavioural response required. For example, a campaign aimed at recruiting new cardholders might have the profile outlined in Table 12.2.

Table 12.1 column two (psychological response) provides a checklist of the possible tasks needed to achieve the objective. These are usually described in terms of psychological tasks that the campaign must perform. Multiple tasks may be required to achieve the objective. For example, in Table 12.2 several tasks are listed. The campaign must persuade non-users of credit cards that they need one; it must make them recognize the brand; it must make them have a positive attitude towards the brand.

Table 12.1 column three (communications stimuli) provides a checklist of stimuli that could be selected to elicit the psychological response. For example, in Table 12.2 the campaign uses a 'hard sell', demonstrating the use of a card and the problems it solves. It also shows that the card is popular and gives the user status among peers. The creative execution is also entertaining.

This campaign could be executed using several different types of creative idea and have many individual executions. The reason for this might be to appeal to different audiences such as young non-users (male and female treated differently) or retired people – see Figure 12.1.

Figure 12.1
Organization of campaigns, creative ideas and executions for credit cards

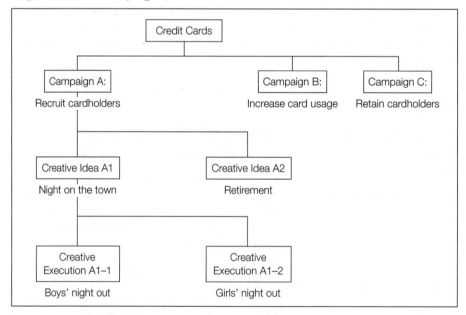

To illustrate the point that a different campaign must be prepared for a different set of objectives and tasks, compare Figure 12.1 with the objectives and tasks for a communication that aims to increase card usage, illustrated in Table 12.3.

Table 12.3
Objectives and tasks of increasing credit card usage

Behavioural response (objective)	Psychological response (tasks)	Communications stimuli
Increase usage of product	Brand awareness (recall 'don't leave home without card') Brand attitude (how versatile card is)	Soft sell Informational Demonstration Entertainment

Comparing Table 12.3 and Figure 12.1 raises the question: 'Can the same creative idea achieve the different objectives and tasks?' In this particular case, it is likely that two different sets of creative ideas will be needed to achieve both sets of objectives and tasks.

Quantifying the objective and task framework is an ideal advocated by many writers on marketing communications. It can be used to estimate the costs of a campaign. The method used is illustrated in the case of recruiting 5,000 new cardholders as shown in Table 12.4.

On the basis of the figures in Table 12.4, the cost per application is £200.00. Without the TV campaign, the direct marketing would have still produced some applications, but the number would have been less. Based on the numbers in the table, we estimate that there would have been 2,679 applications from direct mail without any TV, so the cost per application would be £187.00. The effect of the TV is to increase the response rate for direct mail, and in this case it is a relatively cost-effective way of achieving this aim.

Table 12.4
Objective and tasks method used to estimate costs of recruiting new cardholders

Planned response	Change before → after	Creative executions	Cost estimate
Exposure	15m reached	TV campaign	£500,000
Category need sell	500,000 non-users accept need for card before to 700,000 after	• sells category need (night on the town plus retirement)	
Brand recognition	Among non-users, percentage who recognize our brand increases from 30% to 40%	• plus brand recognition	

▶

Table 12.4
(continued)

Planned response	Change before → after	Creative executions	Cost estimate
Brand attitude – create	Among non-users, percentage who accept that our brand is 'worth considering' increases from 15% to 20%	• plus brand salience	
Exposure	1m reached, of which 100,000 are non-users. About 20,000 of these will have positive attitude	Mailshot targeted at non-users to facilitate purchase	£500,000 at £0.50 per mailing piece
Purchase facilitation	About 25% of those with positive attitude fill out the application form, i.e. 5,000 applications	• with introductory offer	

Creative execution decisions and their effects

Having set the objectives and tasks for a communications campaign, the issue then becomes one of implementation. In general, the effectiveness of a campaign will depend mainly on the following three factors:

- The quality of the creative content;
- The amount of media space used (the 'media tonnage');
- The appropriateness and effectiveness of the media channels chosen.

In this section, we will focus on how the best creative execution can be obtained; we will consider the issues of the amount and type of media in the following section.

The impact of the creative execution

Each year most companies will schedule hundreds, thousands or even more of communications executions, as illustrated in Table 12.5. There will be many different creative executions (in our example TV1, TV2, TV3, MAG4 and OUT5) for each brand or product communication. Differences in creative execution exist because of the variety of media types, but also to introduce variety for the audience and sometimes to convey several different messages. Box 12.1 describes the terminology of creative execution.

Table 12.5
Communications schedule excerpt

Date:	15-Apr	15-Apr	15-Apr	15-Apr
Time:	1.15 pm	1.15 pm	NA	NA
Creative execution	TV1	TV2 TV3	MAG4	OUT5
Media type	Network TV	Network TV	Women's mags	Outdoor
Format	30 sec.	30 & 15 sec.	Colour double page	48-sheet poster
Media	ITV2	Channel 5	*Cosmopolitan*	NA
Position/programme	Emmerdale	Family Affairs	Far forward right-hand page	NA

Box 12.1 Terminology for creative execution

Campaign: The execution of the creative strategy, involving the placement of all creative executions within the strategy in individual media spots.

Creative elements: Important components of a creative execution, such as headlines, tag lines, slogans, benefits claimed, symbols, etc.

Creative execution (or treatment): The tangible communication product, such as a 30-second film, an A4 page or a direct mail enclosure pack.

Creative idea (or theme): Unifying elements of a group of creative executions.

Creative strategy: Unifying elements of a group of creative ideas, aimed at achieving a specific, measurable audience response.

Finished execution: The actual execution that was placed in the media.

Insertion (or placement): The actual running of a finished execution in a medium at a specified time and/or place.

Media spot: Individual elements of media-space and/or time that can be bought from a media owner or media agent.

Rough execution: An inexpensive preliminary to the final execution.

Creative executions are the most basic components of marketing communications. For example, in Table 12.5 there are three television executions (coded TV1, TV2 and TV3), one magazine execution (MAG4) and one outdoor poster execution (OUT5). These executions are all subtly different variants around the main theme (the creative idea) and several creative ideas may be grouped together as a creative strategy, and implemented as a campaign.

The impact of the creative content is seen most easily when media campaigns using different creative contents do not overlap. Good creative content usually provides a combination of the following benefits:

■ Greater maximum uplift;

■ Greater responsiveness;

■ Slower decay rate.

Although effective choice of media channels and media tonnage can offset the effects of poor creative content, the degree of compensation obtained is often both partial and expensive.

Creative execution is an important driver of target audience response. The three aims of creative execution are:

■ To gain attention;

■ To change awareness and attitudes towards the brand; and

■ To promote action.

Response rates differ greatly between good and bad creative executions. This point has profoundly important implications for budgeting. It would be a significant mistake to set marketing budgets on the basis only of audience statistics and other 'hard' data, because if the creative execution is weak, then it needs to be strengthened before continuing to incur marketing expenditure.

In an ideal world, marketing response functions would be widely available and they would provide indisputable evidence of which creative executions were working and which were not. Econometric modelling is a technique that enables data-rich organizations to calculate these response functions.

In most organizations, response models have to be inferred from secondary data. Modelling of creative effects requires a deeper understanding than simply tracking response rates. Tracking 'intermediary' variables that indicate the changes in consumers' awareness and attitudes can be helpful. Three types of factors should be tracked, in recognition of the three creative aims above. These intermediary factors are examined in the next section.

Factors that influence the cost of creative execution are set out as follows.

$$\begin{matrix} \text{Cost} \\ \text{of} \\ \text{creative} \end{matrix} = \begin{matrix} \text{Number} \\ \text{of media} \\ \text{types} \end{matrix} \times \begin{matrix} \text{Number of} \\ \text{executions} \\ \text{per type} \end{matrix} \times \begin{matrix} \text{Cost} \\ \text{per} \\ \text{execution} \end{matrix} \left\{ \begin{matrix} \text{Economies} \\ \text{of scale} \\ \\ \text{Quality of} \\ \text{execution} \end{matrix} \right\}$$

Developing and testing creative executions

The creative team may have developed several ideas and numerous specific elements that may or may not work. Testing helps to provide assurance from the target audience that the communications are 'on strategy'. It is also called pretesting as it happens before the communications are run.

There are three stages that communications pass through, and at each there is a variety of testing methods available. First, *concept development research* helps select creative ideas (how the strategy will be dramatized) and specific elements (headlines, slogans, presenters, celebrities and situations). Second, *rough testing* is conducted with rough executions of the creative content to decide which is worth finishing. Third, *finished testing* is used to screen final creative executions before they go on to media.

Concepts are researched using individual depth interviews amongst the target audience group to obtain a private opinion or rating of each idea presented. An opinion is given about likeability ('I like this ad for the brand'), similarity ('these ideas amount to much the same thing') and convincing ('the claims are believable'). Elements include slogans, headlines, images, people and situations.

Roughs and finished communications are tested, following the concept research, to improve the likelihood that the finished creative executions will work as planned when placed in the media. Rough executions cost about one-fifth of the finished cost, so it is worth testing the roughs before going to full production. After rough testing, several finished executions are then produced to be included in the campaign.

A research sample is recruited that represents the target audience. They are exposed to a simulation of the communication and pre-to-post responses are measured. There are many potential pitfalls to be avoided.

Focus groups are still widely used, and the communication is typically shown for ten minutes or more. However, this approach has serious limitations, as it overexposes the communication and responses are usually exaggerated. Discussion among the group also draws undue attention to the communication.

The low cost of these groups is potentially misleading, for it would be possible to conduct about 100 interviews for the same cost.

The chances of a 'real winner' are about 30% for new brands and 10% for established brands. Individual interviews are more reliable than focus groups, but the test must be designed with care. How the communications are exposed needs care, and in particular the decision on whether to set them in the context of other competing communications. The order and selection of measures is also important. Acceptance and learning from the communication should be tested, along with shifts in awareness, beliefs, attitudes and purchase intention.

Following testing, the researchers assess the test scores and decide which creative executions to accept, which to reject, and where changes should be made. They must also decide the frequency with which each different creative execution will be exposed.

Media decisions and their effects

Rules-of-thumb on media choice

Buying media can be as bewildering as describing creative executions. In particular, describing the media purchase in a meaningful way requires skill and understanding. Some rules-of-thumb are set out in Table 12.6.

Table 12.6
Characteristics of communications media

Medium	Stimuli	Carrying power	Comments
Television	Movement, words, colour, music	Mood, tone, emotion, soft sell, associations	Dramatic, influential but conveys few words
Cinema	Movement, words, colour, music	Mood, tone, emotion, soft sell, associations	Even more dramatic than TV
Radio	Words, music	Mood, tone, emotion, soft sell, associations	Dramatic, can catch people in situ (e.g. driving), conveys few words
Outdoor	Words, colour	Mood, tone, emotion, soft sell, associations	Dramatic, can catch people in situ (e.g. driving), conveys few words

Table 12.6 (continued)

Medium	Stimuli	Carrying power	Comments
Press and magazines	Words, colour	Information, rational, logical, offers, hard sell, associations	Conveys more words, more personal
Web advertising	Words, colour, limited movement	Information, rational, logical, offers, hard sell	Conveys more words, more personal
Sponsorship	Movement, words, colour, music	Mood, tone, emotion, associations	Conveys few words, limited images, associations not always well controlled
Public relations and publicity	Words	Information, rational and emotional, logical, associations	Conveys few words, hard to control, but carries high credibility
Direct mail	Words, colour	Information, rational, logical, offers, hard sell	Conveys more words, even more personal
Email	Words, colour	Information, rational, logical, offers, hard sell	Conveys more words, even more personal
Web response activities	Words, colour, limited movement	Information, rational, logical, offers, hard sell	Conveys more words, even more personal
Personal selling	Words, movement	Information, rational, logical, offers, hard sell	Conveys more words, even more personal
Telephone selling	Words	Information, rational, logical, offers, hard sell	Conveys more words, even more personal
Sales promotion	Words, colour	Information, rational, logical, offers, hard sell	Direct financial offer, in addition to communications

When buying media insertions, the cost depends on a number of factors which are summarized in the formula below.

$$\begin{array}{c}\text{Cost}\\\text{of}\\\text{media}\end{array} = \begin{array}{c}\text{Gross media}\\\text{audience}\\\text{per insertion}\end{array} \times \begin{array}{c}\text{Number}\\\text{of}\\\text{insertions}\end{array} \times \begin{array}{c}\text{Cost}\\\text{per thousand}\\\text{or CPM}\end{array} \left\{ \begin{array}{c}\text{Relative impact}\\\text{of media vehicle}\\\\\text{Size or length of}\\\text{each insertion}\end{array} \right\}$$

The first thing to keep in mind is that the marketer effectively pays for the total media audience whereas their objective is to reach only the target audience within the media audience.

Most media sales are conducted in 'Cost Per Thousand' or CPM. However, this is an almost useless benchmarking statistic because target audience is only a fraction of the media audience upon which CPM is based. A worked example is shown below.

Key concepts in media planning

Three key concepts in media planning are described in Barban *et al.* (1989):

- **Reach**: Defined as the proportion of the target population exposed to the advertising message at least once during a specified period;
- **Frequency**: Defined as the average number of exposures for those members of the target population reached by the advertising message;
- **Continuity**: Refers to how the advertising activity is scheduled over the timespan of the campaign.

In theory, the media planner will wish to reach a high percentage of the target audience (i.e. achieve a high reach) for a high enough number of times to be effective (i.e. at a high frequency) for as much of the campaign as possible. However, this is usually impractical or prohibitively expensive and some compromise has to be sought. We discuss below the nature of the compromises available.

Note also that the definitions of reach and frequency depend in turn upon the definitions of the target audience and the specified period. Unfortunately, all too often there is a lack of clarity about these factors in reported data.

A commonly used term that brings together the concepts of reach and frequency is the Gross Rating Point (GRP). This is defined as the product of reach and frequency, or by the following equation:

$$GRP = Reach \times Frequency$$

GRP is equivalent to the total number of exposures to the advertising message in the target population (sometimes called Opportunities To See, OTS, especially in the context of print media), but expressed as a percentage of the target population. For this reason, it is an important determinant of media price for a defined target audience. Because of its construction, however, it masks whether the GRPs have been achieved via a high reach combined with a low frequency or vice versa. For a given budget that can buy a given number of GRPs, there is always a trade-off between reach and frequency.

Minimum Effective Frequency (MEF) is particularly important in the context of assessing whether advertising has been effective. There is a widespread view that for each media type, a minimum frequency exists for each individual below which the exposure to the advertising message will not have been effective.

Probably the greatest impetus to establishing the concept of MEF was the publication of Michael Naples' book *Effective Frequency: The Relationship Between Frequency and Advertising Awareness* (1979). After presenting many research studies that supported the idea of MEF, Naples arrived at a number of conclusions for media planners:

- One exposure of an advertisement to a target audience within a purchase cycle has little or no effect.

- Most studies reviewed by Naples suggested that two exposures within a purchase cycle are an effective threshold.

- Naples considers three exposures to be optimal.

- Wear-out is not caused by too high a frequency per se; it is caused by copy and content problems, so Naples did not detect a Maximum Effective Frequency (MAEF).

As time passed, media planners have challenged this MEF dogma. The following concerns have been voiced:

- **Purchase cycle frequency**: For any given product, purchase frequency varies greatly from consumer to consumer.

- **Category differences**: Naples' research failed to show differences between product categories and implied that MEF is similar across all products. Given the enormous differences in purchase cycle between cars and cola, planners now doubt that Naples' generalizations can be correct.

- **Threshold**: Direct marketing is effective at the first impression, so why not other media? New product launches are often effective from the first impression. Many now question whether the threshold idea is correct.

- **Creative**: Dull, boring copy could require more repetitions than scintillating creative messages. Yet most research did not address that question.

- **Wear-out**: Again, the evidence for this is debatable.

The debate on MEF is still active and far from resolved. Jones (1999) has used Nielsen household panel research to challenge the Naples rules-of-thumb: 'Effective frequency is provided by a single exposure – one exposure generates the highest proportion of sales . . . Additional exposures add very little to the effect of the first.'

Today many media planners are challenging the importance of 'purchase cycle' and instead argue that media plans should be evaluated in terms of weekly reach points. For example, Batra *et al.* (1996) argue as follows:

- TV: 3–4 exposures per four–week cycle;
- Outdoor: 12 exposures per month;
- Magazines: 3–4 exposures per quarter.

In order to know how many of the target audience have been exposed to the advertising message by at least the effective frequency, the average frequency defined above is not sufficient. What we need is a percentage breakdown of the target audience by number of exposures. This is called the 'frequency distribution'. The frequency distribution then enables us to see what percentage of the target audience has been exposed to the advertising message by at least the number of times indicated by the assumed effective frequency for the media channel. This percentage is often referred to as the 'effective reach'.

Finally, there is the continuity decision for the scheduling of the advertising activity over time. Given that budgetary constraints mean that we often cannot buy the combination of reach and frequency that we would like throughout the campaign, do we settle for less of one or the other (or both), or do we aim for our desired reach and frequency combination for some of the time and sacrifice one or other (or both) to a greater extent for the remainder of the time?

The need to compromise generally forces advertisers to choose between the following three strategies for distributing advertising activity over a campaign period:

- **Flighting**: Bursts of advertising are alternated with periods of no advertising activity.
- **Continuous**: Advertising activity is spread evenly throughout the campaign period.
- **Pulsing**: A continuous base of advertising activity is augmented by intermittent bursts of heavy advertising (e.g. corresponding to expected seasonal peaks in sales).

Payment for marketing communications

Payment has great relevance to the marketing communications industry today, as a consequence of the interest in payment by results. Historically, agencies were paid a percentage commission for buying media time and space (see Box 12.2 for definition of terms). However, as the creative role of the agencies has grown, and their influence as consultants and advisers has soared, questions are being asked about agency objectivity and their self-serving advice. Payment of the agencies has become a highly charged issue.

Box 12.2 Terminology used in payment

Commission: Form of agency remuneration where the agency earns a percentage commission based on the gross cost of the media – traditionally around 15%. So if the rate-card for a page were £100, then that would be the price paid by the client, but to the intermediary agent it would be a 'trade' price of £85 plus £15 commission to the agency.

Cost plus: Form of agency remuneration which is a hybrid of commission and fees.

Fees: Form of agency remuneration based on an agreed work plan and hourly rates for all agency staff. The work plan would be set out in detail, showing the time required from agency staff with different skills and seniority levels.

Payment By Results (PBR): Form of agency remuneration normally used in conjunction with fees and commission. Involves setting quantitative objectives beforehand and quantifying progress against objectives afterwards.

Even before the widespread separation of media agencies from creative ones, bigger clients were becoming increasingly disinclined to allow a full-service agency buying media on its behalf to retain the full 15% commission, which the media owners continued to offer. Once the media agencies had separated, most clients continued to pay commission to their media buyers, but at much more aggressively negotiated levels.

Monthly fees have the advantage of predictability but are not easily geared to reward success, as time is a poor measure of value in creative industries. The question also remains of the 'fair' level for hourly rates. Arthur Andersen, in its highly regarded report *Costing Systems for Advertising Agencies* (1992), recommended that agencies should earn 20% on top of costs as a reasonable goal for specialist advice and consultancy businesses, and this is considered today to be the norm, according to the joint industry guidelines drawn up by the IPA, ISBA, DMA MCCA and PRCA (Joint working party of IPA 2002).

PBR is the fastest growing method of agency remuneration in the UK, USA and Europe. However, few clients employ payment by results as their sole method of remuneration; it is more commonly seen as an element of the main remuneration. It is primarily used to incentivize agency performance.

Results in PBR can mean several things. Results can be measured as sales, but this poses the challenge of linking sales to the marketing communications that drive them and eliminating the effects of factors other than communications. Results can be measured as consumer response – awareness or attitudes. Some companies also include agency service quality as a results measure, but this practice has been criticized.

As clients and agencies grapple with the payment by results issue, there is growing scrutiny of what agencies actually deliver and how much consumers and customers respond to marketing communications.

Tracking your marketing communications

The final stage of planning a communications campaign is planning the tracking activities that will provide the information required to assess whether the implementation has achieved the objectives and tasks.

The effect of media type

The ability to track performance of communications is heavily dependent on the media type (see Table 12.7). For instance, direct response marketing (mail and press where a coded response mechanism is available) has the potential for the responses to be tracked at individual treatment level. Compare this with a brand image advertising campaign, where it is generally impossible to track responses to individual executions and responses to creative ideas cannot usually be tracked.

Table 12.7
Tracking ability by media type

Media type	Tracking ability
Television Cinema Radio Outdoor Press and magazines (indirect)	Creative strategy can be tracked, on the basis of brand sales or product sales, as long as other strategies for the same brand or product are not running concurrently. Econometrics may help disentangle strategies if several are running concurrently. Brand tracking (e.g. awareness or attitudes) can help improve the accuracy of the analysis. Creative ideas and executions cannot generally be separated

Table 12.7
(continued)

Media type	Tracking ability
Web advertising	Viewing of individual web ad executions can be monitored. This can be linked to sales by using econometric analysis
Sponsorship	Brand sales or brand tracking (e.g. awareness or attitudes) can occasionally provide evidence of effectiveness, but it is usually necessary to use econometrics to disentangle the effect of sponsorship from other communications running at the same time
Public relations and publicity	As for sponsorship
Direct mail Email Press and magazines (direct)	Creative executions can be individually tracked using response codes
Web response activities	Creative executions can be tracked to some degree using cookies
Personal selling	Creative executions (in the form of 'detailing') can be tracked at individual customer level using CRM systems and linked to sales responses using econometric methods
Telephone selling	Creative executions (in the form of scripts or call guides) can be tracked at individual customer level and linked to sales responses using econometric methods
Sales promotion	Creative executions can be monitored at individual store level and linked to sales spikes on the basis of EPOS data

Types of tracking activity

Media exposure auditing is the first part of tracking. Every media-buy is negotiated for fulfilment in the future. It is not finished until after fulfilment has been audited. Any number of things can prevent fulfilment: late delivery of the creative execution, a commercial pre-emption due to a news bulletin, a station mislogging a spot, a printing error. Auditing fulfilment provides a degree of assurance that the buy is being fulfilled. If spots are missed or ads misrun, or length, size, timing or position are wrong, makegoods should be immediately negotiated, or cash credits taken if the available makegoods are unacceptable.

Ratings should also be audited to ensure that the negotiated reach, frequency and target audience composition are being delivered. If performance is below plan, for example a programme's ratings are declining, immediate action should be taken. If media performance guarantees were built into the buy during initial negotiation and the post-analysis shows underdelivery relative to the guaranteed level, the buyer should negotiate for bonus (gratis) delivery at a later date to make up for underdelivery.

Processing measures are the second area of tracking. Messages in the real world, not the test lab, have to compete with other communications. Their ability to be processed needs to be measured to improve on the pre-test predictions.

Three measures are commonly tracked: *cut-through*, *recognition* and *recall*. The usual tracking method is the audience survey, where a sample of the population is interviewed periodically. Face-to-face interviews are usual, as it is necessary to show pictures of brands, or brand displays, and examples of ads. Although telephone interviews are used in some countries, they are less reliable.

Cut-through is the toughest test of communication's ability to gain attention. 'What TV ads have you seen for motor lubricants?' is asked, and then 'Can you recall the brand advertised?' Responses are coded for adequate description of the communication's content and scored for correct or incorrect association of the brand.

Recognition is partly a cross-check of media fulfilment – did the message reach the same number of people as planned. 'Have you seen this commercial on TV before?' and if so, 'How many times in total?' Answers are scored for 'Yes', 'Not sure' and 'No' and only the Yes answers should be counted as signifying recognition.

Brand-prompted ad-recall involves showing interviewees a list of brands or a series of pictures of brands and asking 'Which of these brands have you seen or heard advertised recently?' For each brand named, the interviewer asks 'Please describe the advertisement or advertisements for this brand in as much detail as you can remember.' Scoring reflects whether the interviewee recalled sufficient detail to satisfy the analyst that the communication was indeed seen and heard and that the respondent is not simply guessing.

By tracking processing, the communications manager can gain insights about media and message effectiveness. Cut-through questions are media-specific, and they can provide insights about which media are most effective. Day-after recall tests can help determine whether a particular creative execution is ineffective. As a result, the scheduled mix of media and creative executions may require adjustment.

Psychological responses to communications can cover a wide spectrum of possible measures. Two distinct perspectives should be covered – response to the advertising itself (liking it, disliking it, credibility of advert, etc.) and brand perception shifts (awareness, beliefs and attitudes to our brands). *Purchase intentions* are tracked on the global brand tracker.

Trade customer audits and panels provide information about display, stocking and pricing of a defined group of products. This usually consists of specific brands, a range of competitors and specific pack sizes. EPOS data are sometimes used as a detailed source of over-the-counter purchases. Otherwise an audit is necessary, involving physically counting the stocks of the trade customer at the beginning and end of the audit period. Auditors from the research agency visit the panel customers on a regular basis.

Economic response should be measured at two levels: the market and our sales within the market. Market size and growth are especially important as measures of new and developing markets. The reason for this is that sales increases can be the consequence of market growth, and they may not therefore be indicative of the effects of marketing communications.

Surveys of market size are carried out by commercial research firms and also, less frequently, by government agencies. It is important to obtain these data by product type and brand so that shifts from one type of product (e.g. mineral and multigrades) to another (e.g. synthetics) are observed. Expressing sales in terms of market share is a good way of screening out the effect of market size trends.

Sales data are always needed. Fluctuations in sales data over short periods can be caused by several misleading factors, such as variations in time periods (e.g. from 28 to 31 days per month) and supply chain effects that are not necessarily indicative of consumption. Over longer periods, seasonal patterns of consumption can also require skilful interpretation.

Price levels at which products were bought also provide significant economic insights. Care must again be exercised in distinguishing between the consumer price (which is likely to influence purchase decisions), the trade price (which is likely to affect the distribution and display of products), and also any discounts, off-invoice promotions and deals that may apply.

Product mix is another factor to monitor, as it can have dramatic effects on average price, costs and profitability. In many markets, mix changes can be one of the main contributors to profit trends.

Examining the data as described in this section can help managers sort out the communications that work from the ones that don't.

Modelling your marketing communications

If the appropriate tracking data are available, the consumer responses to marketing communications can be identified. It is good practice to measure these responses at the lowest level of detail that the available measurement techniques permit. However, there are several limitations intrinsic to particular communications media and approaches.

Types of response

Some characteristic examples of responses are shown in Figure 12.2.

Sales promotions typically produce a 'spike' response, which can be tracked down to individual product and even store level. Sometimes there is a carryover after the promotion ends, for example as a result of stockpiling. The nature of the offer is critically important, and the relation of promotions to pricing is also important. As pricing is such a specialist subject, we have devoted an entire chapter to it – Chapter 13.

Sponsorship often runs continuously for a long period, say a football season or the motor racing season. Sales responses are thought by some researchers to follow a 'hysteresis' curve, where sales build up after the onset of the sponsorship season and decay after the end of the season.

Advertising of products, and particularly direct response advertising and interactive marketing, follow a peak and decay pattern. Typically the advertising occurs in a burst, and the response to it builds rapidly and then decays gradually. Where sales responses are coded, with a source code, it may be possible to make an accurate link between the specific creative execution and the response it causes. In the case of product advertising, it may still be possible to relate the creative execution to the product sales it causes, assuming that proper records have been archived and also that there was no significant overlap of executions. Often, however, this condition is not met because there are multiple executions running concurrently or with a significant overlap.

Product launch advertising has another response shape altogether. Given that the sales volume starts from a base of zero at the outset, the curve shape is typically that of an adoption curve, as shown in Figure 12.2. The maths of this is characterized as a Bass model, named after F. M. Bass who spent his long career studying this phenomenon. For further details see Lilien and Rangaswamy (1998).

Timescale: short term vs. long term

Many of the examples discussed above have a relatively short-term response lifetime, typically measured in weeks or months rather than years.

Figure 12.2
Shapes of response curves for different communications media

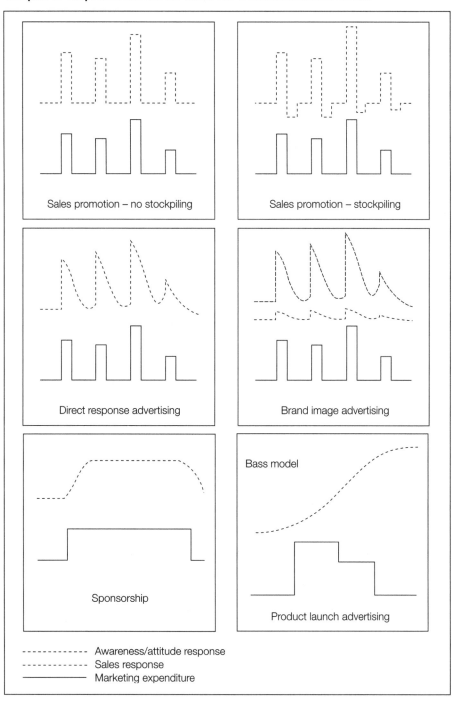

In the case of advertising, for example, the rate at which the effects decay is typically reported to be in the range of 5% to 15% per week. After three months, between 50% and 90% of the effect of a burst of advertising has dissipated.

The timing effect of advertising is usually represented by an 'adstock'. The value of the adstock at the end of each period is calculated by decreasing the value at the beginning of a period by a percentage corresponding to the decay rate, and increasing the value by the amount of marketing expenditure during the period. The adstock is assumed to measure the response to advertising that has accumulated in people's minds.

Brand image advertising is different and is a case that deserves special treatment. It is usually characterized by:

- No offers or call to action;
- No mention of specific products other than the brand.

Brand image advertising may cause short-term sales responses, as indicated in Figure 12.2. However, its main objectives are often more concerned with attitudes towards the brand, leading to:

- Longer-term improvement in sales;
- Support for a premium price for the brand.

Because of the timescales involved and also because all products in the brand portfolio are likely to be affected, the response is likely to suffer more from 'noise' than it would with a short-term, product-specific campaign and is therefore more difficult to quantify.

Two models of the longer-term effects of such advertising are:

- The 'floor-level' model;
- Moving the price-response curve.

When looking at the short-term effects of advertising on an awareness or attitudinal measure of consumer response, it is commonly observed that the response decays to a 'floor' value which is greater than zero in the absence of advertising. The 'floor-level' model asserts that the long-term response of these measures to advertising is that the floor level itself changes. For example, in the absence of advertising for a prolonged period, the 'floor' would decay to zero. Conversely, advertising continued over a long period, even if intermittent, would support a floor level greater than zero. These effects are illustrated in Figure 12.3.

Figure 12.3
Short-term and long-term responses to advertising

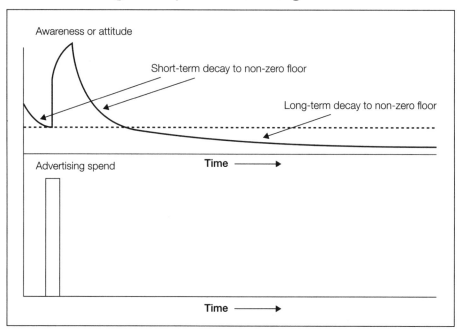

In terms of sales, the effect of brand advertising can be viewed as changing the relationship between sales volume and price, i.e. the demand curve. This is illustrated in Figure 12.4.

Figure 12.4 shows what advertising expenditure does in the long term, if it is effective, is to move the demand curve upwards and to the right.

The implications of this can be assessed by considering the starting point as circle '0' on the 'without advertising' line. The effect of the advertising expenditure is to move all trade-offs between price and sales volumes to the new 'with advertising' curve. Three options are shown:

■ If no change is made to the price, then all of the benefit of the advertising is reflected in increased sales volumes, and the new position for the brand is indicated by circle '1'.

■ If, however, the objective of the advertising expenditure is not to increase sales volume but to obtain a premium price while maintaining the current sales volume, then the price would be increased so that the brand moves to the point indicated by the circle '2'.

■ The above cases are just two options out of an infinite number of possible pricing policy decisions. In practice, neither is likely to be optimal in terms of obtaining the highest return on advertising expenditure. If the original brand position without advertising (circle '0') were optimal, then the optimum new brand position will be between the above two positions, as indicated by circle '3'.

In any specific example, the pricing policy decision that will give the optimum return on advertising expenditure will be determined by the shape of the demand curve and the extent to which the demand curves move in response to the advertising.

Figure 12.4
The long-term effect of brand image advertising on the demand curve

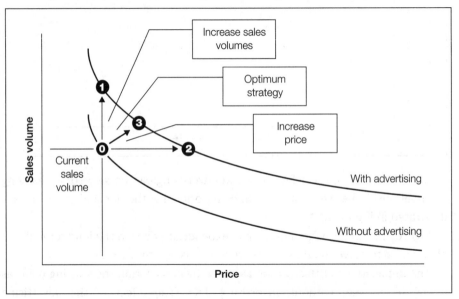

Calculating the payback from your marketing communications

Marketing payback analysis requires that a relationship be determined between communications expenditure and sales responses. The ability to establish such a relationship depends very much on the specificity of the measurement techniques.

Direct response payback analysis

For direct mail and direct response advertising, it is often possible to determine with great precision the source of sales (see Table 12.8).

Table 12.8
Response rate measurement for direct response campaigns

Creative	Media	Response Rate	Expenditure	Sales margin	Expenditure to sales margin ratio
A1–1	M1	7.10%	£50,000	£112,030	45%
A1–2	M1	5.50%	£30,000	£57,750	52%
A1–3	M1	4.30%	£10,000	£15,050	66%
A1–1	M2	5.90%	£40,000	£82,600	48%
A1–2	M2	4.30%	£10,000	£15,050	66%
A1–3	M2	3.10%	£5,000	£5,425	92%
A1–1	M3	7.70%	£100,000	£238,010	42%
A1–2	M3	6.10%	£50,000	£106,750	47%
A1–3	M3	4.90%	£30,000	£34,300	87%

This type of analysis can be used to optimize future campaigns. For example, in Table 12.8, focusing on Creative A1–1 and Media M3 would seem at first sight to be the optimum choice because this offers the lowest expenditure to sales margin ratio. However, there is an important practical limitation in that response rates for media decrease with expenditure.

Assume, for example, that the expenditures on each of the media are doubled, and that the response rates fall to the values shown in Table 12.9.

Table 12.9
The effect of doubling expenditures

Creative	Media	Response rate	Expenditure	Sales margin	Expenditure to sales margin ratio
A1–1	M1	6.60%	£100,000	£201,239	50%
A1–2	M1	5.20%	£60,000	£105,927	57%
A1–3	M1	4.10%	£20,000	£27,770	72%
A1–1	M2	5.50%	£80,000	£148,576	54%
A1–2	M2	3.90%	£20,000	£25,440	79%
A1–3	M2	3.00%	£10,000	£10,177	98%
A1–1	M3	6.20%	£200,000	£344,328	58%
A1–2	M3	5.10%	£100,000	£162,107	62%
A1–3	M3	4.10%	£60,000	£47,604	126%

It is clear that Creative A1–1 Media M3 is no longer the preferred choice. In fact the order of preference has changed completely and it is not even the second choice. The preferred choice now would be Creative A1–1 Media M1.

This raises the question of whether we were correct in assuming that we should put all of our eggs in the Creative A1–1 Media M3 basket in the original table. Using sophisticated mathematical optimization techniques, we can estimate the optimum allocation of spend by modelling the data in the above tables. An illustration is given in Table 12.10 for an overall budget of £100,000.

Table 12.10
Optimum allocation of £100,000

Creative	Media	Response rate	Expenditure	Sales margin	Expenditure to sales margin ratio
A1–1	M1	8.30%	£4,867	£13,560	36%
A1–2	M1	6.22%	£0	£0	
A1–3	M1	4.76%	£0	£0	
A1–1	M2	6.90%	£0	£0	
A1–2	M2	5.41%	£0	£0	
A1–3	M2	3.32%	£0	£0	
A1–1	M3	11.29%	£68,447	£270,924	25%
A1–2	M3	8.56%	£26,686	£90,734	29%
A1–3	M3	8.04%	£0	£0	
Total			**£100,000**	**£375,219**	**27%**

Table 12.10 shows that the optimum allocation of £100,000 involves using three of the nine creatives. The gross margin obtained is £375,219, or more than 50% higher than using Creative A1–1 Media M3 alone (and more than 80% higher than Creative A1–1 Media M1) for the same overall expenditure.

Advertising payback analysis

The response of the target audience to marketing depends on several factors, which are summarized in the formula below.

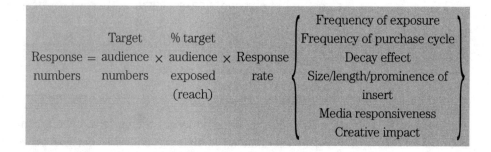

Responses are directly proportional to the exposure level: the size of the target audience multiplied by the percentage that had an opportunity to see the advertising or promotion. This is then multiplied by a response rate that depends on several factors.

Although the response numbers are directly proportional to the target audience numbers, all the target audience is not equally exposed. Three key timing effects must be taken into account:

- Frequency of exposure;
- Frequency of the purchase cycle;
- Decay of response.

Frequency of exposure is a measure of how many times the average target audience individual will see the message in a given time period. Frequency of the purchase cycle is important as a normalizing factor for frequency of exposure. Maximum response occurs at an exposure frequency of about three times within a purchase cycle and then declines (see Figure 12.5).

Figure 12.5
How response varies according to frequency of exposure

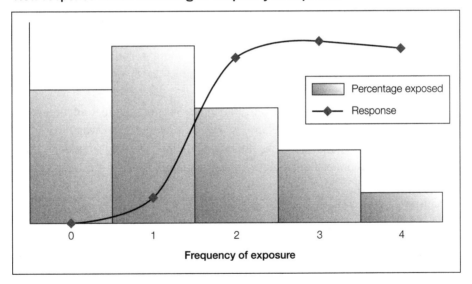

The target audience's exposure varies. In Figure 12.5 a significant percentage is not exposed at all, the largest percentage of the target audience is exposed once per cycle, then the exposure declines.

Response at first increases as the frequency of exposure increases, passes through a maximum and finally declines. In the example, the response is weak for a single exposure and peaks at three exposures.

A marketing plan with a fixed budget can be designed to reach either a lot of people a few times, or a few people a lot of times. This is known as the trade-off between 'reach and frequency' and is an important issue for planners. Average frequency is therefore not a helpful statistic as it ignores the response effect.

A consequence of this is that when marketing budgets get sliced into many little advertising or promotional activities, the response may be of marginal value if the exposures are too small. This has some significant implications for marketing ROME:

> Wasted expenditure is going to occur whenever marketing expenditure levels are (a) below breakeven and (b) above saturation.

As part of the initial phase of performance improvement programmes, many firms rank their activities with a simple dichotomous variable identifying whether an activity is value-adding or non-value-adding. For example, how relatively valuable are trade promotion T-shirts?

Decay is another important effect that needs to be incorporated into ROME models. Response levels decay over time after the initial stimulus is removed.

The size of the insertion, or the broadcast commercial length, and their prominence all have an impact on response numbers. Similarly, media responsiveness is important. Some media are more responsive than others. Finally, the creative effectiveness of the communication needs to be taken into account.

Analyzing these questions is the starting point for eliminating non-value-adding activity, and more generally for improving the way marketing expenditure is managed. While it is difficult to define precisely what constitutes a value-adding or non-value-adding activity, significant insights usually emerge about the more questionable marketing activities, and this helps focus the more exhaustive investigations.

Key points

- Payback is especially important for marketing communications today because of the need to establish yardsticks for Payment By Results (PBR).

- Marketing communications should all have clear objectives and tasks.

- Pre-testing of creative executions needs to follow rigorous best practice in order to be reliable.

- Media planning should be as scientific as possible.

- It is good practice to measure responses to marketing communications at the lowest level of detail that measurement techniques permit (e.g. individual creative execution and media placement wherever possible).

- Modelling of marketing communications can identify significant improvements of media mix.

13

HOW PRICING WORKS

In this chapter we look at how pricing works. In particular, we focus on how to quantify the effect of a change in the price of a brand or product on its sales, on the sales of competing brands or products and on the overall market. We look at how to use these quantifications to maximize profit, and we conclude by considering how price promotions can be incorporated into an integrated pricing framework.

Even if you or your department are not directly responsible for pricing in your company, you should still study this chapter, as pricing decisions will have a fundamental impact on most other areas of marketing payback.

The importance of pricing decisions

Price is one of the most important levers a business possesses. Get pricing wrong and the business can easily fail; get pricing right and the business can be both profitable and growing.

Given the importance of price, it is something of a puzzle that it is accorded less attention by marketing managers than the more exciting areas of advertising and promotions. In the case of commodity markets, this is due to the price being determined externally by the market. A business has no option but to be a price follower. In other cases, especially in B2B sectors, pricing decisions may be taken at the highest level, perhaps as a result of individual contract negotiations. But more generally, especially in consumer markets, pricing policy is a real decision and one that is both central to the prospects of the business and intimately linked with all of the other marketing decisions. Here are ten hard questions to ask about how pricing is managed in your organization:

1. What is the own price elasticity for each of your brands and for each of your main competitors?

2. What are the cross-price elasticities between the major brands competing in your market space?

3. Where do your values for price elasticities come from?

4. What market price elasticities are implied by own price and cross-price elasticities?

5. Do you believe in these values?

6. What is the basis for your price setting?

7. When setting prices, do you maximize revenue or profit?

8. How do own price elasticities for your brands compare with those of your competitors?

9. Do you understand the differences?

10. Do you know how price elasticities in your market space have changed over time?

To answer some of these questions, we look first at how the effects of price can be measured and some of the pitfalls awaiting the unwary. We then look at optimizing pricing policy. Finally, we consider how pricing policy interacts with promotions and advertising.

Price elasticity and its limitations

A typical relationship between price and sales volume is shown in Figure 13.1.

Figure 13.1
The price–demand curve

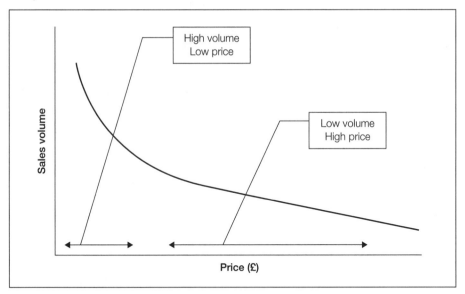

Figure 13.1 shows how the sales volume falls as the price increases, and vice versa. This relationship can also be plotted with the axes transposed, i.e. with price on the vertical axis and sales volume on the horizontal axis. When plotted in this way, it is sometimes referred to as a PQ chart (for price–quantity).

The question is – how do we describe this relationship so that we can use the information to estimate the impact of a price change on sales?

By far the most common way of describing this relationship is *price elasticity*. The concept is simple. If you increase your price by 10% and sales fall by 5%, you have a price elasticity of 0.5. If, under the same circumstances, demand falls by 15%, you have a price elasticity of 1.5.

Price elasticity is an important brand characteristic and will differ from brand to brand. Knowing the price elasticity of each of your brands is therefore a vital piece of information. As we shall see, it can tell you a lot about your competitive position in the marketplace and whether you can improve profitability by increasing or decreasing price.

Box 13.1 Price elasticity terminology

The **price elasticity** of a product is the percentage fall in demand divided by the percentage price increase (calculated on the basis of a small price increase).

A **price-inelastic** brand is one that has a low price elasticity, i.e. a price increase has a relatively small effect on demand).

A **price-elastic** brand is one that has a high price elasticity, i.e. a price increase has a relatively large effect on demand).

In one sense, price elasticity is the ultimate test of brand loyalty. If a brand is price-inelastic, it means that proportionately fewer customers will switch to another brand (or drop out of the market) if the price increases. Conversely, a price-elastic brand is one that will lose many customers if the price increases; it is regarded as something approaching a commodity.

A fatal flaw

Unfortunately, as shown by Merrick (2003), the simplicity and power of the concept of price elasticity are marred by a fatal flaw. This becomes apparent if we use price elasticities to calculate how sales revenue changes with price (see Figure 13.2).

Three cases arise:

1. If the price elasticity is greater than 1, the sales revenue approaches zero at high prices but increases steadily and without limit as the price is reduced. This is because the increase in sales volumes arising from the price reductions more than compensates for the reduction in revenue arising from the reduction in price. Such a model is, of course, improbable given that there is a finite amount of money and demand in the world.

2. Even more problematic is the situation where the price elasticity is less than 1. In this case, sales revenue increases as price increases, again without limit. This is because the reduction in sales volumes arising from the increase in price is less than the increase in revenue arising from the increase in price. If this model were true, we could keep putting up the price and benefiting from increased sales revenues.

3. In the third scenario, if the price elasticity is exactly 1, the sales revenue does not change with price because the reduction in sales volumes is exactly matched by the effect on revenue of the increase in price.

Figure 13.2
The relationship between sales revenue and price

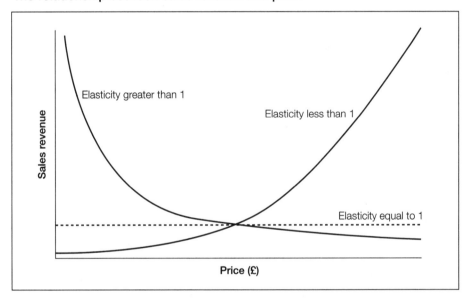

The underlying problem with price elasticities is the assumption that they remain constant over a wide range of prices. Given the analysis above, this clearly cannot be the case. Intuitively, we would expect revenue first to increase as price increases, to go through a maximum, and then to decline steadily at higher price levels (see Figure 13.3).

The implication of the behaviour shown in Figure 13.3 is that the price elasticity increases as price increases. At low prices, it is like the curve for a price elasticity of less than 1, and at high prices it becomes like the curve for a price elasticity of greater than 1. The point of maximum revenue corresponds to a price elasticity of exactly 1.

Figure 13.3
Typical variation of revenue with price

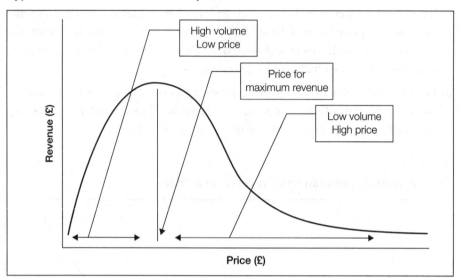

A further problem

A further problem with price elasticities is that we also instinctively assume that sales volume varies smoothly and continuously with price. The frequency with which we see prices such as £1.95 or £99.95 challenges this assumption.

There is no doubt that thresholds for prices – sometimes called price points – are real. The change in sales volume resulting from changing the price from just below a price point to just above a price point is much greater than would be predicted from the price change and typical price elasticity.

The effect of a price point is that the price–demand curve shown in Figure 13.1 is no longer smooth, but instead has a step in it. This creates technical difficulties when trying to describe the behaviour of the market in terms of price elasticities. If price points are believed to be important for a brand, discrete techniques such as conjoint analysis are often used instead.

Optimum pricing

For this section and the rest of this chapter, we will make the following assumptions:

■ The price–demand curve is smooth (i.e. there are no price points), so that we can use a price elasticity approach.

■ Changes in price are relatively small, so that we can assume that the price elasticity is constant.

Subject to these constraints, we can gain valuable insights about optimum pricing, the impact of competitors' pricing and the effect of price on market size.

For example, if we combine these assumptions with a simple fixed cost-variable cost model, we can calculate the price that will maximize profits (assuming that all other factors such as the economic and competitive environments remain constant). Merrick (2004) maintains that the profit-maximizing price depends only on the variable costs and the price elasticity. A mathematical proof is beyond the scope of this book, but the relationship is shown in Figure 13.4.

Figure 13.4
The relationship between the profit maximizing price and the price elasticity

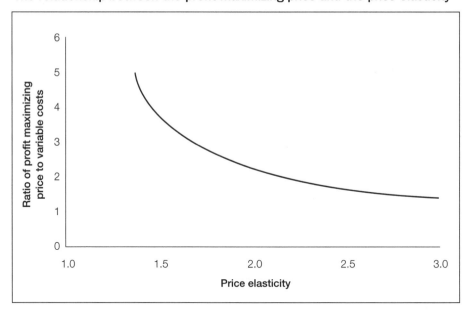

Figure 13.4 shows how the profit maximizing price, expressed as a multiple of the unit variable costs, decreases towards 1 as the price elasticity increases. At a price elasticity of 2, for example, the profit maximizing price is twice the unit variable costs. The model is valid only for price elasticities greater than 1; as noted above, for price elasticities less than 1, revenue increases with price and so there is no optimum price.

A different and sometimes more important decision is whether sales of the product are profitable even if the pricing is optimum. This aspect will depend on a wide range of factors, including competitor price. But this is a separate issue and does not itself affect the optimum price level.

Profit maximization compared with revenue maximization

The optimum pricing model described above was based on the assumption of a constant price elasticity. We now want to consider optimum pricing for the more realistic situation where revenue at first increases with price, reaches a maximum, and then decreases again (as shown in Figure 13.3). If we superimpose a simple fixed cost-variable cost model, we can expect to see the relationships shown in Figure 13.5.

Figure 13.5
How revenues and costs vary with price

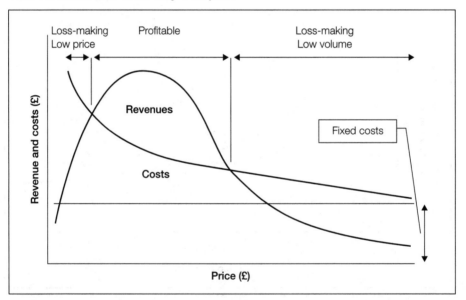

As price increases, sales volumes decrease and variable costs decrease. At high prices, sales volumes and variable costs are both low, and total costs are dominated by the fixed costs.

Revenues exceed costs only at intermediate prices. The business is loss-making when volumes and variable costs are high and, because of the low price, are not covered by revenues. At high prices, volumes and revenues are low and the fixed costs dominate; we have lost the economies of scale and can no longer dilute the fixed costs sufficiently to be profitable.

It is interesting to look at what happens if we start at the high price breakeven point and reduce price steadily. By the time we have reached the point of maximum revenue, costs are increasing and revenues decreasing. This means that we have already passed the point of profit maximization. The following general rule (Merrick 2003) can therefore be deduced.

The price for profit maximization is always higher than the price for revenue maximization.

This is illustrated in Figure 13.6 which shows, for the revenues and costs in Figure 13.5, how profit varies with price.

Figure 13.6
The relationship between revenue maximization and profit maximization

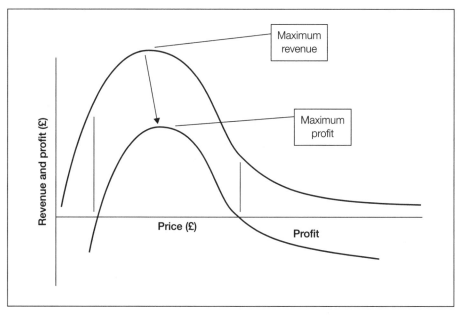

This reinforces the point that we made in Chapter 3; the temptation for marketing managers to focus on revenue maximization, and for bonus schemes to reward this focus, is predictably and consistently suboptimal if sustained over time. It damages profitability and therefore destroys shareholder value. There is no quick and easy substitute for a focus on profitability, and this means ensuring that marketing decisions take into account the cost implications for the business.

What about the competition?

The discussion above of pricing considers only one product or brand in isolation. In this section we look at how the concepts considered above can be extended to describe the effects on your brand of price changes by competing brands.

These effects can be described by defining a cross-price elasticity in the same way that we defined the price elasticity for a single brand. For example, if brand A increases price by 10%, and this results in an increase in sales by brand B of 3%, then we can say that the cross-price elasticity of brand A on brand B is 0.3. The general definition of cross-price elasticity is given below.

> The cross-price elasticity of brand A on brand B is the percentage increase in sales of brand B divided by the percentage increase in price of brand A (calculated on the basis of a small price increase).

Cross-price elasticities are important because they show how your brand can be affected by changes in pricing policy by your competitors. They are most useful when assembled into a table called a cross-price elasticity matrix. An example is illustrated in Table 13.1 for the simple case of just three competing brands.

Table 13.1
A cross-price elasticity matrix

	Brand A	Brand B	Brand C
Brand A	−1.7	0.2	0.4
Brand B	0.8	−2.4	0.5
Brand C	0.7	0.6	−1.9

The elements on the diagonal of the matrix (i.e. −1.7, −2.4, and −1.9) are simply the price elasticities for the three brands themselves, as defined at the beginning of this chapter. These are often referred to as 'own price elasticities' to distinguish them from the other elasticities in the matrix. Note that, by convention, these have a negative sign because an increase in price results in a decrease in sales volume of that brand. For example, for the values in Table 13.1, an increase in the price of brand B of 10% would result in a decrease in sales of brand B of 24%.

The elements not on the diagonal are the cross-price elasticities. These have a positive sign because an increase in the price of one brand will result in an increase in sales of a different brand. For example, for the values in Table 13.1, an increase in the price of brand C of 10% will result in an increase in sales of brand A of 4%.

Note that there is no reason for the cross-price elasticity matrix to be symmetrical – the effect of brand X on brand Y need not be the same as that of brand Y on brand X. In spite of this, it is not uncommon for symmetry to be assumed in analyses in order to reduce the number of variables that need to be considered.

One of the important features of the cross-price elasticity matrix is that it also enables you to calculate which brands will be the winners and losers in terms of market share and revenue share following price changes.

Assume, for example, that the brands in Table 13.1 have the sales volumes and prices shown in Table 13.2.

Table 13.2
Market positions

	Sales volume	Price	Revenue	Market share	Revenue share
Brand A	152.0	44.0	6,688	42.6%	43.5%
Brand B	78.0	48.0	3,744	21.8%	24.3%
Brand C	127.0	39.0	4,953	35.6%	32.2%
Total/Average	**357.0**	**43.1**	**15,385**	**100.0%**	**100.0%**

Given the sales volumes and prices, we can calculate the revenues, market shares and revenue shares (shown in Table 13.2 as shaded areas). We can also calculate the total sales volume and revenue and, from these, the average price of the three brands.

Now let us consider what happens if brand A increases its price by 10%, but brands B and C keep their prices the same. From the cross-price elasticity matrix in Table 13.1, we can see that the effect will be that brand A's sales decrease by 17%, brand B's sales increase by 8%, and brand C's sales increase by 7%.

We can now revise the prices and sales volumes in Table 13.2 and recalculate the revenues, market shares and revenue shares. The results are shown in Table 13.3.

Table 13.3
Market positions after the price change

	Sales volume	Price	Revenue	Market share	Revenue share
Brand A	126.2	48.4	6,108	36.4%	39.5%
Brand B	84.2	48.0	4,042	24.3%	26.2%
Brand C	135.9	39.0	5,300	39.3%	34.3%
Total/Average	**346.3**	**44.6**	**15,450**	**100.0%**	**100.0%**

Comparing Tables 13.2 and 13.3 shows that brand A lost sales of 25.8, with brand B and C gaining sales of 6.2 and 8.9 respectively. In terms of market shares, brand A lost 6.2 percentage points, with brands B and C gaining 2.5 and 3.7 percentage points respectively. We could carry out similar comparisons for revenues and revenue shares.

In the above example, we looked at a simple price change involving just brand A. Clearly, the same method could be applied to look at more complex scenarios with several brands changing price, and also with a more complex markets containing many more brands.

The overall market

Another comparison that we can make using Tables 13.2 and 13.3 is to look at what has happened to the overall market.

The effect of the 10% increase in brand A's price has been to increase the average price in the market across all three brands from 43.1 to 44.6, an increase of 3.5%. At the same time, the total sales volume has decreased from 357.0 to 346.3, a decrease of 3.0%. We can describe this change in terms of a market price elasticity, analogous to the price elasticity of a single brand. In this case, we would calculate the market price elasticity as 3.0 divided by 3.5, i.e. 0.9.

In general, the market price elasticity is defined as follows.

> The market price elasticity is the percentage decrease in total market sales volume divided by the percentage increase in the average price in the market (calculated on the basis of a small price increase).

What has happened, as noted above, is that sales of 6.2 switched from brand A to brand B, and 8.9 switched from brand A to brand C. In total, therefore, sales of 15.1 switched from brand A to other brands as a result of brand A's price increase. But brand A's total loss of sales was 25.8, indicating that the total market size decreased by 10.7. Some of brand A's customers decided not to switch to other brands but to drop out of the market completely.

It is often assumed that the market price elasticity is a characteristic of the market in the same way as a brand price elasticity is a characteristic of a brand. This is not the case, and is at best only an approximation.

If we were to recalculate the effect on the market of, say, brand C increasing its prices by 10% and brands A and B holding their prices constant, we would get a different market price elasticity to that found above. This is not surprising, as there is no reason a priori why all brands should have the same effect on the total market. If we were to assume that all brands were to increase their prices by the same amount, say 10%, in general we would get a different market price elasticity again. So a market price elasticity can only be a rough guide to the response of the overall market size to changes in prices within the market – the more sensitive model is that using cross-price elasticities, described above.

Even with this caveat, there is one area where the market price elasticity is useful. If the market price elasticity is less than 1, then the same analysis that was carried out earlier in this section applies; increases in price bring increasing revenues and decreasing costs, and therefore increasing profits. Clearly, one supplier acting alone is vulnerable. But a market price elasticity of less than 1 provides an incentive for suppliers to form a cartel and is a clear signal that anti-competitive pricing, if it were allowed to take place, would be highly profitable.

Where do price elasticities come from?

The best method of obtaining price elasticities is from econometric analysis, as this approach can take into account all of the other factors that influence sales volumes (e.g. seasonality, trends and advertising).

A good econometric analysis will provide the full matrix of own price and cross-price elasticities shown in Table 13.1. However, unless the data series is unusually detailed and comprehensive, it is often necessary to make additional assumptions or to impose constraints to obtain the full matrix.

But having obtained the full matrix, it is important not to take the results at face value. The effective market price elasticities should be calculated for a range of price changes, following the methodology described above. These then need to be scrutinized and subjected to reality checks before the elasticities can be used to inform policy decisions. The key point is that an arbitrary set of own price and cross-price elasticities may not give credible values for the market price elasticity, even if the values and signs of the own price and cross-price elasticities look satisfactory.

How do price promotions fit in?

We shall look at promotions in more detail in Chapter 14. Here, we would like to consider the narrow topic of price promotions in the context of their being a type of price change and therefore a special case of the price changes considered in the earlier parts of this chapter. For example, some of the more common price promotions are given in Table 13.4, together with the equivalent price change.

Table 13.4
Price promotions and equivalent price reductions

Promotion type	Short form	Price reduction
Buy One Get One Free	BOGOF	50%
Buy Two Get Third Free	B2GTF	33%
Buy One Get One Half Price	B1G1HP	25%
Buy Two Get Third Half Price	B2GTHP	17%

Given the equivalence between price promotions and price changes, the question naturally arises as to what is the equivalent price elasticity for a price promotion. What is interesting and striking is that the price elasticity is usually much higher than the price elasticity that would apply to an 'ordinary' price change for the same product or brand. Price promotion elasticities more than twice as large as the 'ordinary' price elasticity have been found by Finn (2003). This behaviour is surprising because, as discussed earlier in this chapter, we would expect price elasticities to decrease as price decreases.

The relationship between price and sales volume for a price promotion is illustrated by the price–demand curve in Figure 13.7.

Figure 13.7
Price–demand curve for a price promotion

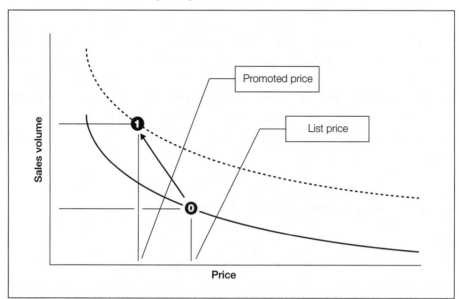

The price and sales volume of the unpromoted product are shown by circle '0'. The overall effect of the promotion is to move the brand to the position shown by circle '1'.

The effect of the price promotion can therefore be represented as moving the brand away from the normal relationship between sales volume and price and onto a different curve for the duration of the promotion. This probably arises for a combination of reasons:

■ The nature of the offer itself – something 'just too good to miss';

■ Increased advertising immediately before and during the promotion;

■ Increased display prominence;

■ Increased distribution.

Price is one of the most important elements of the marketing mix, and one of the least well managed ones. In the next chapter we examine a closely-related decision, the sales promotion decision.

Key points

■ Price elasticities are a useful and simple way of describing the effects of price on sales volumes.

■ They must be used with care, however, as they are valid only within a limited range of price changes and they do not allow for the effect of price points.

■ Price elasticities can be used in simple but robust models to optimize pricing policy.

■ Maximizing revenue is not a valid substitute for maximizing profit – it always gives a lower price, higher volume solution.

■ Price promotions behave like ordinary price changes, but with much higher price elasticities.

14

HOW PROMOTIONS WORK

This chapter looks at the main types of promotions, how they work and what determines their overall effectiveness. We look at consumer promotions and trade promotions separately, and also consider the differences between short-term, medium-term and long-term effects. Finally, we describe a framework for planning promotional campaigns, and discuss how they should be researched, tested and tracked.

Introduction

Prior to the 1990s, advertising was the largest part of the typical FMCG (Fast-Moving Consumer Goods) budget. As short-term pressures and the strength of retailers grew, promotions took more and more of the marketing budget, replacing advertising as the largest component. Jones estimated the ratio of advertising/consumer promotions/trade promotions in a 1997 survey as 24%/26%/50% (see Figure 14.1).

Figure 14.1
Breakdown of typical FMCG marketing budget

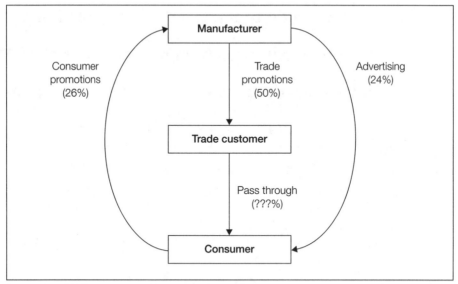

Data from Jones (1999)

It is commonly observed that promotions lead to short, sharp sales spikes. Yet not all volume is profitable volume. From the late 1980s to the present day, a growing weight of academic evidence from fact-based studies of consumer promotion spending effectiveness has revealed an alarming problem (Abraham and Lodish 1990; Ehrenberg *et al.* 1994). For example, Leonard Lodish found that four out of five promotions were unprofitable in an extensive study (Lodish and Lubetkin 1992).

Given the vast spending levels attracted by consumer promotions, it is important to understand what drives companies to use them and what distinguishes the profitable promotions from the unprofitable ones. Before beginning our analysis, it is worth asking ten hard questions about the profitability of your own promotions:

1. Do we believe that our promotions have anything other than a short-term impact?

2. If so, what is the evidence for this?

3. How well do we integrate promotional activity with advertising and display?

4. What percentage of our trade promotional expenditure is passed on to consumers?

5. Do our promotions devalue the brand by encouraging 'bargain hunting'?

6. Can we enhance the loyalty tie-in of our promotions?

7. What analysis supports our choice of promotional offers?

8. Do we understand and take into account the direct and indirect costs of our promotional offers?

9. What process do we use for planning our promotional campaigns?

10. What do we do to research, test and track our promotional campaigns? Is what we do adequate?

Defining sales promotion

Sales promotion is a surprisingly difficult term to pin down. The reason for this is because it includes such a wide variety of activities and techniques. Typical sales promotions can include price-off packs, value packs, coupons, samples, in-pack premiums, self-liquidating premiums, refunds and rebates, contests, sweepstakes, trade shows, continuity plans, warranties and many others.

The term *sales promotion* as used by practising marketers today refers to many kinds of selling incentives and techniques intended to produce immediate or short-term sales effects. The other defining characteristic of sales promotion is that the goal is short term or immediate. Sales promotion is not generally used to generate long-term results or sales in the future, but rather to generate sales results right now.

The distinction between short-term and long-term results may vary with the product category and the particular industry, making a specific time definition somewhat arbitrary. But the important idea is that the goal for sales promotion is results in the current promotional period, not in later time periods.

Sales promotion, then, is a collection of techniques communicated to target audiences to generate short-term sales results. Traditionally, sales promotion has been viewed as a non-recurrent selling activity, and it is often defined as such. However, this view does not reflect the current condition of frequent and repeated sales promotion programmes necessary to maintain business in many product categories. In most cases, sales promotion has become an all-too-recurrent activity, so the idea of a non-recurrent activity is eliminated from the definition here.

What drives you to use promotions?

The simple truth is that promotions are fun to start and challenging to stop. Ambler (1996) comments that 'promotions are no more, and no less, addictive, than cocaine'. Similarly, Ehrenberg *et al.* (1994) comment that 'there are many pressures to promote, acting on middle or junior management'.

Positive reasons for promotional spending cited widely in the literature include:

- Immediate, dramatic consumer sales spike;
- Fear of trade customers (display, listing, stock levels);
- Keeping up with competition;
- Giving salesmen something to say.

Negative reasons for avoiding promotion include the following:

- Stockpiling by consumers cannibalizes the volume advantages of the spike.
- Promotions encourage consumers to become bargain hunters.
- Costs of promotion do not cover profits from the spike.
- Costs associated with supply chain turbulence.

A framework for evaluating promotions

There are many hypotheses available about the effects of promotions, and Table 14.1 provides a framework for evaluating them. Essentially, this shows that there are three ways that promotions can contribute to the ultimate goal of profit, and over three time horizons. If we chart these three avenues to profit against the three time horizons, we get a three-by-three matrix of potential marketing objectives.

Table 14.1
Matrix of potential marketing objectives

	Volume	Price	Cost
Immediate (during the promotion)	*Consumer –* Accelerating purchase; obtaining trial purchase; obtaining share of volume *Trade –* Increasing traffic in channel; obtaining trade support; manipulating trade inventories	*Consumer –* Reducing the net transaction price to the consumer (or increasing the net value, in the case of gifts); deflecting attention from a high price *Trade –* Reducing the off-invoice trade price	Direct cost of promotional incentives, other than off invoice Indirect cost of 'special' manufacturing and packaging Cost of trade promotions not passed on to consumer Indirect cost of supply-chain turbulence
Medium-term (4–16 weeks)	*Consumer –* Decelerating next purchase (stockpiling); encouraging repeat purchase; encouraging more frequent usage; denying volume to competitors *Trade –* Increasing traffic in channel (bargain hunters)	*Consumer –* Encouraging bargain hunting *Trade –* Pressure to reduce prices	Scrapping of unused promotional incentives Repackaging of stock to remove promotional labelling
Long-term (16 weeks to 3 years)	*Consumer –* Increasing consumer loyalty; increasing penetration *Trade –* increasing traffic in channel; increasing trade loyalty; expanding product distribution	*Consumer –* Encouraging bargain hunting; discouraging purchase off-promotion *Trade –* Pressure for more promotions	

Often managers focus on the volume effect of promotions, but the other two are at least as important as methods of driving profits. The basic conceptual differences between consumer and trade effects must also be kept in mind by the analyst.

How can promotions affect your sales volumes?

Consumer purchasing behaviour

By far the most common management expectation about promotions is that they drive sales volume, but this is not necessarily the case. To understand why expectations differ from reality, it is necessary to delve into the extensive literature on consumer purchasing behaviour. However, before doing that, readers unfamiliar with the subject might like to consult a general introduction to the principles and general concepts, such as Robert East's excellent book *Consumer Behaviour* (1997).

Most consumers have a repertoire of two or three brands in a category which they habitually buy over time (Ehrenberg 1988; Brown 1953; Cunningham 1956). The group of brands purchased are called the *brand repertoire*. Multibrand buying may come about for the following reasons:

- Buyers seek variety, for example in beverages and confectionery.
- A preferred brand may not be available.
- A consumer promotion may temporarily attract purchasers.

An understanding of the factors that affect habitual purchase is important if the right marketing decisions are to be made. Is a consumer's brand repertoire the result of variety seeking, bargain seeking (and promotional response) or inability to buy the preferred brand frequently? Answers to these questions relate to marketing mix decisions.

There is no necessity for habitual purchasing to involve strong feelings or cognitive processes. It is quite possible for people to buy regularly a brand they dislike (through economic necessity). People make some brands, such as Guinness, a small part of their portfolio yet continue to buy this brand for a long period of time. People may like a brand but not purchase it through lack of need or opportunity (for example Porsche).

Purchase habits also apply to brands that we routinely do not buy. Most of us will admit to avoiding certain brands that we dislike, but brand avoidance also applies to brands that are unfamiliar to us as individuals.

Most consumers switch their brand choice from purchase to purchase, within their brand repertoire, and stimuli such as sales promotions can trigger such temporary switching. We may also switch to brands that are familiar but not within our brand repertoire. We are much less likely to switch to unfamiliar brands or ones that we actively dislike, except through economic necessity.

Buying a repertoire brand on one occasion does not normally increase the likelihood of buying that brand in the future. While learning theory suggests that there should be a bias towards purchasing the same brand as last time, extensive studies of repeat buying patterns (Bass *et al.* 1984; Ehrenberg 1988) indicate that there is rarely any significant learning effect from individual purchases of consumer products.

Immediate volume effects

'Spikes' in consumer sales volumes are a widely reported effect of promotions and occur for every type of promotional technique. This strongly contrasts with media advertising (but not retail features), where spikes are not observed. The cause of these consumer promotion spikes is hotly debated by researchers, and this issue will be examined later in this chapter. Some examples illustrating this spike effect are shown below.

Responsiveness to consumer promotions varies substantially

Over 20 papers documenting these variations in the USA are cited by Blattberg *et al.* (1995). East (1997) similarly cites numerous studies in Europe. For example (Cotton and Babb 1978), wide variations were found in the sales effects of promotions, ranging from gains of 20% to 400%. Garrick (1986) similarly found that seven instances of a promotion plus an advertising feature produced increases ranging from 43% to 600%. These variations might be explained by the fact that categories have widely different potentials for increased consumption (e.g. toilet paper and petrol, versus beer and confectionery). While increased consumption is only one component of volume increase, it would nevertheless help explain differences in sources of volume.

Short-term sales gain is mostly at the immediate expense of other brands in the consumer repertoire

Consumers switch to another brand in their repertoire if a promotion is attractive, according to research by Bawa and Shoemaker (1987), Grover and Srinivasan (1992) and Neslin and Shoemaker (1989).

Promotions generate relatively few trial purchases

Although sales promotion agencies widely proclaim the effectiveness of promotions to generate trial purchase, empirical evidence shows that this effect is relatively small. A study of 25 brands across four countries using panel data looked at the purchase history of consumers who bought on promotion (Ehrenberg *et al.* 1994). By going back over two years of purchase history, the study established that over 90% who bought on promotion had bought the brand in the past two years (see Figure 14.2 – US and Germany data only). The experience of buying the brand was nothing new to them as they were merely choosing an already familiar brand instead of some other familiar brand which they otherwise would have bought on that particular occasion.

Figure 14.2
Consumers buying on promotion

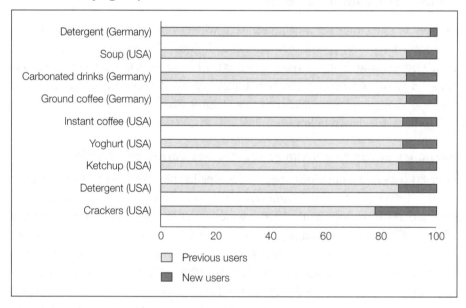

Higher market share brands are proportionally less responsive

Percentage measures of promotional spikes show that spikes are lower for larger brands (even though high-share brands may capture a larger absolute sales volume), because high-share brands have less headroom for expansion. This result was corroborated by Bolton (1989), Bemmaor and Mouchoux (1991) and Vilcassim and Jain (1991). However, the supporting evidence is in terms of percentage increases, and therefore the small-brand advantage should be reviewed against the diseconomies of scale in the set-up cost of small-brand promotions.

Cross-promotional effects are asymmetric, and promoting higher-quality brands impacts weaker brands disproportionately

Promoting certain brands causes customers to switch from a competing brand in greater numbers than would occur if the competing brand were to be promoted instead (Hoch and Banerji 1993). One possible explanation is that asymmetry in switching is due to differences in perceived quality. Research on tea has found this effect, where customers 'trade-up' from private label to a branded tea on promotion, but the reverse effect is less marked (Finn 2003). Asymmetric switching was also observed by Krishnamurthi and Raj (1988), Blattberg and Wisniewski (1989), Cooper (1988) and Walters (1991). Promoting brands perceived to be of higher quality was found to generate more switching in studies by Blattberg and Wisniewski (1989), Kamakura and Russell (1989), Mulhern and Leone (1991) and Allenby and Rossi (1991).

Integrating promotions with advertising and display features yields more than the sum of the individual effects

Most practitioners already recognize the importance of integrated marketing, but the size of the synergistic effect is not so well known. Market researchers IRI have circulated an analysis of these effects based on their 1988 data on sales in 2,400 grocery stores in 66 markets in the USA. Their main findings are shown in Figure 14.3.

Figure 14.3
Comparison of synergistic effects

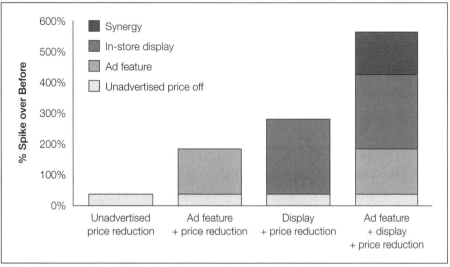

Data from IRI (1989)

Advertised promotions can result in increased trade customer traffic

The positive effect of advertised promotions on traffic was found by Walters and Rinne (1986), Kumar and Leone (1988), Walters and MacKenzie (1988) and Grover and Srinivasan (1992). This finding has practical importance, since the demand for promotions is often significantly influenced by trade customers' insistence on contributions from brand owners to their traffic building, irrespective of cost or benefits to the brand owner.

Medium-term volume effects

Three medium-term volume effects are possible (see Figure 14.4):

- **Peak and trough**: Plotting the data in this case shows a trough after the promotional peak. The reason for this can be because consumers brought forward a purchase to gain from the promotional benefits, but their consumption rate did not increase. Alternatively, limited disposable income may limit consumption levels immediately after promotion.

- **Spike and rise**: Comparing before-and-after sales shows a rise after the promotion. There are two possible explanations for this. First, penetration increased because new buyers were attracted and they continued to repurchase after the promotion. Second, consumption rates among existing buyers rose during the promotion, and then consumption at the faster rate continued after the promotion. This second explanation could in turn be caused by switching repertoire away from competition or by increased consumption (and therefore increased total-category sales).

- **Spike only**: Comparing before-and-after sales shows no change. There are two explanations for this. First, any new consumers attracted to try by the promotion did not repurchase. Second, consumption rate increases among existing buyers did not continue after the promotion.

Before-and-after studies (e.g. Ehrenberg *et al.* 1994) of the medium-term effects of promotions for 25 brands concluded that no significant medium-term effect (neither trough nor uplift) could be detected. In most cases the uplift or trough was less than 5% of the baseline (see Figure 14.5). The average effect across the study was 1% uplift and was not statistically significant.

Other studies drawing similar conclusions include Aaker (1973), Totten and Block (1987), von Gonten (1993) and Bawa and Shoemaker (1987).

Some researchers do find evidence of a trough after purchase (e.g. Blattberg 1981; Neslin *et al.* 1985; Finn 2003). The existence of this trough seems to depend on the category being promoted, and in particular its potential for stockpiling (e.g. off-trade groceries such as tea or beer) or potential for increased consumption (e.g. income constraints causing drinkers to cut back after a spending spree).

Trade traffic may also be changed in the same ways. Increasing trade traffic may result from 'bargain hunting' behaviour as a result of consumers becoming more sensitized to buying on promotion. This effect is likely to impact all brands in the category. While it is of advantage to the trade customer, it only serves to depress prices for the brand owners.

Figure 14.4
Possible impacts over time of promotions on sales volume

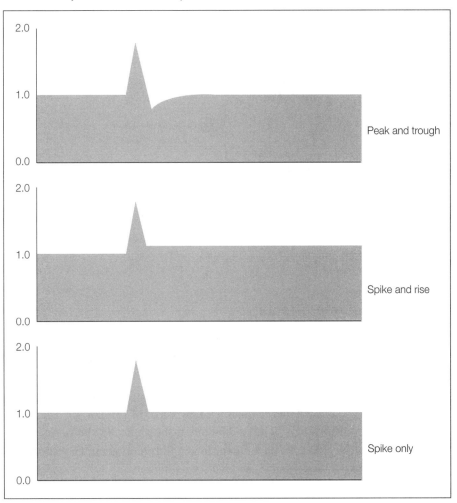

Figure 14.5
Medium-term effects of promotions on sales volumes

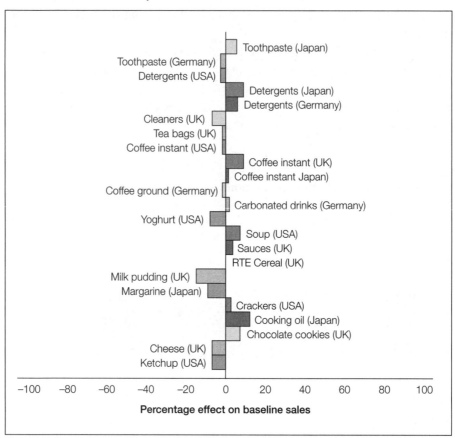

Long-term volume effects

Some promotional activities, such as introductory promotional offers to join a 'club' (e.g. a wine, book or music club) clearly have a long-term effect in recruiting new members who would not otherwise have joined.

For promotions with no loyalty tie-in, the long-term effects are more difficult to identify. For example, whoever begins a new cycle of promotions has a very short-term advantage, due to switching. Some of the gains may be permanent if competitors do not respond. The ambient level of promotions in the category is an important factor in assessing these long-term effects.

The greater the ambient frequency of promotions in the category, the lower the height of the spike

This result is likely to be caused by (a) consumer expectations about promotions (b) changes in the consumer reference price. The empirical results have been documented by Bolton (1989) and Raju (1992).

Brands that promote less often have a lower purchase frequency

This is a consequence of the previous point. The brand's purchase frequency decreases as the category promotion frequency increases, unless the brand increases its promotion frequency to match the category promotion frequency.

Brand penetration seldom increases, as that would require both trial purchases and repurchases

As noted previously, trial is seldom a significant promotional response (although in the case of new products, it may be much more significant, since their baseline starts at zero). To increase penetration, the trial must be succeeded by a repurchase (i.e. a medium-term uplift), and once again empirical research finds this to be a rare effect.

Long-term effects cannot be modelled by examining the spikes, or before–after stats; they are a baseline effect. Only by examining long-term category trends and comparing the brand relative to its competitors can these long-term baseline effects be modelled.

Factors that are likely to be important for long-term modelling include:

- Percentage of category/competitor volume bought on promotion;
- Impact of promotions on brand equity;
- Promotional impact on consumer reference price;
- Impact of promotions on trade customer loyalty.

How can promotions affect your prices?

Types of offer – consumer promotional offers

Consumer promotional offers are incentives that reward end-consumers who buy the end product. Table 14.2 provides a guide to the types of promotional offer that might be appropriate to achieving common objectives for promotional campaigns. The main types of promotional offers are listed in Box 14.1.

Table 14.2

Linking consumer promotions to campaign objectives

Promotional objective	Appropriate promotional offer
Obtaining product trial	Gifts, refund offers, contests, sweepstakes, sampling
Deflecting attention from price	Gifts, refund offers, contests, sweepstakes, sampling
Gaining share of volume from 'deal-seekers'	Price-off, bonus packs, coupons
Accelerating purchase	Price-off, bonus packs, coupons
Encouraging more frequent usage	Continuity plans, loyalty cards
Encouraging repeat usage	Continuity plans, loyalty cards
Denying volume to competition	Price-off, bonus packs, coupons, continuity plans, loyalty cards

Box 14.1 Typical consumer promotional offers

Bonus packs. One way the consumer can be offered a special price is to increase the amount of the product offered for the same price. Bonus packs can also take the form of BOGOF (buy one get one free), buy two get one free, and many variants on this theme. The *advantages* of bonus packs are that they can increase the amount of display space for the product and increase consumption rates, due to the pressure on storage space causing the consumer to use the product faster. The *disadvantages* are that they may well not be profitable – the cost of the extra free product may be more than the value of the extra sales.

Contests and sweepstakes differ in the eligibility rules: contests require that consumers purchasing the product enter, while sweepstakes do not. Some contests require skill, whereas sweepstakes do not. The *advantages* are that they create interest through press and word-of-mouth, plus they can be a source of customer data. The *disadvantages* are the clutter and effort of organizing.

Continuity plans. Continuity plans require the saving of some item relating to the purchase, such as stamps, which may be used for prizes or reduced costs. The *advantage* of using them is that they reward heavy purchasers for being heavy purchasers. The *disadvantage* may be that they do not reward true loyalty, merely heavy purchase.

Coupons. Coupons are by far the most common promotional method in the USA, but their popularity is lower elsewhere. There are two kinds of coupons – manufacturer coupons, where everything is paid by the manufacturer, and trade coupons, which are paid partially by the retailer. The *advantage* may be that only a percentage is redeemed, but the *disadvantages* are that they create clutter and work for those who process them.

Gifts. There are many types of gifts. The *advantages* of gifts are that they can enhance the product's value, if they relate to its brand values or link with sponsorship themes (such as Formula One). The *disadvantages* are that trade customers may resist storing and handling the gift items, and also theft and pilferage can be serious problems.

Loyalty cards are in many ways like electronic continuity plans. They have the additional *advantage* of creating a database, with the possibility of tracking heavy purchasers. Against this must be factored the *disadvantage* of substantial IT cost.

Price-offs. A manufacturer's price-off is printed directly on the product packaging and becomes an integral part of the product's appearance to consumers. Special labels might also be used. The *advantage* of price-offs is that they are easy for the consumer to use and they put the product in direct competition with other products on display. The *disadvantage* is that everyone who buys the product takes advantage of the price reduction, including those who routinely buy the product at the regular price. Trial is therefore restricted mostly to bargain-hunters, who are inherently less likely to stay loyal following the offer.

Refund offers involve the purchaser in sending a proof-of-purchase in return for a reward. They have the *advantage* of rewarding loyal purchasers, but *disadvantages* include a poor record in generating trial purchase.

Sampling provides the consumer with a free sample of the product and is a very effective means of introducing a new product or demonstrating an improvement of an existing product. Typically a small trial size is offered. Although sampling has the *advantage* of starting trial usage, its *disadvantages* are considerable, especially in terms of distribution.

Types of trade offer

In essence, trade promotional offers have many similarities to consumer promotional offers – but their objectives are quite different. Table 14.3 assesses the suitability of trade offers for achieving common objectives set for promotional campaigns, while Box 14.2 lists the typical trade offers available.

Table 14.3
Linking trade promotional offers to campaign objectives

Promotional objective	Appropriate promotional offer
Obtaining trade support	Trade staff gifts, performance-based rewards, events
Manipulating trade inventories	In-channel displays and features
Expanding product distribution	Trade performance-based rewards
Support for in-channel promotions	In-channel price-offs, in-channel displays and features, in-channel advertising

Box 14.2 Typical trade promotional offers

In-channel advertising involves the display of posters and announcements highlighting the product. As with displays and features, the *advantage* is the extra prominence, but the *disadvantage* is that the cost to the manufacturer may exceed the actual creative costs – in effect the manufacturer is making a media-space payment to the trade customer.

In-channel displays and features involve setting up displays of the product – in gondolas or shelf-ends. The *advantage* is the extra prominence the product receives, and hence the possibility of extra sales volume, but manufacturers pay the retailer for the privilege, and the *disadvantage* may be that the money paid exceeds the cost of the actual display mechanism.

In-channel price-offs are where the trade customer marks down the price on the shelf label and price label. Usually it is important to use a large, prominent label to ensure it receives attention. The *advantage* is the extra volume of sales this may generate, but the *disadvantage* is that manufacturers pay the trade customer for the price-off. Often the cost is not fully paid to consumers, and the retailer retains some of the cash benefits.

Trade staff events. Events are sometimes run for trade staff, especially in connection with new product launches. These can include entertainment and also may incorporate gifts. The *advantages* are in the opportunity to train staff to understand the features and benefits of our brands. The *disadvantage* is that the scope for learning in the context of an entertainment may be strictly limited.

Trade staff rewards. Staff in the channel who provide recommendation and other support receive rewards such as gifts, contests and sweepstakes. The *advantages* can be substantial. However, the *disadvantages* include potential anti-trust and regulatory issues, and performance guarantees can be difficult to build into the rewards.

Immediate price effects

Many types of promotions involve a price reduction. For the supplier there is therefore an immediate drop in revenue if the promotion is paid off-invoice. Alternatively, if the payment is made in cash or equivalent, there is an immediate cost effect. Either way, the revenue spike should be counterbalanced against this lost revenue in assessing the effects of the promotion on profits and shareholder value.

Medium-term price effects

The frequency of price deals changes the consumers' reference price

This finding is important because a lower consumer reference price reduces the premium that can be charged for a brand in the marketplace. The effect of deal frequency on consumers' reference price was found by Lattin and Bucklin (1989), Kalwani *et al.* (1990), Kalwani and Yim (1992) and Mayhew and Winer (1992).

Long-term price effects

Consumers become more price-sensitive over time

Long-term exposure of consumers to price promotions makes them more price-sensitive. For products that can be stockpiled, consumers learn to 'lie in wait' for especially good promotions. The evidence for this effect is limited to a few studies (Mela *et al.* 1997, 1998). The generalized applicability of this effect is not certain (Ehrenberg *et al.* 1994).

How can promotions affect your costs?

Promotions add to supplier costs in two ways:

- **Direct costs:** invoiced either by the agency (in the case of gifts, coupons or other incentives) or by the trade customer;

- **Indirect costs:** disruption to supply-chain activities caused by uneven volumes on promotion.

Trade funding can occur in several alternative formats. Chevalier and Curhan (1976) looked at the frequency of occurrence of different types of retailer promotions (see Table 14.4).

Table 14.4
Frequency of retailer promotions

Promotion type	Frequency
Bill-back	49%
Off-invoice	24%
In-ad coupon + bill-back	12%
Off-invoice + bill-back	6%
In-ad coupon + off-invoice	3%
In-ad coupon	3%
Off-invoice + bill-back + in-ad coupon	1%
Free goods	1%
Other	1%
	100%

Trade customers pass through less than 100% of promotions to consumers

Because trade customers are the vehicle for pass-through of promotions, it is important to recognize that most brands receive far less that 100% pass-through. Curhan and Kopp (1986) found that brand characteristics result in different levels of pass-through. The finding that less than 100% of promotions reach the end consumer has been made in several papers, for example Chevalier and Curhan (1976), Curhan and Kopp (1986), Walters (1988) and Blattberg and Neslin (1990).

Other sources of costs that are widely regarded as significant include:

- **The indirect costs of supply chain disruption:** Anecdotal evidence is that Procter & Gamble's decision to adopt 'everyday low pricing' and stop using sales promotions was based largely on the conclusions of its analysis of supply chain disruption costs.

- Trade customers demand more promotions over time: This effect parallels that discussed earlier in the context of consumer promotions.

A framework for managing sales promotions

Sales promotions give financial incentives to consumers and trade customers with one objective – to increase sales rates during the promotional period in a way that generates additional profits that exceed the cost of the promotion. We should only spend money on promotions when we are confident that there will be an economic benefit. However, tying together the costs and profit-effects of promotional activity is far from easy.

The effective management of sales promotions is a hierarchical process, with objectives set for every level. The whole process should be underpinned by an integrated promotional plan, the main steps of which are set out in Figure 14.6.

Figure 14.6
The promotional planning process

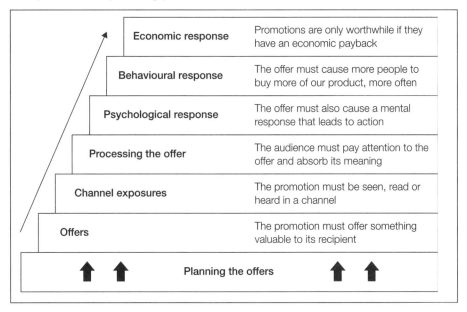

Promotional research, testing and tracking

So far we have explained how our promotional strategies are structured and implemented. This section explains the data collection and analysis methods on which the strategies are based.

Strategy research

Strategy research is essential in order to determine how to split our marketing budget between promotions and communications, and to guide strategic planning for promotions over time.

This type of research is done far too seldom and, as a result, promotions rely too much on hunch, tradition and reaction to trade pressures. If sales promotion is taking a significant share of our marketing expenditure, then it is worth getting the basis right by undertaking some strategy research, either on its own or as part of a wider strategy research programme.

Strategy research ideally consists of three types of analyses: marketing audits, qualitative promotional research and quantitative promotional research.

Marketing audits consist of background research into all the factors that do, or could, affect our profit, sales and market share. Because all parts of the marketing mix are reviewed, the main purpose of the audit is to set the marketing objectives of promotions. In practice, five headline measures are researched in detail:

- **Promotional share of mix** shows how heavily we use sales promotions within our marketing mix. It is our total expenditure on sales promotions divided by our total marketing expenditure. Where competitive intelligence about promotional spending is available, it is important to compare our own mix with that of our competitors.

- **Price-volume** statistics for the entire market and our own sales show the volume of products bought within specific price bands. These statistics are further broken down in terms of product types (e.g. for vehicle lubricants: synthetic, part synthetic, mineral multigrades and monogrades).

- **Percentage bought when on-promotion** is the percentage of sales (both volume and revenue) that are made on the basis of promotional offers. It measures the whole market, not just our brands, and is useful as an indicator of how intensively products are promoted.

- **Share of on-promotion sales**, calculated as the ratio of our sales on-promotion divided by the total sales on-promotion. It indicates whether we are attracting more or less than the average numbers of bargain-hunters in the market.

- **Distribution** (how many trade outlets) **and display** (how many special promotional displays) are useful indicators of trade promotion effectiveness. Researchers should consider providing these figures not only for the most popular products and packs, but also for other product types and packs, especially when it is a key promotional objective to expand the distribution of our full product range.

Qualitative research uses depth interviews and focus groups to develop an understanding of purchase arousals and the factors that motivate brand selection. For example:

- Price partitioning of the market can be assessed – it reflects the differences that buyers perceive in the pricing of products and barriers to substitution.

- Trade customers and their staff can also be included in qualitative studies to ascertain their attitudes and beliefs about the different types of trade promotions.

Quantitative research generally consists of a questionnaire survey with a large number of customers, followed by a statistical analysis of the results. The aim is to classify more precisely the price sensitivity and bargain-hunting behaviour of the consumer population. Trade customers can usefully also be included in these types of surveys.

Testing

The creative team may have developed several promotional ideas and numerous specific elements that may or may not work. Testing helps provide assurance that the promotions are on-strategy.

There is a lot to be understood about the psychological response to promotional offers. They are not simply mechanistic. Four different types of response require different approaches to testing (see Figure 14.7):

- **Immediate value promotions**, such as price-offs and bonus packs, remove the problem of 'high price' and may be perceived as 'good value'. The most usual way of testing alternative offers is to survey a range of offers, with several other closely competing brands – all at their normal prices – then progressively to introduce better and better offers on our brand until an acceptable percentage of the survey sample indicated that they would buy our brand.

- **Future value promotions**, such as samples and trial offers, function by reducing the perceived risk of trying our brand. The major method of testing samples is to place samples at several hundred prospective locations and count the numbers of trials.

- **Gift promotions** are tested in various different ways. Premiums need to be tested first for the appeal of the gift itself – displaying them side-by-side, including gifts that have previously been used with known results. Coupons are tested in much the same way as immediate value promotions.

- **Chance promotions** prizes should be tested and compared for their appeal. Competitions versus sweepstakes should be compared by discussing simulated promotion situations with potential entrants.

Figure 14.7
Types of psychological response to promotional offers

PROMOTION TYPE		EXAMPLES
Problem removal	Immediate value	Price-offs Bonus packs Rebates/refunds Trade coupons
	Future value	Samples, trial packs Warranties Loyalty programmes
Sensory gratification	Gifts	Coupons Premiums Stamps
	Chance	Competitions Sweepstakes

Tracking

After the promotion goes live, it should be tracked. Profit returns on promotions should then be calculated. When promotions are unprofitable, a diagnostic survey of reactions to the promotion should be undertaken to learn the lessons.

The profit return on promotions is relatively straightforward to calculate after the fact, but obviously the return must be estimated beforehand in deciding whether to launch a promotion offer in the first place.

The key figures are:

- Average sales per day when off-promotion (baseline);
- Profit margin per sale when off-promotion;
- Sales per day when on-promotion (baseline plus uplift);
- Profit margin per sale when on-promotion;
- Fixed costs per day of promotion.

From these the promotional payback can be calculated:

$$\text{Profit per day on-promotion} - \text{Profit per day off-promotion}$$

If more profit per day is generated during the promotional period than in the baseline period, then the promotion has positive payback. Extensive research into sales promotions shows that about 80% of all promotions have negative payback. The reasons why companies continue to burn money in this way are:

- Trade customer pressure to run promotions that drive up channel visits (but not supplier profits);

- Sales-based rewards and bonuses that ignore the costs of promotions;

- Failure to analyze promotional payback.

Where negative payback has been established, research can be extremely informative. Follow-up survey interviews with people who did and did not respond to the promotion can be revealing, in particular to discover whether the promotion generated trial purchases, repeats, or both. In-channel observation by the sales force can also furnish useful feedback, and the use of tape recorders to capture comments when people 'think aloud' about the promotion can provide valuable learning.

Key points

- Many promotions do not cover their costs.

- Promotions often produce an immediate and measurable 'spike' in sales volumes, but a positive effect on sales after the promotion has ended is rare and generally small.

- Trial purchases from first-time buyers are in a minority. Most consumers who buy on-promotion have previous experience of the product. They switch temporarily away from other brands in their repertoire (thus temporarily increasing the purchase frequency of the promoted brand, and decreasing the purchase frequency for the rest of the category).

- Frequent promotion by competitors reduces the purchase frequency (and share) for non-promoted brands. Where a significant percentage of category sales is sold on-promotion, brands that do not promote will be 'locked out' during promotional periods, and purchase frequency will fall.

- Sales promotions should not happen on an ad hoc basis, but be implemented via a campaign plan, with every campaign having a specified objective which reflects the overall marketing strategy.

- Sales promotions carried out by and through trade customers require a different type of campaign management and offer from those targeted directly at end consumers.

- Rigorous testing and tracking of responses to individual promotions reduces risk and enables campaigns to be rolled out, withdrawn or fine-tuned to reflect market behaviour.

15

CUSTOMER EQUITY
OPTIMIZATION

This chapter is about accounting for customer relationships and optimizing the payback from them. It is an approach to marketing that applies only to certain sectors of the economy where organizations can track their customers using databases. We have approached it from the angle of an organization that needs to decide how much to spend on acquiring new customers, cross-selling and improving retention rates. An optimum mix that maximizes value exists, and we show how this can be calculated. The chapter ends with a detailed worked example to illustrate the key principles.

What is customer equity optimization?

Customer equity's main thesis is uncomplicated. The customer is a financial asset that firms should measure, manage and maximize, just like any other asset.

> ### Box 15.1 Customer equity terminology
>
> Customer equity management: A dynamic, integrative marketing system that uses financial valuation techniques and data about customers to optimize the acquisition of new customers, their retention, and the selling of additional products to them, and which maximizes the value to the company of the customer relationship throughout the life cycle.
>
> Customer equity optimization: An approach to marketing payback optimization that makes an allowance for future sales from customers in addition to the initial sales that occur at the moment when the customer is first acquired.

The reason why this approach is important to decision makers is that more marketing expenditure is affordable than under traditional accounting approaches. To see how this works, look at Figure 15.1.

The diagonal line on the graph represents the cost of acquiring each customer. Initial acquisition seeks out the most responsive customers and the lowest acquisition costs. When the expenditure level on customer acquisition is increased, then less responsive customers have to be sought, and the acquisition cost per customer rises.

Figure 15.1
Accounting for acquisition expenditure and sales margins

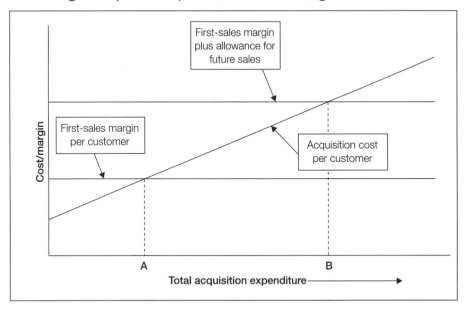

Ignoring future sales, the optimum expenditure would be at level A. The lower horizontal line represents the sales margin obtained from the customer at the time of acquisition. Where this crosses the cost line at expenditure level A, is where short-term profits are maximized. At any higher expenditure level, the cost of acquisition would exceed the incremental sales margin, based on initial sales.

Allowing for future sales, the optimum expenditure would be B. The higher horizontal line represents the sales margin that would be obtained from customers, including an allowance for future sales as well as initial sale. Where this crosses the cost line, at expenditure level B, is where long-term profits are maximized.

Most firms that manage customer relationships have an intuitive grasp of this idea, and yet few have embodied these types of calculations in their budgeting. For example, banks nowadays make a loss on the current accounts of most customers. The only reason why it makes business sense to offer current accounts is because they will subsequently sell other products to their customers, and it is the future sales margins from these products that subsidize the current account. Banks could not afford to withdraw the current account because even though unprofitable in its own right, it is the 'entry product' that most first-time customers want, and without it there would be no customers.

Despite attractive credentials, customer equity accounting is not a panacea to cure all marketing and customer problems. A selection of the main situations where this approach is relevant is shown in Table 15.1.

Table 15.1

Applications of customer equity accounting

Highly relevant/feasible	Medium relevance/feasibility	Low relevance/feasibility
Retail and private banking	Business banking	Corporate banking
Credit cards	Direct insurance	Corporate insurance
Energy (electric and gas)	Insurance – intermediaries	Corporate telecoms
Consumer & SME telecoms	Health services	Grocery products
Catalogue shopping	Automobile sales	Beverages
Internet shopping	IT products	Consumer durables
Membership organizations	Industrial products (high volume)	Other consumer products
Supermarkets (store cards)	Leisure and travel services	Retailers (no store card)
Sales account management (high numbers of customers)	Key account management	Global account management

The main barriers to adopting the customer equity approach are:

- Technical inability to track or model customer contacts and responses through their life stages over several years.

- Single product sales with no opportunity for add-on sales.

- Highly complex customer relationships that cannot be expressed in terms of customer stocks and flows.

The customer equity approach itself is not without inherent limitations, which are principally:

- Market trends are easily overlooked because of undue attention given to existing customers.

- Competitive activity easily overlooked for the same reasons.

- Direct marketing gets undue attention, and other effects such as pricing, offers and above-the-line activity are under-estimated.

These inherent limitations can be overcome by taking an approach to customer equity accounting and modelling that addresses them directly.

Before reading further, here are ten hard questions to ask about customer equity management in your organization:

1. What is the trend in our retention rates?

2. What is the trend in our acquisition costs?

3. What is the trend in the purchase rate for our customers?

4. What is the trend in our variable costs of providing customer service?

5. How do our acquisition costs increase with acquisition spend?

6. Is our customer base too large to be sustainable?

7. Is our customer base too large to be profit maximizing?

8. Is our customer base too small to be profit maximizing?

9. Over what period of time would we want to optimize profits?

10. Do we model customer accounting and the associated financials adequately?

Some worked examples

Shifting to a customer equity focus requires firms to develop new ways of evaluating their business. Although acquisition, retention and cross-selling can be modelled and managed separately, it would be a big mistake to do so, and would probably lead to bad decisions. Two calculations are needed: *customer accounting* and *financial alignment with customer accounting*. To some managers, these will not be familiar calculations, and therefore in this chapter we look at illustrative examples to show how the calculations work, and also to interpret the consequences of this approach.

How to account for the customer base

Customer accounting essentially involves calculating the effects of acquisition, retention, cross-selling and migration on customer numbers.

The 'leaky bucket' model is the starting point. Imagine having to keep the water level constant in a leaky bucket. You need to watch the water level and add water to make good the amount lost through leaks. The customer equivalent is illustrated in Figure 15.2.

The calculations behind the model are easy. However, we recommend applying some modelling discipline to constructing this model: this will prove useful as the models become more complex. Figure 15.3 shows the model structure.

Figure 15.2
The 'leaky bucket' model

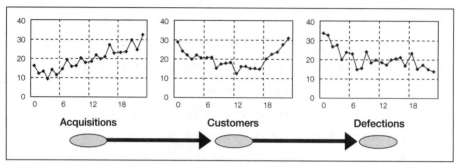

Several points should be noted about the model:

- **Units:** Numbers without units don't tell you much. Although accountants rarely need to show units, other than the currency, in customer accounting they are essential and must be shown, otherwise confusion and misleading conclusions beckon.

- **Calculations:** Showing explicitly how the numbers are calculated is good practice. If a calculation is too complex to show, split it into simpler component calculations on several lines.

- **Assumptions:** Hardwiring assumptions (i.e. using numbers in calculations) is not good practice. All assumptions should be stated explicitly and shown separately.

Having established a structure for the model, it can be populated with numbers. We will use scenarios for this purpose.

The steady-state scenario (Figure 15.4) simply shows the effect of equal acquisition and defection rates. It is intuitively obvious that in this case the number of customers is steady.

Changing the assumptions creates a new scenario, and the calculations become less intuitively obvious. For example, what is the shape of the customer curve when the acquisitions are steady but the defections are rising (as shown in Figure 15.5)?

Although an experienced mathematician would probably be able to answer this from mathematical insight, most others would need to reach for their calculators. We run the calculations and show them diagrammatically in Figure 15.6.

Figure 15.3

Calculations supporting the 'leaky bucket' model

Figure 15.4
Leaky bucket steady-state scenario

				1998	1999	2000	2001	2002
Assumptions								
Retention rate		(A)		80%	80%	80%	80%	80%
Acquisition rate		(B)		20%	20%	20%	20%	20%
Calculations								
Customers – opening balance	Customers	(C)	(F last year)	2,000,000	2,000,000	2,000,000	2,000,000	2,000,000
New customers	Customers/year	(D)	(B) * (C)	400,000	400,000	400,000	400,000	400,000
Retained customers	Customers/year	(E)	(A * (C)	1,600,000	1,600,000	1,600,000	1,600,000	1,600,000
Result								
Customers – closing balance	Customers	(F)	(D) + (E)	2,000,000	2,000,000	2,000,000	2,000,000	2,000,000

Figure 15.5
Steady acquisitions and rising defections scenario

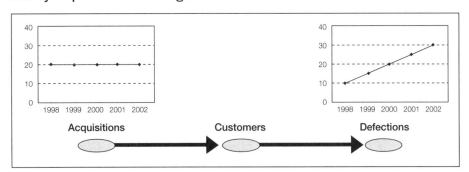

Whether you prefer numbers or graphs is a matter of personal taste, and both have been included above. We find that customer numbers first increase, then reach a maximum, then decline. These behaviours are often not immediately obvious, and our key point here is that customer accounting is something that can and should be calculated. Leaving it to intuition or ignoring it altogether in favour of financial accounting is not an acceptable option.

In this case, examination of the assumptions shows that customer numbers increase because acquisition of new customers exceeds the losses determined by the retention rate. As the retention falls, however, the acquisition rate becomes insufficient to maintain the customer population and numbers begin to fall.

How to align financial and customer accounting

Customer accounting is only an intermediary stage to customer equity modelling. Adding in the financial detail is the next step. Here some of the modelling lessons come in useful. Figure 15.7 shows the financial model as a fuzzy cloud at the outset of the financial modelling process.

In Figure 15.7, the communications that drive the acquisition process are then added explicitly to the previous model (Figure 15.2) because they can be costed, and also because they represent a variable (or input) that can be experimented with and optimized. The fuzzy cloud needs to be filled out, both as a spreadsheet model and schematically.

A simple model of the calculation links between the customer base and the financials is illustrated in Figure 15.8.

Figure 15.6
Calculation supporting the steady acquisitions and rising defections scenario

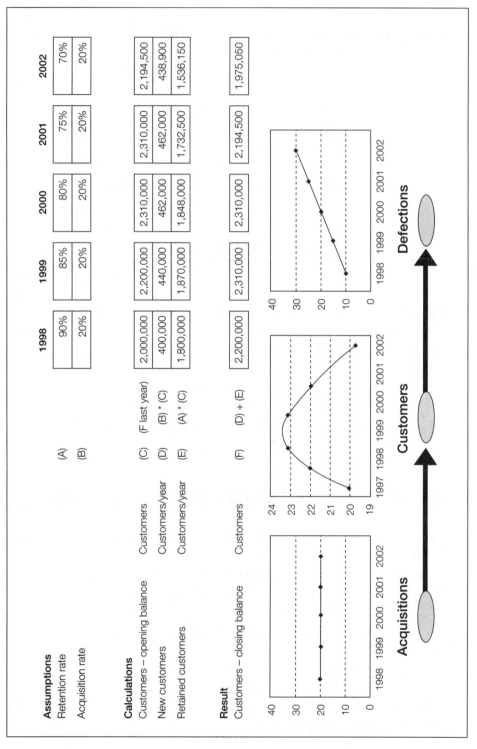

Figure 15.7
Connecting financial and customer models

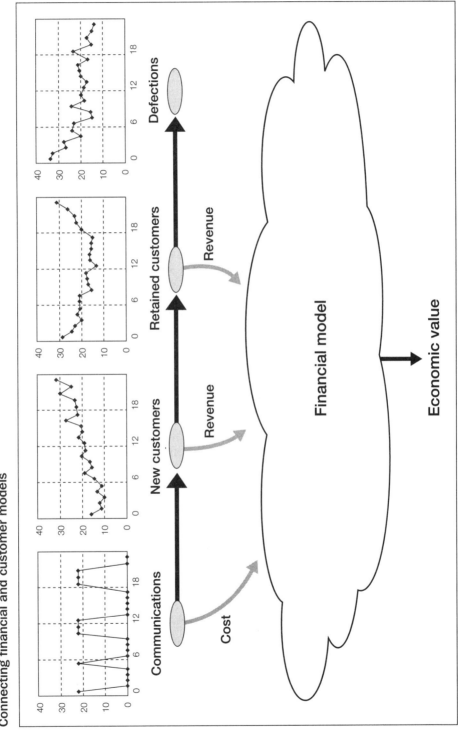

Figure 15.8

Calculation links between the customer base and the financials

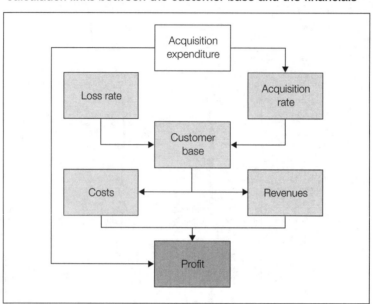

The acquisition expenditure drives the acquisition rate but also, because it is a cost, impacts on profitability. The customer base changes as a result of the net effect of the loss rate and the acquisition rate. Finally, the size of the customer base determines both revenues and costs which, together with the acquisition expenditure, give the profitability. This schematic model can be used as a basis for calculating profitability, for example using a spreadsheet. A sample calculation is shown in Figure 15.9.

The inputs to the model are the acquisition expenditure for each year and the initial customer base. Our customer accounting assumptions are the base acquisition cost, the maximum acquisition rate per year (so that we can allow for an increasing marginal cost of customer acquisition) and the customer loss rate. Our financial assumptions are the purchase rate per customer, the fixed costs of the business and the variable costs per customer. With these assumptions, the figure shows how some relatively simple arithmetic enables us to calculate how the customer base, revenues, costs and profit change year by year.

Figure 15.9

Integrated customer and financial model

				Year 1	Year 2	Year 3	Year 4	Year 5
Inputs								
Acquisition expenditure	£	A		20,000,000	20,000,000	20,000,000	20,000,000	20,000,000
Initial customer base	Customers	B		400,000				
Assumptions								
Base acquisition cost	£/customer	C		80.0	80.0	80.0	80.0	80.0
Maximum acquisition	Customers/year	D		500,000	500,000	500,000	500,000	500,000
Customer losses	%/year	E		20%	20%	20%	20%	20%
Purchase rate	£/customer	F		150.0	150.0	150.0	150.0	150.0
Fixed costs	£	G		10,000,000	10,000,000	10,000,000	10,000,000	10,000,000
Variable costs	£/customer	H		60.0	60.0	60.0	60.0	60.0
Calculations								
Marginal acquisition cost	£/customer	K	$=A/D$	40.0	40.0	40.0	40.0	40.0
Total acquisition cost	£/customer	L	$=C+K$	120.0	120.0	120.0	120.0	120.0
Opening	Customers	M	$=B \text{ or } P(-1)$	400,000	486,667	556,000	611,467	655,840
Losses	Customers	N	$=E*M$	80,000	97,333	111,200	122,293	133,168
Acquisitions	Customers	O	$=A/L$	166,667	166,667	166,667	166,667	166,667
Closing	Customers	P	$=M-N+O$	486,667	556,000	611,467	655,840	691,339
Average	Customers	Q	$=(M+P)/2$	443,333.33	521,333.33	583,733.33	633,653.33	673,589.33
Revenue	£	R	$=F*Q$	66,500,000	78,200,000	87,560,000	95,048,000	101,038,400
Variable costs	£	S	$=H*Q$	26,600,000	31,280,000	35,024,000	38,019,200	40,415,360
Acquisition costs	£	T	$=A$	20,000,000	20,000,000	20,000,000	20,000,000	20,000,000
Fixed costs	£	U	$=G$	10,000,000	10,000,000	10,000,000	10,000,000	10,000,000
Profit (by year)	£	V	$=R-S-T-U$	9,900,000	16,920,000	22,536,000	27,028,800	30,623,040
Total profit for period	£	W	$=V1+V2+V3+V4+V5$	107,007,840				

How to use the model to evaluate alternatives

The 'base case' version of the model shown in Figure 15.9 keeps acquisition expenditure, acquisition costs and customer losses (and therefore the customer retention rate) constant across the 5-year period. As shown in the figure, under these assumptions both the customer base and profits grow steadily over the 5-year period.

Many alternative acquisition expenditure patterns could be investigated using the model structure outlined. In order to provide some interesting and thought-provoking patterns that will help to understand the fundamental business questions, we look at three contrasting scenarios.

1. **Scenario A – Stability:** The acquisition budget is adjusted each year in order to maintain a constant size of customer base (see also the comments on the 'customer base size' myth in Chapter 1).

2. **Scenario B – Growth:** The acquisition budget is kept constant at £50 million per year (rather than the £20 million shown in Figure 15.9) with the objective of growing the customer base.

3. **Scenario C – Profit:** The acquisition budget is set so as to maximize profits over the 5-year period, whatever the consequences for the customer base.

To make the models more interesting, and to yield some useful insights, we now abandon the assumptions in the base case, and consider a situation where two conditions prevail:

- Customer losses increase steadily from 20% to 40% over the 5-year period (and retention rates consequently decline from 80% to 60%) because of growing competition.

- For similar reasons, base acquisition costs increase steadily from £80 to £100 per customer over the period.

The results for Scenario A are shown in Figure 15.10.

The cost of keeping the customer base constant under these assumptions is a steadily increasing expenditure on customer acquisition, both to offset the increasing losses and because of the higher cost of acquisition itself. Although keeping the customer base constant preserves revenues, the increasing costs lead to a steady decline in profits throughout the period.

The results for Scenario B are given in Figure 15.11.

Figure 15.10
Results for the stability scenario

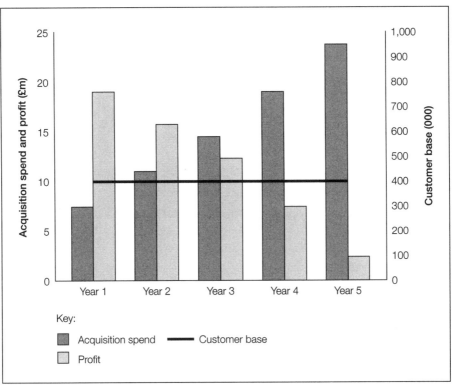

The financial outcome of Scenario B is disastrous. The high acquisition expenditure leads to a loss in the first 2 years. However, the size of the customer base nearly doubles by Year 4 and the higher revenues lead to a return to profitability. By that time, however, the harsher competitive environment means that profits are meagre. In the final year, the customer base declines slightly because even the £50 million acquisition budget is not able to maintain this size of customer base in the face of the higher losses and acquisition costs that apply in Year 5.

The results of Scenario C are shown in Figure 15.12. Here, with profit as the goal, the game plan is very different. This is the classic 'Grow then Milk' strategy. In the first year there is a spurt of acquisition, which gains market share. Thereafter, acquisition is steadily cut back, due to deteriorating market attractiveness.

Figure 15.11
Results for the growth scenario

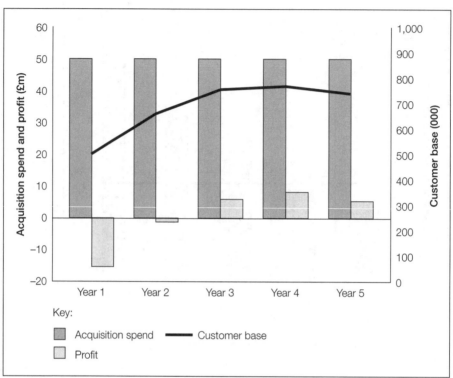

A healthy profit stream emerges in the second year. At the same time, having gained market share early, when the market was attractive, finance pulls back marketing expenditure.

However, this situation is not sustainable in the long term. The initially high share is allowed to decline. Share is conceded to competition because the market attractiveness is declining. Eventually, as size drops, diseconomies of scale will emerge and these will eat profits and the business will eventually need to be shut down.

How to discover what maximizes profits

It is clear that none of the above scenarios is satisfactory. But is there a combination that would offer a stable (and therefore long-term) strategy that would maximize profits? Clearly such a strategy will depend on the assumptions, especially for customer losses (retention rate) and the acquisition cost. We can

Figure 15.12
Results for the profit scenario

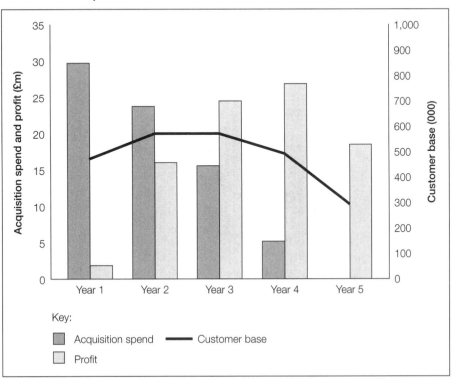

Key:
■ Acquisition spend ▬▬ Customer base
□ Profit

use the model described above to calculate what levels of customer base are supported by various levels of acquisition expenditure and how much profit is made in each case.

To illustrate the point, in Figure 15.13 we show the results based on the assumptions in Year 1 of the previous examples.

First look at the customer base. As we increase the annual acquisition expenditure, the size of the customer base that can be supported increases. Note that these figures refer to a steady-state situation. In any one year, a real company would not necessarily have reached a steady state and may be either growing or shrinking, even with a constant annual spend (as shown in Scenario B). Note also that although the steady-state customer base increases with acquisition expenditure, the rate of increase slows as the costs of acquiring additional customers become ever more expensive.

Now let us compare the profitability of the various levels of acquisition expenditure for a customer base that has reached a steady state. The results are quite revealing – there is a maximum profitability at an acquisition expenditure of about £55 million. Spending less than this quickly reduces profitability as the customer base becomes too small. Above this, the expenditure gradually becomes less and less effective.

Figure 15.13
Customer base and acquisition expenditure

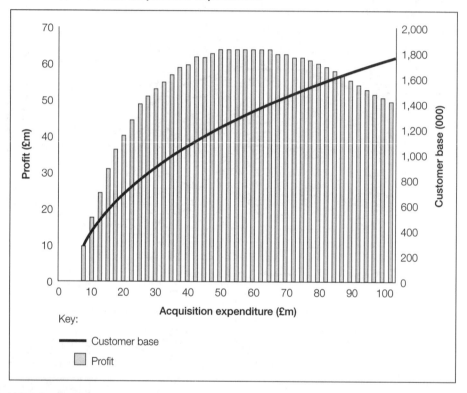

BookCo's optimization of its marketing expenditure

BookCo is one of the world's biggest book clubs. Its business model, that of selling books by mail order to people who join its club, is one that has been around for a long time, but recent changes in its markets and channels have put it under severe financial pressure. This case study is about how a formerly successful company has turned to customer equity modelling techniques, and in particular optimization of its marketing expenditure.

Over the last 5 years, although the total book market has grown, sales of books through direct channels such as book clubs has shrunk. The reason is that major retailers, including supermarket chains, have taken a greater share of the market, especially for popular, best-selling titles which used to be the mainstay of book clubs. BookCo, however, remains the biggest player in the direct sales channel.

BookCo's portfolio ranges from general interest clubs such as BigBooks, through to clubs targeted at special interest or particular age groups (such as trains, military history, cookery books). An important issue to grasp about its business is that although the general clubs have more members, and benefit from negotiating better terms with publishers because of the greater volumes involved, for the most part these clubs are not as profitable as the smaller specialist clubs who, although they have lower volumes, also tend to have higher unit prices and a greater frequency of purchasing.

A further complication is that the general interest clubs have been proved to be the recruiting ground for the special interest clubs, and as such, the general catalogues often carry a selection of special interest titles alongside their general titles. As BookCo is meticulous in tracking customer acquisition costs for each club, management realized that this cross-selling phenomenon makes clear-cut invest/divest decisions particularly difficult.

For all these reasons, BookCo management decided that radically changing the current book club portfolio was not an option, and what they needed was a more sophisticated approach to fine-tuning their customer acquisition and customer maintenance expenditure.

BookCo appointed a new finance director. One of the FD's first moves was to invite us to construct a customer equity optimization model of the business. The solution took the form of an Excel model, which ran on data from BookCo's membership database. It handled data for 30 book clubs (allowing for extra new clubs), 15 media channels and allowed for 450 different recruitment/spend decisions, reflecting the detail with which BookCo managed this part of its operations.

This may appear complex, but what goes on underneath the model is relatively straightforward and can be applied more generally. It helped that BookCo had good base data, however, and this may be a stumbling block for other businesses. In particular, it had a clear idea of the profitability profile of each member over their lifetime as a member, and the recruitment costs by book club and media channel.

However, what management had not done up until this point was to bring all the data together in a form that allowed them to compare club profiles, nor had they made any attempt to use this data to forecast future performance. Our model allowed them to do that, with useful results. An example of how the model was used is shown in Figure 15.14.

The initial optimization resulted in some club closures and the reallocation of acquisition spend away from some club and media channels towards others. This resulted in a deterioration of profitability in the first year compared with the initial budget, but with a much better result in 3 years' time.

One of the key points about this project was that the model was owned and operated by a team within BookCo's management. The use of the model by this team made it possible to have a rational discussion within the organization about the trade-offs between maintaining a large overall membership, and cutting and reallocating acquisition budgets. In the event, an alternative, less radical optimization emerged as a consequence of introducing some constraints into the model. This preferred solution still achieved a substantial improvement in profits in Years 2 and 3, but also improved on the initial budget in Year 1.

The use of the optimization model therefore gave BookCo guidance on:

- The best allocation of media expenditure;
- Which clubs were candidates for closure;
- What would need to happen to overheads as a result of the other changes.

Figure 15.14

The results of three iterations of projected profits

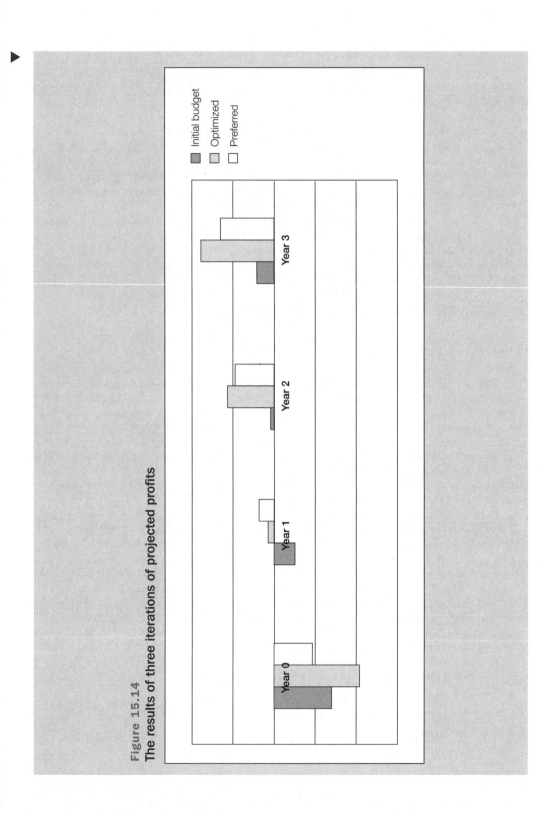

Key points

- Financial planners cannot ignore future sales and should factor them into the breakeven calculations for customer acquisition budgeting.

- Models are needed of the financial performance of all acquisition sources, taking into account the cost of acquisition and current and future sales.

- Response rates and curves must be established for all main customer acquisition sources.

- Future sales estimates must be established for all main customer acquisition sources, based on active life and annual sales rate.

- Add-on sales models are needed to estimate future sales.

- Retention models are needed to estimate the active life of customers by source.

16

GETTING BETTER VALUE FROM MARKETING INFORMATION

This chapter is about extracting more value from marketing information. Marketing information is often hard to understand and it needs squeezing to yield any valuable insights. This requires changes to the normal way that marketing information departments operate, and changes too in marketing decision-making processes. The phrase 'customer insight' is the shorthand used to describe this new approach to handling marketing information.

Too much information, too little insight

Box 16.1 Marketing information terminology

Marketing information: Information needed for marketing decision making. This consists of internal records, collected by accountants, sales and customer service staff, product managers, advertising and promotion managers (see Chapter 20 on marketing bookkeeping and accounting). It also consists of external data, collected by market research firms (see Chapter 5 on measuring how marketing really works) and advertising, media and promotion agencies.

Marketing information system: Consists of people, computers and procedures to collect and integrate data, analyze and interpret data patterns, write reports and presentations, construct models and distribute reports, presentations and models to marketing decision makers.

Market research (MR) department: Managers and staff responsible for commissioning market research from external agencies and distributing results to marketing managers. They usually report to the marketing director and the research specification usually only covers the needs of the marketing department.

Widespread criticisms of marketing information have been around for several decades:

- Marketing managers are frustrated by their existing marketing information.
- Non-marketing managers pay little or no attention to marketing information.
- Marketing research staff and information staff are frustrated by line managers.
- Suppliers do little to add value to the information they provide.

Marketing managers who participated in the Marketing Forum Think-tank in 2002 commented that they had 'not just a data mountain, we've got the Himalayas'. Others said that 'research reports are incomprehensible and go unread' and that 'there is also a strange comfort in lots of data, it makes people feel like they understand and are on top of the business, even though a relatively small percentage may get used' (Hull and Jones 2002).

Top executives who make strategic decisions come in for criticism by marketing for having too little understanding of customers. Ambler (2003) suggests that Boards should have a brand equity scorecard presented to them at regular intervals to keep them better informed. Kaplan and Norton (1996) have suggested that customer loyalty and satisfaction score should be presented to the Board in a balanced scorecard.

Marketing research staff and information staff have always been both critics and criticized, as this old quote from Horne *et al.* (1973) shows:

> There is often competitiveness between the so-called researcher and the marketeer because the more imaginative researchers believe they understand the market better, and are better equipped to make decisions about it, than the marketeer. The purely marketing man is therefore often required to justify his job position by not accepting the advice of the researcher. A frequently heard grumble is that the 'marketing people never read my reports'.

Suppliers of marketing information up to now seem to have taken rather a passive role. Shaw and White (1999) interviewed 30 heads of research firms, finding that the hottest topic on their agenda was cutting the cost of data gathering. The idea of providing added-value services, such as consultancy, was not seen as so important. But slowly things are changing, and are becoming focused around the concept of 'customer insight'. Unfortunately, this is in danger of becoming yet another fad term which could end up meaning not very much instead of spearheading a revolution.

Market research departments are trying to become more impressive and influential by reinventing themselves as 'customer insight' departments. The boundaries between the different internal groups are dissolving – market research, customer satisfaction research and CRM data had traditionally been kept separate. Also, some groups are providing 'added-value' services including data mining, modelling, intranet-bulletins, presentations and consultancy.

Technology firms are now offering tools for generating 'customer insight', as a search on the Internet will quickly reveal. We carried out such a search recently, and many of the first 100 responses came from IT firms. Slogans such as 'pull the trigger on customer insight' and 'real-time customer insight' are being bandied about.

Big consultancies, and little ones too, are evolving their CRM groups into customer insight teams. Unfortunately, closer examination of the service-offers described on the consultants' websites leaves one with the distinct impression that they have not crawled far from the CRM swamp, as this extract from Accenture's website illustrates:

> Having trouble getting through to your target customers? Is ROI on your marketing investments dropping – or can you even measure it? Research by Accenture's Customer Relationship Management service line describes how marketing executives are responding to the challenges, and identifies a new approach – Insight Driven Marketing. (Accenture 2004)

Finally, the market research industry is offering methodological novelties, which claim to get deeper inside consumers' and customers' minds. Phrases such as 'the illogical consumer', 'the customer experience', 'the unconscious mind', 'subliminal messages', 'decoding the emotions' and 'facial action coding systems' are occurring in the sales literature of the research firms. While there are occasionally useful new techniques on offer, often these novelties merely involve the repackaging of existing research methods in zany new gear to make them more appealing to the jaded research buyer. Consequently, the importance of the information they provide is questionable.

Although these moves are evidence that the problem is being recognized and addressed in different ways, the root of the difficulty goes somewhat deeper than this. Line management (in marketing, sales, finance, etc.) have generally taken the view 'I'm not impressed with your data, find something else to impress me'; they rarely see themselves as part of the problem. It is essential that everyone in the marketing decision chain re-examines how they use marketing data, and what data is really needed in their business in order to take good decisions.

This chapter examines all these issues and draws some conclusions about how organizations should respond to these challenges. Before going further, it would be useful to ask ten hard questions about the way market research data is used in your business:

1. What aspects of management decision-making methods and style need to change for marketing information and customer insights to have an impact on business performance?

2. What changes are needed in the working relationships between decision makers and marketing information staff to have the maximum impact on business performance?

3. Which three types of commonly used marketing information are potentially most misused, misleading or misunderstood?

4. Which three pieces of reasonably available marketing information are the most useful?

5. What should the market research industry be doing differently that will have an impact on (client) business performance?

6. Rank sources of commercially valuable and trustworthy customer insights, e.g. existing marketing research staff; market research agency; new, better trained internal team; cross-functional team; external independent consultants. Give reasons.

7. Given the controversy about the relationship between auditing firms and associated consultancies, does the ownership of a market research firm by a creative agency or agency group involve a conflict of interests?

8. Can a market research or media analysis firm be expected to provide an objective view when analyzing the effectiveness of its own creative campaign? Is there a conflict of interests? If so, what can be done to mitigate this problem?

9. Rank the following in order of importance for improving the quality of customer insights: larger expenditure on market research activity; better co-ordination between sources of marketing information; more internal market research staff; training for market research staff; better IT systems; other. Give reasons.

10. Are there any truly innovative approaches to marketing information and customer insights, or should we just focus on getting better at what we currently do? Will developments in technology lead to more or better marketing information or customer insights, or merely exacerbate current problems?

Where should you begin the diagnosis?

It's very tempting to look at marketing information from the perspective shown in Figure 16.1, with information as the starting point on the left, and management decisions as the end point, on the right. While this sequence accurately reflects the sequence of events over time, this mechanistic perspective is unhelpful when trying to improve the effectiveness of the process.

With this perspective, the first questions raised tend to be the wrong ones. It is not our experience that the supply and delivery of marketing information, on a cost-efficient and technically excellent basis, is the primary issue. In our view, the more important issues are that:

- Decision makers make ineffective use of information they possess.
- Insights drawn from existing information are inadequate.

Referring back to Figure 16.1, you should start by looking at the decisions that will be influenced by insights and information, i.e. the right-hand side of the diagram.

This advice may seem surprising, as it's widely assumed that the central problem lies with the information suppliers, their processes, technology and data. We would like to challenge this supply-side assumption. Figure 16.2 is a better framework than Figure 16.1 for diagnosing your problems.

It has been our general experience over 20 years that managers make too little use of the existing marketing information, even when the sources are good. This line of reasoning is supported by observing the contrast between the way managers use information and the way management consultants operate. We have been in numerous companies where management consultants were hired to help managers take difficult decisions. What we have observed is:

- Managers are generally too busy and lack the internal aides to provide an adequate quality of analysis on difficult decisions.
- Consultants have the time and the analytical skills.

We have rarely heard clients say, 'We hired McKinsey [or whoever] because of their great information sources'. Note that the information sources available to the managers and consultants were usually the same. So, in these cases, the information sources are not what make the difference.

Figure 16.1
Conventional view of marketing information

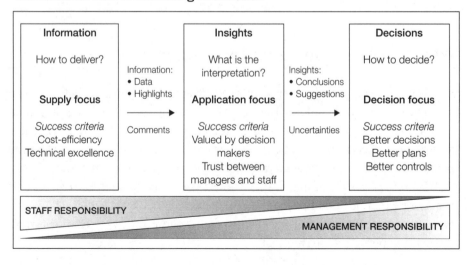

Figure 16.2

A better framework for diagnosing marketing information management

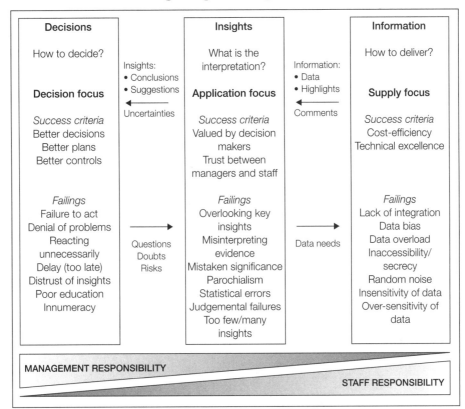

Everyday decisions, which don't require consultants to be hired, must also be looked at. Here the situation tends to be different:

- Managers are generally too busy and lack the staff/aides to extract the insights they need from existing data.

- Internal staff who are responsible for the marketing information and research are seldom accepted by managers as aides and consultants.

This leads us to draw a second conclusion.

> Managers must embrace change in the way they interact with internal staff and aides for any changes in marketing information to yield benefits.

There are several historical precedents to suggest that the central problem is more likely to lie with management than with information suppliers and processors. Particularly important in this case is the observation that, in the world of information systems, benefits arise only when management processes change. The history of IT is littered with failures that arose because managers were not ready and able to use the technology. For example, the 'information centre' was an ill-conceived concept, a sort of information library where staff were hired to act as librarians. Sadly these were disbanded through underutilization. Then there was the Chief Information Officer (CIO), a sort of 'super' IT manager. Unfortunately, too often, as some wag put it, 'CIO really stands for career is over'.

Decision-problem diagnosis

Diagnosing the problems with management decision making – that is, how line managers use information and insights – should be the starting point. Making marketing decisions more effectively is the ultimate goal. To diagnose your organization's problems in this area, some criteria for success and failure are needed:

Success criteria

- Better decisions (marketing and strategic ones);
- Better plans;
- Better controls.

Failure criteria

- Doing things you ought not to have done;
- Failure to act;
- Doing the right things inadequately or by the wrong method;
- Doing the right things too early or too late;
- Doing the right things but irritating those who judge your performance.

Diagnostic workshop questions

Line managers and decision makers generally have some awareness of the areas where their decision making, planning and control may be weak. However, they are often reluctant to openly discuss them.

We have found that running one-day workshops with your top executive group – marketing execs, sales execs, customer service execs, finance execs – can yield some frank opinions if the questions are framed in an appropriate way. We would recommend asking the following list of questions:

- What three aspects of your marketing are most worrying?
- How much money would you estimate to be at risk?
- Where do your plans most often go amiss?
- Are there volatile areas that you manage like a slot-machine?
- Which decisions do you consider involve most luck?
- In which three areas do you feel most out of control?
- Which decisions do you think managers are most complacent about?
- Name three past decisions that you would characterize as 'ill-informed'.
- Name three past mistakes that were quietly buried and forgotten.
- Where ought you to learn much more from past mistakes?
- Which decisions do you consider most scientific?

Case study 16.1

TelCo's value at risk

A telephone company that had ambitious growth plans of a £750 million profit uplift over 5 years suspected that its poor marketing information was going to cause problems and, as a consequence, its growth plan was at risk. So a workshop was held with the top executive team to assess the extent of the problem. The ground rules were:

1. Agree business problems.
2. Quantify benefits of solving the problems.
3. Determine extent to which benefits depend on better marketing information and insights.
4. Headline statement of what needs to be done.

The top executive team defined the problems and estimated value at risk, as shown in Table 16.1. The following comments are important:

- Information would not directly cause these problems to be solved, it would merely *enable* them to be solved.
- Multiple sources of information had to be integrated as part of the solution – market research, customer satisfaction, customer records, call records, service records.
- A mixture of 'big' strategic decisions and 'little' operational decisions were needed to fix the problems.

▶

▶

- Value-at-risk estimates were approximate calculations based on numbers jointly agreed by line managers and finance managers.
- The overall total value at risk was almost half the total planned growth.

This quick analysis galvanized the executive team into action. An important conclusion was that there are no direct benefits from marketing information itself, but information enables marketing to become more competent decision makers.

Table 16.1
Value at risk in TelCo

Headline	Description	Value at risk
New product failures	We are unable to plan, design and launch new products that will yield the planned levels of profits	£120m
New customers unprofitable	We are unable to identify and target the customers with the highest potential profitability	£62m
Cross-selling weak	We are unable to identify and target additional products that customers are likely to buy	£52m
Service problem and retention	We are unable to identify and resolve service problems in a way that will maximize our profits	£44m
Price yield optimization	We are unable to model our pricing structures to yield the maximum profitability	£34m
Channel optimization	We are unable to identify and guide customers to use the channels that will be most profitable for us	£22m

Insight-problem diagnosis

Diagnosing your organization's ability to construct 'insights' can be challenging. In recent years the word 'insight' has come to be much used – and misused – in marketing.

'By 'insight', we really mean a fresh, discerning, penetrating fact that, when combined with insights drawn from a wide variety of sources, inspires ideas and action,' comments Mark Sherrington, former CEO of the consultancy firm Added Value and currently the marketing director of SAB Miller. Sherrington dedicates a whole chapter of his recent book (2003) to this difficult topic. His ideas are provocative, and well worth reading.

Roget's Thesaurus indexes 'insight' against 'discernment, intuition and clairvoyance'. It is inextricably linked with anticipation, astuteness and foresight. To diagnose your organization's issues in creating insights, some criteria for success or failure are needed.

Success criteria

- Anticipating important customer and consumer trends;
- Foreseeing competitive changes;
- Progressing by constantly discovering fresh ways of seeing the market;
- Going beyond superficial analysis and conventional wisdom;
- Focusing on areas with hard-headed commercial significance;
- Observing and learning how to improve on earlier ways of performing.

Sherrington adds the following criterion, which we have characterized in the earlier analysis under implementation: *'inspiring ourselves and others'*. We'd argue that inspiration is in the eye of the beholder. Criticizing those responsible for 'inspiring insights' would be rather unreasonable if the situation existed where management was too dull or dumb to be inspired. We shall return to this issue of inspiration when we examine potential solutions later in this chapter.

Failure criteria

- Stuck in a rut with a fixed view of the market;
- Being distracted by endless trivial discoveries of little significance;
- Being astonished by market and competitive changes after they happen;
- Lacking an effective understanding of the information you already have;
- Unable to connect information and decision making;
- Taking far too much time to search for key facts and figures;
- Unable to see any significant patterns in the data.

Diagnostic workshop questions

Line managers generally have some awareness of the areas where their insights are poor or weak. Staff who are responsible for market research and customer information also have ideas, although there are often gaps between the two perspectives.

We have found that running a second workshop, following the decision-making one, can provide further diagnosis of the problems. We would recommend asking the following questions:

- In what areas are managers and decision makers most out-of-touch?
- What kinds of vital insights are you most lacking?
- What aspects of past performance should you try to learn more from?
- Where do you feel your performance is more luck than judgement?
- Which areas of budget setting rely too much on guesswork?
- Name three past decisions where the 'big picture' was overlooked?
- Where is data overload the most problematic for managers?
- Which areas of existing information are important but neglected?
- What should you be doing differently to improve your foresight?

Case study 16.2

TelCo's second workshop

At the telephone company, a second workshop was held to discover the connections between the business problems and the insights available about customers and the market – see Table 16.2. Here the focus was:

- what we need to be able to do,
- that we can't do now,
- that will enable the business problem to be solved.

Solving the 'new customers unprofitable' problem requires several actions – keeping adequate historical records, constructing a predictive model and optimizing customer acquisition expenditure. Likewise, solving the 'cross-selling weak' problem requires several actions – better customer records, new insights and better decision models. It is our general experience that solving a business problem requires insights from multiple sources; benefits cannot therefore be allocated precisely to particular information sources.

Table 16.2
Linking business issues to marketing insights at TelCo

Headline	Description	Value at risk
New customers unprofitable	We need to be able to optimize the allocation of customer acquisition expenditure by offer and by channel	£62m
	We need to be able to predict the likely response by offer and by channel	
	We need to keep adequate historical records of customer acquisition activity and costs and sources of new customers	
Cross-selling weak	We need to be able to predict what additional products and services each customer will buy	£52m
	We need better insights into the barriers that stop customers from trying out our new products	
	We need to keep information on customer records that will help us predict what they will buy next	

Information-problem diagnosis

Diagnosing your organization's information problems is the final analysis. Most managers have grumbles and misgivings about information sources, and it is relatively easy to find out about them. They should be put into proper perspective, taking into account the findings of the earlier two analyses.

By 'information', we mean a variety of sources which are likely to include:

- Market research – individual questionnaire responses (agency may withhold);
- Market research – continuous tracking tabulations (weekly/monthly/quarterly);
- Market research – test and experiment results;
- Advertising and media agency reports and analyses (of your own campaigns);
- Customer satisfaction surveys;
- CRM reporting and analysis;
- Sales and expenditure reports (weekly or monthly);
- Published research reports and reports that you have commissioned.

To diagnose your organization's problems with information, some criteria for success or failure are necessary.

Success/failure criteria

- Lower/higher cost of data collection;
- More/less data elements available (or more questions in the survey);
- More/less segment analyses available;
- More/less pages of analysis tables;
- More/less integrated information sources;
- Better/worse survey design;
- Larger/smaller sample size;
- Fewer/more errors;
- Faster/slower to make results available;
- Easier/harder access for users.

Diagnostic survey questions

We would recommend that you use a survey rather than a workshop to assess the effectiveness of information sources, as there is too much detail for a group discussion to be an effective approach.

- What kinds of essential information are you lacking?
- Name any information that is surplus to your requirements.
- In which areas are your controls too loose? Where are they too tight?
- Name three or more areas where existing information cannot be trusted.
- Describe any specific problems you have linking together information sources.
- Name any areas where delays in receiving information cause problems.
- Are there areas where the cost of information exceeds its benefits?

At the telephone company example previously cited (Case studies 16.1 and 16.2), specific information sources were identified. The costs of obtaining the new information, or enhancing the quality of existing information, were then assessed in the context of the estimated value at risk. Information management processes and systems were put in place, and as a consequence performance began to improve.

Summarizing your diagnosis

At this point we recommend that you summarize the nature of the changes that you are seeking. Figures 16.3–16.5 illustrate a format that you may wish to adopt.

Figure 16.3
Desirable changes in marketing decision making

FROM	TO
• Intuitive decision making	• Analysis-based decision making
• Managers value experience over formal knowledge	• Managers value formal education too
• Information is used as a political weapon	• Information used impartially and without bias
• Unexpected data trigger rapid reaction	• Data are checked and analyzed before action
• Secrecy surrounds decision making	• Transparency of decision logic
• 'Kill the messenger' syndrome	• Aides pull no punches
• Past mistakes are ignored or over-emphasized	• Past mistakes are assessed carefully
• A state-of-denial often surrounds worrying information	• Management works to solve major problems

Figure 16.4
Desirable changes in marketing insights

FROM	TO
• Market research staff	• Customer insight staff
• Business manager visually scans data for significance	• Support staff act as aides in finding insights
• Information is passive	• Active briefing service is provided
• Data are distributed in bulk for managers to scan	• Data mining by staff to extract key facts
• Data provide a backdrop	• Data fed into models and analyses
• Staff's main training is in survey methods	• Education in business modelling is vital
• Bad forecasts and analyses are quickly forgotten	• Learning and improvement are valued

Figure 16.5
Desirable changes in information management

FROM	TO
• Huge volumes of unfocused data	• Necessary and sufficient data only
• Superficial customer knowledge	• Going deeper inside the customer's mind
• Islands of information	• Data fusion and integration
• 'Well informed' means lots of data	• 'Well informed' means good analysis
• Data gathering continues year after year	• Data gathering stops if it ceases to be useful
• Slow information delivery	• Fast information delivery
• Costs of information exceed benefits	• Benefits exceed costs

Visualizing your best solution

Drawing a schematic representation of the proposed solution can help communicate what is proposed (see Figures 16.6 and 16.7). It also enables managers to discuss some of the practical issues that will need to be addressed to make the solution work effectively in practice.

Specifying the solution

As Figures 16.6 and 16.7 demonstrate, the full solution can require changes in processes, organization and technology. Specifying the solution clearly before embarking on a development programme is important, in order to guide progress.

Figure 16.6
'Before' schematic representation of the solution

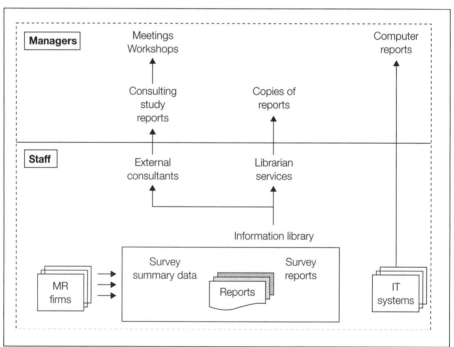

Figure 16.7
'*After*' schematic representation of the solution

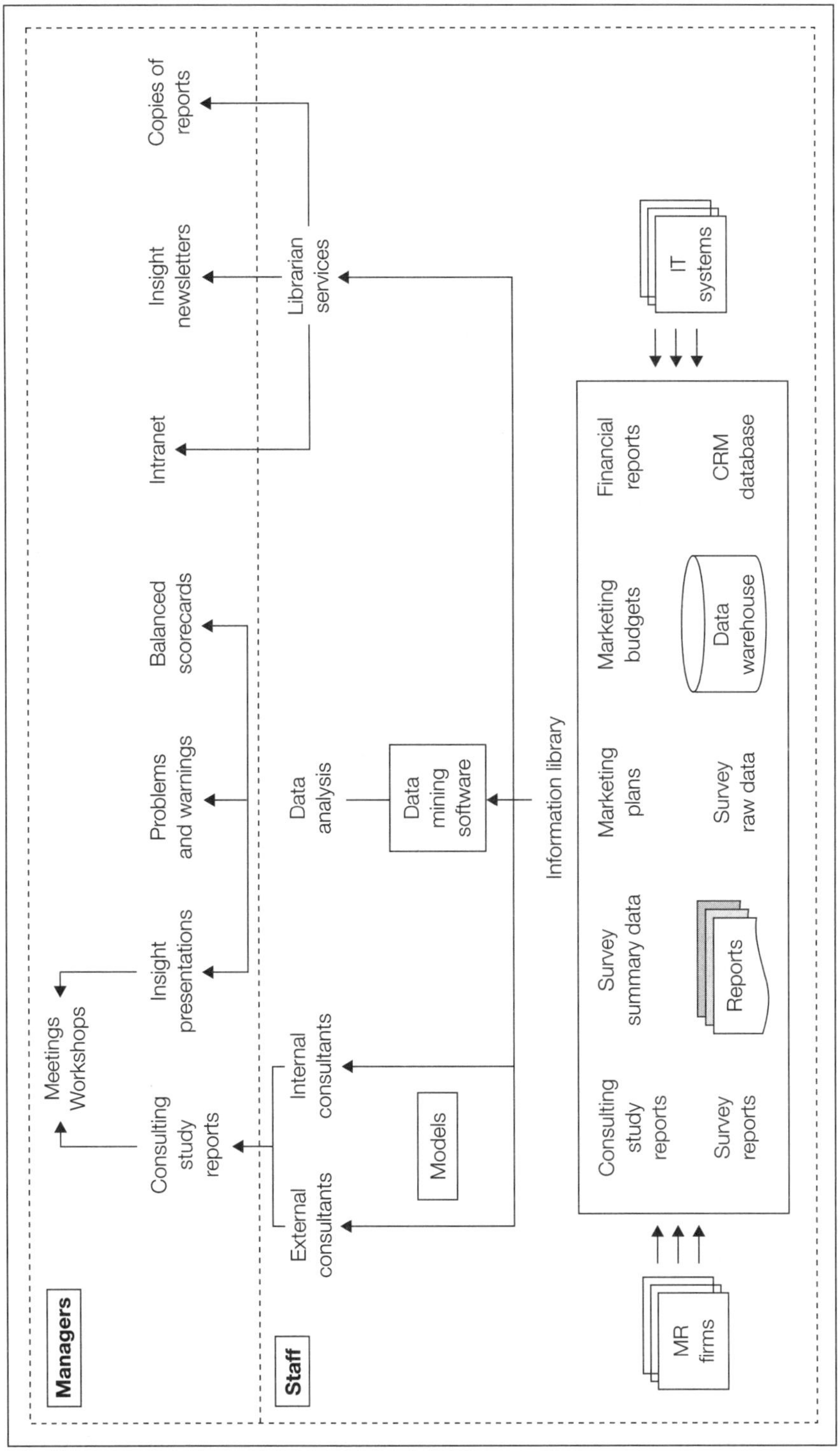

We will use the vision diagram, Figure 16.7, to act as the framework for defining the solution. It is organized into four main components:

- Marketing information library;

- Customer insight people and processes;

- Management tools and techniques;

- Learning and culture change (note: this is critical to success but is not shown explicitly on the diagram).

Each of these is discussed below.

Marketing information library

The main objective is to bring together in a coherently managed way all key marketing information sources. This will typically involve changing from a situation where market research is managed coherently, but other information sources are managed separately, to a situation where:

- Printed reports are stored in one central library, including:
  - Existing market research information sources;
  - New market research reports and studies;
  - Extra market research information from existing sources;
  - Market research summary tables;
  - Consulting study reports;
  - Customer satisfaction survey reports;
  - Marketing plans;
  - Brand plans;
  - Product launch plans.
- Computerized data sources for marketing:
  - Financial reports needed by marketing;
  - CRM data needed by marketing;
  - Survey data needed for analysis by marketing.

New information sources

Market research firms are offering a more varied menu with new information sources. Here is an example:

> Sensory Logic is an East Coast scientific market research business that 'specializes in the analysis of the psycho-physiological responses of consumers to an organization's products and services. Founded by Dan Hill, it believes it has finally developed

something close to the 'introspectometer'. Based on the Facial Action Coding System developed in the 1970s by US Sociologist Paul Ekman (which classified over 3000 facial muscle movements – the 'eyelid tightener' expresses anger, for instance, and the 'nasolabial fold deepener' manifests sadness), the system has 'proven to be highly accurate'. (*www.sensorylogic.com*)

It is not the aim of this book to provide a guide to all these new techniques. We would, however, recommend that you assess these new methods against the 'user requirements' that you have established in your diagnostic studies.

Extra information from existing sources

Buying extra information is always an option. You can increase the survey sample size, add extra segments for analysis, add to the number of survey questions and many more things, all of which cost money. Our advice is to review your diagnosis of information sources and ask yourself the following questions:

- Do users want this extra data?
- Is the data quality bad because of sample problems?
- How important is it to improve the data quality?
- Will the quality improvement cause any changes in your marketing?

Planning and report library

All plans are archived for future reference, as an aid to improving forecasting. This includes marketing plans, brand plans and product launch plans. Typically these are held by line managers and quickly get lost and forgotten. Employing an archivist to keep copies and retrieve information is an important feature of the solution.

Computerized data retrieval

All computerized data sources for marketing are brought together and organized for ease of data retrieval. One of the most common complaints about marketing information is the difficulty of retrieving computerized data. Spreadsheets in particular are rarely maintained and archived in an organized way. CRM data in particular must be managed as an integral part of the whole information library. Coding of this data needs to be consistent with codes and ranges used in market research. Survey data (i.e. copies of questionnaire returns, minus respondent names) provide a rich source of data for analysis. Traditional market research reporting methods tend to ignore key insights that would be disclosed by more sophisticated econometric analysis.

Information management and retrieval skills

Traditional market research staff may lack the skills needed for this broader information role. In particular, the IT skills needed to manage the computerized records will be needed on the team. We would recommend that these skills be within the team, and at the very least that an IT specialist should be seconded to the team.

People and processes

The main objective is:

> To develop internal competencies to provide key customer insights to management.

This will typically involve changing from a situation where marketing research support staff mainly act as 'librarians' for line managers, as well as the interface between market research firms and clients, to a situation where:

- Customer insight staff have an added-value role.
- Data analysts are also part of the team, using data-mining software to discover problems, prepare insight presentations and balanced scorecards.
- Consultants solve business problems for line managers, using similar skills and methods to management consultants.

Customer insight staff

New, different skills are likely to be needed. Market research managers, however skilled and experienced, rarely possess all the skills needed for the new role. New skills required are likely to include:

- IT skills for maintaining the computerized data repositories;
- Data mining for spotting opportunities and threats;
- Econometric analysis and model construction;
- Business know-how to offer practical consultancy advice.

Data analysis resources

One of the widely proclaimed capabilities of this new approach is the application of data-mining systems to identify opportunities and threats. Routine duties are likely to include:

- Insight presentations made on a regular basis to the line managers;
- Construction of models and management tools.

The track record of data mining is not proven, and there is still a great deal of scepticism surrounding the subject. Erik Brynjolfsson, professor of information systems at MIT Sloan School, has noted: 'The same dollar spent on the same system may give a competitive advantage to one company but only expensive paperweights to another' (Brynjolfsson and Hitt 1996).

Consultants

Another feature of the customer insight approach is the possibility of offering internal consultancy. Routine duties are likely to include:

- Problem solving on the basis of a brief agreed with a line manager;
- Construction of models and management tools.

Internal consultancies have come and gone in many businesses. The Operational Research (OR) boom of the 1960s and 1970s ebbed away in the 1980s and 1990s and today OR groups are a rarity in business. Perhaps the most widespread consultancy in business today is the spreadsheet modelling groups found in the finance departments of many larger organizations. Some of this expertise needs to be transferred to the marketing area.

Case study 16.3

Nokia consumer insights

World leader in mobile communications, Nokia, has a Consumer Insights division of 30 people. It was established in 2001 and absorbed the old market research function. Its remit includes product conception and design and interpreting the attitudes and behaviour of consumers. It tries to track and forecast changes in long-term consumer motivation. Its aim is to provide internal consultancy to Nokia's managers. Market research firms are retained for their data collection and tabulation roles, but are not expected to provide added-value. 'They lack real understanding of Nokia's business needs and where the company is heading,' comments Jane Hanford, head of brand and customer understanding. (BMRA 2004b)

External consultancies do offer an alternative to having the resources in-house. Management consultancies, such as McKinsey, are now offering 'customer insight' as one of their service lines. Some market research firms and advertising agencies also offer consultancy advice, but few appear to have invested in the heavyweight skills that their management consulting rivals offer. There is also a group of specialist marketing consultancies offering a range of services, some of which appear to compete with their bigger management consultancy cousins.

Management tools and techniques

The main objective is:

> **To provide management with tools and techniques that will enable them to improve their marketing plans, controls and decision making.**

This will typically involve changing from a situation where photocopies of market research reports are the main source of marketing data, and staff are used as 'librarians' to retrieve facts and figures from the research library, to a situation where:

- Many sources of printed marketing information are received.
- Workshops and presentations by customer insight team are used to brief management on trends and emerging issues.
- Computers are used to access marketing information.
- Models are used as aids to problem solving.
- Staff are used as consultants and are valued as advisers.

Newsletters, bulletins and intranets

Disseminating 'insights' is a challenge in today's business environment, where managers are drowning in information. We would strongly recommend that consultation takes place between the line managers who will receive this additional information and the customer insight team who produce it.

Balanced scorecards

One of the silver-bullet solutions widely hyped today is the balanced scorecard. Many companies have adopted this approach, alongside their traditional reporting systems. Extra non-financial data are added to conventional financial data. However, the non-financial data still tend to be ignored. If a balanced scorecard is to be successful, it needs to replace the financial systems, as advocated by the Beyond Budgeting Round Table (*www.bbrt.co.uk*). If you are planning to use scorecards, make sure that your management fully understands the drastic implications.

Insight presentations

PowerPoint slides can impart information in a dramatic and interactive way that written reports cannot. An alternative to newsletters, etc. is to make a regular presentation. Market research firms already make such presentations to their clients. However, informal feedback to the Value Based Marketing Forum indicates that clients find these dull and uninspiring. Management is looking for something more exciting.

Before you add another presentation to management's busy diaries, ask yourself: 'How will my presentation be more interesting and better received than the usual research briefings?' Ask the audience what they really want to hear, but also make your own mind up, as audiences can be fickle.

Opportunity alerts and threat warnings

One of the ideas about data-mining analysts is that they ought to spot opportunities and threats. A practical problem with this idea is what method should be used to communicate these opportunities and threats. Insight presentations (see above) may provide a forum for debating the opportunities and threats discovered by the analysts. However, the 'not invented here' mindset in many organizations can be a practical hindrance for ideas discovered by staff to find acceptance among line managers. Ask yourself whether these insights are worth paying for. Heed the comments of sceptics, such as Tim Ambler (1996): 'Does it need paid research? Read the Sunday papers instead.'

Management tools

A valuable role of the consultant-analyst is to develop practical tools for managers to use in their decision making.

Case study 16.4

Diageo's Activity Evaluator

Global drinks company Diageo has introduced a new decision-analysis procedure called the Activity Evaluator, which is used as a control on all marketing proposals. Managers have to forecast, before they run any new activity, what will be its effects. They must also determine how the effects are to be measured. Often there is a requirement for research – before/during/after – to measure the incremental effects. Expenditure and resources for the Activity Evaluator are set aside as a routine component of every marketing activity budget.

Econometric modelling

Econometric modelling can yield even greater insights than more simple analyses and presentations. However, greater skills are likely to be required.

Case study 16.5

Kraft's use of modelling methods

Consumer food manufacturer Kraft routinely uses modelling methods to extract insights about the effectiveness of its marketing activities. Tom Lloyd holds the post of Group Market Analytics Manager. His role is to ensure that the response to every element of the marketing mix is understood by decision makers – advertising, consumer promotion, trade promotion, pricing, new product development. He offers the following advice to anyone who is planning to establish their own modelling capabilities:

1. Start with the problem, not the tool (avoid the man with the model – if all you have is a hammer, every problem looks like a nail).
2. Don't get sidetracked by black-box debates (steer clear of anybody who says that you just feed raw data in, press a button and the answers come out).
3. Choose your modeller carefully – buy in the quality of work you need.
4. Model-fits are just the starting point (ask about the forecasting strength of the model).
5. Use your logic and ask stupid questions (if it doesn't feel right, say so).

Learning and culture change

Managers generally don't have terrific quantitative skills with regard to marketing information. For this reason, organizations are establishing management training in marketing numeracy. This can be a substantial investment, both in terms of expenditure and management time and commitment.

Case study 16.6

Diageo Way of Brand Building (DWBB)

Diageo was formed by a merger in October 1997 and 18 months later, the marketing directors of the four component organizations got together and put together a common way of doing marketing. This evolved into a comprehensive corporate programme, called the Diageo Way of Brand Building (DWBB).

It was recognized from the outset that quantitative skills were needed. Over 3,000 people from within the company have attended, including finance and HR in addition to marketing and sales. Several analysis tools and templates are incorporated in DWBB and these are now embedded in the fabric of everyday decision making.

Staff who inspire line managers

A challenge of the insight area is: 'How can staff inspire managers?' As Mark Sherrington (2003) suggests, if insights do not inspire managers they are likely to be ignored. Training of staff in consultancy methods is one potential way of solving the problem. The idea is that if consultants can inspire confidence and interest, then perhaps they have something to teach the staff team.

A new skills profile

Organizations that are planning to establish an insight capability will need to establish a new kind of staff skills profile from whatever existed previously. This will affect hiring and career progression.

Case study 16.7

BAA research

The British Airports Authority (BAA) has established a research function with a skills profile that is significantly different from that of the traditional research department. Under Stan Maiden, research director, is a team whose skills include:

- forecasting;
- statistics;
- operational research/model construction;
- market research.

BAA has responsibility for the flow of 128 million passengers each year through seven airports, making it the largest such organization in the world. It has to sift out problems in 35 different aspects of service across 11 air terminals. The team are very proactive in making recommendations to management to improve performance in many different aspects of the operation. Their role is to solve problems as diverse as the siting of escalators to the packaging of whisky bottles. They also manage a field force of 160 interviewers at seven airports, as well as numerous 'observers' who count people when they are walking, queuing, visiting, buying, in addition to other issues such as, vehicles, cars, lorries, taxis, car-parking spaces and baggage. For difficult quantitative analysis, they sometimes commission work with an external consultancy, otherwise they do the analysis themselves. (BMRA 2004a)

The case for change

Having diagnosed the problems and outlined the solutions, the next step should be to estimate costs and resources, discuss and agree your priorities and weigh up the case for change.

Cost of change

Solutions come in many forms: some involve money, others headcount, while others have no budgeted cost but do require time and attention. Use Table 16.3 to shortlist your own requirements and the estimated costs and resources.

Table 16.3
Calculating the costs of sourcing marketing information

EXPENDITURE REQUIRED:	
New information sources	
Extra information from existing sources	
More analysis and better presentation of existing data	
Models constructed from existing data	
Consultancy from external organizations to provide insights	
Learning and education for marketing line managers in quantitative planning, control and decision-analysis methods	
Learning and education for non-marketing managers	
Skills training for internal staff in analysis methods	
HEADCOUNT REQUIRED:	
Extra staff to develop insights from the data	
ORGANIZATIONAL CHANGE REQUIRED:	
Establishing a Customer Insight department	
HR INTERVENTION REQUIRED:	
Redefining the job of the marketing research manager	
Establishing a better career path for marketing research and information specialists	
Establishing management selection and career progression criteria based on analytical decision-making competencies	
IT ASSISTANCE REQUIRED:	
Developing an integrated data source	
Developing an intranet for publishing the 'insights' and giving online access to reports and other information sources	

Each of these now needs assessing in the light of the diagnostic work you will already have undertaken. You may also want to group these changes into projects and prepare a presentation showing your vision of the future capabilities.

Cost–benefit analysis

A cost–benefit analysis is likely to be needed to obtain the budgets and resources. Key areas of the benefits analysis are:

- Value at risk:
  - Doing things wrong;
  - Failure to act;
  - Doing the right things but ineffectively;
  - Doing things too late;
- Time savings for managers.

The decision-problems diagnosis exercise, described earlier, should provide you with some estimates of these benefits.

Agreeing the need for change

Having specified the solution, its costs and benefits, the final step is to gain agreement for the changes to happen. Some important points to note are:

- Sponsorship for customer insight needs to come from the top.
- The cost–benefit case must be understood and agreed by all parties, especially finance.
- Decision makers must change and become more accountable for marketing decisions.
- Marketing research must change and deliver better and more customer insights.

Marketing information is an essential resource that needs to be managed better than it is today in most organizations. The changes required are not cosmetic ones, and involve transforming the market research function from its present role to that of a Customer Insight department. New skills will need bringing together, from finance, marketing, sales and service.

Key points

- Marketing information has long been the focus of criticism, but recently companies have been responding by upgrading their marketing information functions to make them more value-adding.

- 'Customer insight' has become the shorthand used to describe the new approach.

- Ingredients of the new solution include:
  - Enhanced analysis and interpretation of marketing information;
  - Better communication of the research 'headlines';
  - More skilled analysts inside the company;
  - Managers more skilled at using customer insights in decision making.

- Companies should not jump on the customer-insight bandwagon without first diagnosing their own particular requirements and the feasibility of the solution 'taking root' in their organizational culture.

- A process is needed to manage information, transform it into customer insights and embed the insights in decision making. Problems can occur at any or all three stages in the process.

- Diagnosis of requirements should begin with an examination of the problems with embedding customer insights in decision making. Decision makers should be encouraged to reflect on these problems and assess the amount of value at risk as a result of these problems.

- Diagnosis should then progress to 'customer insights' and problems with the process that creates them.

- Diagnosis should finally cover the information itself. There are often many problems with information sources, and it is important to put them in perspective by relating them to the decisions and customer insights that the information supports.

- A summary diagnosis should then by prepared, showing the main changes envisaged.

- Next, a vision of the solution should be prepared. This usually takes the form of a schematic diagram, showing the situation before and after the envisaged changes.

- Costs and benefits of the solution should be estimated next and a case for change prepared.

- Agreeing the vision and a 'case for change' are the final steps. The changes should be explained, discussed and agreed with senior management to make sure that they will make productive use of the customer insights.

part III:

FINANCIAL PLANNING
AND CONTROL

17

THE NUMBER WIZARD'S TOOLBOX

This chapter is about modelling marketing payback using spreadsheets. It is intended to provide some discipline in a usually disorderly domain. If you can do the things in this chapter, you will be able to do everything in this book.

Spreadsheets are familiar to most managers, yet few use more than 10% of their power, and even fewer use them with discipline. There are two messages to take away from this chapter: use spreadsheets much more often, and apply the same discipline to modelling as you would to any other area of management.

Why you must become a better model maker

First a word of apology. In the previous chapters, we happily discussed ideas and issues. In this chapter, we are going to ask you to actually do something. We will start gently, but in the second half of the chapter, we want you to experiment with spreadsheets. We will try to explain everything in plain English before degenerating into the 'press this' and 'click that' of books for computer dummies. We think that if you have made it this far, you will probably find this easy. Moreover, if you are already slick with spreadsheets, you will find this a doddle.

You may already be asking nervously: 'Why should I bother with all this, it sounds difficult?' Here are six good reasons why using a standard PC with the software that probably came with it can give you many advantages over calculator, pen and paper:

1. You can tell the PC to do all the arithmetic for you, and even build in cross-checks to ensure it has done it right.

2. You can do what-if analysis and watch how changes ripple through to the bottom line.

3. You can update the assumptions over the coming months and make your forecast respond to changing circumstances.

4. You can link and copy tables into your Word documents and PowerPoint presentations, and produce wonderfully neat results on paper.

5. Once you have set up the template, you can use it over and over again for years to come.

6. You can email it to colleagues for them to share your insights and knowledge.

Lots of managers have already realized this. If you look at the office of a numbers wiz, you will find one main tool – a PC loaded with spreadsheet software, such as Microsoft Excel. PCs used by finance managers will also contain electronic accounting packages. If you look really hard, you will also find some obscure statistical package, such as SAS or SPSS. Calculators are still used sometimes, but the humble spreadsheet fulfils the calculator's role and does much more.

However, before getting carried away with enthusiasm, don't imagine that spreadsheets are a panacea. Spreadsheets can help every manager manage better, but only if they are used in a disciplined way.

More haste less speed should be in the mind of every modeller. Yet in the heat of decision making, when an urgent response to a question is needed, a spreadsheet is hastily constructed and emailed to interested parties. The result is rarely satisfactory for the following reasons:

- Nobody documents their models.
- No one else can understand your model.
- It prints awkwardly, across several badly presented pages.
- Formulae are overwritten with constants by people who try to use it.
- You can't understand it yourself in three months' time.

On the other hand, a properly constructed model will provide the following long-term and short-term benefits to people other than the modeller. They should be able to see:

- How the model works;
- What the inputs and assumptions are;
- That the model is carrying out the calculations intended.

In addition, a good model will be:

- Robust;
- Easily changed and updated;
- Able to present the results clearly.

Growing evidence suggests that poor discipline in spreadsheet modelling results in serious errors. John Sterman, a professor at the Massachusetts Institute of Technology (MIT) has commented that 'as a result of the introduction of the spreadsheet, the average quality of financial models has plummeted and many models are not only useless but downright harmful to decision makers' (Sterman 2000).

Few spreadsheet builders and users are aware of these potential pitfalls, and fewer still are aware that the powerful techniques covered in this chapter can be used to reduce the sources of errors.

Before reading on, ask these ten hard questions on your own modelling skills:

1. Why don't I make better use of my spreadsheet?

2. Do I trust the models I use?

3. Have the models I use been constructed well?

4. Do I use modelling enough for evaluating alternatives?

5. Are model inputs easy to enter?

6. Are assumptions kept together in one place and protected from change?

7. Are formula calculations kept together in one place and checked for errors?

8. Are results presented in a clear way?

9. Have models been tested and checked thoroughly before they are circulated for use?

10. Is my modelling team adequately trained?

The perfect model and its structure

Any numerical model has four main functional components: input numbers, assumption numbers, calculations and outputs (numbers and charts). This is illustrated in Figure 17.1.

Investment of time in the design of a model and its layout will facilitate understanding and simplify maintenance. We discuss each of these components of a model below, and make recommendations for good design practice for spreadsheet models.

Inputs

Inputs are numbers that are entered by users of the model. They are usually the variables that will be changed as part of what-if analysis. For example, marketing expenditure is often an input variable in marketing payback models.

An obvious point, but one that is often missed, is that users of a model need to be able to find the input cells easily. It is therefore good to put them together, on one sheet if possible, at or near the beginning of the workbook. It is also good practice for these cells to be given a distinctive background colour that will distinguish them from the other parts of the spreadsheet.

Figure 17.1
Block diagram of model structure

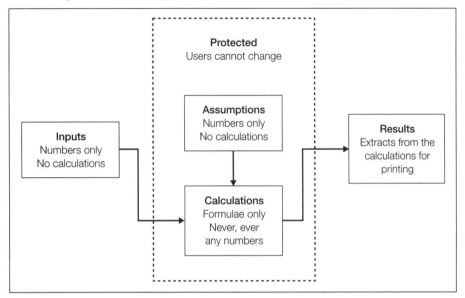

We recommend below that all sheets in a workbook should be protected. Input cells should be the only cells that are not locked, and therefore the only cells that can be changed by a user without unprotecting the workbook.

The designers of a model have the best idea of how it should be used and, in particular, what range of values is valid for each of the input variables. These ranges of validity should be built into the design of the model using spreadsheet features such as 'data validation'. This will minimize the risk that the model will be used outside its range of validity and produce flawed results. Without such checks, at best the flawed results will be noticed and will undermine the credibility of the model. At worst, they will not be noticed and used as the basis for important business decisions.

Assumptions

Assumptions are numbers that are entered when the model is constructed and then held fixed. For example, market growth forecasts are sometimes included as assumptions in marketing payback models. Conversion factors should always be entered explicitly in the assumptions section.

Again, the assumptions should be kept together, on one sheet if possible. Given that documenting spreadsheet models is rare indeed, at least the assumptions sheet (if well designed) can provide a comprehensive list of all the numerical assumptions in the model other than the input values used for a particular run.

We recommend that assumption cells are locked so that they cannot easily be changed by accident, and that they are given a distinctive background colour (different to that used for the input cells) to highlight that they contain numbers rather than formulae.

Calculations

The calculation section is the heart of the model; it is the engine that contains the formulae that calculate outputs from the model, based on the input values and the assumptions.

These formulae should never, ever contain explicit numbers. All of the components of a formula should be references to cells. If you need a constant in a formula, you should include the constant in the inputs section or assumptions section and make an indirect reference to it. This is for two good reasons:

- It retains the status of the assumptions section as a complete record of all of the numerical assumptions other than the input values.
- If you start including constants in formulae, you can easily get to the position where you are using different values for the same parameter in different formulae in different parts of the spreadsheet. Your model is no longer self-consistent. What is especially threatening about this type of error is that it is extremely difficult to spot.

One of the most common errors in spreadsheet models is that formulae become overtyped with constants. It is for this reason that we recommend protecting all sheets in a workbook and ensuring that all cells other than input cells are locked.

One of the common frustrations in modifying other people's spreadsheets (or even maintaining your own spreadsheet) is working out what the formulae in the calculations are actually doing. One way of making a model much more transparent and easy to maintain is to use the feature available in most modern spreadsheets to name cells. The formula to calculate profit then looks something like this:

=Price*Volume

The above formula is much easier to understand and check than, for example:

=Sheet3!G53*Sheet7!C27

Results

The results section of a spreadsheet model contains the tables and charts that you want to use to present the outcomes predicted by the model. Modern spreadsheets have a wide range of features that enable these outputs to be attractively designed and presented.

It is good practice not to carry out substantive calculations (i.e. calculations other than those needed for presentational purposes) in the results section, but instead to make simple references to cells in the calculations section. The reason for this is that you (or your colleagues) are more likely, over time, to want to make changes to how the results are presented than to the calculation engine itself. Having developed and checked the calculation engine to make certain that it is correct, you want to leave it alone to minimize the risk that changes will introduce errors.

Applications of modelling

Not all models are equal, and several different types can be constructed. The most common of these are illustrated in Figure 17.2 and described below.

The 'what-if' model

This is the basic type of model described in the previous section. The user decides on a set of input values and uses the model to calculate the results. The model can be run many times to investigate 'what-if' other sets of input values were to apply.

Each of the other types of model in the figure requires the construction of a 'what-if' model as a precursor.

The scenario model

This is no more than a 'what-if' model constructed to investigate a structured set of input values that represent different but plausible views of the future. The scenarios are often given names like 'Base case', 'Status quo', 'Going for growth', 'Downside risk'. By running a series of scenarios such as these, the model can be used to map out a range of possible outcomes and thereby provide an informed view on the robustness of the plan or project, or the prospects for the business.

Figure 17.2
Four common applications of modelling

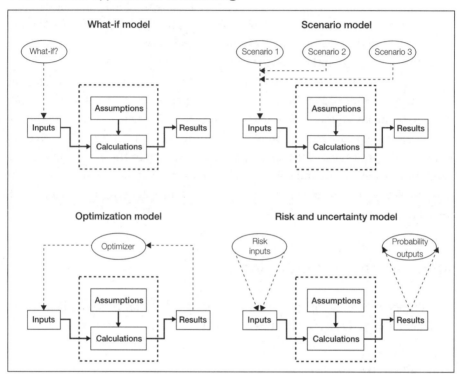

It is good practice to embed the scenarios in the model so that they can be revisited and fine-tuned. The low-tech way of doing this is simply to save different versions of the model with appropriate names.

The main objection to this is not that it is wasteful – computer storage is relatively cheap nowadays. It is that if a refinement to the calculations is needed (or, dare we say it, if an error in the model is uncovered), then the appropriate changes have to made in each copy of the model used for the different scenarios. It is generally better, therefore, to embed all of the scenarios in one copy of the model. There are various ways of doing this, including using the built-in scenario manager that is part of most spreadsheet packages.

The optimization model

This type of model turns the 'what-if' model on its head. Instead of specifying the inputs, we tell the model what type of outputs we would like, and ask the computer to choose the set of input values that delivers these outputs, often subject to some constraints.

For example, suppose that we had a 'what-if' model that required (amongst other factors) advertising spends and the prices for a set of brands as input variables and the total revenue and profit as part of the results. Configuring this as an optimization model could then involve specifying that we require the total profit to be maximized, subject to the total advertising spend being less than or equal to the budgeted amount. Although this may sound intimidating to spreadsheet novices, it is in fact quite easy to do because spreadsheets usually have a built-in solver capability to facilitate exactly this type of modelling.

There is, however, an important health warning associated with optimization models. Most models of interest will be non-linear (meaning that the results do not increase or decrease directly in proportion to the input values). In this situation, it is possible that the optimization process will either not converge at all, or may converge to a 'local' maximum or minimum rather than the global optimum. A good analogy here is mountaineering: you may have reached the top of a mountain, but you may not be on the top of the highest peak in the region.

The following strategies can help to reduce (but not eliminate entirely) this problem:

- Make sure that you have a good understanding of the situation that you are trying to model and, as part of this, spend time playing with the model in 'what-if' mode to understand how it responds to different combinations of input variables.

- Choose the constraints carefully to ensure, as far as possible, that the model will be searching for a solution in a feasible (and sensible) region. In the example given above, you may have to specify that advertising spends cannot be negative. The model will not otherwise know this and may therefore conclude that the best option for unattractive brands is for the media agency to pay for the privilege of running an advertising campaign!

- When you have obtained an estimate of the optimum, use the model again in 'what-if' mode to explore the region around the optimum. If the optimum is near a cliff-edge, you may decide that a suboptimal solution is better, given the uncertainties in the model and its data.

The risk and uncertainty model

In this type of model, we do not know exactly the values to specify for the input variables. What we do know, however, is something about the probability that they will be in a certain range. This problem may sound like a difficult one to crack. The 'good news' is that various techniques that go by exotic names such as Monte Carlo analysis or Latin Hypercube analysis have been developed to model this situation, and can be used in ordinary spreadsheets given a 'what-if' model as the starting point. The 'bad news', perhaps not unexpectedly, is that the results from this type of model are of the same form as the inputs, i.e. they are not an exact prediction of, for example, a profit figure. Rather, they specify the probability that the value will be in a certain range (for example, that the profit margin will be greater than a certain percentage).

Modelling do's and don'ts

Over the years, we have collected a set of spreadsheet modelling 'do's and don'ts', based partly on looking at a wide range of other people's models but, more especially, on trying to learn from our own mistakes. These are summarized in Table 17.1.

Table 17.1
Ten do's and don'ts of spreadsheet modelling

Design point	Rationale
1. DO clearly separate out the inputs, assumptions, calculations and results.	Both you and other users need to be able to find these key sections quickly and easily.
2. DON'T use constants in formulae – put all constants in the assumptions (or inputs) section and make indirect references.	Otherwise you risk creating a model that is not self-consistent and for which the assumptions section is not a complete list of the assumptions in the model.
3. DO label cells, rows and columns fully.	You (and others) will need reminders of how the model is working. Make sure that the units of each value are clear. Use the comment facility if necessary to document the source of the data in the assumptions or the calculation method employed.
4. DON'T write long or wide spreadsheets.	They are difficult to navigate and check, and are awkward to print. Where possible, break the calculations up into submodels on separate sheets.
5. DO include range checking for input variables.	Otherwise the model may be used outside its range of validity and produce flawed results.

Table 17.1
(continued)

Design point	Rationale
6. DON'T write spreadsheet models that depend on a circular calculation (i.e. one where the result of the calculation is used indirectly as an input to the calculation).	Such models are difficult to understand and check, may contain unintended circular calculations which are not apparent, may not converge fully to the answer, and can be slow to recalculate.
7. DO protect every sheet in the workbook.	This will reduce the risk of users inadvertently overtyping formulae with constants or changing the assumptions. The input cells should, of course, be unlocked so that values can be entered. It also helps to identify the input cells by giving them a distinctive background colour.
8. DON'T write long or complicated formulae for calculations.	They are difficult to understand, check and modify. Instead, break the calculations down into easy stages, using intermediate variables where necessary. Also, use range names to make the formulae more transparent.
9. DO build in charts to your spreadsheet.	Not only do they help to communicate the results of your model, they can assist you in sense-checking the results during the model development phase.
10. DON'T include substantive calculations in the results section	Making the results section completely separate from the calculations section will enable you and colleagues to change the former without disturbing and possibly introducing errors into the latter.

Case study example

The case study example is a spreadsheet that you can construct and which, with a few assumptions, you can use to get a feeling for the effects of changes in price and marketing spend on profitability.

The starting point for the brand or business is referred to as the 'base case' and all of the parameters in the model are defined by reference to this base case.

The inputs to the model are:

■ A price change (as a percentage of the base case price);

■ A change in marketing expenditure (as a percentage of the base case marketing expenditure).

The assumptions in the model are:

- The base case fixed costs (as a percentage of the base case revenue);
- The base case variable costs (as a percentage of the base case revenue);
- The base case marketing spend (as a percentage of the base case revenue);
- The base case profit (as a percentage of the base case revenue), i.e. the profit margin;
- A price elasticity (this is the factor that you multiply the price change by to get the change in sales volume – see Chapter 13);
- The maximum increase in sales volume that you could achieve through marketing expenditure, if money were no object (as a percentage of the base case volume);
- The amount of marketing expenditure that you would need to obtain half of the maximum increase in sales volume (as a percentage of the base case revenue).

The results produced by the model are:

- The volume (as a percentage of the base case volume);
- The profit (as a percentage of the base case revenue);
- The change in profit (as a percentage of the base case revenue).

The steps to build the model

Building the model is a simple four-step process. The steps refer to the completed model shown in Table 17.2.

- **Step 1:** Type the headings into the spreadsheet, just as they are shown in the table.
- **Step 2:** For the inputs and assumptions sections, type the numbers shown in the table into the corresponding cells. You will then be able to check your answers against those in the table.
- **Step 3:** For the calculations sections and the results sections, type in the formulae using the table as a guide. Interpret the references in the table as follows. If, in your spreadsheet, the cell containing the input value of the price change (–5.0% in the table) is cell E4, then this is the cell referred to as A in the table. Similarly if, in your spreadsheet, the cell containing the assumption for the price elasticity (–1.75 in the table) is cell E15, then this

cell is referred to as G in the table. The formula that you type in your spreadsheet to calculate the 'Volume change due to price change' would then be =E4*E15. In the table, this cell is referred to as K and contains the value 8.8%.

■ **Step 4**: Check your answers against those in the table.

Congratulations! You are now ready to use the model!

Table 17.2
The spreadsheet marketing model

Factors	Units	Ref.	Calculation	Result
Inputs				
Price change	% base case price	A		−5.0%
Marketing spend change	% base case marketing spend	B		20.0%
Assumptions				
Base case financial structure				
Fixed costs	% base case revenue	C		40.0%
Variable costs	% base case revenue	D		20.0%
Marketing spend	% base case revenue	E		10.0%
Profit	% base case revenue	F		30.0%
Elasticities				
Price elasticity		G		−1.75
Max increase in volume due to marketing spend	% base case volume	H		40%
Marketing spend for half max volume increase	% base case revenue	J		15%
Calculations				
Price				
Volume change due to price change	% base case volume	K	= A * G	8.8%
New volume due to price change	% base case volume	L	= 1 + K	108.8%
Marketing				
Change in marketing spend	% base case revenue	M	= B * E	2.00%
New marketing spend	% base case revenue	N	= 1 + M	12.0%
Reference marketing spend	% base case revenue	P	= J + N	27.0%
Marketing elasticity		Q	= H / P	148.1%
Volume change due to marketing spend change	% base case volume	R	= M * Q	3.0%

Table 17.2
(continued)

Factors	Units	Ref.	Calculation	Result
New volume due to marketing spend change	% base case volume	S	$= 1 + R$	103.0%
Revenue				
New volume	% base case volume	T	$= L * S$	112.0%
New price	% base case price	U	$= 1 + A$	95.0%
New revenue	% base case revenue	V	$= T * U$	106.4%
Variable costs				
New variable costs	% base case revenue	W	$= D * T$	22.4%
Profit				
Revenue	% base case revenue	V	$= V$	106.4%
Variable costs	% base case revenue	W	$= W$	22.4%
Fixed costs	% base case revenue	C	$= C$	40.0%
Marketing spend	% base case revenue	N	$= N$	12.0%
Profit	% base case revenue	X	$= V - W - C - N$	32.0%
Results				
Volume	% base case volume	T	$= T$	112.0%
Profit	% base case revenue	X	$= X$	32.0%
Change in profit	% base case revenue	Y	$= X - F$	2.0%

Using the model

We suggest that you use the model as follows:

- First, keep the assumptions as in the table. This will enable you to get a feel of how the model works.

- Try separate changes to price and marketing spend and look at the effects on volume and profit.

- Are the results sensible?

- Now change price and marketing spend together and look at the effects on volume and profit.

- Are the results sensible?

- Are the results obvious?

- Can you pick a combination of price and marketing spend changes that maximize profit?

- Now that you have a feel for how the model works, try changing the assumptions to align them with your own brands or business.

Self-assessment exercise

You may find it useful to have a discussion with colleagues, or run a workshop, to assess your own modelling abilities and make recommendations for improvements. If you do this as a workshop, you should split up into syndicates, and each should choose a topic to define best practice in:

1. Scoping and defining models;

2. Sourcing assumptions and data;

3. Packages and tools to assist model solutions;

4. Generating conclusions from models;

5. Presenting ideas and seeking buy-in.

Each syndicate should ask themselves:

- What have you done that was successful?

- What did you do that was unsuccessful (hence what should have been done or been avoided)?

- What references or research can you suggest?

- Are there any useful websites, books or companies you have used?

You may find the points in Box 17.1 useful to guide your discussion on each theme.

Box 17.1 Checklist for assessing modelling capabilities

1. Scoping and defining models:

- Who should be involved in scoping and defining marketing models?

- What is the most effective process to use?

- What problems have you encountered?

2. Sourcing and packaging assumptions and data:

- Who owns the data you need for your model, internally and externally?

- Do the data need cleaning before you can use them? Is this a problem?

- Do you have too much data, or get distracted by non-critical data?

- Are assumptions made explicit?

▶

▶ 3. Packages and tools to assist model solutions:

   ■ Who knows about modelling software in the company?

   ■ Who would make the business/IT case for purchasing and/or making the software available to users?

   ■ Would you even try to do the technical aspects of modelling in-house, or would you use external experts?

   ■ What tools and packages have you used successfully?

4. Generating conclusions:

   ■ What defines success?

   ■ What sensitivities do you build into models?

   ■ What risk factors are important?

5. Presenting ideas and seeking buy-in:

   ■ What are the best ways of explaining models, and the conclusions drawn from them, to a non-specialist audience?

   ■ How can you ensure the modelling process remains dynamic over time?

Key points

■ Spreadsheet models are not inherently difficult to master nor are they impenetrable.

■ Many spreadsheet models are, however, poorly designed.

■ Good model design means a model that can easily be understood by others.

■ Good model design also means that your model is more likely to be carrying out the calculations that you think it is.

■ Clear layout and labelling are key elements of good model design.

■ Even simple 'what-if' models can provide valuable insights into marketing and business processes.

■ Spreadsheets are also capable of handling the more complex situations of optimization and risk and uncertainty modelling.

18

MARKETING PLANNING

What is marketing planning?

Establishing the planning timetable

Step 1: Organizing the planning process

Step 2: Assembling a fact base

Steps 3 and 4: Preparing the baseline forecast and
options for investigation

Step 5: Constructing a marketing plan simulator

Step 6: Selecting the best plan

Step 7: Writing the plan report

Step 8: Getting approval

Key points

This chapter is about writing a marketing plan. Many busy executives confronted with a demand for a plan want only to get one on paper as soon as possible. The trouble is they fall into planning traps. The aim of this chapter is to help you avoid the planning traps and produce a useful document that you will be proud of and your colleagues will value.

What is marketing planning?

> I am good at creating advertising messages and criticizing them, I can run my own department, but I am not very good at writing down my own plans. (Marketing Director of a major brewer)

Planners face several real problems and they also worry about various non-issues – getting ideas together in a well-organized argument and writing them up into a useful document, these are real problems. Getting consensus and buy-in can also be problematic. This chapter will concentrate on helping you solve these real problems.

It is not our prime intention in this chapter to provide detailed instructions on how you should perform the analysis of history and trends that precede the writing of the plan. Nor will it tell you about how to produce charts and PowerPoint slides. If you have read the chapters preceding this one, you will have had plenty of suggestions about analysis methods. However, before reading further, it may be useful to remind yourself of the terminology used in marketing planning (see Box 18.1).

Box 18.1 Marketing planning terminology

Financial plan: Report that sets out the best method of managing the company's finances over a specific future period, say 3 years.

Marketing plan simulator: Spreadsheet model that allows the planner to try out alternative plans and estimate their effects on sales and profits.

Marketing plan: Report that sets out the best method for running your marketing activity, assets and resources over a specific future time period, say 3 years, given the forecast changes in the market.

Marketing planning: Process of thinking ahead about the changes to current marketing activities, assets and resources that will be needed in the future to

> support the firm's revenue and profit objectives, given the forecast changes in the market.
>
> **Strategic plan:** Report that sets out the best method for running the entire business over a specific future time period, say 3 years, given the forecast changes externally and internally.

Planning is thinking. It is not primarily about writing – that comes after the thinking. It is not primarily about PowerPoint slides. The planning process requires you to take sufficient time away from office administrivia to actually think! Few executives realize this, and fewer actually do it.

> **Planning should be 80% thinking and 20% writing and charting.**

A marketing plan usually reviews the past history of your marketing and sets out a general strategic marketing plan, for say 3 years, with a more detailed tactical marketing plan for the coming year. The most important issues vary from company to company, but in general the key focus is on market opportunities and threats, product brand portfolio and marketing expenditure allocation.

There is no unique formula for preparing a marketing plan. There is no perfect size or level of detail. There is no single magic list of contents. There is not even a single ideal way of ordering the content. However, by understanding the intended audience for the plan, the expected uses and overall purposes, it is possible for any competent person to write a satisfactory marketing plan. Start by asking yourself ten hard questions about the way you go about the task at the moment:

1. Do we even have a marketing plan?
2. Have the planners assembled a fact base?
3. Have the planners prepared a baseline forecast of likely changes in the market?
4. Have lessons from previous marketing plans been taken into account?
5. Are market response models used in the planning process?
6. Have alternatives and scenarios been considered?
7. Are planning assumptions recorded?
8. Is there a report that explains the plan to management?
9. Is there a realistic timetable for constructing the plan?
10. Is the approval process for the plan an effective one?

Establishing the planning timetable

A cause of confusion among managers is the process of planning. What do you do first? When will there be time to do everything? How can we cut corners? Can I afford to be absent from some steps? Who can I trust? Who will get blamed if it goes wrong? Will I even be here when the problems emerge?

The biggest problem is the many hours, days and weeks that are invested in the process but do not show up in the finished product, i.e. the plan report. It is like cooking a meal – choosing a menu, all the shopping, selecting ingredients, substituting missing ingredients, chopping, heating, simmering, mixing, cleaning up and serving – and at the end, it seems, nobody is aware of the effort. But of course, that is not the true picture. The quality of the preparation and skill of the cook are reflected in the quality and success of the end product. The same is true of marketing planning.

Too many managers treat marketing planning cynically as an unwelcome and optional task that is imposed on them by someone else. They allocate time to the approval of the plan, and a little time to its writing, but fail to recognize the effort needed to undertake the process thoroughly. Consequently many plans are rushed, slipshod and illogical, and provide nothing useful to the organization. Preparations take time and the calendar for planning needs to become a standard part of the manager's annual diary.

If you are apprehensive about the planning process, you need not only a series of steps but also some indication of how long each step is likely to take. This depends, of course, on the size and complexity of your business.

If your planning is embryonic, do not try to get the planning process perfect first time – perfection isn't a reasonable expectation. Do not allow the process to be held up by the lack of extensive data. Instead, use the judgement of managers and make reasonable assumptions on the move. You can always improve your plans later in the light of better data, and your planning skills will get better over time. Use the checklist in Table 18.1 to help you set a realistic calendar for marketing planning.

Work *backwards* from when your plan is to be approved and set yourself a deadline for completion, naming individuals and tasks, and an approximate number of man-days effort. Remember that people have other responsibilities, and time for seasonal activities and holidays should be realistically incorporated. Most organizations should be working to at least a 3-month period for constructing their plan. In complex organizations, 6 months might be more realistic.

Table 18.1

Reverse scheduling through the steps in the marketing planning process

Step 8: Getting approval for the plan

- Circulating plan report
- Preparing PowerPoint slides
- Presentation and discussion
- Revising the plan
- Approval of revised plan

Deadline:_____

People involved_____

Effort required_____

Step 7: Writing the plan report

- Agreeing table of contents
- Writing first draft
- Preparing charts, tables and graphs
- Reviewing first draft and agreeing amendments
- Finalizing plan report

Deadline:_____

People involved_____

Effort required_____

Step 6: Selecting the best plan

- Running planning workshops
- What-if analysis
- Discussion among planning team
- Calculation of plan forecast
- Downside risk assessment
- Approval of best plan by planning team

Deadline:_____

People involved_____

Effort required_____

Step 5: Constructing a marketing plan simulator

- Reviewing modelling requirements
- Prototype models
- Final models

Deadline:_____

People involved_____

Effort required_____

Step 4: Identifying options for investigation

- Workshops to discuss potential changes
- Prioritizing changes for investigation
- Approving modelling requirements

Deadline:_____

People involved_____

Effort required_____

Step 3: Preparing the baseline forecast

- Analyzing the trends and correlations
- Constructing a spreadsheet model
- Documenting forecasting assumptions
- Preparing a baseline forecast
- Disseminating it to the planning team

Deadline:_____

People involved_____

Effort required_____

Step 2: Assembling the fact base

- Collecting key facts and figures
- Consolidating the master spreadsheet
- Learning from history
- Preparing charts of key facts and figures
- Disseminating them to the planning team

Deadline:_____

People involved_____

Effort required_____

▶

Table 18.1
(continued)

Step 1: Organizing the planning process	Deadline:_____
	People involved_____
	Effort required_____

Step 1: Organizing the planning process

A marketing plan is often thought to be a political document that passes the 'thud' test and enables the marketer to obtain approval from the Board with the minimum of pain. Yet in reality marketing plan reports are used for many different purposes and it is difficult to summarize what constitutes a good plan (see Box 18.2). Sometimes it may be necessary to produce more than one version of the plan report to cater for the needs of different readerships.

Box 18.2 What makes a good marketing plan?

- Definition of how your future marketing will change from your past marketing;

- A logical explanation of why your future activities are in the best interests of the company and its shareholders;

- A request for funding;

- A framework for budget approval;

- A reference document informing your colleagues and external agencies about the logic behind any marketing changes in coming years;

- Convergence between the sales revenue forecasts of finance and marketing;

- Convergence between the product/market plans of marketing and strategic planning;

- A yardstick for measuring marketing performance;

- Quantitative 'what-if' analysis showing how your plan will cause performance to improve;

- Alignment between words and numbers;

- Sufficient realism about the past and current situation;

- Successful anticipation of future changes;

- Imaginative challenging of the status quo;

- Not fixing what ain't broke.

There can be a huge difference between a logically argued plan and just a plan. What you need to explain in the plan is why your proposal is in the best interests of the company. There can be a huge difference between an undocumented explanation and a documented plan. The formal exercise of distilling plans on paper helps highlight risks and uncover inconsistencies.

There is always a budgetary motive lurking somewhere behind a plan. The plan might be used to argue the case for a bigger budget. The plan might also be used to justify grabbing a chunk of someone else's budget. Therefore the plan needs to talk the language of finance as well as the language of marketing. Sometimes it may be necessary to prepare a finance supplement to the marketing plan.

It hardly needs to be said that a plan needs to provide a framework for approval. The group marketing director usually approves business unit marketing plans. The Board of Directors usually approves the marketing plan. However, the approval process can be disconnected, with the finance director approving the numbers and the Board approving the words. Aligning words and numbers in the marketing plan is therefore important. It may also be necessary to prepare business cases for any significant approvals that are part of the planning process.

A plan can provide a useful reference document informing your colleagues and external agencies about the logic behind any marketing changes in coming years. However, to achieve this aim, it may be necessary to prepare a separate document to communicate the plan to a wider audience.

Marketing plans need to converge with strategic plans and financial plans, but often they do not. The marketing planning process needs to ensure that there is sufficient realism in the company's financial plans, and it is particularly important that there is convergence between sales revenue forecasts from different departments. There also needs to be convergence between the views of strategic planners about mergers and acquisitions and major product launches and the views of marketing about their viability in the marketplace.

Marketing plans should provide yardsticks against which marketing performance can be measured. That means that they must contain numbers and targets, both financial and non-financial. They must distinguish clearly between results that are caused by marketing and ones that marketing does not cause.

Quantitative models and what-if analyses should underlie the numbers in the plan. There is nothing worse than a plan whose numbers are plucked out of thin air. The modelling techniques that you have encountered earlier in this book can all contribute to the planning process.

Words in plans need to be aligned with the numbers. We have seen numerous plans where there is a major disconnect between the words and numbers. Often it is the job of finance to check the numbers (and they do not read the words) and the Board of Directors reads the words (but they do not check them for consistency with the numbers)!

Realism must be the watchword. Past performance is often a good guide to the future, and major step changes in performance, or 'hockey stick' graphs, should be investigated for feasibility. Future performance can often be modelled, and rigorous modelling should be employed in forecasting the future.

> The plan should not merely reflect the status quo plus a small incremental change. Be prepared to challenge the status quo but, conversely, don't instigate change for its own sake.

Step 2: Assembling a fact base

Many facts and figures can be studied by the planning team. A rule-of-thumb for deciding what facts are needed is to collect enough to carry out a SWOT analysis. Although we do not recommend that your analysis of Strengths, Weaknesses, Opportunities and Threats should appear in any detail in the marketing plan, doing a SWOT analysis is a good way of getting the planning team to think.

- Strengths and weaknesses are internal factors over which you have some control and influence.
- Opportunities and threats are external factors that you may react to but you cannot control.

Among the many authors on marketing planning, McDonald (1999) has produced by far the most comprehensive and practical guide, including many templates for various parts of the process (e.g. see Tables 18.2 to 18.7).

Strengths in the marketplace (i.e. the degree to which you can take advantage of a market opportunity) can be assessed by *competitive position* analysis. It is a judgemental assessment of an organization's ability to satisfy market needs relative to competitors and will differ by market/segment opportunity. Start by creating a form similar to that in Table 18.2 for each product-market in which you participate.

Table 18.2
Competitive position data collection

Product-market:		Relative competitive strength scores:				
Critical success factor (CSF)	Weight	Self	Competitor A	Competitor B	Competitor C	Competitor D
Total	100%					

Source: After McDonald (1999)

In column 1 (critical success factors or CSFs) indicate how customers choose between rival suppliers in the product-market. Each product-market will probably have different CSFs, or at least different weightings. There are not normally more than five or six key factors, though there may be many other factors that contribute to success. In column 2, indicate the relative importance of the factors to the customer by allocating weights out of 100. Across the top of the table, list your key competitors in the product-market, e.g. 'comp. 1', 'comp. 2', etc. Then, decide how your customers would score you and each of your competitors out of 10 on each of the CSFs. Enter the scores on the form.

Whenever market research can be used to validate these judgements, use it. If there is no independent market research for important product-markets, beware of just accepting the views of managers. In situations of poor data, the best approach is to obtain the views of colleagues closest to the customers – remembering those involved in product delivery, service, etc. as well as sales. Do not allow your marketing department to complete this form in isolation. In industrial markets, asking a few key customers to complete the form can provide some objectivity, as well as building the relationship. Multiply each score by the weight, and add up the weighted scores in each column.

Opportunities to enter new markets, or to develop new offers in existing ones, can be assessed using *market attractiveness* as a measure of the potential of the marketplace to yield growth in sales and profits. The criteria themselves will, of course, be determined by the organization being benchmarked and will be relevant to the objectives the organization is trying to achieve. The method is as follows.

Construct a chart similar to Table 18.3, starting by listing a few key market attractiveness factors for the SBU or brand being benchmarked in column 1. To identify these factors, ask what attracts management of this SBU or brand to one product-market rather than another. For example, market size, market growth, market profitability. Factors should be independent of each other. For example, if you have a market size factor and a potential profit factor, use an estimate of potential unit margins to measure potential profit, as otherwise the market size would effectively be counted twice.

Indicate the relative importance of the factors when comparing product-markets by allocating weights out of 100 in column 2. List the various product-markets that are being compared across the top of the table: 'product-market 1', etc. Score each product-market out of 10 on each factor, where 10 is highly attractive. Multiply each score by the factor's weight, and add up the scores for the product-market in the 'total' row at the bottom. The factors should not have anything to do with your current position in the market. It would be a mistake to regard a market as unattractive just because you are not currently strong in it. For example, a profitability factor should relate to industry average profitability or the profitability of the market leader, not to your current profitability.

Table 18.3
Market attractiveness data collection

Attractiveness factor	Weight	Market attractiveness factors score				
		Prod-mkt 1	Prod-mkt 2	Prod-mkt 3	Prod-mkt 4	Prod-mkt 5
Growth						
Size						
Profit potential						
etc.						
Total	100%					

Source: After McDonald (1999)

Market attractiveness is a combination of a number of factors, as illustrated in Table 18.3. These factors, however, can usually be summarized under three headings:

- **Growth rate:** Expected average annual growth rate of revenue spent by that segment (e.g. % growth 2001 over 2000, plus % growth 2002 over 2001, plus % growth 2003 over 2002, divided by 3). If preferred, compound average growth rate could be used.

- **Accessible market size:** An attractive market is not only large, it can also be accessed. One way of calculating this is to estimate the total revenue of the segment in year t+3, where t0 is the current year, less revenue which is impossible to access, regardless of investment made. Alternatively, total market size can be used, which is the most frequent method, as it does not involve any managerial judgement to be made that could distort the truth. This latter method is the preferred method.

- **Profit potential:** This is much more difficult to deal with and will vary considerably, according to industry. A simple way of calculating it is to use the weighted required return on sales (ROS) that the company would find attractive. Thus, in Table 18.3: >15% = high in attractiveness; 15%–10% = medium; <10% = low.

Another way of doing this calculation is to use Porter's Five Forces model (Porter 1980) to estimate the profit potential of a segment, as shown in Table 18.4.

Table 18.4
Estimating profit potential of segments – 1

Five Forces	Weight	Profit-potential factors score				
		Prod-mkt 1	Prod-mkt 2	Prod-mkt 3	Prod-mkt 4	Prod-mkt 5
1. Intensity of competition						
2. Threat of substitutes						
3. Threat of new entrants						
4. Power of suppliers						
5. Power of customers						
Total	100%					

Source: After McDonald (1999)

Alternatively, a combination of these and industry-specific factors could be used. In the case of the pharmaceutical sector, for example, the factors could be as outlined in Table 18.5.

Table 18.5
Estimating profit potential of segments – 2

Profit-potential factors	Weight	Profit-potential factors score				
		Prod-mkt 1	Prod-mkt 2	Prod-mkt 3	Prod-mkt 4	Prod-mkt 5
Competitive intensity						
Price potential						
Unmet medical needs						
etc.						
Total	100%					

Source: After McDonald (1999)

These scores are clearly a proxy for profit potential. Each is weighted according to its importance. The weights add up to 100 in order to give a profit potential factor score, as in the Porter's Five Forces example above.

Steps 3 and 4: Preparing the baseline forecast and options for investigation

A baseline performance forecast is a prediction of how the business will perform if marketing carries on in the same way in the future as it has in the past. On the face of it, such a forecast is simple, being an extrapolation of past performance.

Fill in the form shown in Table 18.6 for each product-market as far as you are able. Enter latest estimates for the year in progress, and historical figures as far back as you have them (3 years is often a realistic target).

Then enter 'trend' figures of the market size for each year of the planning period (e.g. 3 years ahead), and forecasts of what sales will be on current trends, assuming no remedial action is taken – not what you would like to achieve.

Market size represents the total purchases made by customers in this product-market from your company or from your competitors. Use either volume figures or revenue figures, or both, depending on what data are available. 'Volume' represents the number of 'units' sold, e.g. computers, mortgages or days of training. Enter margin figures if available for the product-market. 'Margin' can be defined in whatever way you find most appropriate, e.g. marketing contribution in the case of a sales and marketing business unit, provided you are consistent. If you have made important assumptions when forecasting, make a note of these on a separate sheet.

Table 18.6
Collection of baseline data

Year	Market size (volume)	Market size (revenue)	Our sales (volume)	Our sales (revenue)	Our % margin	Largest competitor's sales volume	Largest competitor's revenue
Y–3							
Y–2							
Y–1							
Y–0							
Y+1							
Y+2							
Y+3							

Key:
Y–3 to Y–1: Historical data
Y–0: This year
Y+0 to Y+3: Forecasts

Source: After McDonald (1999)

Step 5: Constructing a marketing plan simulator

The team discussing and selecting the best plan will want to assess the financial impact of the options they are evaluating. Spreadsheet models offer the best tools available for carrying out these what-if analyses.

Preparation of spreadsheet models is vital before the workshops. Although it is possible to construct spreadsheet models on the run during a workshop, this can be a risky thing to do. Our advice would always be to construct spreadsheet models before the workshop.

Chapter 17 has provided you with all you need to know to begin construction of your 'marketing plan simulator'. We call it that because it is a model specifically constructed to evaluate those options that are being tested in the planning process. You probably have business models in finance or even in marketing, but don't make the mistake of assuming that any old model will be up to the job. It is likely that you will need to construct a model specifically for the purpose of marketing planning.

Finding a suitable modeller during the planning season can be tough. Spreadsheet skills are in high demand at this time, so book your resources well in advance. Don't settle for a spreadsheet specialist who does not understand marketing, or who has only basic spreadsheet knowledge. Delivering poorly constructed models that are not user-friendly will only antagonize the planning team.

For example, Figure 18.1 illustrates a model that qualifies as poorly constructed. The layout is haphazard and it is not clear which cells are inputs to the model and which numbers are calculated. There are no units or definitions shown, and the chart is not labelled. It is going to take anyone other than the author more than a little time and some considerable pain to find their way around a spreadsheet model that shares these features!

Step 6: Selecting the best plan

A common cause of confusion is what is 'the plan', and what are its 'results'. So let's reiterate: the plan is the best method of running your marketing activity. It's the things you will do in the future.

Focus is vital in planning. There will be so many things that you will do in the future that you cannot state all of them. Some details will have to be omitted. The question is, which details should you include in the plan?

Our advice would be that the overall marketing plan should attempt to make the best decision about the following topics:

- Expenditure allocation (see Chapter 8);
- Brand identity and image changes (see Chapter 9);
- Product brand portfolio changes (see Chapter 10).

In planning terms, you must decide whether you expect to need a makeover for your brand(s). Is it becoming tired and worn out? What direction should the changes take? Don't, however, attempt to define the new identity in detail in the plan.

Product brand portfolio changes also need to be planned. Should your portfolio be extended, stretched, or gaps filled? Should the length of the product lines be lengthened, with new varieties or pack variants, or should it be consolidated?

Expenditure will need to be reallocated to increase payback. Two levels of reallocation should be assessed – (a) strategic allocation by product/market and (b) tactical allocation by mix element.

Workshops are a good way of debating the options and reaching consensus on the best plan. Begin by reviewing the brand identity and image and changes that are required. Then look at the portfolio. Finally look at expenditure allocation. Make sure that enough time has been allowed for each set of decisions.

You should then document the risks that you believe are associated with each decision – see Table 18.7.

Figure 18.1

Example of a poorly constructed spreadsheet model

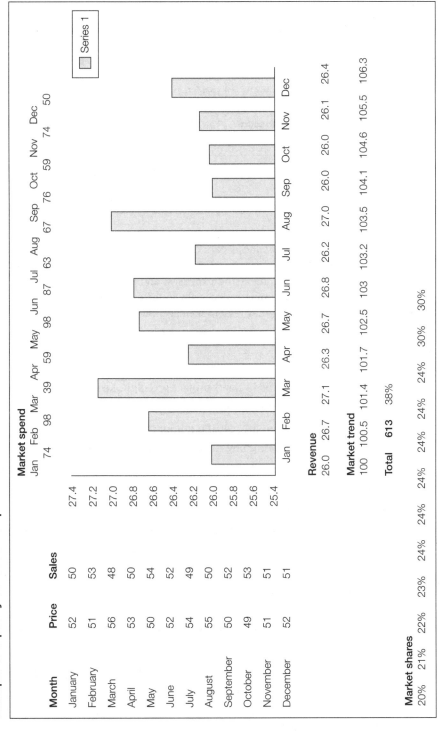

Month	Price	Sales			
January	52	50			27.4
February	51	53			27.2
March	56	48			27.0
April	53	50			26.8
May	50	54			26.6
June	52	52			26.4
July	54	49			26.2
August	55	50			26.0
September	50	52			25.8
October	49	53			25.6
November	51	51			25.4
December	52	51			

Market spend

	Jan	Feb	Mar	Apr	May	Jun	Jul	Aug	Sep	Oct	Nov	Dec
	74	98	39	59	98	87	63	67	76	59	74	50

Revenue

	Jan	Feb	Mar	Apr	May	Jun	Jul	Aug	Sep	Oct	Nov	Dec
	26.0	26.7	27.1	26.3	26.7	26.8	26.2	27.0	26.0	26.0	26.1	26.4

Market trend

100	100.5	101.4	101.7	102.5	103	103.2	103.5	104.1	104.6	105.5	106.3

Total 613   38%

Market shares

20%	21%	22%	23%	24%	24%	24%	24%	24%	24%	30%	30%

Table 18.7

Suggested downside risk assessment format

Key assumption	Basis of assumption	What event would have to happen to make this strategy unattractive?	Risk of such an event occurring (%) High (7–10) Medium (4–6) Low (0–3)	Impact if event occurs	Trigger point for action	Actual contingency action proposed
1.						
2.						

Source: After McDonald (1999)

Cooper (1993) additionally comments about the risk inherent in valuation models:

> [These] models require financial data as input. Someone must make estimates of expected sales in Year 1, Year 2 and so on; and estimates are required for selling prices, production costs, marketing expenses, and investment outlays. Often these variables are difficult to estimate, especially in the early stage of a project. And even when estimates are made, they tend to be inaccurate.

Cooper's advice in these situations is to minimize risk by staged implementation of strategies:

1. When the uncertainties of [a new] project are high, keep the amounts at stake low. When you don't know where you are going, take small steps.

2. As the uncertainties decrease, let the amounts at stake increase. As you learn more about where you are going, take bigger and bigger steps.

3. Incrementalize the [project] progress into a series of steps or stages. Each step should be more costly than the one before.

4. View each stage as a means of reducing uncertainty. Remember that information is the key to uncertainty reduction. Each stage in the process that creates an expenditure must reduce uncertainty by an equivalent amount. 'Buy a series of looks' at the project's outcome.

5. Provide for timely evaluation, decision and bail-out points. These decision points pull together all the new information from the previous stage and pose the questions 'Are we still in the game? Should we proceed to the next stage or kill the project now?'

The high risks associated with new product development are well documented in the academic literature. Baker (1983), for example, reviews about 20 studies of new product failure. It appears to be normal that less than one in five will succeed. As Schon (1967) comments on marketing risks:

> In the absence of any clear criteria of success and failure and of adequate statistics
> . . . It is at any rate more accurate to say 'Almost nothing new works' than to say 'Most
> new developments succeed'.

Investors are conscious of this high failure rate, and they adjust their investment criteria accordingly. Ward (2003) suggests that management accountants who appraise marketing strategies should tailor their investment criteria similarly, according to the inherent marketing risks.

Step 7: Writing the plan report

> Everyone knew what Walt [Disney] wanted. Everyone had objectives. Both were
> communicated all the way down the line. The management layer was flat and
> responsibilities were well defined. We had a good self image and the company ran
> well. (Quoted in Stutely 1999)

This quote from a former Walt Disney executive makes two important points. Walt must have known what he wanted before it could be communicated. Knowing what you want is what planning is all about. Walt was also a visionary. Although the movie business requires meticulous planning to turn a dry script into a lively strip of celluloid, Walt delegated most of the detailed stuff and spent most of his time on the vision.

The marketing director should take overall responsibility for the marketing plan. Like Walt, he must know what he wants. His conviction must be based on thinking and analysis. However, he will need an experienced planner to take the time to translate his vision into a well-reasoned planning narrative. He will also need to delegate some of the exploration and investigation to a planning team.

The marketing plan should be inviting to read and easy to understand. Having put a great deal of effort into the planning process, the planning team will want to communicate its ideas as concisely and effectively as possible. This might sound obvious, but as one wit quipped: 'Once you put our plan down, you just can't pick it up.'

A plan to plagiarize

Certainly, emphatically, unquestionably, the last thing that we want you to do is copy a marketing plan. It must be your own creation. However, you will find the list of contents in Box 18.3 useful as a framework if you are very rushed.

Box 18.3 Table of contents of a typical marketing plan

1. Cover

2. Table of Contents

3. Executive Summary

4. Baseline Performance Forecast (how business will evolve if nothing internally changes)

5. Your Plan (to outperform the baseline)

6. Plan Performance Forecast (how business will perform if you carry out the plan)

7. Controls and Risk Management

8. Appendices (for example):

- Approvals List (for changes needing higher approval)

- Expanded Analysis

- Associated Information

- Financial Plan

- Strategic Plan

- Situation Review and SWOT Analysis

- Marketing Planning Fact Base

- Marketing Plan Simulator

- Supplementary Business Cases (for changes needing higher approval)

- Departmental Plans – advertising, direct marketing, customer service, etc.

- Brand Plans (for all major brands)

It hardly needs to be stated that the plan should have a *cover*, showing the date, version and author. While it is rare for a plan to be professionally printed, it should nevertheless look and feel professional; a *table of contents* will help reinforce this impression.

The *executive summary* will create a first impression and so it is important that the main conclusions that you want readers to reach are clearly stated in language they can understand. Don't be afraid to include a short glossary if there are any key terms that need explaining, especially of any metrics, but don't burden readers with a lot of jargon.

The *baseline performance forecast* is where you tell readers what you predict will happen if the company carries on as it has in the past. It is useful here to examine past trends as well as projecting the future.

The *body of the plan* comes next. Here you are saying what you plan to do. It should cover the longer term, say 3 years or perhaps 5, and also give a more detailed plan for the coming 12 months. Include numbers, tables and charts sparingly to make points. Focus on changes from past activities, not on the continuation of the status quo.

A *plan performance forecast*, illustrating how the plan will affect performance, comes next. Use tables and charts to illustrate the mechanism by which your plan will outperform the baseline forecast.

Risks and controls should be identified in the final section, to show that you recognize that the world is a risky place and demonstrate that you plan to be in control of future eventualities. Controls that you will put in place should also be identified here.

Appendices should be used to hold the more detailed material (e.g. situation and SWOT analysis; marketing planning fact base) that some readers may wish to refer to, but the average reader will not want to review. Associated information also needs to be archived, as when plans get reviewed in the future, it is important to have evidence about how the conclusions in the plan were reached.

Step 8: Getting approval

You can be sure that your marketing plan will be given some attention. You can also be sure that readers will not study it in its entirety. The best you can hope for is that they will grasp some of the points you are making.

So, think about the people who will be reading the plan report and who will be listening to you making a presentation. If you are fighting in a tough political atmosphere, do not let the plan be discussed too freely in advance of your presentation. Idle chatter gives your opponents too much opportunity to pick holes in your plan!

People who influence your plan's approval

Chief executive:

Will the chief executive form his/her own opinion or will he/she seek the approval of finance or other power brokers?

Finance director (or CFO):

- Does the finance director have the power to overrule or, worse, ignore the sales forecasts and budget proposals in your plan?
- Have you been invited to review their forecasts?
- What are the finance director's views on pricing changes?
- Have you taken the time to review his/her financial plans?
- Will he/she have their staff check your numbers?

Sales director:

- How will the sales director respond to the sales forecast in your plan?
- Have you sought his/her approval before the meeting?
- Have you discussed his/her plans for sales promotion and distribution?
- Even if he/she indicates prior approval, do you trust them?

Strategic planning director:

Does the strategic planning director's plans for mergers, acquisitions and product development align with your plans?

- Has he/she even shared their plans with you?
- Have you bothered to read their plans?

Customer service director:

- How will the customer service director respond to your views on customer service?
- Does he/she have the resources to make changes to service levels that your plan indicates?

There are two worst-case scenarios. One is that your plan is rejected or you are told to go back to the drawing board. This you can deal with by redrafting the report or revising some of the calculations. The second, more threatening scenario is that your plans are ignored by finance, sales and other departments. So, despite your efforts, it does not get you budget approval, nor does it have the support of the sales team who follow their own, independent path.

Whatever the case, the most likely reasons for your plan failing to gain the approval you desire are shown in Box 18.4 below.

Box 18.4 Twelve reasons why plans fail at first glance

1. Presentation too scruffy – or too slick (it feels false).

2. Text too long, too many generalizations, too much waffle.

3. Text too short, too weak, too vague.

4. Whatever the length, there are too few hard facts.

5. There are major errors of fact.

6. Specific omissions suggest that vital insights are missing.

7. Words and numbers are not consistent.

8. Numbers are easily contradicted by simple calculations.

9. Optimism about the future neglects past failures.

10. No assessment of risks and planning assumptions.

11. Plans obviously presented to obtain financial support but don't align with departmental expectations.

12. Plans produced by staff without sufficient input from line management.

Source: After Stutely (1999)

Marketing planning is a vitally important task that often declines into a worthless chore. Becoming an effective planner requires teamwork, between marketing and finance, and the blending of presentational and analytical skills.

Key points

- Marketing planning is the process of thinking ahead about improvements to current marketing activities, assets and resources.
- Marketing plans are reports setting out the best method of running your marketing.
- Book enough time away from the office to think effectively about your plans.
- Anticipate the opposition that your plan will face in the approval process.

- Disapproval of your plan is often expressed by ignoring it.

- Make the marketing plan report interesting, readable and useful.

- Establish a process for debating alternatives and selecting the best plan.

- Decide how you will manage and control the risks of the plan.

- Construct models to make sure the numbers in the plan make sense.

- Construct a baseline forecast that reflects past trends externally and internally.

- Do a SWOT analysis after you have done the baseline forecast as it will help you decide where improvements are most needed.

- Check that the numbers in the plan are consistent with the words.

- Make sure that the plan recognizes and assesses the inherent risks.

19

BETTER BUDGETING

Budgeting couldn't be worse, according to a broad cross-section of managers, so it can only get better. The aim of this chapter is to help you make the marketing budgeting process better. We look at the process and how it should be improved. We offer practical hints to help you get budget approval without too much pain. We examine the claims being made today about 'better budgeting' and ask whether this medicine will cure the ills of marketing.

An overview of the budget cycle

Budgeting is more than just a boring errand we have to run for the finance department. Budgeting can help our marketing payback improve. Sometimes when we budget, we catch expenditure misallocations. It's a lot better to catch errors in a budget than to have problems later. And good budgeting will typically show up marketing waste of 20% to 30%.

Timing is an important consideration in good budgeting (see Table 19.1). Late starting of the process causes slipshod, hurried calculations. Early starting of the process results in the budget being out of date before it starts.

A timetable is generally set by the finance department to ensure that everyone does their homework at the right time. It usually covers an 18-month cycle, with the budget covering 12 months. In this illustration, we begin the process in mid-2004. The logical steps in the process are shown in Figure 19.1.

Usually each department prepares a monthly memorandum comparing results with budget and commenting on differences. Around July 2004, there is a review meeting, in which managers discuss the lessons learnt from the first 6 months trading, and to inform senior managers about the priorities for improvement in 2005.

A memorandum is issued around this time setting out guidelines for the 2005 budget and showing departmental heads the operating board's expectations about improvements in 2005. A flurry of analysis is triggered by this memo, as departments prepare their budget submissions for 2005. By November, all submissions should have been received, and the review and approval process begins.

Sales forecasts are the first to be approved as they form the logical foundation for all the variable cost budgets. Because marketing expenditure is a major driver of sales revenues, it would be logical to approve it at the same time as the sales forecast, but this rarely happens.

After the sales forecast is agreed, there is usually a long and detailed round of discussions of the operating costs – variable and fixed – and eventually these are approved.

Table 19.1

Normal budget cycle

Date	2004 budget	2005 budget	2006 budget
Jul. 2004	Detailed review of first 6 months feeds into 2005 target setting	Senior executives set direction of improvement for 2005:	
Aug.	Managers report 7 months to end of July	• Sales growth • Cost savings • Marketing expenditure limits	
Sep.	Managers report 8 months to end of August	Directional plans are communicated to departments	
Oct.	Managers report 9 months to end of September	Departments prepare activity plans to achieve directional improvements	
Nov.	Managers report 10 months to end of October	Departments submit plans, committees debate, plans are revised and eventually approved as budgets	
Dec.	Managers report 11 months to end of November		
Jan. 2005	Full review of 2004 budget results	New budget year begins. 2005 budgets may be revised in light of 2004 results	
Feb. to Jun.		Managers submit month-end reports showing results versus budgets. April review is more detailed	
Jul.		Detailed review of first 6 months feeds into 2006 target setting	Senior executives set direction of improvement for 2006: • Sales growth • Cost savings • Marketing expenditure limits
Aug. to Dec.		Managers report months 7 to 11 showing performance relative to budget. October review is more detailed	
Jan. 2006		Full review of 2005 budget results	New budget year begins. 2006 budgets may be revised in light of 2005 results

Source: After Stutely (2003)

Figure 19.1

The normal budget preparation, submission and approval sequence

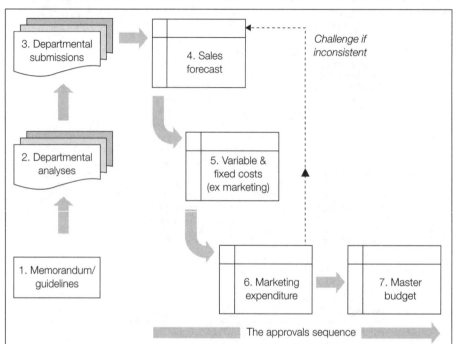

By the time the marketing submission comes to be approved it is early December. Marketing approval is the last thing standing in the way of the master budget being approved, and by this time in the year, the budget committee is not in any mood for protracted debate and negotiation. The marketing budget is therefore often treated as a 'balancing item' or a 'discretionary expense' that can be cut arbitrarily to help the budget committee reach an acceptable total in the master budget.

Yet meddling arbitrarily with the marketing budget is likely to have a detrimental effect on the sales forecast, so the marketing budget team should ideally be prepared to challenge any meddling, on the grounds that changing the marketing budget is likely to invalidate the sales forecast. Yet at this stage in the cycle, it would be a heroic marketing director who had the audacity to speak up, as such whistle-blowing would overturn the whole approval timetable.

Consequently, most sales forecasts and marketing expenditure budgets are based on a flawed process, which by its very nature encourages systematic bias. Cynicism is endemic among marketing managers ensnared in this process. Marketing habitually leaves its submission to the last possible moment, and makes only the most superficial of analyses in support of the budget submission. Marketing budget analysis is shallow, and often late, precisely because of the bitter experience that it will be subjected to arbitrary meddling by the budget committee. Check through our list of ten hard questions to ask about the way marketing budgeting is handled in your organization:

1. Should the marketing budget be approved at the same time as the sales forecast, at the start of the budgeting approval timetable?

2. Can marketing bring forward its budgeting submission date to meet this deadline?

3. Can we replace our sales forecasting procedure with marketing simulation models?

4. Does the finance department accept the principle of 'rightsizing' the marketing budget?

5. If we revise downwards the marketing budget, do we also revise downward the sales forecast?

6. Is our marketing budget set on the basis of maximizing profits or volume?

7. If I had to hack out 10% of marketing spending, what would I cut? If I had 10% more budget, where would I spend it?

8. Is our budgeting process useful as a control tool, or is it merely something to help the finance department report to bankers and investors?

9. Does budgeting form part of a wider set of performance measures? Are non-financial performance indicators treated as seriously as financial ones?

10. Is marketing risk modelled correctly? What is the most important message from the marketing risk assessment?

Transforming your budgeting process

These problems cry out for solution. Marketing payback improvement becomes unworkable with such a flawed process. The financial inefficiency and wastefulness of this flawed process is substantial.

Good and bad news await. The good news is that budgeting processes in many companies are being modified, computerized and revolutionized. The bad news is that the better budgeting bandwagon has many passengers, and marketing is not generally high on the better budgeting agenda. We shall address this issue later in this chapter, but for now we will take you through an improved process of marketing budgeting, as set out in Figure 19.2.

Figure 19.2
An improved preparation, submission and approval sequence

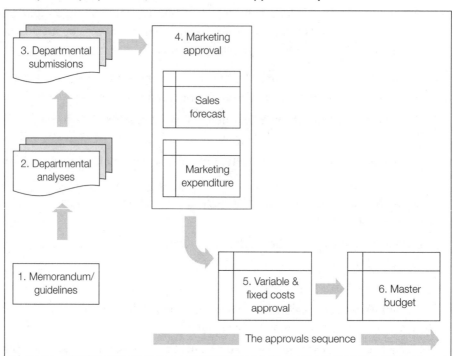

Setting guidelines for budgeting

Around the middle of the year, a memo will arrive announcing the start of the process (Figure 19.3). Guidelines are often attached, in the case of bigger organizations, setting out the methods that you are expected to use to arrive at the budget submission and describing the approval process.

When you receive this, don't immediately deputize the role of marketing budget coordinator to a scapegoat, a secretary or a proxy in finance. Don't think we're joking about this. We have often found that marketing directors actively stay away from any direct involvement in the budgeting process, other than the ceremonial roles of signing off the submission before it goes to finance and presenting the submission to the Board, surrounded by 'staffers', who are the people who actually understand the submission.

The timetable is important. You need to check that the marketing expenditure submission is connected to the sales forecast (as in Figure 19.2), and not an afterthought that is slipped in at the end of the budgeting process (as in Figure 19.1). If this is not the case, you need to take steps to get the timetable changed.

Figure 19.3
Typical mid-year budgeting memo

MEMO

From: Budget Coordinator
To: Marketing Director
Date: 1 July 2004
Subject: Annual Budget for 2005

Please attend the first budget meeting of 2004, which will be held in the Boardroom on 2 August. I am attaching:

1. Timetable for budgeting process
2. Proposed roles and responsibilities
3. Guidelines on preparation of budget submissions
4. Definitions of expenditure categories
5. Guidelines for the approval process
6. Draft strategic plan for 2005–8
7. Provisional performance improvement targets set by the Board.

Proposed roles are important too. The leadership of the sales forecasting committee is especially important. Often marketing is outnumbered by other departments, such as manufacturing or operations, finance, R&D and the sales department. Ideally marketing should chair this committee, and take responsibility for the construction of sales forecasting models.

Guidelines for preparation of budget submissions need to follow the principles that we set out in Chapter 8:

- The principle of rightsizing expenditure allocation;

- The principle of no expenditure rationing;

- The principle of waste elimination;

- The principle of funding projects not people;

- The principle of consolidating and fragmenting.

Definitions of expenditure categories should meet marketing's needs, but often they don't. A common problem that needs to be solved is the splitting of major marketing items into sufficient detail, while not over-analyzing trivial items.

The approval of your marketing expenditure submission should come early in the approval schedule, and it should be linked to the approval of the sales forecast. There needs to be a process of challenging the submission, to check that it is robust, but it is important that those doing the challenging understand the links between marketing expenditure and sales revenues, and ideally use simulation models to carry out what-if analyses.

Finally, the provisional performance improvement targets set by the Board should be recognized as provisional. It will be hard for them to best-guess the sources of improvement and it would be a mistake for them to pressurize managers into dreaming up fantastic budgets that are divorced from reality, just to make the Board happy. A memo such as that shown in Figure 19.4 would be problematic and should be challenged.

Figure 19.4
Moving the goalposts on marketing revenues and costs

MEMO

From: Company Secretary
To: Marketing Director
Date: 1 July 2004
Subject: Provisional Performance Improvements for 2005

At the Board meeting of 23rd June, we resolved that the following performance improvements targets apply to marketing:

1. Revenues need to increase by 5 per cent.
2. Advertising budgets are extravagant and savings of 10 per cent must be found.

You are required to complete a detailed submission showing where the revenue increases and advertising savings can be obtained.

Such a memo, however well intentioned, is likely to cause marketing to invent a fictitious set of figures that have no roots in reality. Meddling in marketing's affairs is bad for everyone. A far better approach is for the company secretary to send the memo outlined in Figure 19.5.

This approach gives the Board the freedom to set a profit target, but leaves marketing the choice of how it is to be achieved. In order to separate the marketing decisions from operational ones, the fixed and variable costs that are to be used in the marketing calculations are the 2004 standard costs, which are known at July 2004.

Figure 19.5
Formal resolutions on the marketing budget

MEMO

From: Company Secretary
To: Marketing Director
Date: 1 July 2004
Subject: Provisional Performance Improvements for 2005

At the Board meeting of 23rd June, we resolved that the following performance improvements targets apply to marketing:

(£m)	2003 Results	2004 Projected Results	2005 Budget
Revenue	225.35	218.00	*Marketing estimate*
Variable costs	135.21	146.06	At 2004 unit costs
Fixed costs (ex marketing)	22.32	25.04	As 2004
Marketing	11.27	10.90	*Marketing estimate*
Profits	56.55	36.00	55.00

Please make your submission in a way that clearly demonstrates the sources of performance improvement.

Analyzing marketing budgets

The most common method of budget analysis is also one of the most corrosive ways of impairing management's thought process. It is budgeting by proforma (see Table 19.2).

Table 19.2
Budget proformas can impair your thinking

(£m)	2004 Budget	2004 Forecast	2005 Budget	Variance	Variance %
Sales revenue	230.00	218.00			
Variable costs	135.00	146.06			
Fixed (ex mkting)	22.00	25.04			
Advertising	5.00	5.00			
Direct marketing	6.00	5.00			
PR	1.00	0.40			
Market research	1.00	0.50			
Total marketing	13.00	10.90			
Profits	60.00	36.00			

This form-filling approach trivializes budgeting by reducing it to an arithmetic routine in which management thinking and analysis are largely unnecessary. The spreadsheet calculates the row and column totals and all that managers have to do is make up some numbers that add up to the desired total.

The main merit of the approach is its convenience. It limits the complexity of the spreadsheet models that finance managers have to construct, and it avoids the need for finance managers to learn the complexities of how the business actually works. At its most basic, budget modelling reduces business to a series of pluses and minuses with no intrinsic meaning.

Numbers don't create numbers

When setting budgets, it is important to remember that we are not saying that one number causes another, or that past numbers cause future numbers. The patterns in the numbers are reflections of management decisions, and their only significance is as outcomes of more complex business processes. For example, we can determine that the relationship between direct marketing expenditure and initial sales revenue is 1:2, but if competition enters the market, then that ratio will change, so our management decisions would have to change. Be sure you understand what's happening in the business that causes the patterns of numbers and trends.

Last year's budget is an unsatisfactory basis for comparison. It is likely to differ from last year's actual figures. Investors are unlikely to be interested in budgets as a basis for assessing progress. However, marketing planners often find it convenient to use the previous year's plans as their starting point. This year's marketing plan is therefore likely to be based on an adjustment to last year's plan. It is a significant mistake to use last year's plan as the starting point.

Last year's actual results are a better basis for comparison. Investors are more likely to use actual historical progress as a criterion for evaluating performance. However, actual historical results provide a poor basis for estimating future results. Revenues in particular can be dragged up or down by trends in consumer demand. These historical trends must be taken into account when setting targets for future performance.

Baseline forecasts are the best starting point for comparison, if you must use a form-filling approach. Investment analysts are likely to take forecasts of market and industry trends as the starting point of their performance reviews. Box 19.1 explains some terms you are likely to encounter in budgeting decisions.

Box 19.1 Terminology used in budgeting

Baseline forecast: A prediction of future performance based on the assumption that the business will operate in the same way in the future as it has done in the past.

Benchmarking: Comparison of the resource consumption rates of different firms within a market.

Block budget: The opposite of a line item budget. You are given a block of money. You present the details of your plan in line items. But later on you are free to move money from one line to another. As long as you don't overspend the block of budgeted money, there is no reason for your superior to ask questions. The technical term for such an authorized transfer of funds is *virement*.

Common size statements: Financial statements expressed in component percentages.

Component percentages: The presentation of the components of financial statements in percentage form, to aid comparability when business units or brands differ in size.

Controllability: In an ideal world, responsibility reports submitted to managers should reflect only those revenues and costs under their control. In a sense the term 'controllable' is a misnomer because no item is completely under the control of one manager. The term is widely used to refer to any item that is affected by a manager's decisions, even if it is not totally controlled.

Line item budget: A budget where each item is named, as is the limit to expenditure for that item. Authority to move money from one line to another must be granted at a higher level.

Comparison between business units and brands

When comparing business units and sub-units that differ in size, accountants and investment analysts often apply percentage relationships called *component percentages* to operating statements. The resulting statements are called *common size statements*.

An illustration of this technique is shown in Table 19.3. Last year's results are shown on a percentage basis, as are industry average figures. The result of this comparison is that marketing costs and promotions and discounts are found to be higher than industry averages, and they are therefore cut to put them more closely in line with industry averages. This technique of assessing advertising budgets is sometimes referred to as the A/S (advertising/sales) method.

Table 19.3
Component percentages analysis

	Last year	Budget	Industry
Gross revenue	100%	100%	100%
Promotions and discounts	12%	11%	10%
Net revenue	88%	89%	90%
Cost of sales	51%	51%	51%
Gross profit	37%	38%	39%
Marketing	12%	10%	8%
Overheads	11%	11%	11%
Net profit	14%	17%	20%

Component percentages have several weaknesses as a basis for comparison:

- **Accounting methods:** These vary from company to company and sometimes from business unit to business unit within the same company.

- **Conglomerates:** Some companies (such as General Electric) defy industry classification. When a firm is involved in many different markets, comparative analysis can be misleading or extremely difficult to interpret.

- **Market dominance:** Some companies (such as Microsoft) are dominant in a sector to such a large extent that it can be misleading to compare them to the market norm. Even in less extreme circumstances, percentage comparisons can be misleading when comparing dominant brands with less dominant ones (see Table 19.4).

Another technique that is widely used is to make direct comparisons with competitors. In advertising, benchmark figures are published by MEAL (Media Expenditure Analysis Ltd.) and these comparisons are commonly quoted as a basis for comparison.

However, benchmarking also has several weaknesses as a basis for comparison:

- **Linking growth to its drivers:** Growth objectives vary from company to company and brand to brand. Different resource levels will be required to drive growth, depending on circumstances.

- Allocation across brands, products and mix elements: Total marketing budget allocation will vary from company to company. No two companies are sufficiently similar that a direct comparison of total budgets is useful.

Table 19.4
Component percentages analysis in a conglomerate

	Beer			Wine		
	Last year	Budget	Industry	Last year	Budget	Industry
Gross revenue	100%	100%	100%	100%	100%	100%
Promotions and discounts	12%	11%	12%	12%	11%	8%
Net revenue	88%	89%	88%	88%	89%	92%
Cost of sales	40%	40%	40%	61%	61%	61%
Gross profit	48%	49%	48%	27%	28%	31%
Marketing	12%	10%	12%	12%	10%	4%
Overheads	13%	13%	13%	10%	10%	10%
Net profit	23%	26%	23%	5%	8%	17%

Linking progress to its sources

When predicting future progress, it is good practice to explain the sources of progress. Sources of progress come in two kinds: uncontrollable and controllable.

Uncontrollable factors include market demand growth and decline, seasonality, consumer preference changes, competitive activity and intensity changes. These factors often have a dramatic effect on sales revenues, but they are not under the control of management.

When declaring progress in the form of sales volume budgets and product mix percentages, it is important to declare how much of the progress is assumed to be caused by uncontrollable factors (see Table 19.5).

Controllable factors that are the sources of volume and revenue changes come in five main varieties (see Table 19.6). Financial numbers provide an inadequate way of quantifying them.

Table 19.5
Uncontrollable factors influencing budget progress

Factor	Comment	Recommendation
Uncontrollable market growth	Changes in market growth rates are likely to be reflected in sales results. Market growth rate is not recorded in cost accounting systems	Market growth assumptions should be recorded and modelled as part of the budgeting process
Product mix preference	Changes in consumer preference for particular product types can have an important effect, especially when there are significant differences in product profitability	Product mix assumptions (at market level) should be recorded and modelled as part of the budgeting process

Table 19.6
Controllable factors influencing budget progress

Factor	Comment	Recommendation
Rate of resource consumption	Changing the speed with which resources such as advertising media are consumed is often directly responsible for driving changes in revenue growth. Inflation in media costs and other resource costs over time means that financial trends do not adequately quantify the trends in resource consumption	Actual levels of resource consumption should also be budgeted. For example, GRPs, numbers of mailing items
Efficiency of resource consumption	Marketing mix elements have efficiency measures as well as resource consumption rates. The response rate to advertising media is a measure of its efficiency. Efficiencies are sometimes referred to as **elasticities.**	Efficiency (ratio) assumptions should be explicitly stated in budget calculations
Allocation of resource consumption	Changing the allocation of marketing resources across the product range can directly drive revenue growth. Although the mix of consumer–product–preference is an uncontrollable factor, responding to this uncontrollable change by shifting the product resource allocation can enable a company to increase its share of consumer preference	Mix of resource allocation assumed in budget calculations should be stated explicitly

Table 19.6
(continued)

Factor	Comment	Recommendation
Prices	Reducing the price of a product or service can be a source of sales revenue growth (or decline if the price is raised). Price is not a resource, hence it is not recorded in the cost accounting system	For price effects to be analyzed effectively, special systems must be set up to track price changes
Promotional intensity	Increasing the proportion of the product that is sold on promotions can directly drive revenue growth. Price promotions are not resources, hence they are not recorded by cost accounting methods	For promotional effects to be analyzed effectively, special systems must be set up to track promotional intensity

Our conclusion is that non-financial assumptions about sources of volume and revenue changes must be modelled explicitly as part of the budgeting process. These key assumptions should then be tracked, and variances between non-financial assumptions and actuals should be reported in the budgeting cycle.

Using a spreadsheet model

Spreadsheets take a lot of the tedium out of setting a budget. Many managers take the time to learn advanced spreadsheet modelling by taking two or three days of classes or reading a book on spreadsheet modelling.

Choosing an appropriate level of detail

The smart manager does not use percentage increases across all items as a quick way of creating a budget figure. Managers need to make changes at a more detailed level, and to set priorities that reflect the situation for each major item in the budget.

What is the right level of detail for budgeting? Too much detail will result in time wasted on trivial calculations and responding to trivial variances. Too little detail and control will be weak.

Choose an appropriate mix of line items and blocks for your marketing budget. Use your intelligence to assess what needs to be itemized and what can be blocked.

Allocating budgets to time periods

Allocating the annual budgets to months (or even weeks) is necessary in order to make the management reporting work. This allocation generally happens towards the end of the budgeting process and is often rushed. Anomalies and imperfections can be introduced into the budget schedule as a consequence of several factors:

- **Seasonal demand patterns:** They may be oversimplified or even overlooked. As a consequence, actual results will fluctuate in ways that the budget does not.

- **There are not four weeks in a month:** A very common estimating mistake is to think quickly, 'there are 12 months in a year, so an annual budget of £1560 divides into £130 per month'.

- **Delays between orders, delivery and invoices:** These matter much more when the timescale is a month (or a week) than they do over the whole year.

Taking the time necessary to develop a realistic budget schedule is all that is needed to avoid these problems. Spreadsheets are important tools for the budget scheduler. However, it is vitally important that the modeller uses good assumptions, and doesn't take too many shortcuts.

Finally, check all the figures and assumptions carefully before making the budget submission. Use a buddy-check to make sure that the figures you have produced can be verified and that the report you have written makes sense.

After you have printed everything, let it sit overnight and look at it in the morning. With fresh eyes you can catch the mistakes that you hadn't noticed – like a misspelling of the finance director's name in the list of recipients!

Presenting, revising and approving the budget

Creating a budget submission involves a lot of detailed work. While we're making the budget, most of our attention is on thinking carefully, calculating correctly and getting the figures right. And that's exactly what we should be doing. However, at the submission point we must change our focus. We need to look at the whole package, think about our audience and decide how to present the budget submission. You need to think about how to make your submission relevant and clear. You need to think about how much detail to present, and to whom.

Be prepared to give explanations and support for your submission. Getting it approved early in the approval schedule, alongside the revenue budget, is likely to help. Be prepared for presentations to three audiences, and tailor the submission document to each:

- The budgets committee;
- The sales forecasting subcommittee;
- The financial analysts.

A written budget submission will usually be needed for the budgets committee, which is essentially a more detailed version of the marketing plan. The advice given in the chapter on marketing planning will also come in handy for the budget committees. A PowerPoint presentation is likely to be needed for both the budget committee and the sales forecasting subcommittee.

The sales forecasting subcommittee will want to go into more detail about your assumptions and your methods of calculation. They will also have interests that go beyond marketing, such as capacity planning. The sales forecast will be rendered invalid if there is not enough capacity available in the future to meet demand.

A detailed review of your plan is also likely to be performed by financial analysts. Be prepared to share with them the models you used in calculating the numbers. Familiarizing them with the models is important, so allow enough time in the process for them to be properly briefed.

Box 19.2 Getting the marketing budget approved

1. Remind your audience where you came in on budget last year and where things went wrong.

2. Explain where past misses were the result of uncontrollable external factors, such as competitor activity.

3. Make it clear how what you learned from last year's budgeting exercise will make this year's budget more reliable.

4. Teach the uninitiated – explain, explain, explain.

5. Distinguish between essentials and nice-to-have.

6. Identify risks explicitly and plan mitigating action.

7. Walk them through your submission step by step.

8. Be ready to show that you have considered alternatives and your submission is the one with the best profit forecast.

Source: After Stutely (2003)

Should you bin your budget?

If you've reached this point, you are probably feeling anxious about the amount of work that faces you. Wouldn't it be nice if budgeting wasn't necessary? Well, there is a debate raging in financial circles on just this topic, so we'll fill you in on the details and let you judge for yourself.

Today, more and more experts are joining the chorus of criticism, suggesting in increasingly loud tones that it's time for a major overhaul of our budgeting systems. Consider the titles of some of the following recent articles:

- 'Why Budgeting Kills Your Company' (Loren 2003)
- 'The Case Against Budgeting' (Krell 2003)
- 'Budgets Roll with the Times' (Hunt 2003)
- 'Should You Shoot Your Budget?' (Brodrick 2003)
- 'Is Planning a Waste of Time?' (Taub 2003)

These few articles, all appearing within a few weeks of each other – together with the publication of a recent book, *Beyond Budgeting* (Hope and Fraser 2003) – suggest that a major trend is afoot. Perhaps Krell puts it best:

> Two simple messages course through the 100–plus candid remarks survey respondents provided. The budgeting process takes far too long, and the end result is stale by the time it is completed. Businesses need more agile forecasting and reforecasting capabilities, but the organizational barriers to those capabilities are formidable. Judging from the responses, generating a brighter budgeting and forecasting future will require companies to make significant behavioural and procedural changes and upgrade their tool set. (Krell 2003)

Marketing is an area where budgeting is especially unsatisfactory. The existence of the marketing budgeting problem has been known for many years. The problem has remained largely unsolved because marketing has not had enough influence to drive the reform of its own budgeting. Over 30 years ago, marketing budgeting and control faced criticisms such as:

> A profit wall has two sides: on the one is the accountant, on the other the marketing man, and their views of the wall may be quite different. I believe that the accountant should go to the other side of the wall to view the problems from there. (Bain 1970)

> . . . finance and marketing are as non-integrated as cats and dogs. (Field and Gabhart 1971)

Ward (1996), in a recent review of the situation, suggests that the accounting profession is slow and conservative in its response to the needs of marketing:

Some companies are attempting to tackle this area, but even in most of these leading companies, the sophistication of the marketing evaluation techniques is far ahead of the corresponding financial analysis. This whole area of marketing accounting represents one of the most important development opportunities for financial managers who wish to make a major strategic contribution to their companies.

In a later paper, Ward (1999) mentions that a new job role of marketing finance manager is being created in some organizations to address this issue. But he comments:

Many businesses are taking critical marketing decisions with very little strategic financial evaluation, because they do not have suitably tailored marketing accounting systems. In such businesses there is no real 'strategic control' over marketing.

Wilson (1999) has also proposed the idea that a 'marketing controller' function should be established within marketing departments, staffed by a management accountant. The role would be to support marketing decision making by supplying information, cost estimates and expert opinions about the financial implications of marketing decisions.

Most accountants are not yet in tune with marketing . . . It is from the point of view of operating managers located within these departments that the quality of the controller's service will be determined: if he or she is not supplying information that helps them to perform more effectively given their problems as they see them, then the controller in turn is not performing effectively. The link between information and action cannot be stressed too highly: the controller supplies the information, but if it is to lead to appropriate action it must be relevant to the circumstances within which the action must take place.

Ambler (2003) suggests the opposite arrangement, that marketing information become the responsibility of the finance department, including market research 'where a separate market information function does not exist, there is much to be said for giving the job to the chief financial officer (CFO)'.

Will this nascent movement to abolish traditional budgeting processes – and adopt better ones – reach the heights of some of the other major enterprise initiatives of the past decade, such as enterprise resource planning (ERP), supply chain management and world class manufacturing?

The 'better budgeting' agenda

'Better budgeting' has become a catchphrase in the business press. It sets an agenda around process streamlining, new technology and interpersonal skills for accountants.

A review of the literature on budgeting and the websites of the major consultants and systems houses provides evidence of these themes:

'Reduce management time' (Accenture website, 19 November 2003)

'Month-end close cut from 10 days to 3 days' (Oracle website, 19 November 2003)

'Real-time control and accountability' (Peoplesoft website, 19 November 2003)

'Streamline financial data consolidation' (Hyperion website, 19 November 2003)

'Fixed targets are a thing of the past' (SAP website, 19 November 2003)

'Budgeting abolished' (BBRT website, 19 November 2003).

Most reforms of budgeting are reflecting these concerns with people and processes, which raises two questions:

- Are budgeting reforms going to benefit marketing?
- Will budgeting reforms improve profitability?

At the beginning of this section it was argued that the first priority in business should be to maximize profits, yet profit maximization and improvement are peripheral to the reforms that are generally happening in budgeting. We can see no mechanism by which faster budgeting closes will make companies much more profitable. Nor can we see how reducing the hassle of budgeting will drive significantly more profits.

Marketing is a major driver of profits. It is unlikely to benefit significantly from the current approach to budgeting reforms. Budget reforms today have no specific marketing angle. It is hard to see how today's budgeting reforms are important to the objectives of marketing or profitability.

Marketing budgeting reform is therefore likely to need a separate project. We believe that it should not be subsumed under the existing better budgeting programmes.

Key points

Our review of the budget setting process provided some important lessons:

- Numbers don't create numbers – be sure you understand what causes the pattern of numbers.
- Check with accounting for last year's actual figures – don't rely on last year's marketing plan.
- Create a baseline forecast.
- Choose the right level of detail for your budgets.
- Compare yourself with other companies and brands using component percentages and benchmark ratios, but think before you match competition.
- Record budgeting assumptions about trends in market size and product mix.
- Use objective and task calculations to determine resource consumption rates.
- Record the assumptions about the efficiency ratios, marketing mix, prices and promotions that underpin your budget calculations.
- Learn to use spreadsheets as modelling tools, not just adding machines.
- Don't take unnecessary shortcuts in preparing the budget spreadsheet.
- Take time to prepare for the approval process.

20

MARKETING BOOKKEEPING AND ACCOUNTING

This chapter is about keeping financial records for marketing. These are the nuts and bolts of marketing payback. The analysis comes after the record keeping. Even if you are in a large organization supported by teams of accountants, you will need to read this chapter and gain an understanding of the special requirements of marketing bookkeeping and accounting and how it differs from more conventional accounting. Please take particular note of the comments about the need for you to keep your own records, and to stay on top of the details.

The marketing shoebox

Suppose you have committed to making your marketing more accountable, just as we suggested right at the beginning of this book. Then you will need to have a reliable source of information. You may imagine that your accounting system is that source of information. After all, your company has probably paid substantial sums of money for systems and consultancy that are supposed to 'modernize' your accounting. You may imagine that all the information you need is sitting inside the computer system, awaiting your commands like a genie in a bottle.

This Aladdin's dream is just a fantasy, unfortunately. In reality, accounting systems (or enterprise resource planning (ERP) systems as they seem to be called by the computer boffins nowadays) seldom provide adequate support for the information needs of marketing. While supply chain, manufacturing, logistics and distribution all have ample support in today's modern ERP system, marketing is neglected. Nor will you find what you want in the CRM system that your company may also have bought.

In this chapter, we are going to ask you to do something rather boring. In the previous chapters we talked about strategic planning and sophisticated analyses. Here we are going to suggest that you collect some information for yourself and put it onto a spreadsheet to analyze yourself. We will try to explain each task in plain language without using too much of the obscure language of accounting (but see Box 20.1 for a few useful definitions).

Box 20.1 Terminology used in marketing bookkeeping

Account: A list of explicit transactions and associated adjustments (date, description, associated amount).

Accounting: The occupation of recording and auditing business transactions and preparing financial reports for a business.

Accrual: Accounting system in which business transactions are tracked when commitments are made.

Adjustments: Used to refine the accountant's accuracy by making allowance for events such as the passage of time, which are temporarily ignored in day-to-day bookkeeping procedures. They are prepared from special schedules or memoranda, such as an agency payment schedule.

Bookkeeping: The occupation of recording business transactions in a regular and systematic way, to show the state of the business in which they occur.

Business transaction: Something that is transacted, such as a purchase or a sale.

Explicit transactions: A business transaction that is supported by explicit evidence of the transaction in the form of vouchers, such as sales or purchase invoices. It always consists of a date, description and associated amount, but it may also carry a code such as product code, campaign code or source code, which may be used to analyze the transactions.

Fixed costs: Costs that are not immediately affected by changes in sales volume, at least over a specified range of output.

Track: To track business transactions means making sure we have good records about what we are spending and what sales we are obtaining, and how closely they match our plans.

Variable costs: Costs that are proportional to sales volumes (such as raw materials).

Voucher: A document serving as evidence for some claimed transaction, such as the receipt or expenditure of money.

In our status-conscious companies, the important but humble art of bookkeeping has been neglected in favour of the grander-sounding topic of accounting. You may be surprised to hear that few textbooks on accounting make any reference whatever to bookkeeping.

Suppose you want to obtain the accounting information needed to do the analyses we have referred to throughout the book, but you are quite busy enough without wanting to spend much time dealing with a task such as bookkeeping. Here is the secret. Every time you authorize a payment, write the full details on a sheet of paper (preprinted vouchers are useful for this), staple any supporting documents to it and drop it into a shoebox.

Most marketing managers give the contents of this shoebox to their accountants once a week and let the professionals worry about posting records, writing cheques, claiming VAT and so on. However, if you want to stay on top of your marketing bookkeeping and accounting, you must keep your own records on a PC even if you pass on the shoebox and let your accountant handle all the nasty, fiddly stuff. Some of the data your accountant enters will be useful to you, and vice versa, so you may wish to establish an arrangement for sharing it, as shown in Figure 20.1.

Figure 20.1
The marketing shoebox and its data entry

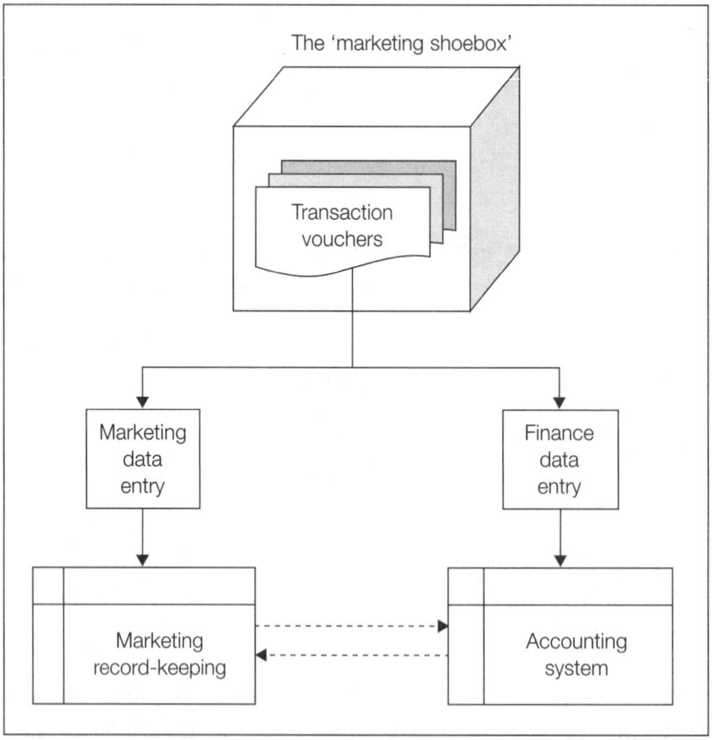

Splitting a single payment

Suppose you've received a single agency invoice for services rendered. Rather than call this a general advertising expense, you could split it by campaign. You could also split the media expenditure element from the creative fees. You could record these items on the accounting system, if the system can accept this level of detail. Alternatively, you may need to record the items on the marketing record-keeping system if the accounting system is unable to record this level of detail.

Using splits is a good way to track marketing transactions. It allows you to track items at a level of detail that is meaningful to marketing, rather than just the detail that the accountants need to know.

Before reading further, ask yourself ten hard questions about how marketing bookkeeping is handled in your company:

1. Do marketing and finance separate responsibilities for marketing bookkeeping? Could the same person be recording information for marketing analysis and financial analysis?

2. Can marketing obtain archived financial data going back 10 years?

3. Can we obtain volumes, prices and promotion details associated with sales transactions?

4. Does the finance department provide adequate data on variable and fixed costs to support marketing analysis?

5. Is there a voucher (e.g. agency invoice) for every marketing expense? Are vouchers properly recorded by the marketing department for subsequent analysis?

6. Do agencies provide information on a regular basis so that you can track marketing expense commitments?

7. Do agencies regularly provide detailed schedules of activities (e.g. media exposures) and associated costs, so that marketing can analyze the cause-and-effect relationships between marketing expenditures and sales responses?

8. Are we using technology effectively to record the information we need?

9. Does the finance department understand the importance of keeping this information?

10. Have we involved our purchasing department effectively in this process?

Getting started

Probably the hardest part of marketing bookkeeping is getting started. It's especially difficult if you are in the habit of handing the shoebox to your beancounters without doing any analysis work yourself. Nobody wants to add work to their busy schedules, especially not boring bookkeeping. But that's precisely the challenge you face to get the information you need.

If you are going to keep your own marketing records, you'll need a computer system for data entry. Our advice to you is to start with a spreadsheet. Although your accounting system may be flexible enough to accommodate your marketing information needs, our experience is that you will suffer massive delays if you have to wait for the IT department to make the necessary adaptations. Far better to get started with a spreadsheet-based system and then work up to something fancier once your procedure is tested and running smoothly.

When you first sit down with a blank spreadsheet and wonder what information you should be recording yourself, it is worth looking at the chart of accounts produced by finance. Some of the information you need may already be available using your existing accounting system (see Table 20.1). Alternatively, by amending the chart of accounts, it may be possible to get the information you need out of your accounting system.

Table 20.1
Chart of accounts review

Sales revenue	Description	Analysis codes and information required by marketing
Sales revenue	This is the revenue earned during the period, calculated on an accrual basis. Off-invoice promotions and discounts are incorporated in the revenue figure but are usually not explicitly reported. It may be allocated to specific products, but some organizations do not split revenue in enough detail for marketing accounting	Date/description/amount Product code Price Quantity of product sold Promotions and discounts Campaign source code (where available) Customer identification
Variable costs		
Variable cost of goods sold	These are the variable costs of the goods associated with the revenue earned, calculated on a standard-cost basis. There may be many specific subaccounts, the details of which are unimportant to marketing	Date/description/amount Product code
Fixed costs (ex marketing)		
Fixed costs	These are the fixed costs excluding all the marketing expenses shown below. There are many specific subaccounts, the details of which are unimportant to marketing	Date/description/amount

Table 20.1
(continued)

Sales revenue	Description	Analysis codes and information required by marketing
Marketing expenses		
Advertising costs	This is the payment to advertising agencies, often calculated on an accrual basis	Date/description/amount Commitment by month Spend by month Split by product (where available) Split by campaign Split by media/creative Split by media vehicle Media weight lay-down by week
Media costs	This is the payment to media agencies	As for advertising costs
Sponsorship costs	This is the payment to a sponsorship agency, or direct to the sponsoring organization, often calculated on an accrual basis	Date/description/amount Split by product (where available)
PR costs	This is the payment to the PR agency, calculated on an accrual basis	Date/description/amount Split by product (where available)
Sales promotion	This is the payment to a sales promotion agency, calculated on an accrual basis	Date/description/amount Commitment by month Split by product (where available) Spend by month Split by campaign Split by trade outlet
Trade promotion – direct payment	This is the payment to a trade customer to pay for sales promotion, or incentives, calculated on an accrual basis	Date/description/amount Commitment by month Split by product (where available) Spend by month Split by reason for payment Split by trade customer

You may wish to make an improvement to the arrangement in Figure 20.1 by combining the data-entry activities (see Figure 20.2). This arrangement has the advantage that data is only entered once into the systems. The complications are (a) you will have to agree to joint resourcing with finance (b) whoever does the data-entry job will need broader skills, as the information they produce is intended for finance and marketing users.

Figure 20.2
The ideal 'single source of data entry'

Analyzing sales volumes and revenues

It is time now to pull those figures out of the shoebox and check whether they provide the details you are going to need for marketing analysis. If you check Table 20.1, you will see that sales revenues need to be recorded in more detail than is conventional in normal accounting practice to provide the data needed for marketing analysis. Some of the details that are likely to be required by marketing are shown in Figure 20.3.

Revenue depends on volume and price, and may also be affected by promotions. The price that you could charge depends on the concept that economists call *price elasticity*. Products that are price elastic are sensitive to changes in price; take a pound off and sales will skyrocket.

Promotions have an even more dramatic effect on sales volumes. Hence it is essential for marketing to know how much of the total sales volume was obtained at various levels of promotion. Gifts and other promotional incentives also make a big difference.

Figure 20.3
Sales details likely to be needed for marketing analysis

Sales invoice	

Product code:
     123456
	Date:
	     20 Apr 04

Quantity:
     10
	Description:
	     Widgets Large Black

Promotional gift:
     Mini Tool Box
	Price:
	     £10.00

Campaign source code:
     DMail23
	Special offer:
	     £1.00 for 10 units and above

Customer ID:
     John Smith (A/C 123321)
	Amount:
	     £90.00

Generally, for a transaction like the one in Figure 20.3, bookkeeping will record a sale net of promotions, so a figure of £90. Alternatively, they may credit sales with £100 and then post a contra charge of £10 to sales – promotions. The promotional gift is likely to be recorded in the accounts as a sale of an item 'Mini Tool Box Set' with sales revenue of £0.00, if it is recorded in the sales ledger at all.

From a marketing analysis perspective, it is far more satisfactory to know all the details shown in Figure 20.3, rather than the conventional figures that your accounts contain. You will also get far greater insights if your finance people provide this data at individual transaction level, rather than summary sales figures. As we will see in the next chapter, correlations and trends are far more likely to be revealed by detailed transaction data.

Calculating variable costs

It hardly needs to be said that you need to know the cost of one unit of your product. Apart from anything else, you will use this figure in your profit maximization calculations. In keeping with true accounting traditions, this figure is not as clear-cut as might be expected. We will describe the calculations for a manufacturing business. The same logic applies if you are providing services or reselling someone else's products.

For a period such as a year, the cost of factors consumed in producing one widget is derived by dividing total costs by the number of items. For example, if the number of widgets produced is 100,000, the cost of factors consumed in producing one widget is:

Variable cost of goods sold:

Direct raw materials	£300,000
Packing	£50,000
Direct labour	£100,000
Variable factory overhead	£20,000
Freight	£30,000
Variable warehousing overhead	£20,000
Spoilage	£10,000
Variable administrative costs	£10,000
Total variable costs	**£540,000**

$$\text{Unit cost} = \text{Total variable cost / volume of production}$$
$$= £540,000 / 100,000$$
$$= £5.40$$

This is the variable cost of one unit. It does not tell you what sales price is needed for profitability because marketing and fixed costs are not included, and clearly you want to cover these in order to stay in business.

Calculating fixed costs

Fixed costs are the other element, apart from marketing expenditure, that is needed to calculate profits. An example may clarify the difference between fixed and variable costs.

Fixed costs:

Factory supervision	£1,400,000
Factory rent	£500,000
Equipment depreciation	£1,500,000
Fixed administrative overheads	£3,300,000
Office rent	£500,000
Total fixed costs	**£7,200,000**

Suppose a factory is rented to produce widgets. The total cost of £500,000 is not affected by the number of widgets sold. The unit cost apportioned to the widgets depends on the number of widgets. For example, if 5% of the factory output is widgets, then the unit cost of factory rent applicable to each widget is £0.25. Table 20.2 summarizes the key relationships.

Table 20.2
How variable and fixed costs are related to volume

	If sales volume increases	
	Total cost	Cost per unit
Variable costs	Increases	No change
Fixed costs	No change	Decreases

Calculating marketing accruals and commitments

We return now to the shoebox, and look at the various expenses it contains. If you record all the transactions on the dates on the vouchers (agency invoices, etc.) you will not be following the procedure that your accountants are likely to follow. They are likely to follow an accruals procedure.

You might have heard of accrual accounting. Take the example of an advertising agency that undertakes a campaign that starts in one accounting period and ends in another. You are contracted to pay the agency at a series of stages during the project. The amount 'due' each month is recognized as a cost to the business, even though it may not have been invoiced or paid. This is known as an accrual.

Non-accountants often misunderstand the accruals idea because there is a tendency to think of a company's expenses in a given period as being the same as the cash it pays out during that period. This is almost never the case. The process typically follows these steps:

1. **Decision to buy:** This includes allocating funds, say for advertising, and agreeing terms with the agency. It may include a contract and a purchase order or payment schedule.

2. **Receiving the items:** This includes receiving the roughs, the finished creative executions, and checking to make sure that the media schedule was correctly executed and at the quality agreed. The schedule is marked 'received'.

3. **Approving payment:** The schedule and agency invoice are brought together and checked. The account codes for the advertising are marked.

4. **Making payment:** The payment can now be made into the agency's bank account.

Each week you can identify the status of each purchase. If you add up all the current expenses, then you can find the status for each line item. For example, let's say we have agreed a media budget of £1,000,000. Earlier in the year we spent £350,000. At the beginning of the month, the agency made a forward commitment for media of £400,000. The status of the media account is shown in Table 20.3.

Table 20.3
Media schedule status in May

	Period	Budgeted	Spent	Committed	Available
Campaign budget	Jan.	£1,000,000			
Media expenditure	Feb.		£120,000		
	Mar.		£120,000		
	Apr.		£110,000		
Media 'commitments'	May			£100,000	
	Jun.			£100,000	
	Jul.			£100,000	
	Aug.			£100,000	
Media 'commitments'	Sep.				
	Oct.				£250,000
	Nov.				
	Dec.				
Total		**£1,000,000**	**£350,000**	**£400,000**	**£250,000**

In practice, of course, nothing is completely committed – schedules can be 'deferred' and campaigns pulled, even at the last minute. There may, of course, be financial penalties to pay.

The table refers only to media expenditure – 'media' for this purpose being a broadcast media that can be purchased by an agency. In addition, it will be necessary to track expenditure and forward 'commitments' for production of the creative content and, of course, agency fees. The agency has a vital role to play in providing this schedule each period. It is not something that your accountants can prepare on their own.

Purchasing managers in some companies become involved with marketing expenditure tracking. Something that you should get them to help with is setting up a system of commitment reporting which the agencies use. Each month, the agencies should send you a schedule similar to Table 20.3, and you will enter it into your marketing record-keeping system.

Tracking marketing activities and associated costs

Marketing expenditure and activity tracking data should generally be captured in as much detail as practical. Computer storage is relatively cheap. Having to go back and try to get data about past performance that was not captured at the time is at best time-consuming, and usually expensive. It may not even be possible, leaving the potentially even more expensive situation of having to make decisions about future strategy without being able to learn the lessons of the past.

In general, the type of data that should be collected falls into three categories:

1. expenditures;

2. scale of activity;

3. type of activity.

At a minimum, the data should be collected separately at the following level of disaggregation:

- by market;

- by brand;

- by period (weekly data is superior to monthly);

- by location;

- by creative content (for media).

Many agencies have a proprietary data system. It is always worth asking your agency about their data systems, and understanding the opportunities and constraints that may exist as a result of how the agency captures, stores and accesses media data.

A key parameter for all media purchases is the *unit cost*. Historically, media costs have often increased more quickly than inflation. The media agency should be able to supply data on media inflation rates.

Some examples of the scale and type of activity are given in Table 20.4, together with comments on data collection. The list is not intended to be comprehensive, but should provide a minimum checklist that can be used as a starting point for developing a data collection system.

Table 20.4
Marketing data collection

Type of marketing expenditure	Data series and comments

TV advertising	Spend
	Activity measured by GRPs
	  (note different definitions, e.g. spot weighted)
	Target audience (e.g. housewives)
	Cost per week and cost per GRP
	Perhaps frequency and reach, but this leads to a
	  lot of data

Non-TV advertising, including press, radio, outdoor, cinema	Spend
	Differentiate between time when billed and time
	  when impact made
	Activity measured by GRPs is possible in theory,
	  but difficult in practice
	Audience size and demographics

Sponsorship	Spend Dates of sponsorship events Sponsorship ratings GRPs for TV sponsorship can be estimated

Public relations	Press mentions broken down by positive,
	  negative, neutral
	Affinity with the brand
	Highly disaggregated data are often available,
	  especially if the tracking service is bought in

Sales promotions	Spend (total)
	Price reductions by SKU, retail outlet, display
	  (e.g. Wal-Mart: Sweet & Crunchy 1.49–0.99:
	  end gondola)
	Percentage sold through promoting outlets
	Cost of special packaging
	Returns
	Data on both own promotions and those of
	  competitors

Trade promotions	Spend (total) Cost by type of promotion and trade outlet Data on both own promotions and those of competitors
Direct mail	Spend Mail out Door drops Replies, in what time, to what level of offer

Table 20.4
(continued)

Type of marketing expenditure	Data series and comments
Call centres	Spend Activity level Responses
Website activity	Spend Site visits Responses

Key: GRP = gross rating point: SKU = stock-keeping unit

Bookkeeping is one of the boring-but-necessary chores that every manager must undertake. Bad bookkeeping undermines the effectiveness of management. In this regard, marketing is perhaps the worst offender in most businesses, and marketing records are often the most incomplete and inaccurately kept. The problem is not one of technique or method, it is simply a matter of discipline and habit.

Key points

- The sooner you start, the easier it will be.
- Capturing the data on a computer is essential if you are going to use it for the analyses discussed in other chapters.
- Spreadsheets are an easy and useful way to begin.
- CRM and ERP systems are unlikely to provide the solution you require.
- Sales record keeping will need to be enhanced to provide the necessary information.
- Your agencies will need to provide better information about their costs, the activities (e.g. advertising exposures and promotional displays), and the forward commitments.
- Setting up these record-keeping systems is likely to be a joint project requiring resources from finance and marketing, the agencies and possibly the sales department (for recording discounts and promotions).

21

WHEN RESULTS GO WRONG

This chapter looks at what to do when results go wrong. We look at how you can use variances to measure how badly wrong the results are, and how you can separate out variances to identify the underlying reasons why the results are wrong. Finally, we look at some of the courses of action that you should follow in selecting corrective actions.

Will management reporting alert you to a crisis?

Most of us take management reporting for granted. Large heaps of printed budget reports are a familiar sight in most offices. The endless rounds of budget meetings are a feature of the calendar for much of the management year. We saw in Chapter 19 that most of the reform of budgeting that is taking place today is focused on process streamlining and people issues, not root and branch reform. Unfortunately, our investigation of the tools and techniques that are routinely used in budgeting lead us to the following three conclusions:

- Imperfections of the simple tools are probably more critical than the process and people issues currently being addressed because they have a directly harmful effect on profits.

- Ignoring these imperfections in budgeting tools because nothing is ever perfect is a perilous strategy.

- Imperfections and their harmful effects on profits can be ameliorated by better design of existing tools and augmenting them with more advanced methods.

Management reporting is assumed to have good characteristics as a profit-maximizing tool. Sometimes these are explicitly stated, more often implicitly assumed (see Table 21.1).

Our analysis demonstrates that management reporting is often riddled with critical imperfections. These are not fussy trivia, they are substantive problems that can seriously damage the quest for high profits and lead to dysfunctional decision making.

Management reporting certainly needs to be better. The problems identified above arise because of bad budget information or unwise application. Our review of the agendas behind the slogans 'better budgeting' and 'beyond budgeting' suggests that their prospects of removing the imperfections noted above are poor. Too much importance is given in 'better budgeting' to the speed of the process and the people issues; too little importance is given to the information itself. What is actually needed is better information and the better application of information.

Table 21.1
Profit information provided by management reporting

	Ideal	Imperfection
Profit maximization	Follows as a consequence of correcting unfavourable variances	Suboptimal profits are likely to result from reacting to all 'unfavourable' variances
Direction of improvement	Variance sign (+ve or −ve) offers guidance on the direction of change that will maximize profits	Suboptimal profits are likely to result from reacting independently to each variance
Responsibility separation	Can report unambiguously the consequences of individual manager's decisions and actions	Interdependencies between departments and decisions
Hierarchy of optimization	Can optimize the whole by optimizing subordinate levels	Optimization is not hierarchical
No false alarms	Variances always result from genuine problems	False alarms are common. Managers learn to ignore them
Early warnings	Always sufficient time to correct problems	Too little too late
Fairness	Budgeting provides a fair basis for comparing the performance of different managers	Management by fear

What happens in your company? Here are ten hard questions to ask about the management reporting in your organization:

1. Do you believe the numbers you get? Do you trust your instinct if you think a number doesn't look right, and get it checked for accuracy?

2. Are you comparing enough? One number in isolation is fairly meaningless.

3. Have they told you the whole truth? What other facts and figures have been expediently overlooked?

4. Is the timing correct? What about short or long months? Have the transactions been booked to the right period?

5. Have your planning assumptions changed? Do you even need to monitor the assumptions?

6. How does the top-line variance break down into component variances?

7. What assumptions are made to break down variances where the components are not additive?

8. Have product mix variances been investigated?

9. Are you sure that you know which variances are relevant and, within these, which are 'good' and which are 'bad'?

10. What approach do you adopt to decide what corrective action is needed?

Reporting against budget

Once the budget year is in full swing, each month managers tend to receive a reporting pack comparing what actually happened with what was budgeted. Managers are often asked to write a short commentary explaining the difference between the two. It will be a rare month when results are exactly on budget. Essentially, they are being asked to comment on a variance analysis.

> **Variance analysis** is an accounting technique that permits the close examination of the differences between budgeted information and actual information. It is used to investigate the causes of differences that are deemed significant, and breaks them down into categories that are potentially meaningful for managerial action.

Most variance reports are likely to be similar to the one in Table 21.2.

Table 21.2
Variances showing failures to hit targets, size and directions of error

£m	This month				Year to date			
	Actual[1]	Budget[2]	VAR[3]	%[4]	Actual[1]	Budget[2]	VAR[3]	%[4]
Revenue	22.0	20.0	2.0F	10%	114.1	120.0	5.9U	5%
Cost	18.3	16.7	1.6U	10%	95.1	100.0	4.9F	5%
Profit	3.7	3.3	0.4F	12%	19.0	20.0	1.0U	5%

Key:
F = Favourable
U = Unfavourable
1. Results are shown in the first column – what actually happened. They are sometimes referred to as the 'out-turn'.
2. Budgets are shown in the second column.
3. Variances are shown in the third column as absolute differences between out-turn and budget.
4. Variances expressed as percentages of the budget are shown in the fourth column.

Achieving or exceeding budget has been accorded a central role in managing for profit. Variance analysis is the tool of choice for determining whether the budget has been met, and by what margin. Its apparent simplicity contributes to its popularity.

Accountants conventionally comment on variances in terms of whether they are favourable or unfavourable, as shown in Table 21.2. Revenue in excess of budget is classified as favourable (F), and below budget is unfavourable (U).

Cost in excess of budget is classified as unfavourable, and below budget is favourable.

Yet this very simplicity gives managers a sense of false security about variance analysis and its widespread use can damage profits in both the short term and the long. What is needed is:

- A wider understanding of the imperfections and limitations of variance analysis and the critical impact they have on profit maximization;

- More cautious use of variance figures within management reports to avoid the misdirection and false alarms that they can cause;

- Introduction of more sophisticated modelling within the management reporting programs to supplement the overly simplistic variance calculations.

Checking results for accuracy

When results differ from budgets, the first step is to check the figures for accuracy before panicking and taking remedial action. Surprisingly often, wrong results come from bad bookkeeping.

The mechanics of bookkeeping can introduce complications and anomalies into the results. Results are categorized and allocated to a time period before reporting (see Table 21.3). Period closing inflexibility can result in errors remaining frozen within the official records.

Table 21.3
Bookkeeping categorizes transactions and allocates them to time periods

(£m)	Jan.	Feb.	Mar.	Apr.	May	Jun.
Revenue	16.2	20.2	16.9	21.1	17.6	22.0
Cost	13.5	16.9	14.1	17.6	14.7	18.3
Profit	2.7	3.4	2.8	3.5	2.9	3.7

Complications and anomalies can arise for several reasons:

- **Revenue miscategorization:** Records are not always detailed enough and sometimes inaccuracies occur. These are not always corrected, since a detailed split of revenues is not required for statutory financial reporting.

- **Sales price and promotion ignorance:** Absence of this information is common, since prices and promotions do not generally need to be recorded for statutory reporting. In the USA, new accounting regulations have forced firms to improve this area of record keeping.

- **Revenue mistiming:** Delays between orders, delivery and invoicing can result in revenues being allocated to the wrong time periods. The proper way to track income projections from a contract is to divide estimated income into two categories: committed (for signed and binding contracts) and possible (for contracts under negotiation).

- **Cost abridgement:** Records are not detailed enough and are reported only in summary categories. Agency invoices in particular are often not analyzed in as much detail as marketing requires.

- **Cost miscategorization:** Records are not allocated to the correct marketing activity. If this is not discovered until long after the period closes, the correct figure may never appear in official records.

- **Cost mistiming:** Delays between purchase commitments, purchase orders, purchase invoices and payments can cause records to be allocated to the wrong time period.

- **Period closing:** Errors that are not corrected before the period close may remain on the system.

- **Blackout periods:** A period of time set by the accounting department or senior management during which you may not make purchases, even though allocation has been approved.

- **Year end spending:** Although it is not good business practice, many firms figure that if you don't spend your budget, it will be cut next year. Hurrying to spend at year end may result in distortions being introduced and costs being miscoded.

These complications and anomalies can generally be avoided by stipulating more rigorous bookkeeping procedures. The priority for such improvements needs to be understood and accepted by accounting management if the necessary changes are to occur. Most can be solved through time and effort and better systems, such as:

- Better bookkeeping procedures – front and back office; enterprise resource planning (ERP) and customer relationship management (CRM) projects can provide the impetus;

- Extra record-keeping systems for non-financial data.

Separating the variances into hierarchies of effects

Our minds routinely categorize effects into hierarchies (see Figure 21.1). Delegation is a practical manifestation of this tendency.

Figure 21.1
Hierarchies of effects

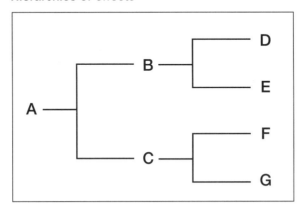

We often idealize these hierarchies, and convince ourselves that our business works in this hierarchical way. McKinsey & Co has coined the acronym MECE to describe an ideal hierarchy. MECE stands for 'mutually exclusive, collectively exhaustive'. In Figure 21.1, the variance A can be divided into factors B and C, and further subdivided into D and E plus F and G, which are all mutually exclusive. Factors D, E, F and G are collectively exhaustive if only these four factors, and no more, are needed to explain A.

Although we often assume that variance analysis behaves in this MECE way, perfect MECE is rarely found in practice. MECE imperfections have extremely important consequences and must not be ignored.

Separating the effect of marketing from other factors is an important requirement of variance analysis. What is possible is the separation of profit variance into components associated with revenues and other components associated with costs. This is represented schematically in Figure 21.2. Putting Figure 21.2 into words can help explain the logic.

Price variance has a directly calculable effect on revenue (the revenue difference percentage is directly proportional to the price difference percentage), which in turn has a calculable effect on profit variance. This can be calculated by multiplying the revenue variance by the budgeted profit margin, expressed as a fraction of the revenue.

Figure 21.2
Separation of profit variance into component parts

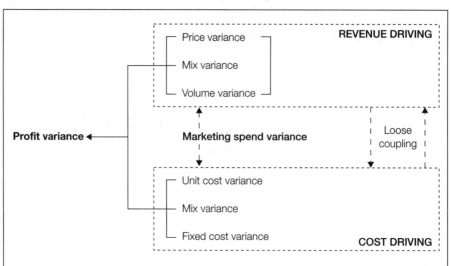

Volume variance has a similar effect. The revenue difference percentage is directly proportional to the volume difference percentage. The profit variance can then be calculated using the same method as for price variance.

Product-mix variance is the third of the revenue effects. It is likely to be less familiar to most readers, since relatively few companies report product-mix variances. It arises when the actual product mix is different from that assumed in budget calculations. This can result in a profit variance if the profit margin differs from product to product. For example, if the product mix shifts towards high-profit-margin products, a positive profit variance will result.

The cost variances work in a similar way. Variable cost variances (i.e. unit costs) arise when actual variable costs are different from budgeted. The impact on profits can be calculated by multiplying the unit cost variance by the budgeted sales volume. Fixed cost variances are even simpler. A variance in fixed costs shows directly as a variance in profits.

Marketing expenditure, it should be noted, can be categorized as a revenue driver and also a cost driver. The reason is that cutting marketing expenditure is likely to have a direct effect on revenue, unlike all other cost elements. For this reason, marketing expenditure has a unique position in cost accounting.

Volume variances, time patterns and their sources

Volume variances have numerous sources. Many are uncontrollable while others are controllable. Separating the total volume variance into its component parts is important. Time patterns offer important clues to interpreting volumes.

The main *uncontrollable variances* are driven by market forecasting problems:

- **Long-term market forecasts:** For example, based on product life cycles, the economy, legislation and regulation are all important ingredients in volume forecasts.

- **Seasonal demand forecast:** Often related to factors such as weather, temperature, rain. Errors in these forecasts over a year can have a significant effect on the annual forecast and it is important to try to separate out the effect.

- **Special event forecast:** (e.g. Easter, Christmas, Wimbledon, Cup Final, other events). Some key events can have a huge impact on short-term demand, and it is important to separate out these special events from the general pattern of consumption.

- **Weekly demand patterns:** Weekend shopping and weekday shopping have been evolving, so it important to understand how these changing patterns affect volumes.

Even though these market forecasting variances are not strictly controllable, they are still important to the business and point to the need to take all practical steps to improve the forecasting techniques used so that the errors are reduced in the future.

Controllable volume variances can generally be separated into two parts:

- **Short-term volume spikes:** Short-term spikes in sales volume or customer acquisition are often the result of campaigns. Advertising, direct marketing and sales promotion can all contribute to a spike in sales.

- **Long-term share trends:** Slow changes in market share cannot be fully explained in terms of sales campaigns and often signal more fundamental shifts in brand preference.

Grey areas in reconciling variances to sources

We often use spreadsheets like adding machines, and it is common to assume that variances are naturally additive. Indeed many variances are additive, for example, variances expressed in purely monetary terms (e.g. revenues and costs) and sales volumes are all additive.

Unfortunately, there are also several important cases where variances do not combine additively. This is generally the case where the components are multiplied or divided. Common examples are:

- Revenue (calculated by multiplying price and sales volume);
- Market share (calculated by dividing brand sales volume by total sales volume for the market).

Indeed, all ratios involve division and therefore none is additive.

The importance of this is that, where a number is made up of components that are not additive, it is impossible to allocate the variance accurately and unambiguously between the components. We always get what is called a 'grey area'. An example, based on revenue, volume and price is given in Figure 21.3.

Figure 21.3
Grey areas in separating revenue variance into volume and price effects

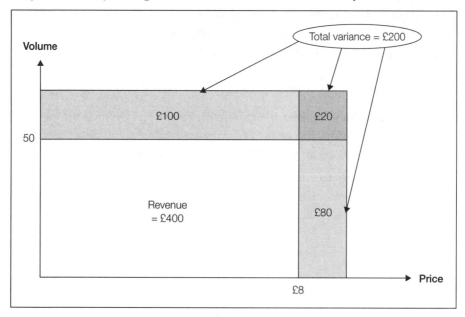

For the case illustrated in Figure 21.3, the total revenue variance of £200 (i.e. 50%) has been caused by a combination of volume variance (rising from 50 to 62.5, an increase of 25%) and a price variance (rising from £8 to £9.60, an increase of 20%).

Clearly, the 50% revenue increase is not quite the sum of the 25% volume increase and the 20% price increase. Part of the revenue variance (i.e. 5% or £20 as shown in the grey box in the top right of Figure 21.3) is unaccounted for. The greater the percentage changes, the larger will be the grey area, and vice versa.

Even when there is a grey area, accountants generally prefer to reconcile all variances to a 'source'. In our example, the 5% can either be accounted for as volume variance, or equally well as price variance.

Managers need to understand that these grey areas exist naturally, and that reconciling variances to source is inevitably an inexact process.

Product mix variance

Profit variances arise for reasons other than volume, price and cost. Most important is the difference between budgeted product mix and actual.

Consider a situation where we have two products, product 1 and product 2. One definition of product mix is the proportion of the total sales volume accounted for by product 1. We could, of course, equally well have chosen the proportion accounted for by product 2.

For example, if beer is sold in six-packs (with sales of 15 million pints annually) and 24-packs (with sales of 5 million pints annually), then the mix of six-packs is 0.75 or 75% expressed as a percentage.

The profit earned on each product is the product volume multiplied by the contribution margin, less the fixed costs. The effect of changes in mix on the average contribution margin is shown schematically in Figure 21.4.

For example, if the contribution margin for six-packs is 20p per pint, and for 24-packs is 10p per pint, then increasing the mix of six-packs from 0.75 to 0.80 will increase the average contribution from 17.5p to 18p.

What makes the product mix an interesting and useful parameter is that profit variances arising from changes in product mix are directly proportional to the change in mix. Figure 21.4 can be generalized to any number of products, and the relationship remains a linear one. The effect of mix can be separated out from the volume and price effects, with the caveat that grey areas persist in all these calculations due to interactions between price, volume and mix.

Figure 21.4
Average contribution margins for different product mixes

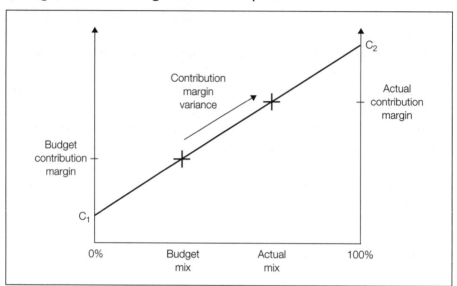

Marketing expenditure variances, ratios and trade-offs

Marketing expenditure is an important driver of revenues, so it is essential to monitor it and report variances. There are four important aspects of this:

- The rate of marketing expenditure can have a direct effect on sales, particularly in the case of direct marketing, sales promotion and other sales driving factors. Use your intelligence when reviewing marketing expenditure variance, and look for revenue variances that may be caused by the expenditure variance.

- The cost of marketing changes over time must be monitored and reported. For example, media cost inflation has far exceeded general inflation. Linking marketing expenditure to the activity it buys (e.g. GRPs or direct mail volumes) provides useful insights.

- Marketing mix is also important, especially the mix of short-term sales drivers (such as direct marketing, sales promotion) to longer-term growth drivers (such as advertising). This mix is sometimes referred to as the ATL% (meaning above-the-line spending as a percentage of total). Again look for revenue variances that may be caused by changes in the marketing mix.

- Efficiency is the final factor. This is usually measured as a ratio of outputs to inputs. For example, direct mail response rate is a measure of efficiency. Tracking and reporting these efficiencies over time is useful.

Finally, a word of caution is necessary about efficiency variances. Ratios often are linked, and an efficiency achieved in one area may adversely affect performance in another area (see Table 21.4). A favourable or unfavourable label should not cause managers in one area to jump to conclusions. By themselves, variances should merely raise questions – they are attention directors, not problem solvers.

Responding to variances and maximizing profits

Deciding how to respond whenever a budget target is missed is a critical problem in budgeting. There is surprisingly little guidance in budgeting education and practice to assist in solving it.

When we find that there is a variance, we often make incorrect assumptions that lead us to make bad decisions. We need to remember:

- **Call for action:** 'Corrective' action is *not* always needed whenever a variance is reported.
- **Directionality:** The sign of the variance does not always dictate the action needed.
- **Balancing the budget:** It is not necessary to adjust the figures so that the original budget is exactly achieved.

Variances do not always mean that something is wrong. Things may indeed be very right. In Table 21.2, the 10% unfavourable cost variance this month occurred because 10% more product than planned was sold. The sign of the variance does not immediately dictate the direction of action required. Since customers paid for their purchases, that means the business is doing better than planned. Saving money isn't always a good thing.

When actual and budgeted figures differ, the experienced manager generally asks 'Why?' In the case of Table 21.2, the only question may be: 'Can we do a better job of revenue forecasting next time?' Once we know why the variance has occurred, then we can think about corrective action.

When does a variance matter? Some variances matter, others really don't. Also the size of the variance may matter as much as the percentage. A 100% variance on monthly media expenses is not surprising, as you don't buy media every

Table 21.4
Trade-offs between marketing expenditure and other budgets

Department	Wants	Which causes	To be less good at
Marketing	Customers to receive personalized service	Operations	Containing costs by spending less time with each customer
Finance	Pricing to cover short-term costs	Sales	Negotiating to secure long-term customer loyalty
Credit control	Credit limits to reflect financial risk criteria	Sales	Winning business from long-term prospects
Computing	Databases to be shared across departments	All other departments	Reducing their overheads
Manufacturing	Standard product features	Product development	Creating a competitive product range
Purchasing	Lowest cost bids	Manufacturing	Quality control, failure and defect reduction
Sales	Enquiries to be qualified by whoever takes the message	Operations	Reducing cost of telephone time and effort
Advertising	Long-term budgets to support brand development	All other departments	Obtaining funding for other valid investments
Operations	Standardized service to meet ISO9000	Marketing	Offering differentiated service levels to various market segments

month, and you didn't have an exact media schedule at budgeting time. But if your plans change and you have a large percentage media variance for the whole year, that may be important. Use your intelligence when interpreting variances.

How corrective action should be selected

When variances are reported, management must decide what corrective action, if any, is appropriate. One approach is to assess where you want to be by the end of the year, and then analyze how you are going to get there. In Table 21.5, three options are considered at a point halfway through the year:

- **Balancing the budget:** Aiming for rest-of-year figures that exactly restore the actuals at end of year to the original budgeted level.

- **Best possible result:** Analyzing the situation, you notice that there is an upward trend in revenues, and if that continues to the end of the year, you will be able to beat the budget.

- **Revise the budget:** Taking account of the poor results, you revise management's expectations downwards.

Table 21.5
Assess the options for where you want to be by the end of the year

	Year to date			1. Balanced budget – rest of year		2. Best possible result – rest of year		3. Revise the budget – full year
	Actual	Budget	VAR	Target	VAR	Target	VAR	Budget
Revenue	114.1	120	5.9U	125.9	5.9	128.9	8.9	228.2
Cost	95.1	100	4.9F	104.9	4.9	106.4	6.4	190.2
Profit	19.0	20	1.0U	21	1.0	22.5	2.5	38.0

Key: U = Unfavourable
       F = Favourable

The trouble with traffic light reporting

Favourable (F) and unfavourable (U) variances are widely used labels, and form part of the examples used in this chapter. Traffic light reporting is a modern implementation of this concept. Unfavourable variances are reported in RED, favourable variances are shown as GREEN. Software from companies such as Cognos, Hyperion, Comshare, Oracle Financials, SAP BW, and many other packages now boast the traffic light feature. Even the humble spreadsheet can be used to set up traffic light reporting.

Yet traffic light reporting is a technologists' solution that drives bad and dysfunctional decisions. Reacting to traffic lights can easily result in bad decisions and wrong corrective actions. The reason for this is to do with optimization; Figure 21.5 shows how this problem arises.

Figure 21.5
The 'right' price on a price–profit curve

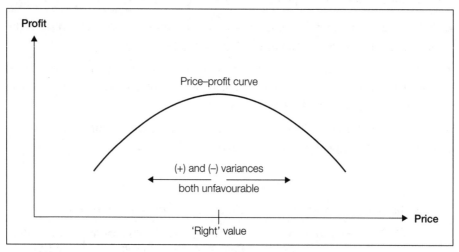

Budgets are often set on the basis of the 'right' value for factors such as price, marketing expenditure, etc. Yet if these factors have been chosen in such a way as to optimize profits, then (+) and (−) variances will both result in lower profits because they move away from the peak in the profit curve. The trouble with the traffic light concept is that it assumes that 'up is good' and 'down is bad' (or vice versa). Figure 21.5 shows that this is very misleading. In traffic light terms, it means that RED is bad, but GREEN is also bad! Variance analysis is indicative, not conclusive. You must apply your intelligence to variances, and not simply respond to the traffic lights.

Balancing the budget

'Balancing the budget' is a widely used method, yet it is seldom mentioned in accounting literature. The idea is simple and appealing to some finance managers. If variances during one part of the year are unfavourable, then variances should have the equal and opposite value for the rest of the year. Figure 21.5 includes an example of this practice.

Part of the appeal of this approach to finance managers is that there is no requirement for them to learn about the underlying business issues causing the variances. They simply manage by the numbers. And counting beans can be very therapeutic. However, dangers and risks with the beancounter's balanced budget are numerous:

- **Unfeasible commitments:** Corrective action that will restore the original budget may be impossible if circumstances have changed.

- **Postponing inevitable problems:** Cost-cutting of marketing budgets is a common example of balancing the budgets. This can cause unfavourable revenue variances at a later date.

- **Slackening off:** Opportunities to beat the budget can get overlooked. Where there is a favourable trend in the year to date, it may be considered acceptable to slacken off during the rest of the year.

- **Offloading problems:** Where there are trade-offs between departments, aiming to balance budgets can lead one department to offload its problems onto another.

- **Financial myopia:** Too much focus on the numbers and too little attention paid to their causes.

While the balanced budget is not always a bad idea, managers should act intelligently and look for the issues noted here before committing to a balanced budget.

Best possible result

The risk with the 'best possible result' approach is clear. The apparent trend may be illusory, or may just be short term. This can leave a situation similar to that of the 'big hairy audacious goals' method of budget setting that we discuss in Chapter 3. Managers down the line feel faced with 'Mission Impossible' targets and become demotivated.

In short, if you plan on the best possible result, you may be setting yourself up for the biggest possible disappointment. But, more than that, in the process you may take decisions that are suboptimal and damaging to the business.

On the other hand, if your projections are correct, you will have taken full advantage of an opportunity that the other approaches will have missed. All the more reason then to:

- Understand the underlying reasons for the variances;
- Make your decisions on corrective actions with the support of a well-constructed spreadsheet model.

Revise the budget

Having assessed budget variances, you may decide to revise your budget. Three main techniques are available:

1. **Flexible budgeting:** Revised budget that recognizes the impact of sales volume changes during the year on costs and revenues.
2. **Rolling forecasting:** Extending the planning horizon so that it always extends beyond the end of the current accounting period. The review process tends to be limited to the preparation of revised financial estimates.
3. **Rolling budgeting:** Review of financial projections is complemented by a review of strategic options and plans. Rolling forecasts are an element.

What is important in all three cases is that whoever sets the revised budgets does so intelligently. The danger is that they will cut marketing budgets without thinking about the consequences, which may result in:

- Balancing the budgets purely numerically;
- Maximizing net marketing contribution;
- Maximizing the return on marketing expenditure.

In every case, the likelihood is that the profit will not in fact be maximized by this course of action. Far better to develop a model that will enable profits to be maximized.

Key points

- Corrective action is *not* needed whenever a variance is reported.
- Determining what constitutes a significant variance is important.
- You cannot assume that the sign of the variance (+ve/–ve) necessarily indicates the direction of the solution.
- Overemphasizing the 'responsibility' aspect of budget subvariances can backfire by causing dysfunctional decisions by managers.

- Ignoring the linkages across departmental boundaries can result in managers optimizing their own area of 'responsibility' and damaging overall profitability.

- Volume variances have many uncontrollable causes which need to be taken into account in interpreting the revenue variance.

- Overemphasizing every financial variance to the detriment or even exclusion of non-financial considerations can be very harmful to profits.

- It is important to understand the causes of the variances and, in particular, to make sure that they are due to real problems.

- The process of assessing possible corrective actions is simplified by separating uncontrollable sources of variance from controllable factors.

- It is not good practice to make infeasible commitments in order to 'balance the budget', nor to adopt solutions today that store up problems for tomorrow nor to offload your problems onto other departments.

- Don't slacken off when you are ahead of budget.

- The best strategy is to maximize profits, not volume or revenue.

- Take care that contribution or ROME numbers don't distort your profit perspective.

- Revise budgets only on the basis of rigorous modelling and what-if analyses.

22

TWENTY THINGS YOU'LL
DO DIFFERENTLY

1. Marketing will gain back its lost credibility by coping with numerical issues as competently as finance (Chapter 2).

2. Marketing will get a grip on how brands drive profitability, including all the technical issues of measuring, modelling and accounting (Chapter 3).

3. Marketing will learn objective lessons from past experience and use them to plan future marketing activity (Chapter 4).

4. Marketing research will be used as an investigation to discover how marketing really works and not simply to feel the comfort of lots of data (Chapter 5).

5. Forecasting and predictive modelling will be used routinely in decision making and marketing managers will become technically competent in these areas (Chapter 6).

6. Decision making will be audited and recurring problems will be solved (Chapter 7).

7. Marketing budgets will be 'rightsized' based on revenue growth plans, not capped based on historical precedent (Chapter 8).

8. Brand identity changes will be evaluated using strategic research to assess the artistry of the design agency (Chapter 9).

9. Decisions to expand or rationalize the product range will be based on hard analysis and not simply as a reflex reaction to competitor or channel pressure (Chapter 10).

10. Marketing will be responsible for evaluating and maximizing brand valuation (Chapter 11).

11. Advertising and marketing communications campaigns will be managed to maximize their payback, and not merely based on artistic merit (Chapter 12).

12. Prices will be set to maximize profits and not merely to boost volume or unit margin (Chapter 13).

13. Sales promotions will be undertaken to maximize profits and not as a reflex reaction to competition or channel pressure (Chapter 14).

14. Customer acquisition and retention will be managed to maximize long-term profits and not merely to maintain a fixed number of customers or fixed revenues (Chapter 15).

15. Market research staff will be upgraded and combined with finance staff to form a 'Revenue Insights' team (Chapter 16).

16. Modelling staff will learn how to construct models that are reusable and auditable, and that will inspire the confidence of senior decision makers (Chapter 17).

17. Marketing plans will be written that give clear justification for marketing activity and expenditure and set targets against which success will be evaluated (Chapter 18).

18. Marketing budgets will be determined at the start of the corporate budgeting cycle as part of the revenue forecasting activity (Chapter 19).

19. Marketing will keep complete and accurate records of all its key activities and expenditures that can be used to evaluate its financial performance (Chapter 20).

20. Management reporting will be used responsibly to provide early warnings, and not as a stick with which to beat staff when things go wrong (Chapter 21).

REFERENCES

Aaker, D. A., 'Toward a normative model of promotional decision making', *Management Science*, 19(6): 593, 1973.

Aaker, D. A., *Managing Brand Equity*, Free Press, 1991.

Aaker, D. A., *Building Strong Brands*, Free Press, 1996.

Abraham, M. M. and Lodish, L. M., 'Getting the Most out of Advertising and Promotion', *Harvard Business Review*, 68(3): 50, 1990.

Accenture, *Using Customer Insights to Build Brand Loyalty and Increase Marketing ROI*, Accenture website, 2004.
http://www.accenture.com/xdoc/en/newsroom/epresskit/insight/epres_insight_markstudy.pdf

Adams, J. T., *Hamiltonian Principles*, Simon Publications, 2001.

Allenby, G. M. and Rossi, P. E., 'Quality Perceptions and Asymmetric Switching between Brands', *Marketing Science*, 10(3): 185–205, 1991.

Ambler, T., *Marketing: From Advertising to Zen*, FT Pitman Publishing, 1996.

Ambler, T., *Marketing and the Bottom Line*, 1st edn, FT Prentice Hall, 2000.

Ambler, T., *Marketing and the Bottom Line*, 2nd edn, FT Prentice Hall, 2003.

Argyris, C., *On Organisational Learning*, Blackwell, 1998.

Arkes, H. R., 'Overconfidence in Judgemental Forecasting', in: Armstrong, J. S. (ed.), *Principles of Forecasting*, Kluwer Academic Press, 2001.

Arthur Andersen, *Costing Systems for Advertising Agencies*, IPA Publications 1992.

Baghai, M., Coley, S. and White, D., *The Alchemy of Growth*, Perseus, (1999).

Bain, N. C., 'The Accountant's Contribution to Marketing Decisions', *Accountants Journal (NZ)*, 49: 46–50, 1970.

Baker, M. J., *Market Development*, Penguin, 1983.

Baker, S., 'Defining a Marketing Paradigm', Cranfield School of Management, working paper, 2000.

Barban, A. M., Cristol, S. M. and Kopec, F. J., *Essentials of Media Planning*, NTC Business Books, 1989.

Barnard, N. R., Presentation to Centre for Marketing and Communication, London Business School, 1987.

Barnard, N. R., Barwise, T. P. and Ehrenberg, A. S. C., 'Reinterviews in Attitude Research', *MRS Conference Proceedings*, Brighton, 1986.

Barwise, T. P. and Ehrenberg, A. S. C., 'Consumer Beliefs and Brand Usage', *Journal of the Market Research Society*, 1985; 27: 81–93, 1985.

Bass, F. M., Givon, M. M., Kaiwani, M. U., Reibstein, D. and Wright, G. P., 'An Investigation into the Order of the Brand Choice Process', *Marketing Science*, 3: 267–87, 1984.

Batra, R., Myers, J. and Aaker, D., *Advertising Management*, Prentice Hall, 1996.

Bawa, K. and Shoemaker, R. W., 'The Effects of a Direct Mail Coupon on Brand Choice Behavior', *Journal of Marketing Research*, 24(4): 370, 1987.

Bemmaor, A. C. and Mouchoux, D., 'Measuring the Short-term Effect of In-store Promotion and Retail Advertising on Brand Sales: a Factorial Experiment', *Journal of Marketing Research*, 28:(2) 202–14, 1991.

Bird, D., 'If You Can, Do, If You Can't You're Too Costly', *Marketing*, 29 January 1998.

Blattberg, R. C., 'A Theoretical and Empirical Evaluation of Price Deals for Consumer Non-durables', *Journal of Marketing*, 45: 116–29, 1981.

Blattberg, R. C. and Neslin, S. A., *Sales Promotion Concepts, Methods, and Strategies*, Prentice Hall, 1990.

Blattberg, R. C. and Wisniewski, K. J., 'Price-Induced Patterns of Competition', *Marketing Science*, 8(4): 291, 1989.

Blattberg, R. C., Briesch, R., and Fox, E. J., 'How Promotions Work', *Marketing Science*, 14(3): G122, 1995.

Blattberg, R. C., Getz, G. and Thomas, J. S., *Customer Equity – Building and Managing Relationships as Valuable Assets*, Harvard Business School Press, 2001.

Blue Sky Consulting, *The True Cost of Staff Turnover*, http://www.blue-sky.co.uk/in_in.html

BMRA, (British Market Research Association), 'The Sky's the Limit: Research at BAA', *MR Business*, 30, 1 February 2004(a).

BMRA, (British Market Research Association), 'Insight at Nokia', *MR Business*, 31, 27 February 2004(b).

Bolton, R. N., 'The Relationship between Market Characteristics and Promotional Price', *Marketing Science*, 8(2): 153, 1989.

Booz Allen and Hamilton, *New Product Development in the 1980s*, Booz Allen and Hamilton Inc, 1982.

Borin, N., Van Vranken, C. and Farris, P. W., 'A Pilot Test of Discrimination in the Japanese Distribution System', *Journal of Retailing*, 67(1): 93–106, 1991.

Brady, J. and Davis, I., 'Marketing's Mid-life Crisis', *McKinsey Quarterly*, 2: 17–28, 1993.

Broadbent, S., *The Advertising Budget: The Advertiser's Guide to Budget Determination*, NTC Publications, 1989.

Brodrick, J., 'Should You Shoot Your Budget?' *BetterManagement.com*, 29 August 2003.

Bronnenberg, B. J., Mahajan, V. and Vanhonacker, W. R., 'The Emergence of Market Structure in New Repeat Purchase Categories', *Journal of Marketing Research*, 37: 1116–31, 2000.

Brown, G. H., 'Brand Loyalty', *Advertising Age*, 24. Reproduced in: Ehrenberg, A. S. C. and Pyatt, F. G. (eds), *Consumer Behaviour*, Penguin, 1953.

Brynjolfsson, E. and Hitt, L., 'The Customer Counts', *Information Week*, 9 September, 1996.

BusinessWeek, 'Brands in an Age of Anti-Americanism', 2 August 2004.

Butterfield, L., 'How Advertising Affects Share Price', *ADVALUE*, 5, February 2000.

Buzzell, R. D. and Gale, B.T., *The PIMS Principles*, Free Press, 1987.

Carlzon, J., *Moments of Truth*, HarperCollins, 1989.

Chevalier, M. and Curhan, R. C., 'Retail Promotions as a Function of Trade Promotions', *Sloan Management Review*, 18: 19, 1976.

Clancy, K. J. and Krieg, P. C., *Counterintuitive Marketing: Achieve Great Results Using Uncommon Sense*, Free Press, 2000.

Clancy, K. J. and Shulman, R. S., *Marketing Myths that Are Killing Business*, McGraw-Hill, 1994.

Clark, B. H., 'Marketing Performance Measures: History and Inter-relationships', *Journal of Marketing Management*, 15: 711–32, 1999.

Colley, R. H., *Defining Advertising Goals for Measuring Advertising Results*, Association of National Advertisers, New York, 1961.

Cooper, L. G., 'Competitive Maps: The Structure Underlying Asymmetric Cross Elasticities', *Management Science*, 34(6): 707, 1988.

Cooper, R. G., *Winning at New Products*, Addison Wesley, 1993.

Coopers & Lybrand, *Marketing at the Crossroads*, Coopers & Lybrand, 1994.

Copeland, T., Koller, T. and Murrin, J., *Valuation: Measuring and Managing the Value of Companies*, 3rd edn, Wiley, 2000.

Corstjens, J. and Corstjens, M., *Store Wars*, Wiley, 1995.

Corstjens, M. and Merrihue, J., 'Optimal Marketing', *Harvard Business Review*, 81, October 2003.

Cotton, B. C. and Babb, E. M., 'Consumer Response to Promotional Deals', *Journal of Marketing*, 42(3): 109, 1978.

Court, D. C., Leiter, M. G. and Loch, M. A., 'Brand Leverage', *McKinsey Quarterly*, 2: 100–110, 1999.

Covey, S., *Seven Habits of Highly Effective People*, Free Press, 1990.

Cox, K. K., 'The Responsiveness of Food Sales to Shelf Space Changes in Supermarkets', *Journal of Marketing Research*, 1: 63–67, 1964.

Cox, K. K., 'The Effect of Shelf Space upon Sales of Branded Products', *Journal of Marketing Research*, 7: 55–58, 1970.

Crawford, C., 'Marketing Research and the New Product Failure Rate', *Journal of Marketing*, 41, April: 51–61, 1977.

Cunningham, R. M., 'Brand Loyalty – What/Where/How much?', *Harvard Business Review*, 34: 116–28, 1956.

Curhan, R. C., 'The Relationship between Shelf Space and Unit Sales in Supermarkets', *Journal of Marketing Research*, 9: 406–12, 1972.

Curhan, R. C., 'Shelf Space Elasticity: Reply', *Journal of Marketing Research*, 11: 221–2, 1974a.

Curhan, R. C., 'The Effects of Merchandising and Temporary Promotional Activities on the Sale of Fresh Fruits and Vegetables in Supermarkets', *Journal of Marketing Research*, 11, 1974b.

Curhan, R. C. and Kopp, R. J., *Factors Influencing Grocery Retailers' Support of Trade Promotions*, Marketing Science Institute, July 1986.

Davidow, W. and Uttal, B., *Total Customer Service: The Ultimate Weapon*, Harper Perennial, 1989.

Davidson, H., *Even More Offensive Marketing*, Penguin, 1997.

Davidson, H., 'Transforming the Value of Company Reports through Marketing Measurement', *Journal of Marketing Management*, 15: 757–78, 1999.

Day, G., *Market Driven Strategy*, Free Press, 1990.

Doyle, P., *Marketing Management and Strategy*, 2nd edn, Prentice Hall, 1998.

Doyle, P., 'How Shareholder Value Analysis Re-defines Marketing', *Market Leader*, 16–25, 2000.

Dresdner Kleinwort Benson and Interbrand, *Brands in Financial Services – Where's the Beef?* 1997.

DTI, *Value Added Scoreboard 2004*, www.innovation.gov.uk

Eagly, A. H. and Chaiken, S., *The Psychology of Attitudes*, Harcourt Brace Jovanovitch, 1993.

East, R., *Consumer Behaviour*, Prentice Hall, 1997.

Ehrenberg, A. S. C., *Repeat Buying: Theory and Applications*, 2nd edn, Charles Griffin and Co., 1988.

Ehrenberg, A. S. C. and Uncles, M. D., *Dirichlet-type Markets: A Review*, South Bank University Business School working paper, 1996.

Ehrenberg, A. S. C., Hammond, K. and Goodhardt, G. J., 'The After-effects of Price-related Consumer Promotions', *Journal of Advertising Research*, 34(4): 11, 1994.

Ehrenberg, A. S. C., Barnard, N. and Scriven, J., 'Differentiation or Salience?', *Journal of Advertising Research*, 37(6): 7, 1997.

Ellison, L., quoted on www.ssi-world.com, 2004.

Farley, J. U. and Leavitt, H. J., 'A Model of Distribution of Branded Products in Jamaica', *Journal of Marketing Research*, 5(4): 362–69, 1968.

Farris, P. W., Olver, J. and de Kluyver, C., 'The Relationship between Distribution and Market Share', *Marketing Science*, 8 (2): 107–28, 1989.

Feldwick, P., 'Brand Equity: Do We Really Need It?' in: Jones, J. P. (ed.), *How to Use Advertising to Build Strong Brands*, Sage, 1999.

Field, G. A. and Gabhart, D. R. L., 'Cultural Lag and Homeostasis in Accounting Theory and Practice', *MSY Business Topics*, 19(3): 31–37, 1971.

Fildes, R. and Hastings R., 'The Organisation and Improvement of Market Forecasting', *Journal of the Operational Research Society*, 1994.

Fill, C., *Marketing Communications*, Prentice Hall, 1999.

Finn, B., *A Model of the Tea Market*, presentation to Cranfield School of Management's Marketing Value Added Best Practice Club, 2003.

Finn, B., Presentation to Value Based Marketing Forum, City Business School, London, March 2004.

Frank, R. E. and Massey, W. F., 'Shelf Position and Space Effects on Sales', *Journal of Marketing Research*, 7: 59–66, 1970.

Frigstad, D., *Customer Engineering: Cutting-Edge Selling Strategies*, PSI Successful Business Library, Oasis Press, 1995.

Gabor, A. and Granger C. W. J., 'On the Price Consciousness of Consumers', *Applied Statistics*, 10(3): 170–88, 1961.

Gale, B., *Managing Customer Value: Creating Quality and Service that Customers Can See*, Free Press, 1994.

Gardner, Sir Roy, 'Marketers Must Be More than Functional Specialists to Win Over Chief Executives', *Market Leader*, 24, 2004.

Garrick, G. 'Spend Better Advertising Dollars, Not More', paper presented to the Advertising Research Foundation Electronic Media Workshop, New York, 11 December 1986.

Grande, C., 'Relief on Intellectual Property', *Financial Times*, 7 March 2001.

Gregory, J., 'How Advertising Impacts on Share Price', *ADVALUE*, 2 April 1999.

Grover, R. and Srinivasan, V., 'Evaluating the Multiple Effects of Retail Promotions on Branding', *Journal of Marketing Research*, 29(1): 76–89, 1992.

Gupta, S., 'Impact of Sales Promotions on When, What, and How Much', *Journal of Marketing Research*, 25(4): 342–355, 1988.

Haig, M., *Brand Failures: the Truth about the 100 Biggest Branding Mistakes of All Time*, Kogan Page, 2003.

Haigh, D., *Brand Valuation, a Review of Current Practice*, Institute of Practitioners in Advertising, November 1996.

Haigh, D., *The Brand Finance Report*, Brand Finance, 1999.

Hartley, R. F., *Marketing Mistakes*, Wiley, 1995.

Hoch, S. J. and Banerji, S., 'When Do Private Labels Succeed?' *Sloan Management Review*, 34(4): 57, 1993.

Holmes, M. and Cook, L., *Econometrics Explained*, IPA Publications, 2004.

Hope, J. and Fraser, J., *Beyond Budgeting*, Harvard Business School Press, 2003.

Horne, A., Morgan, J. and Page, J., 'Where Do We Go From Here?' *Journal of the Market Research Society*, 16(3): 157–81, 1973.

Hull, J. and Jones, J., 'Think-tank Findings – Marketing Accountability', *Marketing Forum Insights*, 2, 2002.

Hunt, S., 'Budgets Roll with the Times', *Optimize*, August 2003.

IRI, *Larger sample, stronger proof of P-O-P effectiveness*, Reprint from IRI which enlarges on a report that first appeared in *P-O-P Times* Mar/Apr: 28–32, 1989.

Joint working party of IPA, ISBA DMA MCCA and PRCA, *The Guide: Joint Industry Guidelines on Agency Search, Selection and Relationship Management*, ISBA, 2002.

Jones, J. P., *How to Use Advertising to Build Strong Brands*, Sage, 1999.

Kalwani, M. U. and Yim, C. K., 'Consumer Price and Promotion Expectations: An Experimental Survey', *Journal of Marketing Research*, 29(1): 90–100, 1992.

Kalwani, M. U., Yim C. K., Rinne, H. J. and Sugita, Y., 'A Price Expectations Model of Customer Brand Choice', *Journal of Marketing Research*, 27(3): 251–263, 1990.

Kalyanaram, G., Robinson, W. T. and Urban, G. L., 'Order of Market Entry: Established Empirical Generalisations, Emerging Empirical Generalisations, and Future Research', *Marketing Science*, 14(2): G212–21, 1995.

Kamakura, W. A. and Russell, G. J., 'A Probabilistic Choice Model For Market Segmentation and Elasticity Structure', *Journal of Marketing Research*, 26(4): 379–390, 1989.

Kaplan, R. S. and Norton, D. P., *The Balanced Scorecard*, Harvard Business School Press, 1996.

Kay, J., *Foundations of Corporate Success*, Oxford University Press, 1993.

Kennedy, J. R., 'The Effect of Display Location on the Sales and Pilferage of Cigarettes', *Journal of Marketing Research*, 7(2): 210–15, 1970.

Korgaonkar, P. K., Lund, D. and Price, B., 'A Structural Equations Approach toward Examination of Store Attitude and Store Patronage Behavior', *Journal of Retailing*, 2: 39–60, 1985.

Kotler, P., *Marketing Management: Analysis, Planning and Control*, 7th edn, Prentice Hall, 1991.

Kotzan, J. A. and Evanson, R. V., 'Responsiveness of Drug Store Sales to Shelf Space Allocation', *Journal of Marketing Research*, 6: 465–69, 1969.

KPMG, *Finance Directors Survey*, KPMG, 1996.

Krell, E., 'The Case Against Budgeting', *Business Finance*, July 2003.

Krishnamurthi, L. and Raj, S. P., 'A Model of Brand Choice and Purchase Quantity Price Sensitivities', *Marketing Science*, 7(1): 1, 1988.

Kumar, V. and Leone, R. P., 'Measuring the Effect of Retail Store Promotions on Brand and Store Substitution', *Journal of Marketing Research*, 25(2): 178–185, 1988.

Lattin, J. M. and Bucklin, R. E., 'Reference Effects of Price and Promotion on Brand Choice Behavior', *Journal of Marketing Research*, 26: 299–310, 1989.

Lavidge, R. J. and Steiner, G. A., 'A Model for Predictive Measurements of Advertising Effectiveness', *Journal of Marketing*, 25: 59–62, 1961.

Leone, R. P. and Schultz, R. L., 'A Study of Marketing Generalisations', *Journal of Marketing*, 44: 101–18, 1980.

Levitt, T., 'The Globalisation of Markets', *Harvard Business Review*, 61(3): 92–102, 1983.

Lilien, G. L. and Rangaswamy, A., *Marketing Engineering – Computer Assisted Marketing Analysis and Planning*, Addison Wesley, 1998.

Lodish, L. M. and Lubetkin, B., 'How Advertising Works. General Truths? Nine Key Findings from IRI Test Data', *Admap*, 9–15, 1992.

Lodish, L. M., Curtiss, E., Ness, M. and Simpson, M. K., 'Sales Force Sizing and Deployment Using a Decision Calculus Model at Syntex Laboratories', *Interfaces*, 18(1): 5–20, 1988.

Lodish, L. M., Abraham, M. M., Livelsberger J. and Lubetkin B., 'A Summary of Fifty-five in-market Experimental Estimates of the Long-term Effect of TV Advertising', *Marketing Science*, 14(3): G133, 1995.

Lomax, W., Hammond, K., Clemente, M. and East, R., 'New Entrants in a Mature Market: an Empirical Study of the Detergent Market', *Journal of Marketing Management*, 1996.

Loren, G., 'Why Budgeting Kills Your Company', *Harvard Business School Working Knowledge*, 11 August 2003.

Low, G. S. and Lamb, C. W. Jr., 'The Measurement and Dimensionality of Brand Associations', *Journal of Product and Brand Management*, 9(6): 350, 2000.

MacDonald, G. and Lush, J., 'Walkers Crisps: Garymania – how an already successful brand benefited from famous advertising', in: Duckworth, G. (ed.) *Advertising Works 9*, NTC Publications, 1997.

Makridakis, S. and Gaba, A., 'Judgement: Its Role and Value for Strategy', in: Wright, G. and Goodwin, P. (eds), *Forecasting with Judgement*, Wiley, 1998.

Malcolm, R., *100% Marketing*, The Brands Lecture, the British Brands Group, 2003.

Mayhew, G. E. and Winer, R. S., 'An Empirical Analysis of Internal and External Reference', *Journal of Consumer Research*, 19(1): 62, 1992.

McDonald, M. H. B., *Marketing Plans*, 4th edn, Butterworth-Heinemann, 1999.

McDonald, M. H. B., 'On the Right Track – Whether CRM Provides an Opportunity or Threat to Your Organization Is Your Call', *Marketing Business*, April: 28–31, 2000.

Mela, C. F., Gupta, S. and Lehmann, D. R., 'The Long-term Impact of Promotion and Advertising on Consumer Brand Choice', *Journal of Marketing Research*, 34: 248–261, 1997.

Mela C. F., Jedidi, K. and Bowman, D., 'The Long-term Impact of Promotions on Consumer Stockpiling Behavior', *Journal of Marketing Research*, 35: 250–262, 1998.

Mercer, D., *Management's Commitment to Marketing Theory Compared with Actual Practice*, Marketing Education Group (MEG) Conference, July 1996.

Merrick, D., Personal Communication, 2004.

Merrick, D., *Guidelines for Marketing Spending Effectiveness*, Presentation to Cranfield School of Management's Marketing Value Added Best Practice Club, 2003.

Merrick, D. and Weaver, K., 'Budget Allocation in Practice', Paper presented to the Marketing Value Added Best Practice Club, Cranfield School of Management, 14 February 2001.

Moore, W. L. and Pessemier, E. A., *Product Planning and Management*, McGraw-Hill, 1993.

Mulhern, F. J. and Leone, R. P., 'Implicit Price Bundling of Retail Products: A Multiproduct Approach', *Journal of Marketing*, 55(4): 63, 1991.

Muller, R. W., Kline, G. E. and Trout, J. J., 'Customers Buy 22% More When Shelves are Well Stocked', *Progressive Grocer*, 32: 40–48, 1953.

Naples, M. J., *Effective Frequency: The Relationship between Frequency and Advertising Awareness*, Association of National Advertisers, 1979.

Narasimhan, C., Neslin S. A. and Sen, S. K., 'Promotional Elasticities and Category Characteristics', *Journal of Marketing*, 60(2): 17, 1996.

Neslin, S. A. and Shoemaker, R. W., 'An Alternative Explanation for Lower Repeat Rates after Promotions', *Journal of Marketing Research*, 26(2): 205–213, 1989.

Neslin, S. A., Henderson, C. and Quelch, J., 'Consumer Promotions and the Acceleration of Product Purchases', *Marketing Science*, 4(2): 147, 1985.

Nuttall, C., 'The Relationship between Sales and Distribution of Certain Confectionery

Lines', *Commentary*, 7(4): 272–85, 1965.

Parsons, L. J., 'An Econometric Analysis of Advertising, Retail Availability, and Sales of a New Brand', *Management Science*, 20: 938–47, 1974.

Pauli, H. and Hoecker, R. W., *Better Utilisation of Selling Space in Food Stores*, Marketing Research Report No. 30, United States Government Printing Office, 1952.

Peppers, D. and Rogers, M., *The One-to-one Future: Building Business Relationships One Customer at a Time*, Piatkus Books, 1996.

Perrier, R., *Brand Valuation*, Business Books Limited, 1996.

Peters, T., *Thriving on Chaos*, Pan, 1987.

Pickering, J. F., 'Purchase Expectations and the Demand for Consumer Durables', *Journal of Economic Psychology*, 5(4): 342–52, 1984.

Piercy, N., *Market-Led Strategic Change*, Butterworth-Heinemann, 1992.

Porter, M., 'How Competitive Forces Shape Strategy', *Harvard Business Review*, March–April 1979.

Porter, M., *Competitive Strategy: Techniques for Analyzing Industries and Competitors*, Free Press, 1980.

Powell, G., *Return on Marketing Investment*, RPI Press, 2002.

Progressive Grocer, 'The Colonial Study', *Progressive Grocer*, 42: 43, 1963.

Raju, J. S., 'The Effect of Price Promotions on Variability in Product Category Sales', *Marketing Science*, 11(3): 207, 1992.

Rangaswamy, A., Prabhakant, S. and Zoltners, A., 'An Integrated Model-based Approach for Sales Force Restructuring', *Marketing Science*, 9: 279–98, 1990.

Rapp, S. and Collins, T., *Maximarketing*, McGraw-Hill, 1987.

Ratchford, B. T., 'New Insights about the FCB Grid', *Journal of Advertising Research*, 1987.

Reibstein, D. J. and Farris, P. W., 'Market Share and Distribution', *Marketing Science*, 14(3): G190–202, 1995.

Reichheld, F., *The Loyalty Effect*, Harvard Business School Press, 1996.

Reichheld, F. and Sasser, E., 'Zero Customer Defections', *Harvard Business Review*, September–October: 105–111, 1990.

Ries, A. L. and Trout, J., *The 22 Immutable Laws of Marketing*, HarperCollins, 1993.

Riley-Smith, P., 'Do Shoppers Look at Prices?', *Proceedings of the Market Research Conference*, March 1984.

Rossiter, J. R. and Percy, L., *Advertising Communications and Promotion Management*, McGraw-Hill, 1997.

Russo, J. E. and Schoemaker P. J. H., *Decision Traps*, Simon & Schuster, 1989.

Sandell, R., *The Dynamic Relationship between Attitudes and Choice Behavior in the Light of Cross-lagged Panel Correlations*, Dept. of Psychology, University of Stockholm, Report no. 581, 1981.

Schon, D. A., *Technology and Change*, Delacorte Press, 1967.

Schultz, D. E. and Walters, J. S., *Measuring Brand Communication*, Association of National Advertisers, 1997.

Scriven, J. and Ehrenberg, A., 'Brand Loyalty: Now You See It, Now You Don't', *Marketing and Research Today*, May 1994.

Sewell, C. and Brown, P. B., *Customers for Life*, Doubleday, 1990.

Shaw, J., *Customer Inspired Quality: Looking Backward through the Telescope*, Jossey-Bass, 1996.

Shaw, R., *Computer Aided Marketing and Selling*, Butterworth-Heinemann, 1991.

Shaw, R., *Guide to Creating a Fact Base for Marketing Spend Evaluation,* Cranfield School of Management, 2003.

Shaw, R. and Finn, B., *Guide to Good Forecasting and Predictive Modelling*, Cranfield School of Management, June 2003.

Shaw, R. and Fisk, P., 'How Effectively Does Marketing Drive Business Success?', *Marketing Forum Insights*, 2002.

Shaw, R. and Mazur, L., *Marketing Accountability*, FT Reports, 1997.

Shaw, R. and Radford, C., *Marketing Influence Study*, Marketing Forum, 1997.

Shaw, R. and Stone, M., *Database Marketing*, Wiley, 1990.

Shaw, R. and White, C., 'Improving Marketing Accountability through Better Management of the Market Research Process', *Journal of Marketing Management*, 15: 8, 857–80, 1999.

Sherrington, M., *Added Value*, Palgrave Macmillan, 2003.

Sherrod, B., *Blackie Sherrod at Large,* Eakin Press, 2003.

Silverman, G., 'The Bean Counters Get into Creative Accounting', *Financial Times*, 2 September 2004.

Srivastava, R. K. and Shocker, A. D., *Brand Equity: a Perspective on its Meaning and Measurement,* Marketing Science Institute, Working Paper, 1991.

Sterman, J. D., *Business Dynamics – Systems Thinking and Modelling for a Complex World*, Irwin McGraw-Hill, 2000.

Stubbs, J., *Marketing Marketing,* Marketing Forum Proceedings, 1997.

Stutely, R., *The Definitive Business Plan*, FT Prentice Hall, 1999.

Stutely, R., *The Definitive Guide to Managing the Numbers*, FT Prentice Hall, 2003.

Taub, S., 'Is Planning a Waste of Time?', *CFO.com*, 12 August 2003.

Terazono, E., 'Always on the Outside Looking in', *Financial Times*, 2004.

Totten, J. C. and Block, M. P., *Analyzing Sales Promotion: Text and Cases*, Commerce Communications Inc., 1987.

Upchurch, A., *Management Accounting Principles and Practice*, FT Prentice Hall, 1998.

Vaughn, R., 'How Advertising Works: a Planning Model', *Journal of Advertising Research,* 1980.

Vaughn, R., 'How Advertising Works: a Planning Model – Revisited', *Journal of Advertising Research,* 1986.

Verbeke, W., Clement, F. and Farris, P. W., 'Product Availability and Market Share in an Oligopolistic Market', *International Review Retail, Distribution and Consumer Research,* 4 (3): 277–96, 1994.

Vilcassim, N. J. and Jain, D. C., 'Modelling Purchasing Timing and Brand Switching Behaviour Incorporating Scanner Panel Data', *Journal of Marketing Research*, 28: 29–41, 1991.

von Braun, C.-F., *The Innovation War*, Prentice Hall, 1997.

von Gonten, M. F., 'Long Term Promotional Effects Using Panel Data', *Proceedings of the Fifth Annual Advertising and Promotion Workshop New York,* Advertising Research Foundation, 1993.

Walters, R. G., 'Retail Promotions and Retail Store Performance: A Test of Store Performance', *Journal of Retailing*, 64(2): 153, 1988.

Walters, R. G., 'An Empirical Investigation into Retailer Response to Manufacturer Trade Promotions', *Journal of Retailing*, 65(2): 253–72, 1989.

Walters, R. G., 'Assessing the Impact of Retail Price Promotions on Product Substitution', *Journal of Marketing,* 55(2): 17, 1991.

Walters, R. G. and MacKenzie, S. B., 'A Structural Equations Analysis of the Impact of Price Promotions', *Journal of Marketing Research*, 25(1): 51, 1988.

Walters, R. G. and Rinne, H. J., 'An Empirical Investigation into the Impact of Price Promotions on Retail', *Journal of Retailing*, 62(3): 3, 237–66, 1986.

Ward, K., *Accounting for Marketing Strategies*, in: Drury, C. (ed.) *Management Accounting Handbook*, Butterworth-Heinemann, 1996.

Ward, K., 'Controlling Marketing', in: Baker, M. J. (ed.), *The Marketing Book*, 4th edn, Butterworth-Heinemann, 1999.

Ward, K., *Marketing Finance: Turning Marketing Strategies into Shareholder Value*, Butterworth-Heinemann, 2003.

Warren, K., *Competitive Strategy Dynamics*, Wiley, 2002.

Whitely, R., *Customer-Centered Growth: Five Proven Strategies for Building Competitive Advantage*, Perseus Publishing, 1997.

Wiersema, F., *Customer Intimacy: Pick Your Partners, Shape Your Culture, Win Together*, National Book Network, 1996.

Wilson, R., *Accounting for Marketing*, Thomson Business Press, 1999.

Wright, G. and Goodwin, P., *Forecasting with Judgment*, Wiley, 1998.

Zenith Optimedia, http://www.zenithoptimedia.com/dec03.doc and http://zenithoptimedia.com/apr04.doc

INDEX

Note: **bold** page numbers indicate chapters; *italics* indicate definitions. Only firms mentioned more than once have been included.